The Illustrated
Bulfinch's Mythology

THE AGE
OF
CHIVALRY

The Illustrated
Bulfinch's Mythology

THE AGE
OF
CHIVALRY

Illustrations by
Giovanni Caselli

Macmillan • USA

MACMILLAN
A Simon & Schuster Macmillan Company
1633 Broadway
New York, NY 10019–6785

Library of Congress Cataloging-in-Publication Data

Bulfinch, Thomas, 1796–1867.
    [Age of chivalry]
    The illustrated Bulfinch's Mythology. The age of chivalry /
Thomas Bulfinch ; illustrated by Giovanni Caselli.
        p.   cm.
    Includes index.
    ISBN 0-02-861478-X
    1. Arthurian romances.   2. Mythology, Celtic, in literature.
I. Title.
PN685.B86   1997
398.2'094'02—dc21   97–16730
                                                                     CIP

1 3 5 7 9 10 8 6 4 2

AN EDDISON•SADD EDITION
Edited, designed, and produced by
Eddison Sadd Editions Limited
St. Chad's House,
148 King's Cross Road
London WC1X 9DH

Phototypeset in Bauer Bodoni BT using QuarkXPress on Apple Macintosh
Origination through Imago Publishing Ltd, UK
Printed by Dai Nippon Printing Company, Hong Kong

EDITOR'S NOTE

In this new edition of Bulfinch's classic work, we have faithfully reproduced his original version of the text in a fresh typeface and layout that we trust will appeal to you, the modern reader. We have retained certain peculiarities of style and spelling that reflect the custom of his time: for example, the use of Roman names to identify Greek gods, goddesses, and heroes; and Guenever for Guinevere, Isoude for Isolde. We feel that retaining these features helps preserve the essential spirit and character of Bulfinch's writing. You will notice that Bulfinch weaves his literary and artistic associations within his stories. We have not attempted to highlight these, believing that you will quickly become familiar with his style. Similarly, the captions to the new illustrations are designed to be non-intrusive. Where the layout allows, the underlining of text will relate directly to the illustration on the same two-page spread, but where, due to design limitations, an illustration is found on the previous or following page, a cross reference in the margin will lead you to the image. Finally, the footnotes are Bulfinch's, as he wrote them.

Giovanni Caselli has based his map of *The Wanderings of Ulysses* on pages 174–5
in *The Age of Fable* on the work of Pierre Grimal, and that of *King Arthur's Britain*
on page 8 of *The Age of Chivalry* on the work of Leslie Alcock and Geffrey Ashe.

Illustration on page 2: "… he (Geraint) rushed upon him (the Knight of the Sparrow-hawk), and gave him a blow so severe, and furious, and fierce, upon the face of his shield …" *(Text on page 131)*

CONTENTS

THOMAS BULFINCH

THOMAS BULFINCH was born on July 15, 1796, in Boston, Massachusetts, the son of Charles Bulfinch, an eminent architect, and Hannah Apthorp. One of eleven children, Thomas was devoted to his family and had a happy childhood.

From his schooldays spent at the Boston Latin School, he acquired his taste for the classics, which was to influence the later, and most significant, part of his life. After graduating in classical studies from Harvard in 1814, he held a succession of jobs. He taught for one year at the Boston Latin School, and for a while assisted his elder brother, who owned a store.

When Bulfinch's father was invited by U.S. President James Monroe, in 1817, to be the architect of the Capitol in Washington, Thomas joined him in the U.S. a year later. There he entered into several business ventures, but all were unsuccessful.

In autobiographical notes written for a school yearbook, Thomas expressed his own judgment on this period of his life: "My tastes had always been literary, which may in part account for my ill success in commerce." Finally, in 1837, at the age of 41, he accepted a job as clerk in the Merchant's Bank of Boston, where he worked for thirty years, in the same position.

Thomas Bulfinch remained a bachelor, living with his parents until their death, and then alone. He lived a routine, quiet existence. His work at the bank was not demanding and he spent his leisure time in classical studies. A scholar and teacher at heart, he was a voracious reader; but he was also a judicious student of history, a good translator, and a man of taste and knowledge in art.

It was in his late fifties that Bulfinch began his magnus opus. His purpose was to retell in his own words, the traditional accounts of European mythology, in order to familiarize his contemporary Americans with the extensive heritage of classical literary culture. *The Age of Fable*, published in 1855, followed by *The Age of Chivalry* in 1858, and *Legends of Charlemagne* in 1862, demonstrated his wide knowledge, not only of the classics, but of European literature and contemporary poets as well. In his preface Bulfinch wrote, "Without a knowledge of mythology much of the elegant literature of our own language cannot be understood and appreciated. Our book is not for the learned ... but for the reader of English literature, of either sex, who wishes to comprehend the allusions so frequently made by public speakers, lecturers, essayists, and poets, and those which occur in polite conversation." The three volumes were an instant success and merged into the classic known ever since as *Bulfinch's Mythology*.

Thomas Bulfinch died on May 27, 1867, at the age of seventy-one. For him mythology was a marvelous cultural vision. And although his life seems to contain very little, his three volumes of mythology alone have made him unforgettable, a man for the ages.

FOREWORD

Western literature, drama, music, and the visual arts, are all imbued in classical myths and medieval legends. As early as 1855, Thomas Bulfinch conceived the three volumes of his classical Mythology—*The Age of Fable*, *The Age of Chivalry*, and *Legends of Charlemagne*—with precisely this in mind. His very purpose was to point out how Shakespeare, Milton, and Tennyson in England, Longfellow and Lowell in America, and the great Italian poets, Dante and Ariosto, made constant references to the classical myths of Greece and Rome, and to the legends of later times, such as *Le Morte d'Arthur*, the *Chanson de Roland*, and many others. Musicians, musical dramatists and visual artists did, as well—even more so.

Myths and legends are vital to the life of a nation: They provide a sense of continuity, and constitute a source of patterns and rules of behavior. And, although what constitutes today's myths is often somewhat controversial, the fact is our own society is as dependent on its modern myths as the Greeks and the Romans, the Vikings or the Hindus, were dependent on theirs.

I was very ignorant of British and Celtic archaeology and tradition when I first settled in England in 1970. This was a wind-swept, green island, with neat undulating countryside and orderly architecture, far removed, it seemed, from my Mediterranean world where I was still studying Classical archaeology and making frequent trips to Florence to research the ailing culture of the Tuscan peasants.

To get a good taste of my new home, I decided to visit the real countryside Thomas Hardy had made known through his fiction as "Wessex." I wandered through Hampshire and Wiltshire; I visited Stonehenge, Avebury, Silbury Hill, West Kennet Long Barrow, the Ridgeway, and Marlborough. Soon after, I joined the local Archaeological Society and took part in the dig of Celtic forts and Celto-Roman farms. I also joined the Museum Ethnographers' Group and contributed several paintings to the exhibits of civic museums in England and Wales.

It became clear to me how, at some time after the barbarian invasions that followed the fall of the Roman Empire, civilized, Christian Britons must have felt proud of their heritage as distinct from that of the pagan Saxons or Vikings, or the Celtic pagans. During this time the legendary King Arthur and his knights could have developed from a real King Arthur of the South Britons, as proud subjects exaggerated the deeds and exploits of their leader, until some of the stories became so widely repeated they became part of French medieval tradition.

When I was invited to illustrate Bulfinch's second volume, *The Age of Chivalry* or *Legends of King Arthur*, I found it a daunting task. I wanted my illustrations to be as historically accurate as possible. The subject of King Arthur had already been wonderfully illustrated by both great Victorian artists and many modern British artists. Almost all these had dressed their characters in the splendid costumes and armor of the later Middle Ages—the fourteenth and fifteenth centuries. This choice was probably dictated by the fact that the extant texts had been written or revised during that period, and often make references to arms and armor familiar to the writers. Almost nothing was known, until the 1960s, of pre-Saxon and early Saxon costume in the British Isles.

But since the stories themselves and the characters whose deeds they describe, true or fictional, lived in late Roman or early Saxon times (between the fifth and sixth centuries A.D.), I have attempted to re-create costumes that might have been in fashion during Arthurian time, and filled the gaps with elements from my own imagination.

In illustrating the Arthurian legends I have not attempted to disguise my sources, wherever there were any. While the illustration work for this volume is solely of my own creation, I am indebted to the many fine artists before me who have researched and illustrated these magnificent stories.

GIOVANNI CASELLI.
MALTA, MAY 1997

7

King Arthur's Britain

KEY
▲ = Arthurian sites
• = main cities

NORTH SEA

SCOTLAND

▲ Arthur's Court

Hadrian's Wall

RHEGED
▲ Round Table

York

IRELAND

Chester

WALES

Caerleon ▲

London

Bath
ATLANTIC OCEAN

Glastonbury

▲ Winchester

CORNWALL

Isle of Avalon

▲ St. Michael's Mount

ENGLISH CHANNEL

PREFACE

I N a former work the compiler of this volume endeavored to impart the pleasures of classical learning to the English reader, by presenting the stories of Pagan mythology in a form adapted to modern taste. In the present volume the attempt has been made to treat in the same way the stories of the second "age of fable," the age which witnessed the dawn of the several states of Modern Europe.

It is believed that this presentation of a literature which held unrivalled sway over the imaginations of our ancestors, for many centuries, will not be without benefit to the reader, in addition to the amusement it may afford. The tales, though not to be trusted for their facts, are worthy of all credit as pictures of manners; and it is beginning to be held that the manners and modes of thinking of an age are a more important part of its history than the conflicts of its peoples, generally leading to no result. Besides this, the literature of romance is a treasure-house of poetical material, to which modern poets frequently resort. The Italian poets, Dante and Ariosto, the English, Spenser, Scott, and Tennyson, and our own Longfellow and Lowell, are examples of this.

These legends are so connected with each other, so consistently adapted to a group of characters strongly individualized in Arthur, Launcelot, and their compeers, and so lighted up by the fires of imagination and invention, that they seem as well adapted to the poet's purpose as the legends of the Greek and Roman mythology. And if every well-educated young person is expected to know the story of the Golden Fleece, why is the quest of the Sangreal less worthy of his acquaintance? Or if an allusion to the shield of Achilles ought not to pass unapprehended, why should one to Excalibur, the famous sword of Arthur:

> "Of Arthur, who, to upper light restored,
> With that terrific sword,
> Which yet he brandishes for future war,
> Shall lift his country's fame above the polar star?"[1]

It is an additional recommendation of our subject, that it tends to cherish in our minds the idea of the source from which we sprung. We are entitled to our full share in the glories and recollections of the land of our forefathers, down to the time of colonization thence. The associations which spring from this source must be fruitful of good influences; among which not the least valuable is the increased enjoyment which such associations afford to the American traveller when he visits England, and sets his foot upon any of her renowned localities.

The readers of Tennyson are invited to peruse in these legends the originals of those stories which the poet has clothed in the drapery of verse, and given to the public in his "Idylls of the King," and in shorter poems. Perhaps some of them may be found more intelligible for our plain narrative of the same events.

THOMAS BULFINCH.
BOSTON, 1858

---

[1]Wordsworth.

PART ONE

KING ARTHUR AND HIS KNIGHTS

CHAPTER I

INTRODUCTION

ON the decline of the Roman power, about five centuries after Christ, the countries of Northern Europe were left almost destitute of a national government. Numerous chiefs, more or less powerful, held local sway, as far as each could enforce his dominion, and occasionally those chiefs would unite for a common object; but, in ordinary times, they were much more likely to be found in hostility to one another. In such a state of things, the rights of the humbler classes of society were at the mercy of every assailant; and it is plain that, without some check upon the lawless power of the chiefs, society must have relapsed into barbarism. Such checks were found, first, in the rivalry of the chiefs themselves, whose mutual jealousy made them restraints upon one another; secondly, in the influence of the Church, which, by every motive, pure or selfish, was pledged to interpose for the protection of the weak; and lastly, in the generosity and sense of right which, however crushed under the weight of passion and selfishness, dwell naturally in the heart of man. From this last source sprang Chivalry, which framed an ideal of the heroic character, combining invincible strength and valor, justice, modesty, loyalty to superiors, courtesy to equals, compassion to weakness, and devotedness to the Church; an ideal which, if never met with in real life, was acknowledged by all as the highest model for emulation.

The word Chivalry is derived from the French *cheval*, a horse. The word *knight*, which originally meant boy or servant, was particularly applied to a young man after he was admitted to the privilege of bearing arms. This privilege was conferred on youths of family and fortune only, for the mass of the people were not furnished with arms. The knight then was a mounted warrior, a man of rank, or in the service and maintenance of some man of rank, generally possessing some independent means of support, but often relying mainly on the gratitude of those whom he served for the supply of his wants, and often, no doubt, resorting to the means which power confers on its possessor.

In time of war the knight was, with his followers, in the camp of his sovereign, or commanding in the field, or holding some castle for him.

In time of peace he was often in attendance at his sovereign's court, gracing with his presence the banquets and tournaments with which princes cheered their leisure. Or he was traversing the country in quest of adventure, professedly bent on redressing wrongs and enforcing rights, sometimes in fulfilment of some vow of religion or of love. These wandering knights were called knights-errant; they were welcome guests in the castles of the nobility, for their presence enlivened the dulness of those secluded abodes, and they were received with honor at the abbeys, which often owed the best part of their revenues to the patronage of the knights; but if no castle or abbey or hermitage were at hand, their hardy habits made it not intolerable to them to lie down, supperless, at the foot of some wayside cross, and pass the night.

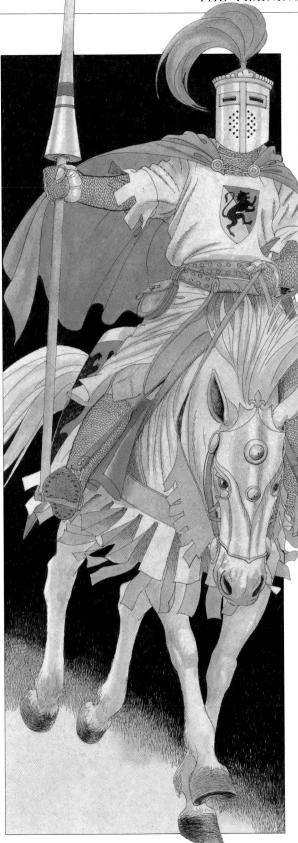

It is evident that the justice administered by such an instrumentality must have been of the rudest description. The force whose legitimate purpose was to redress wrongs, might easily be perverted to inflict them. Accordingly, we find in the romances, which, however fabulous in facts, are true as pictures of manners, that a knightly castle was often a terror to the surrounding country; that its dungeons were full of oppressed knights and ladies, waiting for some champion to appear to set them free, or to be ransomed with money; that hosts of idle retainers were ever at hand to enforce their lord's behests, regardless of law and justice; and that the rights of the unarmed multitude were of no account. This contrariety of fact and theory in regard to chivalry will account for the opposite impressions which exist in men's minds respecting it. While it has been the theme of the most fervid eulogium on the one part, it has been as eagerly denounced on the other. On a cool estimate, we cannot but see reason to congratulate ourselves that it has given way in modern times to the reign of law, and that the civil magistrate, if less picturesque, has taken the place of the mailed champion.

THE TRAINING OF A KNIGHT

THE preparatory education of candidates for knighthood was long and arduous. At seven years of age the noble children were usually removed from their father's house to the court or castle of their future patron, and placed under the care of a governor, who taught them the first articles of religion, and respect and reverence for their lords and superiors, and initiated them in the ceremonies of a court. They were called *pages*, *valets* or *varlets*, and their office was to carve, to wait at table, and to perform other menial services which were not then considered humiliating. In their leisure hours they learned to dance and play on the harp, were instructed in the mysteries of *woods* and *rivers*, that is, in hunting, falconry, and fishing, and in wrestling, tilting with spears, and performing other military exercises on horseback. At fourteen the page became an esquire, and began a course of severer and more laborious exercises. To vault on a horse in heavy armor; to run, to scale walls, and spring over ditches, under the same encumbrance; to wrestle, to wield the battle-axe for a length of time, without raising the visor or taking breath to perform with grace all the evolutions of horsemanship,—were necessary preliminaries to the reception of knighthood, which was usually conferred at twenty-one years of age, when the young man's education was supposed to be completed. In the meantime, the esquires were no less assiduously engaged in acquiring all those refinements of civility which formed what was in that age called *courtesy*. The same castle in which they received their education was usually thronged with young persons of the other sex, and the page was encouraged, at a very early age, to select some lady of the court as the mistress of his heart, to whom he was taught to refer all his sentiments, words and actions. The service of his mistress was the glory and occupation of a knight, and her smiles, bestowed at once by affection and gratitude, were held out as the recompense of his well-directed valor. Religion united its influence with those of loyalty and love, and the order of knighthood, endowed with all the sanctity and religious awe that attended the priesthood, became an object of ambition to the greatest sovereigns.

The ceremonies of initiation were peculiarly solemn. After undergoing a severe fast, and spending whole nights in prayer, the candidate confessed, and received the sacrament. He then clothed himself in snow-white garments, and repaired to the church, or the hall, where the ceremony was to take place, bearing a knightly sword suspended from his neck, which the officiating priest took and blessed, and then returned to him. The candidate then with folded arms, knelt before the presiding knight, who, after some questions about his motives and purposes in requesting admission, administered to him the oaths, and granted his request. Some of the knights present, sometimes even ladies and damsels, handed to him in

succession the spurs, the coat of mail, the hauberk, the armlet and gauntlet, and lastly he girded on the sword. He then knelt again before the president, who, rising from his seat, gave him the "accolade," which consisted of three strokes, with the flat of a sword, on the shoulder or neck of the candidate, accompanied by the words: "In the name of God, of St. Michael, and St. George, I make thee a knight; be valiant, courteous, and loyal!" Then he received his helmet, his shield, and spear; and thus the investiture ended.

FREEMEN, VILLAINS, SERFS, AND CLERKS

THE other classes of which society was composed were, first, *freemen*, owners of small portions of land, independent, though they sometimes voluntarily became the vassals of their more opulent neighbors, whose power was necessary for their protection. The other two classes, which were much the most numerous, were either serfs or villains, both of which were slaves.

The *serfs* were in the lowest state of slavery. All the fruits of their labor belonged to the master whose land they tilled, and by whom they were fed and clothed.

The *villains* were less degraded. Their situation seems to have resembled that of the Russian peasants at this day. Like the serfs, they were attached to the soil, and were transferred with it by purchase; but they paid only a fixed rent to the landlord, and had a right to dispose of any surplus that might arise from their industry.

The term *clerk* was of very extensive import. It comprehended originally, such persons only as belonged to the clergy, or clerical order, among whom, however, might be found a multitude of married persons, artisans or others. But in process of time a much wider rule was established; every one that could read being accounted a *clerk*, or *clericus*, and allowed the "benefit of clergy," that is, exemption from capital and some other forms of punishment, in case of crime.

TOURNAMENTS

THE splendid pageant of a tournament between knights, its gaudy accessories and trappings, and its chivalrous regulations, originated in France. Tournaments were repeatedly condemned by the Church, probably on account of the quarrels they led to, and the often fatal results. The "joust," or "just," was different from the tournament. In these, knights fought with their lances, and their object was to unhorse their antagonists; while the tournaments were intended for a display of skill and address in evolutions, and with various weapons, and greater courtesy was observed in the regulations. By these it was forbidden to wound the horse, or to use the point of the sword, or to strike a knight after he had raised his visor, or unlaced his helmet. The ladies encouraged their knights in these exercises; they bestowed prizes, and the conqueror's feats were the theme of romance and song. The stands overlooking the ground, of course, were varied in the shapes of towers, terraces, galleries, and pensile gardens, magnificently decorated with tapestry, pavilions, and banners. Every combatant proclaimed the name of the lady whose *servant d'amour* he was. He was wont to look up to the stand, and strengthen his courage by the sight of the bright eyes that were raining their influence on him from above. The knights also carried *favors*, consisting of scarfs, veils, sleeves, bracelet, clasps,—in short, some piece of female habiliment,—attached to their helmets, shields, or armor. If, during, the combat, any of these appendages were dropped or lost, the fair donor would at times send her knight new ones, especially if pleased with his exertions.

MAIL ARMOR

MAIL armor, of which the hauberk is a species, and which derived its name from *maille*, a French word for mesh, was of two kinds, *plate* or *scale* mail, and *chain* mail. It was originally used for the protection of the body only, reaching no lower than the knees. It was shaped like a carter's frock, and bound round the waist by a girdle. Gloves and hose of mail were afterwards added, and a hood, which, when necessary, was drawn over the head, leaving the face alone uncovered. To protect the skin from the impression of the iron network of the chain mail, a quilted lining was employed, which, however, was insufficient, and the bath was used to efface the marks of the armor.

The hauberk was a complete covering of double chain mail. Some hauberks opened before, like a modern coat; others were closed like a shirt.

The chain mail of which they were composed was formed by a number of iron links, each link having others inserted into it, the whole exhibiting a kind of network, of which (in some instances at least) the meshes were circular, with each link separately riveted.

The hauberk was proof against the most violent blow of a sword; but the point of a lance might pass through the meshes, or drive the iron into the flesh. To guard against this, a thick and well-stuffed doublet was worn underneath, under which was commonly added an iron breastplate. Hence the expression "to pierce both plate and mail," so common in the earlier poets.

Mail armor continued in general use till about the year 1300, when it was gradually supplanted by plate armor, or suits consisting of pieces or plates of solid iron, adapted to the different parts of the body.

Shields were generally made of wood, covered with leather, or some similar substance. To secure them, in some sort, from being cut through by the sword, they were surrounded with a hoop of metal.

HELMETS

THE helmet was composed of two parts: the *headpiece*, which was strengthened within by several circles of iron; and the *visor*, which, as the name implies, was a sort of grating to see through, so contrived as, by sliding in a groove, or turning on a pivot, to be raised or lowered at pleasure. Some helmets had a further improvement called a *bever*, from the Italian *bevere*, to drink. The *ventayle*, or "air-passage," is another name for this.

To secure the helmet from the possibility of falling, or of being struck off, it was tied by several laces to the meshes of the hauberk; consequently, when a knight was overthrown, it was necessary to undo these laces before he could be put to death; though this was sometimes effected by lifting up the skirt of the hauberk, and stabbing, him in the belly. The instrument of death was a small dagger, worn on the right side.

ROMANCES

IN ages when there were no books, when noblemen and princes themselves could not read, history or tradition was monopolized by the storytellers. They inherited generation after generation, the wondrous tales of their predecessors, which they retailed to the public with such additions of their own as their acquired information supplied them with. Anachronisms became of course very common, and errors of geography, of locality, of manners, equally so. Spurious genealogies were invented, in which Arthur and his knights, and Charlemagne and his paladins, were made to derive their descent from Æneas, Hector, or some other of the Trojan heroes.

With regard to the derivation of the word *Romance*, we trace it to the fact that the dialects which were formed in Western Europe, from the admixture of Latin with the native languages, took the name of *Langue Romaine*. The French language was divided into two dialects. The river Loire was their common boundary. In the provinces to the south of that river the affirmative, *yes*, was expressed by the word *oc*; in the north it was called *oil* (*oui*); and hence Dante has named the southern language *langue d'oc*, and the northern *langue d'oil*. The latter, which was carried into England by the Normans, and is the origin of the present French, may be called the French Romane; and the former the Provençal, or Provencial Romane, because it was spoken by the people of Provence and Languedoc, southern provinces of France.

These dialects were soon distinguished by very opposite characters. A soft and enervating climate, a spirit of commerce encouraged by an easy communication with other maritime nations, the influx of wealth, and a more settled government, may have tended to polish and soften the diction of the Provencials, whose poets, under the name of Trou- badours, were the masters of the Italians, and par- ticularly of Petrarch. Their favorite pieces were *Sirventes* (satirical pieces), love-songs, and *Tensons*, which last were a sort of dialogue in verse between two poets, who questioned each other on some refined points of love's casuistry. It seems the Provencials were so completely absorbed in these delicate questions as to neglect and despise the com- position of fabulous histories of adventure and knighthood, which they left in a great measure to the poets of the northern part of the kingdom, called Trouveurs.

At a time when chivalry excited universal admira- tion, and when all the efforts of that chivalry were directed against the enemies of religion, it was natur- al that literature should receive the same impulse, and that history and fable should be ransacked to furnish examples of courage and piety that might excite increased emulation. Arthur and Charlemagne were the two heroes selected for this purpose. Arthur's pretensions were that he was a brave, though not always a successful warrior; he had with- stood with great resolution the arms of the infidels, that is to say of the Saxons; and his memory was held in the highest estimation by his countrymen, the Britons, who carried with them into Wales, and into the kindred country of Armorica, or Brittany, the memory of his exploits, which their national vanity insensibly exaggerated, till the little prince of the Silures (South Wales) was magnified into the con- queror of England, of Gaul, and of the greater part of Europe. His genealogy was gradually carried up to an imaginary Brutus, and to the period of the Trojan war, and a sort of chronicle was composed in the Welsh, or Armorican language, which, under the pompous title of the History of the Kings of Britain, was translated into Latin by Geoffrey of Monmouth, about the year 1150. The Welsh critics consider the material of the work to have been an older history, written by St. Talian, bishop of St. Asaph, in the seventh century.

As to Charlemagne, though his real merits were sufficient to secure his immortality, it was impossible that his holy wars against the Saracens should not become a favorite topic for fiction. Accordingly, the fabulous history of these wars was written, probably towards the close of the eleventh century, by a monk, who, thinking it would add dignity to his work to embellish it with a contemporary name, boldly ascribed it to Turpin, who was archbishop of Rheims about the year 773.

These fabulous chronicles were for a while imprisoned in languages of local only or of professional access. Both Turpin and Geoffrey might indeed be read by ecclesiastics, the sole Latin scholars of those times, and Geoffrey's British original would contribute to the gratification of Welshmen; but neither could become extensively popular till translated into some language of general and familiar use. The Anglo-Saxon was at that time used only by a conquered and enslaved nation; the Spanish and Italian languages were not yet formed; the Norman French alone was spoken and understood by the nobility in the greater part of Europe, and therefore was a proper vehicle for the new mode of composition.

That language was fashionable in England before the Conquest, and became, after that event, the only language used at the court of London. As the various conquests of the Normans, and the enthusiastic valor of that extraordinary people, had familiarized the minds of men with the most marvellous events, their poets eagerly seized the fabulous legends of Arthur and Charlemagne, translated them into the language of the day, and soon produced a variety of imitations. The adventures attributed to these monarchs, and to their distinguished warriors, together with those of many other traditionary or imaginary heroes, composed by degrees that formidable body of marvellous histories which, from the dialect in which the most ancient of them were written, were called Romances.

METRICAL ROMANCES

THE earliest form in which romances appear is that of a rude kind of verse. In this form it is supposed they were sung or recited at the feasts of princes and knights in their baronial halls. The following specimen of the language and style of Robert de Beauvais, who flourished in 1257, is from Sir Walter Scott's introduction to the Romance of Sir Tristram:

"Ne voil pas emmi dire,
Ici diverse la matyere,
Entre ceus qui solent cunter,
E de la cunte Tristran parler."

"I will not say too much about it,
So diverse is the matter,
Among those who are in the habit of telling
And relating the story of Tristran."

This is a specimen of the language which was in use among the nobility of England in the ages immediately after the Norman conquest. The following is a specimen of the English that existed at the same time among the common people. Robert de Brunne, speaking of his Latin and French authorities, says:

"Als thai haf wryten and sayd
Haf I alle in myn Inglis layd,
In symple speeche as I couthe,
That is lightest in manne's mouthe.
Alle for the luf of symple men,
That strange Inglis cannot ken."

—the "strange Inglis" being the language of the previous specimen. It was not till toward the end of the thirteenth century that the *prose* romances began to appear. These works generally began with disowning and discrediting the sources from which in reality they drew their sole information. As every romance was supposed to be a real history, the compilers of those in prose would have forfeited all credit if they had announced themselves as mere copyists of the minstrels. On the contrary, they usually state that, as the popular poems upon the matter in question contain many "lesings," they had been induced to translate the real and true history of such or such a knight from the original Latin or Greek, or from the ancient British or Armorican authorities, which authorities existed only in their own assertion.

A specimen of the style of the prose romance may be found in the following extract from one of the most celebrated and latest of them, the Morte d'Arthur of Sir Thomas Mallory, of the date of 1485. From this work much of the contents of this volume has been drawn, with as close an adherence to the original style as was thought consistent with our plan of adapting our narrative to the taste of modern readers.

"It is notoyrly knowen thorugh the vnyuersal world that there been IX worthy and the best that ever were. That is to wete thre paynyms, thre Jewes, and thre crysten men. As for the paynyms, they were tofore the Incarnacyon of Cryst whiche were named, the fyrst Hector of Troye; the second Alysaunder the grete, and the thyrd Julyus Cezar, Emperour of Rome, of whome thystoryes ben well kno and had. And as for the thre Jewes whyche also were tofore thyncarnacyon of our Lord, of whome the fyrst was Duc Josue, whyche brought the chyldren of Israhel into the londe of beheste; the second Dauyd, kyng of Jherusalem, and the thyrd Judas Machabeus; of these thre the byble reherceth al theyr noble hystoryes and actes. And sythe the sayd Incarnacyon haue ben the noble crysten men stalled and admytted thorugh the vnyuersal world to the nombre of the IX beste and worthy, of whome was fyrst the noble Arthur, whose noble actes I purpose to wryte in this present book here folowyng. The second was Charlemayn, or Charles the grete, of whome thystorye is had in many places both in frensshe and englysshe, and the thyrd and last was Godefray of Boloyn."

THE MABINOGEON

IT has been well known to the literati and antiquarians of Europe, that there exist in the great public libraries voluminous manuscripts of romances and tales once popular, but which on the invention of printing had already become antiquated and fallen into neglect. They were therefore never printed, and seldom perused even by the learned, until about half a century ago, when attention was again directed to them, and they were found very curious monuments of ancient manners, habits, and modes of thinking. Several have since been edited, some by individuals, as Sir Walter Scott and the poet Southey, others by antiquarian societies. The class of readers which could be counted on for such publications was so small that no inducement of profit could be found to tempt editors and publishers to give them to the world. It was therefore only a few, and those the most accessible, which were put in print. There was a class of manuscripts of this kind which were known, or rather suspected, to be both curious and valuable, but which it seemed almost hopeless ever to see in fair printed English. These were the Welsh popular tales, called Mabinogeon, a plural word, the singular being Mabinogi, a tale. Manuscripts of these were contained in the Bodleian Library at Oxford, and elsewhere, but the difficulty was to find translators and editors. The Welsh is a spoken language among the peasantry of Wales, but is entirely neglected among the learned, unless they are natives of the principality. Of the few Welsh scholars none were found who took sufficient interest in this branch of learning to give these productions to the English public. Southey and Scott, and others who, like them, loved the old romantic legends of their country, often urged upon the Welsh literati the duty of reproducing the Mabinogeon. Southey, in the preface to his edition of Morte d'Arthur, says: "The specimens which I have seen are exceedingly curious; nor is there a greater desideratum in British literature than an edition of these tales, with a literal version, and such comments as Mr. Davies of all men is best qualified to give. Certain it is that many of the Round Table fictions originated in Wales, or in Bretagne, and probably might still be traced there."

Again, in a letter to Sir Charles W. W. Wynn, dated 1819, he says:

"I begin almost to despair of ever seeing more of the Mabinogeon; and yet, if some competent Welshman could be found to edit it carefully, with as literal a version as possible, I am sure it might be made worth his while by a subscription, printing a small edition at a high price, perhaps two hundred at five guineas. I myself would gladly subscribe at that price per volume for sure an edition of the whole of your genuine remains in prose and verse. Till some such collection is made, the 'gentlemen of Wales' ought to be prohibited from wearing a leek; ay, and interdicted from toasting cheese also. Your bards would have met with better usage if they had been Scotchmen."

Sharon Turner and Sir Walter Scott also expressed a similar wish for the publication of the Welsh manuscripts. The former took part in an attempt to effect it, through the instrumentality of a Mr. Owen, a Welshman, but, we judge, by what Southey says of him, imperfectly acquainted with English. Southey's language is, "William Owen lent me three parts of the Mabinogeon, delightfully translated into so Welsh an idiom and syntax that such a translation is as instructive as an original." In another letter he adds, "Let Sharon make his language grammatical, but not alter their idiom in the slightest point."

It is possible Mr. Owen did not proceed far in an undertaking which, so executed, could expect but little popular patronage. It was not till an individual should appear possessed of the requisite knowledge of the two languages, of enthusiasm sufficient for the task, and of pecuniary resources sufficient to be independent of the booksellers and of the reading public, that such a work could be confidently expected. Such an individual has, since Southey's day and Scott's, appeared in the person of Lady Charlotte Guest, an English lady united to a gentleman of property in Wales, who, having acquired the language of the principality, and become enthusiastically fond of its literary treasures, has given them to the English reader, in a dress which the printer's and the engraver's arts have done their best to adorn. In four royal octave volumes containing the Welsh originals, the translation, and ample illustrations from French, German, and other contemporary and affiliated literature, the Mabinogeon is spread before us. To the antiquarian and the student of language and ethnology an invaluable treasure, it yet can hardly, in such a form, win its way to popular acquaintance. We claim no other merit than that of bringing it to the knowledge of our readers, of abridging its details, of selecting its most attractive portions, and of faithfully preserving throughout the style in which Lady Guest has clothed her legends. For this service we hope that our readers will confess we have laid them under no light obligation.

Chapter II

The Mythical History of England

ACCORDING to the earliest accounts, Albion, a giant, and son of Neptune, a contemporary of Hercules, ruled over the island, to which he gave his name. Presuming to oppose the progress of Hercules in his western march, he was slain by him.

Another story is that Histion, the son of Japhet, the son of Noah, had four sons,—Francus, Romanus, Alemannus, and Britto, from whom descended the French, Roman, German, and British people.

Rejecting these and other like stories, Milton gives more regard to the story of Brutus, the Trojan, which, he says, is supported by "descents of ancestry long continued, laws and exploits not plainly seeming to be borrowed or devised, which on the common belief have wrought no small impression; defended by many, denied utterly by few." The principal authority is Geoffrey of Monmouth, whose history, written in the twelfth century, purports to be a translation of a history of Britain, brought over from the opposite shore of France, which, under the name of Brittany, was chiefly peopled by natives of Britain, who from time to time emigrated thither, driven from their own country by the inroads of the Picts and Scots. According to this authority, Brutus was the son of Silvius, and he of Ascanius, the son of Æneas, whose flight from Troy and settlement in Italy will be found narrated in "The Age of Fable."

Brutus, at the age of fifteen, attending his father to the chase, unfortunately killed him with an arrow.

Banished therefor by his kindred, he sought refuge in that part of Greece where Helenus, with a band of Trojan exiles, had become established. But Helenus was now dead, and the descendants of the Trojans were oppressed by Pandrasus, the king of the country. Brutus, being kindly received among them, so throve in virtue and in arms as to win the regard of all the eminent of the land above all others of his age. In consequence of this the Trojans not only began to hope, but secretly to persuade him to lead them the way to liberty. To encourage them they had the promise of help from Assaracus, a noble Greek youth, whose mother was a Trojan. He had suffered wrong at the hands of the king, and for that reason the more willingly cast in his lot with the Trojan exiles.

Choosing a fit opportunity, Brutus with his countrymen withdrew to the woods and hills, as the safest place from which to expostulate, and sent this message to Pandrasus: "That the Trojans, holding it unworthy of their ancestors to serve in a foreign land, had retreated to the woods, choosing rather a savage life than a slavish one. If that displeased him, then, with his leave, they would depart to some other country." Pandrasus, not expecting so bold a message from the sons of captives, went in pursuit of them, with such forces as he could gather, and met them on the banks of the Achelous, where Brutus got the advantage, and took the king captive. The result was, that the terms demanded by the Trojans were granted; the king gave his daughter Imogen in marriage to Brutus, and furnished shipping, money, and fit provision for them all to depart from the land.

The marriage being solemnized, and shipping from all parts got together, the Trojans, in a fleet of no less than three hundred and twenty sail, betook themselves to the sea. On the third day they arrived at a certain island, which they found destitute of inhabitants, though there were appearances of former habitation, and among the ruins a temple of Diana. Brutus, here performing sacrifice at the shrine of the goddess, invoked an oracle for his guidance, in these lines:

"Goddess of shades, and huntress, who at will
Walk'st on the rolling sphere, and through the deep;
On thy third realm, the earth, look now and tell
What land, what seat of rest, thou bidd'st me seek;

What certain seat where I may worship thee
For aye, with temples vowed and virgin choirs."

To whom, sleeping before the altar, Diana, in a vision thus answered:

"Brutus! far to the west, in the ocean wide,
Beyond the realm of Gaul, a land there lies,
Seagirt it lies, where giants dwelt of old;
Now, void, it fits thy people: thither bend
Thy course; there shalt thou find a lasting seat;
There to thy sons another Troy shall rise,
And kings be born of thee, whose dreaded might
Shall save the world, and conquer nations bold."

Brutus, guided now, as he thought, by Divine direction, sped his course towards the west, and, arriving at a place on the Tyrrhene sea, found there the descendants of certain Trojans who with Antenor came into Italy, of whom Corineus was the chief. These joined company, and the ships pursued their way till they arrived at the mouth of the river Loire, in France, where the expedition landed, with a view to a settlement, but were so rudely assaulted by the inhabitants that they put to sea again, and arrived at a part of the coast of Britain now called Devonshire, where Brutus felt convinced that he had found the promised end of his voyage, landed his colony, and took possession.

The island, not yet Britain, but Albion, was in a manner desert and inhospitable, occupied only by a remnant of the giant race whose excessive force and tyranny had destroyed the others. The Trojans encountered these and extirpated them, Corineus in particular signalizing himself by his exploits against them; from whom Cornwall takes its name, for that region fell to his lot, and there the hugest giants dwelt, lurking in rocks and caves, till Corineus rid the land of them.

Brutus built his capital city, and called it Trojanova (New Troy), changed in time to Trinovantum, now London;[1] and, having governed the isle twenty-four years, died, leaving three sons, Locrine, Albanact,

and Camber. Locrine had the middle part, Camber the west, called Cambria from him, and Albanact Albania, now Scotland. Locrine was married to Guendolen, the daughter of Corineus; but, having seen a fair maid named Estrildis, who had been brought captive from Germany, he became enamored of her, and had by her a daughter, whose name was Sabra. This matter was kept secret while Corineus lived; but after his death, Locrine divorced Guendolen, and made Estrildis his queen. Guendolen, all in rage, departed to Cornwall, where Madan, her son, lived, who had been brought up by Corineus, his grandfather. Gathering an army of her father's friends and subjects, she gave battle to her husband's forces, and Locrine was slain. Guendolen caused her rival, Estrildis, with her daughter Sabra, to be thrown into the river, from which cause the river thenceforth bore the maiden's name, which by length of time is now changed into Sabrina or Severn. Milton alludes to this in his address to the river:

"Severn swift, guilty of maiden's death";

—and in his "Comus" tells the story with a slight variation, thus:

"There is a gentle nymph not far from hence,
That with moist curb sways the smooth Severn
  stream;
Sabrina is her name, a virgin pure:
Whilom she was the daughter of Locrine,
That had the sceptre from his father, Brute.
She, guiltless damsel, flying the mad pursuit
Of her enragéd step-dame, Guendolen,
Commended her fair innocence to the flood,
That stayed her flight with his cross-flowing course.
The water-nymphs that in the bottom played
Held up their pearléd wrists and took her in,
Bearing her straight to aged Nereus' hall,
Who, piteous of her woes, reared her lank head,
And gave her to his daughters to imbathe
In nectared layers strewed with asphodel,
And through the porch and inlet of each sense
Dropped in ambrosial oils till she revived,
And underwent a quick, immortal change,
Made goddess of the river," etc.

20 ▷

---

[1] "For noble Britons sprong from Trojans bold,
  And Troynovant was built of old Troy's ashes cold."
  Spenser, Book III, Canto IX. 38

If our readers ask when all this took place, we must answer, in the first place, that mythology is not careful of dates; and next that, as Brutus was the great-grandson of Æneas, it must have been not far from a century subsequent to the Trojan war, or about 1100 years before the invasion of the island by Julius Cæsar. This long interval is filled with the names of princes whose chief occupation was in warring with one another. Some few, whose names remain connected with places, or embalmed in literature, we will mention.

BLADUD

BLADUD built the city of Bath, and dedicated the medicinal waters to Minerva. He was a man of great invention, and practised the arts of magic, till, having made him wings to fly, he fell down upon the temple of Apollo, in Trinovant, and so died, after twenty years' reign.

LEIR

LEIR, who next reigned, built Leicester, and called it after his name. He had no male issue, but only three daughters. When grown old, he determined to divide his kingdom among his daughters, and bestow them in marriage. But first, to try which of them loved him best, he determined to ask them solemnly in order, and judge of the warmth of their affection by their answers. Goneril, the eldest, knowing well her father's weakness, made answer that she loved him, "above her soul." "Since thou so honorest my declining age," said the old man, "to thee and to thy husband I give the third part of my realm." Such good success for a few words soon uttered was ample instruction to Regan, the second daughter, what to say. She therefore, to the same question replied, that "she loved him more than all the world beside;" and so received an equal reward with her sister. But Cordeilla, the youngest, and hitherto the best beloved, too honest to profess in words more than she felt in her heart, was not moved from the solid purpose of a sincere and virtuous answer, and replied: "Father, my love towards you is as my duty bids. They who pretend beyond this flatter." When the old man, sorry to hear this, and wishing her to recall these words, persisted in asking, she still restrained her expressions so as to say rather less than more than the truth. Then Leir, all in a passion, burst forth: "Since thou hast not reverenced thy aged father like thy sisters, think not to have any part in my kingdom or what else I have;"—and without delay, giving in marriage his other daughters, Goneril to the duke of Albany, and Regan to the duke of Cornwall, he divided his kingdom between them. Cordeilla, portionless, married the prince of France, who shortly after succeeded his father upon the throne.

King Leir went to reside with his eldest daughter, attended only by a hundred knights. But in a short time his attendants, being complained of as too numerous and disorderly, are reduced to thirty. Resenting that affront, the old king betakes him to his second daughter; but she, instead of soothing his wounded pride, takes part with her sister, and refuses to admit a retinue of more than five. Then back he returns to the other, who now will not receive him with more than one attendant. Then the remembrance of Cordeilla comes to his thoughts, and he takes his journey into France to seek her, with little hope of kind consideration from one whom he had so injured, but to pay her the last recompense he can render,—confession of his injustice. When Cordeilla is informed of his approach, and of his sad condition, she pours forth true filial tears. And, not willing that her own or others' eyes should see him in that forlorn condition, she sends one of her trusted servants to meet him, and convey him privately to some comfortable abode, and to furnish him with such state as befitted his dignity. After which Cordeilla, with the king her husband, went in state to meet him, and, after an honorable reception, the king permitted his wife Cordeilla to go with an army and set her father again upon his throne. They prospered, subdued the wicked sisters and their consorts, and Leir obtained the crown and held it three years. Cordeilla succeeded him, and reigned five years; but the sons of her sisters, after that, rebelled against her, and she lost both her crown and life.

Shakespeare has chosen this story as the subject of his tragedy of King Lear, varying its details in some respects. The madness of Lear, and the ill success of Cordeilla's attempt to reinstate her father, are the principal variations, and those in the names will also be noticed. Our narrative is drawn from Milton's History; and thus the reader will perceive that the story of Leir has had the distinguished honor of being told by the two acknowledged chiefs of British literature.

FERREX AND PORREX

FERREX AND PORREX were brothers, who held the kingdom after Leir. They quarrelled about the supremacy, and Porrex expelled his brother, who, obtaining aid from Suard, king of the Franks, returned and made war upon Porrex. Ferrex was slain in battle, and his forces dispersed. When their mother came to hear of her son's death, who was her favorite, she fell into a great rage, and conceived a mortal hatred against the survivor. She took, therefore, her opportunity when he was asleep, fell upon him, and, with the assistance of her women, tore him

in pieces. This horrid story would not be worth relating, were it not for the fact that it has furnished the plot for the first tragedy which was written in the English language. It was entitled Gorboduc, but in the second edition Ferrex and Porrex, and was the production of Thomas Sackville, afterwards earl of Dorset, and Thomas Norton, a barrister. Its date was 1561.

DUNWALLO MOLMUTIUS

THIS is the next name of note. Molmutius established the Molmutine laws, which bestowed the privilege of sanctuary on temples, cities, and the roads leading to them, and gave the same protection to ploughs, extending a religious sanction to the labors of the field. Shakespeare alludes to him in Cymbeline, Act III, Sc. I.:

"Molmutius made our laws;
Who was the first of Britain which did put
His brows within a golden crown, and called
Himself a king."

BRENNUS AND BELINUS

THE sons of Molmutius, succeeded him. They quarrelled, and Brennus was driven out of the island, and took refuge in Gaul, where he met with such favor from the king of the Allobroges, that he gave him his daughter in marriage, and made him his partner on the throne. Brennus is the name which the Roman historians give to the famous leader of the Gauls who took Rome in the time of Camillus. Geoffrey of Monmouth claims the glory of the conquest for the British prince, after he had become king of the Allobroges.

ELIDURE

AFTER Belinus and Brennus there reigned several kings of little note, and then came Elidure. Arthgallo, his brother, being king, gave great offence to his powerful nobles, who rose against him, deposed him, and advanced Elidure to the throne. Arthgallo fled, and endeavored to find assistance in the neighboring kingdoms to reinstate him, but found none. Elidure reigned prosperously and wisely. After five years' possession of the kingdom, one day, when hunting, he met in the forest his brother, Arthgallo, who had been deposed. After long wandering, unable longer to bear the poverty to which he was reduced, he had returned to Britain, with only ten followers, designing to repair to those who had formerly been his friends. Elidure, at the sight of his brother in distress, forgetting all animosities, ran to him, and embraced him. He took Arthgallo home with him, and concealed him in the palace. After this he feigned himself sick, and, calling his nobles about him, induced them, partly by persuasion, partly by force, to consent to his abdicating the kingdom, and reinstating his brother on the throne. The agreement being ratified, Elidure took the crown from his own head, and put it on his brother's head. Arthgallo after this reigned ten years, well and wisely, exercising strict justice towards all men.

He died, and left the kingdom to his sons, who reigned with various fortunes, but were not long-lived, and left no offspring, so that Elidure was again advanced to the throne, and finished the course of his life in just and virtuous actions, receiving the name of *the pious*, from the love and admiration of his subjects.

Wordsworth has taken the story of Artegal and Elidure for the subject of a poem, which is No.2 of "Poems founded on the Affections."

LUD

AFTER Elidure the Chronicle names many kings, but none of special note, till we come to Lud, who greatly enlarged Trinovant, his capital, and surrounded it with a wall. He changed its name, bestowing upon it his own, so that thenceforth it was called Lud's town, afterwards London. Lud was buried by the gate of the city called after him Ludgate. He had two sons, but they were not old enough at the time of their father's death to sustain the cares of government, and therefore their uncle Caswallaun, or

Cassibellaunus, succeeded to the kingdom. He was a brave and magnificent prince, so that his fame reached to distant countries.

CASSIBELLAUNUS

ABOUT this time it happened (as is found in the Roman histories) that Julius Cæsar, having subdued Gaul, came to the shore opposite Britain. And having resolved to add this island also to his conquest, he prepared ships and transported his army across the sea, to the mouth of the river Thames. Here he was met by Cassibellaunus, with all his forces, and a battle ensued, in which Nennius, the brother of Cassibellaunus, engaged in single combat with Cæsar. After several furious blows given and received, the sword of Cæsar stuck so fast in the shield of Nennius, that it could not be pulled out, and, the combatants being separated by the intervention of the troops, Nennius remained possessed of this trophy. At last, after the greater part of the day was spent, the Britons poured in so fast that Cæsar was forced to retire to his camp and fleet. And finding it useless to continue the war any longer at that time, he returned to Gaul.

Shakespeare alludes to Cassibellaunus, in Cymbeline:

"The famed Cassibelan, who was once at point
(O giglot fortune!) to master Cæsar's sword,
Made Lud's town with rejoicing fires bright,
And Britons strut with courage."

KYMBELINUS, OR CYMBELINE

CÆSAR, on a second invasion of the island, was more fortunate, and compelled the Britons to pay tribute. Cymbeline, the nephew of the king, was delivered to the Romans as a hostage for the faithful fulfilment of the treaty, and, being carried to Rome by Cæsar, he was there brought up in the Roman arts and accomplishments. Being afterwards restored to his country, and placed on the throne, he was attached to the Romans, and continued through all his reign at peace with them. His sons, Guiderius and Arviragus, who make their appearance in Shakespeare's play of Cymbeline, succeeded their father, and, refusing to pay tribute to the Romans, brought on another invasion. Guiderius was slain, but Arviragus afterward made terms with the Romans, and reigned prosperously many years.

ARMORICA

THE next event of note is the conquest and colonization of Armorica, by Maximus, a Roman general, and Conan, lord of Miniadoc or Denbigh land, in Wales. The name of the country was changed to Brittany, or Lesser Britain; and so completely was it possessed by the British colonists, that the language became assimilated to that spoken in Wales, and it is said that to this day the peasantry of the two countries can understand each other when speaking their native language.

The Romans eventually succeeded in establishing themselves in the island, and after the lapse of several generations they became blended with the natives so that no distinction existed between the two races. When at length the Roman armies were withdrawn from Britain, their departure was a matter of regret to the inhabitants, as it left them without protection against the barbarous tribes, Scots, Picts, and Norwegians, who harassed the country incessantly. This was the state of things when the era of King Arthur began.

The Adventure of Albion, the giant, with Hercules is alluded to by Spenser, Faery Queene, Book IV., Canto XI.:

"For Albion the son of Neptune was;
Who for the proof of his great puissance,
Out of his Albion did on dry foot pass,
Into old Gaul that now is cleped France,
To fight with Hercules, that did advance
To vanquish all the world with matchless might;
And there his mortal part by great mischance
Was slain."

CHAPTER III

ARTHUR

WE shall begin our history of King Arthur by giving those particulars of his life which appear to rest on historical evidence; and then proceed to record those legends concerning him which form the earliest portion of British literature.

Arthur was a prince of the tribe of Britons called Silures, whose country was South Wales,—the son of Uther, named Pendragon, a title given to an elective sovereign, paramount over the many kings of Britain. He appears to have commenced his martial career about the year 500, and was raised to the Pendragonship about ten years later. He is said to have gained twelve victories over the Saxons. The most important of them was that of Badon, by some supposed to be Bath, by others Berkshire. This was the last of his battles with the Saxons, and checked their progress so effectually that Arthur experienced no more annoyance from them, and reigned in peace, until the revolt of his nephew Modred, twenty years later, which led to the fatal battle of Camlan, in Cornwall, in 542. Modred was slain, and Arthur, mortally wounded, was conveyed by sea to Glastonbury, where he died, and was buried. Tradition preserved the memory of the place of his interment within the abbey as we are told by Giraldus Cambrensis, who was present when the grave was opened by command of Henry II in 1150, and saw the bones and sword of the monarch, and a leaden cross let into his tombstone, with the inscription in rude Roman letters, "Here lies buried the famous King Arthur, in the island Avalonia." This story has been elegantly versified by Warton. A popular traditional belief was long entertained among the Britons that Arthur was not dead but had been carried off to be healed of his wounds in Fairy-land, and that he would reappear to avenge his countrymen, and reinstate them in the sovereignty of Britain. In Warton's Ode a bard relates to King Henry the traditional story of Arthur's death, and closes with these lines:

"Yet in vain a paynim foe
Armed with fate the mighty blow;
For when he fell, the Elfin queen,

All in secret and unseen,
O'er the fainting hero threw
Her mantle of ambrosial blue,
And bade her spirits bear him far,
In Merlin's agate-axled car,
To her green isle's enamelled steep,
Far in the navel of the deep.
O'er his wounds she sprinkled dew
From flowers that in Arabia grew.

· · · · · · ·

There he reigns a mighty king,
Thence to Britain shall return,
If right prophetic rolls I learn,
Borne on victory's spreading plume,
His ancient sceptre to resume,
His knightly table to restore,
And brave the tournaments of yore."

After this narration another bard came forward, who recited a different story:

"When Arthur bowed his haughty crest,
No princess veiled in azure vest
Snatched him, by Merlin's powerful spell,
In groves of golden bliss to dwell;
But when he fell, with winged speed,
Hi-champions, on a milk-white steed,
From the battle's hurricane
Bore him to Joseph's towered fane,[1]

In the fair vale of Avalon;
There, with chanted orison
And the long blaze of tapers clear,
The stoled fathers met the bier;

---

[1] Glastonbury Abbey, said to be founded by Joseph of Atimathea, in a spot anciently called the island or valley of Avalonia.

Tennyson, in his Palace of Art, alludes to the legend of Arthur's rescue by the Faery queen, thus:

"Or mythic Uther's deeply wounded son,
  In some fair space of sloping greens,
Lay dozing in the vale of Avalon.
  And watched by weeping queens."

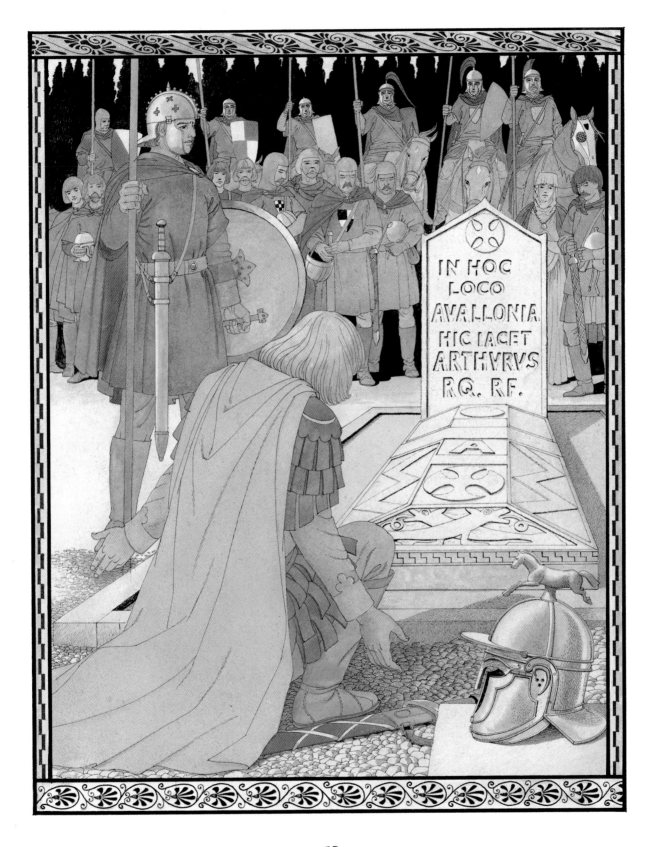

Through the dim aisles, in order dread
Of martial woe, the chief they led,
And deep entombed in holy ground,
Before the altar's solemn bound."

It must not be concealed, that the very existence of Arthur has been denied by some. Milton says of him: "As to Arthur, more renowned in songs and romances than in true stories, who he was, and whether ever any such reigned in Britain, hath been doubted heretofore, and may again, with good reason." Modern critics, however, admit that there was a prince of this name, and find proof of it in the frequent mention of him in the writings of the Welsh bards. But the Arthur of romance, according to Mr. Owen, a Welsh scholar and antiquarian, is a mythological person. "Arthur," he says, "is the Great Bear, as the name literally implies (Arctos, Arcturus), and perhaps this constellation, being so near the pole, and visibly describing a circle in a small space, is the origin of the famous Round Table." Let us now turn to the history of King Arthur, as recorded by the romantic chroniclers.

Constans, king of Britain, had three sons, Moines, Ambrosius, otherwise called Uther, and Pendragon. Moines, soon after his accession to the crown, was vanquished by the Saxons, in consequence of the treachery of his seneschal, Vortigern, and growing unpopular through misfortune, he was killed by his subjects, and the traitor Vortigern chosen in his place.

Vortigern was soon after defeated in a great battle by Uther and Pendragon, the surviving brothers of Moines, and Pendragon ascended the throne.

This prince had great confidence in the wisdom of Merlin, and made him his chief adviser. About this time a dreadful war arose between the Saxons and Britons. Merlin obliged the royal brothers to swear fidelity to each other, but predicted that one of them must fall in the first battle. The Saxons were routed, and Pendragon, being slain, was succeeded by Uther, who now assumed, in addition to his own name, the appellation of Pendragon.

Merlin still continued a favorite counsellor. At the request of Uther, he transported by magic art enormous stones from Ireland to form the sepulchre of Pendragon. These stones constitute the monument now called Stonehenge, on Salisbury Plain.

Merlin next proceeded to Carlisle to prepare the Round Table at which he seated an assemblage of the great nobles of the country. The companions admitted to this high order were bound by oath to assist each other at the hazard of their own lives, to attempt singly the most perilous adventures, to lead, when necessary, a life of monastic solitude, to fly to arms at the first summons, and never to retire from battle till they had defeated the enemy, unless night intervened and separated the combatants.

Soon after this institution, the king invited all his barons to the celebration of a great festival, which he proposed holding annually at Carlisle.

As the knights had obtained the sovereign's permission to bring their ladies along with them, the beautiful Igerne accompanied her husband, Gerlois, duke of Tintadiel, to one of these anniversaries. The king became deeply enamored of the duchess, and disclosed his passion; but Igerne repelled his advances, and revealed his solicitations to her husband. On hearing this, the duke instantly removed from court with Igerne, and without taking leave of Uther. The king complained to his council of this want of duty, and they decided that the duke should be summoned to court, and, if refractory, should be treated as a rebel. As he refused to obey the citation, the king carried war into the estates of his vassal, and besieged him in the strong castle of Tintadiel. Merlin transformed the king into the likeness of Gerlois, and enabled him to have many stolen interviews with Igerne. At length the duke was killed in battle, and the king espoused Igerne.

From this union sprang Arthur, who succeeded his father, Uther, upon the throne.

ARTHUR CHOSEN KING

ARTHUR, though only fifteen years old at his father's death, was elected king, at a general meeting of the nobles. It was not done without opposition, for there were many ambitious competitors; but Bishop Brice, a person of great sanctity, on Christmas eve addressed the assembly, and represented that it would well become them, at that solemn season, to put up their prayers for some token which should manifest the intentions of Providence respecting their future sovereign. This was done, and with such success, that the service was scarcely ended, when a miraculous stone was discovered, before the church door, and in the stone was firmly fixed a sword, with the following words engraven on its hilt:

> "I am hight Escalibore,
> Unto a king fair tresore."

Bishop Brice, after exhorting the assembly to offer up their thanksgivings for this signal miracle, proposed a law, that whoever should be able to draw out the sword from the stone, should be acknowledged as sovereign of the Britons; and his proposal was decreed by general acclamation. The tributary kings of Uther, and the most famous knights, successively put their strength to the proof, but the miraculous sword resisted all their efforts. It stood till Candlemas; it stood till Easter, and till Pentecost, when the best knights in the kingdom usually assembled for the annual tournament. Arthur, who was at that time serving in the capacity of squire to his foster-brother, Sir Kay, attended his master to the lists. Sir Kay fought with great valor and success, but had the misfortune to break his sword, and sent Arthur to his mother for a new one. Arthur hastened home, but did not find the lady; but having observed near the church a sword sticking in a stone, he galloped to the place, drew out the sword with great ease, and delivered it to his master. Sir Kay would willingly have assumed to himself the distinction conferred by the possession of the sword; but when, to confirm the doubters, the sword was replaced in the stone, he was utterly unable to withdraw it, and it would yield a second time to no hand but Arthur's. Thus decisively pointed out by heaven as their king, Arthur was by general consent proclaimed as such, and an early day appointed for his solemn coronation.

Immediately after his election to the crown, Arthur found himself opposed by eleven kings and one duke, who with a vast army were actually encamped in the forest of Rockingham. By Merlin's advice Arthur sent an embassy to Brittany to solicit aid of King Ban and King Bohort, two of the best knights in the world. They accepted the call, and with a powerful army crossed the sea, landing at Portsmouth, where they were received with great rejoicing. The rebel kings

28 ▷

were still superior in numbers; but Merlin by a powerful enchantment, caused all their tents to fall down at once, and in the confusion Arthur with his allies fell upon them and totally routed them.

After defeating the rebels, Arthur took the field against the Saxons. As they were too strong for him unaided, he sent an embassy to Armorica, beseeching the assistance of Hoel, who soon after brought over an army to his aid. The two kings joined their forces, and sought the enemy, whom they met, and both sides prepared for a decisive engagement. "Arthur himself," as Geoffrey of Monmouth relates, "dressed in a breastplate worthy of so great a king, places on his head a golden helmet engraved with the semblance of a dragon. Over his shoulders he throws his shield called Priwen, on which a picture of the Holy Virgin constantly recalled her to his memory. Girt with Caliburn, a most excellent sword, and fabricated in the isle of Avalon, he graces his right hand with the lance named Ron. This was a long and broad spear, well contrived for slaughter." After a severe conflict, Arthur, calling on the name of the Virgin, rushes into the midst of his enemies, and destroys multitudes of them with the formidable Caliburn, and puts the rest to flight. Hoel, being detained by sickness, took no part in this battle.

This is called the victory of Mount Badon, and, however disguised by fable, it is regarded by historians as a real event.

The feats performed by Arthur at the battle of Badon Mount are thus celebrated in Drayton's verse:

"They sung how he himself at Badon bore, that day,
When at the glorious goal his British scepter lay;
Two dais together how the battle stronglie stood;
Pendragon's worthie son, who waded there in blood,
Three hundred Saxons slew with his owne valiant
    hand."

Song IV

MERLIN

"—The most famous man of all those times,
Merlin, who knew the range of all their arts,
Had built the King his havens, ships and halls,

Was also Bard, and knew the starry heavens;
The people called him wizard."

Tennyson

Now Merlin, of whom we have already heard somewhat and shall hear more, was the son of no mortal father, but of an Incubus, one of a class of beings not absolutely wicked, but far from good, who inhabit the regions of the air. Merlin's mother was a virtuous young woman, who, on the birth of her son, intrusted him to a priest, who hurried him to the baptismal fount, and so saved him from sharing the lot of his father, though he retained many marks of his unearthly origin.

At this time Vortigern reigned in Britain. He was a usurper, who had caused the death of his sovereign, Moines, and driven the two brothers of the late king, whose names were Uther and Pendragon, into banishment. Vortigern, who lived in constant fear of the return of the rightful heirs of the kingdom, began to erect a strong tower for defence. The edifice, when brought by the workmen to a certain height, three times fell to the ground, without any apparent cause. The king consulted his astrologers on this wonderful event, and learned from them that it would be necessary to bathe the cornerstone of the foundation with the blood of a child born without a mortal father.

In search of such an infant, Vortigern sent his messengers all over the kingdom, and they by accident discovered Merlin, whose lineage seemed to point him out as the individual wanted. They took him to the king; but Merlin, young as he was, explained to the king the absurdity of attempting to rescue the fabric by such means, for he told him the true cause of the instability of the tower was its being placed over the den of two immense dragons, whose combats shook the earth above them. The king ordered his workmen to dig beneath the tower, and when they had done so they discovered two enormous serpents, the one white as milk, the other red as fire. The multitude looked on with amazement, <u>till the serpents, slowly rising from their den, and expanding their enormous folds, began the combat, when every one fled in terror</u>, except Merlin, who stood by clapping his hands and cheering on the conflict. The red dragon was slain, and the white one, gliding through a cleft in the rock, disappeared.

These animals typified, as Merlin afterwards explained, the invasion of Uther and Pendragon, the rightful princes, who soon after landed with a great army. Vortigern was defeated, and afterwards burned alive in the castle he had taken such pains to construct. On the death of Vortigern, Pendragon ascended the throne. Merlin became his chief adviser, and often assisted the king by his magical arts. Among other endowments, he had the power to transform himself into any shape he pleased. At one time he appeared as a dwarf, at others as a damsel, a page, or even a greyhound or a stag. This faculty he often employed for the service of the king, and sometimes also for the diversion of the court and the sovereign.

Merlin continued to be a favorite counsellor through the reigns of Pendragon, Uther, and Arthur, and at last disappeared from view, and was no more found among men, through the treachery of his mistress, Viviane, the Fairy, which happened in this wise.

Merlin, having become enamored of the fair Viviane, the Lady of the Lake, was weak enough to impart to her various important secrets of his art, being impelled by a fatal destiny, of which he was at the same time fully aware. The lady, however, was not content with his devotion, unbounded as it seems to have been, but "cast about," the Romance tells us, how she might "detain him for evermore," and one day addressed him in these terms: "Sir, I would that we should make a fair place and a suitable, so contrived by art and by cunning that it might never be undone, and that you and I should be there in joy and solace." "My lady," said Merlin, "I will do all this." "Sir," said she, "I would not have you do it, but you shall teach me, and I will do it, and then it will be more to my mind." "I grant you this," said Merlin. Then he began to devise, and the damsel put it all in writing. And when he had devised the whole, then had the damsel full great joy, and showed him greater semblance of love than she had ever before made, and they sojourned together a long while. At length it fell out that, as they were going one day in hand through the forest of Brécéliande, they found a bush of white-thorn, which was laden with flowers; and they seated themselves, under the shade of this white-thorn, upon the grass, and Merlin laid his head upon the damsel's lap, and fell asleep. Then the damsel rose, and made a ring with her wimple round the bush, and round Merlin, and began her enchantments, such as he himself had taught her; and nine times she made the ring, and nine times she made the enchantment, and then she went and sat down by him, and placed his head again upon her lap. And when he awoke, and looked round him, it seemed to him that he was enclosed in the strongest tower in the world, and laid upon a fair bed. Then said he to the dame: "My lady, you have deceived me, unless you abide with me, for no one hath power to unmake this tower but you alone." She then promised that she would be often there, and in this she held her covenant with him. And Merlin never went out of that tower where his Mistress Viviane had enclosed him; but she entered and went out again when she listed.

After this event Merlin was never more known to hold converse with any mortal but Viviane, except on one occasion. Arthur, having for some time missed him from his court, sent several of his knights in search of him, and among the number Sir Gawain, who met with a very unpleasant adventure while engaged in this quest. Happening to pass a damsel on his road, and neglecting to salute her, she revenged herself for his incivility by transforming him into a hideous dwarf. He was bewailing aloud his evil fortune as he went through the forest of Brécéliande, when suddenly he heard the voice of one groaning on his right hand; and, looking that way, he could see nothing save a kind of smoke, which seemed like air, and through which he could not pass. Merlin then addressed him from out the smoke, and told him by what misadventure he was imprisoned there. "Ah, sir!" he added, "you will never see me more, and that grieves me, but I cannot remedy it; I shall never more speak to you, nor to any other person, save only my mistress. But do thou hasten to King Arthur, and charge him from me to undertake, without delay, the quest of the Sacred Graal. The knight is already born, and has received knighthood at his hands, who is destined to accomplish this quest." And after this he comforted Gawain under his transformation, assuring him that he should speedily be disenchanted; and he predicted to him that he should find the king at Carduel, in Wales, on his return, and that all the other knights who had been on like quest would arrive there the same day as himself. And all this came to pass as Merlin had said.

Merlin is frequently introduced in the tales of chivalry, but it is chiefly on great occasions, and at a period subsequent to his death, or magical disappearance. In the romantic poems of Italy, and in Spenser, Merlin is chiefly represented as a magical artist. Spenser represents him as the artificer of the impenetrable shield and other armor of Prince Arthur (Faery Queene, Book I., Canto vii.), and of a mirror, in which a damsel viewed her lover's shade. The Fountain of Love, in the Orlando Innamorato, is described as his work; and in the poem of Ariosto we are told of a hall adorned with prophetic paintings, which demons had executed in a single night, under the direction of Merlin.

The following legend is from Spenser's Faery Queene (Book III., Canto iii.):

CAER-MERDIN, OR CAERMARTHEN (IN WALES), MERLIN'S TOWER, AND THE IMPRISONED FIENDS

Forthwith themselves disguising both, in straunge
And base attire, that none might them bewray,
To Maridunum, that is now by chaunge
Of name Caer-Merdin called, they took their way:
There the wise Merlin, whylome wont (they say)
To make his wonne, low underneath the ground
In a deep delve, far from the view of day,
That of no living wight he mote be found,
Whenso he counselled with his sprights encompassed round.

And if thou ever happen that same way
To travel, go to see that dreadful place:
It is a hideous hollow cave (they say)
Under a rock that lies a little space,
From the swift Barry, tombling down apace
Amongst the woody hills of Dynevor;
But dare not thou, I charge, in any case,
To enter into that same baleful bower,
For fear the cruel fiends should thee unwares devour.

But standing high aloft, low lay thine ear,
And there such ghastly noise of iron chains
And brazen cauldrons thou shalt rumbling hear,

Which thousand sprites with long enduring pains
Do toss, that it will stun thy feeble brains;
And oftentimes great groans, and grievous stounds,
When too huge toil and labor them constrains;
And oftentimes loud strokes and ringing sounds
From under that deep rock most horribly rebounds.

The cause some say is this. A little while
Before that Merlin died, he did intend
A brazen wall in compas to compile
About Caermerdin, and did it commend
Unto these sprites to bring to perfect end;
During which work the Lady of the Lake,
Whom long he loved, for him in haste did send;
Who, thereby forced his workmen to forsake,
Them bound till his return their labor not to slack.

In the meantime, through that false lady's train,
He was surprised, and buried under beare,[1]
Ne ever to his work returned again;
Natheless those fiends may not their work forbear,
So greatly his commandëment they fear;
But there do toil and travail day and night,
Until that brazen wall they up do rear.
For Merlin had in magic more insight
Than ever him before or after living wight.

GUENEVER

"Leodogran, the Ring of Cameliard,
Had one fair daughter, and none other child,
And she was fairest of all flesh on earth,
Guenevere, and in her his one delight."

Tennyson

MERLIN had planned for Arthur a marriage with the daughter of King Laodegan[2] of Carmalide. By his advice Arthur paid a visit to the court of that

---

[1] *Buried under beare.* Buried under something which enclosed him like a coffin or bier.

[2] The spelling of these proper names is very often only a matter of taste. I think, however, *Leodogran* and *Guenevere* are less common than *Laodegan* and *Guenever*.

sovereign, attended only by Merlin and by thirty-nine knights whom the magician had selected for that service. On their arrival they found Laodegan and his peers sitting in council, endeavoring, but with small prospect of success, to devise means for resisting the impending attack of Ryence, king of Ireland, who, with fifteen tributary kings and an almost innumerable army, had nearly surrounded the city. Merlin, who acted as leader of the band of British knights, announced them as strangers, who came to offer the king their services in his wars; but under the express condition that they should be at liberty to conceal their names and quality until they should think proper to divulge them. These terms were thought very strange, but were thankfully accepted, and the strangers, after taking the usual oath to the king, retired to the lodging which Merlin had prepared for them.

A few days after this, the enemy, regardless of a truce into which they had entered with King Laodegan, suddenly issued from their camp and made an attempt to surprise the city. Cleodalis, the king's general, assembled the royal forces with all possible despatch. Arthur and his companions also flew to arms, and Merlin appeared at their head, bearing a standard on which was emblazoned a terrific dragon. Merlin advanced to the gate, and commanded the porter to open it, which the porter refused to do, without the king's order. Merlin thereupon took up the gate, with all its appurtenances of locks, bars, and bolts, and directed his troop to pass through, after which he replaced it in perfect order. He then set spurs to his horse, and dashed, at the head of the little troop, into a body of two thousand Pagans. The disparity of numbers being so enormous, Merlin cast a spell upon the enemy, so as to prevent their seeing the small number of their assailants; notwithstanding which the British knights were hard pressed. But the people of the city, who saw from the walls this unequal contest, were ashamed of leaving the small body of strangers to their fate, so they opened the gate and sallied forth. The numbers were now more nearly equal, and Merlin revoked his spell, so that the two armies encountered on fair terms. Where Arthur, Ban, Bohort, and the rest fought, the king's army had the advantage; but in another part of the field the king himself was surrounded and carried off by the enemy. This sad sight was seen by Guenever, the fair daughter of the king, who stood on the city wall and looked at the battle. She was in dreadful distress, tore her hair, and swooned away.

But Merlin, aware of what passed in every part of the field, suddenly collected his knights, led them out of the battle, intercepted the passage of the party who were carrying away the king, charged them with irresistible impetuosity, cut in pieces or dispersed the whole escort, and rescued the king. In the fight Arthur encountered Caulang, a giant fifteen feet high, and the fair Guenever, who already began to feel a strong interest in the handsome young stranger, trembled for the issue of the contest. But Arthur, dealing a dreadful blow on the shoulder of the monster, cut through his neck so that his head hung over on one side, and in this condition his horse carried him about the field, to the great horror and dismay of the Pagans. Guenever could not refrain from expressing aloud her wish that the gentle knight, who dealt with giants so dexterously, were destined to become her husband, and the wish was echoed by her attendants. The enemy soon turned their backs, and fled with precipitation, closely pursued by Laodegan and his allies.

After the battle Arthur was disarmed and conducted to the bath by the Princess Guenever, while his friends were attended by the other ladies of the court. After the bath the knights were conducted to a magnificent entertainment, at which they were diligently served by the same fair attendants. Laodegan, more and more anxious to know the name and quality of his generous deliverers, and occasionally forming a secret wish that the chief of his guests might be captivated by the charms of his daughter, appeared silent and pensive, and was scarcely roused from his reverie by the banter of his courtiers. Arthur, having had an opportunity of explaining to Guenever his great esteem for her merit, was in the joy of his heart, and was still further delighted by hearing from Merlin the late exploits of Gawain at London, by means of which his immediate return to his dominions was rendered unnecessary, and he was left at liberty to protract his stay at the court of Laodegan. Every day contributed to increase the admiration of the whole court for the gallant strangers, and the passion of Guenever for their chief; and when at last Merlin announced to the king that the object of the visit of the party was to procure a bride for their leader, Laodegan at once presented Guenever to Arthur, telling him that, whatever might be his rank, his merit was sufficient to entitle him to the possession of the heiress of Carmalide. Arthur accepted the lady with the utmost gratitude, and Merlin then proceeded to satisfy the king of the rank of his son-in-law; upon which Laodegan, with all his barons, hastened to do homage to their lawful sovereign, the successor of Uther Pendragon. The fair Guenever was then solemnly betrothed to Arthur, and a magnificent festival was proclaimed, which lasted seven days. At the end of that time, the enemy appearing again with renewed force, it became necessary to resume military operations.[1]

We must now relate what took place at or near London while Arthur was absent from his capital. At this very time a band of young heroes were on their way to Arthur's court, for the purpose of receiving knighthood from him. They were Gawain and his three brothers, nephews of Arthur, sons of King Lot, and Galachin, another nephew, son of King Nanters. King Lot had been one of the rebel chiefs whom Arthur had defeated, but he now hoped by means of the young men to be reconciled to his brother-in-law. He equipped his sons and his nephew with the utmost magnificence, giving them a splendid retinue of young men, sons of earls and barons, all mounted on the best horses, with complete suits of choice armor. They numbered in all seven hundred, but only nine had yet received the order of knighthood; the rest were candidates for that honor, and anxious to earn it by an early encounter with the enemy. Gawain, the leader, was a knight of wonderful strength; but what was most remarkable about him was that his strength was greater at certain hours of the day than at others. From nine o'clock till noon his strength was doubled, and so it was from three to evensong; for the rest of the time it was less remarkable,

though at all times surpassing that of ordinary men.

After a march of three days they arrived in the vicinity of London, where they expected to find Arthur and his court; and very unexpectedly fell in with a large convoy belonging to the enemy, consisting of numerous carts and wagons, all loaded with provisions, and escorted by three thousand men, who had been collecting spoil from all the country round. A single charge from Gawain's impetuous cavalry was sufficient to disperse the escort and to recover the convoy, which was instantly despatched to London. But before long a body of seven thousand fresh soldiers advanced to the attack of the five princes and their little army. Gawain, singling out a chief named Choas, of gigantic size, began the battle by splitting him from the crown of the head to the breast. Galachin encountered King Sanagran, who was also very huge, and cut off his head. Agrivain and Gaheris also performed prodigies of valor. Thus they kept the great army of assailants at bay, though hard pressed, till of a sudden they perceived a strong body of the citizens advancing from London, where the convoy which had been recovered by Gawain had arrived, and informed the mayor and citizens of the danger of their deliverer. The arrival of the Londoners soon decided the contest. The enemy fled in all directions, and Gawain and his friends, escorted by the grateful citizens, entered London, and were received with acclamations. 34 ▷

After the great victory of Mount Badon, by which the Saxons were for the time effectually put down, Arthur turned his arms against the Scots and Picts, whom he routed at Lake Lomond, and compelled to sue for mercy. He then went to York to keep his Christmas, and employed himself in restoring the Christian churches which the Pagans had rifled and overthrown. The following summer he conquered Ireland, and then made a voyage with his fleet to Iceland, which he also subdued. The kings of Gothland and of the Orkneys came voluntarily and made their submission, promising to pay tribute. Then he returned to Britain, where, having established the kingdom, he dwelt twelve years in peace.

During this time he invited over to him all persons whatsoever that were famous for valor in foreign nations, and augmented the number of his domestics,

---

[1]Guenever, the name of Arthur's queen, also written Genievre and Geneura, is familiar to all who are conversant with chivalric lore. It is to her adventures, and those of her true knight, Sir Launcelot, that Dante alludes in the beautiful episode of Francesca da Rimini.

and introduced such politeness into his court as people of the remotest countries thought worthy of their imitation. So that there was not a nobleman who thought himself of any consideration unless his clothes and arms were made in the same fashion as those of Arthur's knights.

Finding himself so powerful at home, Arthur began to form designs for extending his power abroad. So, having prepared his fleet, he first attempted Norway, that he might procure the crown of it for Lot, his sister's husband. Arthur landed in Norway, fought a great battle with the king of that country, defeated him, and pursued the victory till he had reduced the whole country under his dominion and established Lot upon the throne. Then Arthur made a voyage to Gaul and laid siege to the city of Paris. Gaul was at that time a Roman province, and governed by Flollo, the Tribune. When the siege of Paris had continued a month, and the people began to suffer from famine, Flollo challenged Arthur to single combat, proposing to decide the conquest in that way. Arthur gladly accepted the challenge, and slew his adversary in the contest, upon which the citizens surrendered the city to him. After the victory Arthur divided his army into two parts, one of which he committed to the conduct of Hoel, whom he ordered to march into Aquitaine, while he with the other part should endeavor to subdue the other provinces. At the end of nine years, in which time all the parts of Gaul were entirely reduced, Arthur returned to Paris, where he kept his court, and calling an assembly of the clergy and people, established peace and the just administration of the laws in that kingdom. Then he bestowed Normandy upon Bedivere, his butler, and the province of Andegavia upon Kay, his steward,[1] and several others upon his great men that attended him. And,

---

[1]This name, in the French romances, is spelled Queux, which means *head cook*. This would seem to imply that it was a title, and not a name; yet the personage who bore it is never mentioned by any other. He is the chief, if not the only, comic character among the heroes of Arthur's court. He is the Seneschal or Steward, his duties also embracing those of chief of the cooks. In the romances his general character is a compound of valor and buffoonery, always ready to fight, and generally getting the worst of the battle. He is also sarcastic and abusive in his remarks, by which he often gets into trouble. Yet Arthur seems to have an attachment to him and often takes his advice, which is generally wrong.

having settled the peace of the cities and countries, he returned back in the beginning of spring to Britain.

Upon the approach of the feast of Pentecost, Arthur, the better to demonstrate his joy after such triumphant successes, and for the more solemn observation of that festival, and reconciling the minds of the princes that were now subject to him, resolved during that season to hold a magnificent court, to place the crown upon his head, and to invite all the kings and dukes under his subjection to the solemnity. And he pitched upon Caerleon, the City of Legions, as the proper place for his purpose. For, besides its great wealth above the other cities,[1] its situation upon the river Usk, near the Severn sea, was most pleasant and fit for so great a solemnity. For on one side it was washed by that noble river, so that the kings and princes from the countries beyond the seas might have the convenience of sailing up to it. On the other side the beauty of the meadows and groves, and magnificence of the royal palaces, with lofty gilded roofs that adorned it, made it even rival the grandeur of Rome. It was also famous for two churches, whereof one was adorned with a choir of virgins, who devoted themselves wholly to the service of God, and the other maintained a convent of priests. Besides, there was a college of two hundred philosophers, who, being learned in astronomy and the other arts, were diligent in observing the courses of the stars, and gave Arthur true predictions of the events that would happen. In this place, therefore, which afforded such delights, were preparations made for the ensuing festival.

---

[1]Several cities are allotted to King Arthur by the romance-writers. The principal are Caerleon, Camelot, and Carlisle.

Caerleon derives its name from its having been the station of one of the legions during the dominion of the Romans. It is called by Latin writers Urbs Legionum, the City of Legions,—the former word being rendered into Welsh by *Caer*, meaning city, and the latter contracted into *lleon*. The river Usk retains its name in modern geography, and there is a town or City of Caerleon upon it, though the city of Cardiff is thought to be the scene of Arthur's Court. Chester also bears the Welsh name of Caerleon; for Chester, derived from *castra*, Latin for *camp*, is the designation of military headquarters.

Camelot is thought to be Winchester.

Shalott is Guildford.

Hamo's Port is Southampton.

Carlisle is the city still retaining that name, near the Scottish border. But this name is also sometimes applied to other places, which were, like itself, military stations.

Ambassadors were then sent into several kingdoms, to invite to court the princes both of Gaul and of the adjacent islands. Accordingly there came Augusel, king of Albania, now Scotland, Cadwallo, king of Venedotia, now North Wales, Sater, king of Demetia, now South Wales; also the archbishops of the metropolitan sees, London and York, and Dubricius, bishop of Caerleon, the City of Legions. This prelate, who was primate of Britain, was so eminent for his piety that he could cure any sick person by his prayers. There were also the counts of the principal cities, and many other worthies of no less dignity.

From the adjacent islands came Guillamurius, king of Ireland; Gunfasius, king of the Orkneys, Malvasius, king of Iceland, Lot, king of Norway, Bedivere the butler, duke of Normandy, Kay the sewer, duke of Andegavia; also the twelve peers of Gaul, and Hoel, duke of the Armorican Britons, with his nobility, who came with such a train of mules, horses, and rich furniture, as is difficult to describe. Besides these, there remained no prince of any consideration on this side of Spain who came not upon this invitation, and no wonder, when Arthur's munificence, which was celebrated over the whole world, made him beloved by all people.

When all were assembled, upon the day of the solemnity, the archbishops were conducted to the palace in order to place the crown upon the king's head. Then Dubricius, inasmuch as the court was held in his diocese, made himself ready to celebrate the office. As soon as the king was invested with his royal habiliments, he was conducted in great pomp to the metropolitan church, having four kings, viz., of Albania, Cornwall, Demetia, and Venedotia, bearing four golden swords before him. On another part was the queen, dressed out in her richest ornaments, conducted by the archbishops and bishops to the Church of Virgins; the four queens, also, of the kings last mentioned, bearing before her four white doves, according to ancient custom. When the whole procession was ended, so transporting was the harmony of the musical instruments and voices, whereof there was a vast variety in both churches, that the knights who attended were in doubt which to prefer, and therefore crowded from one to the other by turns, and were far from being tired of the solemnity, though the whole day had been spent in it. At last, when divine service was over at both churches, the king and queen put off their crowns, and, putting on their lighter ornaments, went to the banquet. When they had all taken their seats according to precedence, Kay the sewer, in rich robes of ermine, with a thousand young noblemen all in like manner clothed in rich attire, served up the dishes. From another part Bedivere the butler was followed by the same number of attendants, who waited with all kinds of cups and drinking-vessels. And there was food and drink in abundance, and everything was of the best kind, and served in the best manner. For at that time Britain had arrived at such a pitch of grandeur that in riches, luxury, and politeness it far surpassed all other kingdoms.

As soon as the banquets were over they went into the fields without the city, to divert themselves with various sports, such as shooting with bows and arrows, tossing the pike, casting of heavy stones and rocks, playing at dice, and the like, and all these inoffensively, and without quarrelling. In this manner were three days spent, and after that they separated, and the kings and noblemen departed to their several homes.

After this Arthur reigned five years in peace. Then came ambassadors from Lucius Tiberius, Procurator under Leo, Emperor of Rome, demanding tribute. But Arthur refused to pay tribute, and prepared for war. As soon as the necessary dispositions were made, he committed the government of his kingdom to his nephew Modred and to Queen Guenever, and marched with his army to Hamo's Port, where the wind stood fair for him. The army crossed over in safety, and landed at the mouth of the river Barba. And there they pitched their tents to wait the arrival of the kings of the islands.

As soon as all the forces were arrived, Arthur marched forward to Augustodunum, and encamped on the banks of the river Alba. Here repeated battles were fought, in all which the Britons, under their valiant leaders, Hoel, duke of Armorica, and Gawain, nephew to Arthur, had the advantage. At length Lucius Tiberius determined to retreat, and wait for the Emperor Leo to join him with fresh troops. But Arthur, anticipating this event, took possession of a certain valley, and closed up the way of retreat to Lucius, compelling him to fight a decisive battle, in which Arthur lost some of the bravest of his knights and most faithful followers. But on the other hand Lucius Tiberius was slain, and his army totally defeated. The fugitives dispersed over the country, some to the by-ways and woods, some to the cities and towns, and all other places where they could hope for safety.

Arthur stayed in those parts till the next winter was over, and employed his time in restoring order and settling the government. He then returned into England, and celebrated his victories with great splendor.

Then the king established all his knights, and to them that were not rich he gave lands, and charged them all never to do outrage nor murder, and always to flee treason; also, by no means to be cruel, but to give mercy unto him that asked mercy, upon pain of forfeiture of their worship and lordship; and always to do ladies, damsels, and gentlewomen service, upon pain of death. Also that no man take battle in a wrongful quarrel, for no law, nor for any world's goods. Unto this were all the knights sworn of the Table Round, both old and young. And at every year were they sworn at the high feast of Pentecost.

KING ARTHUR SLAYS THE GIANT OF ST. MICHAEL'S MOUNT

WHILE the army was encamped in Brittany, awaiting the arrival of the kings, there came a countryman to Arthur, and told him that a giant, whose cave was in a neighboring mountain, called St. Michael's Mount, had for a long time been accustomed to carry off the children of the peasants, to devour them. "And now he hath taken the duchess of Brittany, as she rode with her attendants, and hath carried her away in spite of all they could do." "Now, fellow," said King Arthur, "canst thou bring me there where this giant haunteth?" "Yea, sure," said the good man; "lo, yonder where thou seest two great fires, there shalt thou find him, and more treasure than I suppose is in all France beside." Then the king called to him Sir Bedivere and Sir Kay, and commanded them to make ready horse and harness for himself and them; for after evening he would ride on pilgrimage to St. Michael's Mount.

So they three departed, and rode forth till they came to the foot of the mount. And there the king commanded them to tarry, for he would himself go up into that mount. So he ascended the hill till he came to a great fire, and there he found an aged woman sitting by a new-made grave, making great sorrow. Then King Arthur saluted her, and demanded of her wherefore she made such lamentation; to whom she answered: "Sir knight, speak low, for yonder is a devil, and if he hear thee speak he will come and destroy thee. For ye cannot make resistance to him, he is so fierce and so strong. He hath murdered the duchess, which here lieth, who was the fairest of all the world, wife to Sir Hoel, duke of Brittany." "Dame," said the king, "I come from the noble conqueror, King Arthur, to treat with that tyrant." "Fie on such treaties," said she; "he setteth not by the king, nor by no man else." "Well," said Arthur, "I will accomplish my message for all your fearful words." So he went forth by the crest of the hill, and saw where the giant sat at supper, gnawing on the limb of a man, and baking his broad limbs at the fire, and three fair damsels lying bound, whose lot it was to be devoured in their turn. When King Arthur beheld that he had great compassion on them, so that his heart bled for sorrow. Then he hailed the giant, saying, "He that all the world ruleth give thee short life and shameful death. Why hast thou murdered this duchess? Therefore come forth, thou caitiff, for this day thou shalt die by my hand." Then the giant started up, and took a great club, and smote at the king, and smote off his coronal; and then the king struck him in the belly with his sword, and made a fearful wound. Then the giant threw away his club, and caught the king in his arms, so that he crushed his ribs. Then the three maidens kneeled down and prayed for help and comfort for Arthur. And Arthur weltered and wrenched, so that he was one while under, and another time above. And so weltering and wallowing they rolled down the hill, and ever as they weltered Arthur smote him with his dagger; and it fortuned they came to the place where the two knights were. And when they saw the king fast in the giant's arms they came and loosed him. Then the king commanded Sir Kay to smite off the giant's head, and to set it on the truncheon of a spear, and fix it on the barbican, that all the people might see and behold it. This was done, and anon it was known through all the country, wherefore the people came and thanked the king. And he said, "Give your thanks to God; and take ye the giant's spoil and divide it among you." And King Arthur caused a church to be built on that hill in honor of St. Michael.

KING ARTHUR GETS A SWORD FROM THE LADY OF THE LAKE

ONE day King Arthur rode forth, and on a sudden he was ware of three churls chasing Merlin to have slain him. And the king rode unto them and bade them, "Flee, churls!" Then were they afraid when they saw a knight, and fled. "O Merlin," said Arthur, "here hadst thou been slain, for all thy crafts, had I not been by." "Nay," said Merlin, "not so, for I could save myself if I would; but thou art more near thy death than I am." So, as they went thus talking, King Arthur perceived where sat a knight on horseback, as if to guard the pass. "Sir knight," said Arthur, "for what cause abidest thou here?" Then the knight said, "There may no knight ride this way unless he joust with me, for such is the custom of the pass." "I will amend that custom," said the king. Then they ran together, and they met so hard that their spears were shivered. Then they drew their swords and fought a strong battle, with many great strokes. But at length the sword of the knight smote King Arthur's sword in two pieces. Then said the knight unto Arthur, "Thou art in my power, whether to save thee or slay thee, and unless thou yield thee as overcome and recreant thou shalt die." "As for death," said King Arthur, "welcome be it when it cometh; but to yield me unto thee as recreant I will not." Then he leapt upon the knight, and took him by the middle and threw him down; but the knight was a passing strong man, and anon he brought Arthur under him, and would have razed off his helm to slay him. Then said Merlin, "Knight, hold thy hand, for this knight is a man of more worship than thou art aware of." "Why, who is he?" said the knight. "It is King Arthur." Then would he have slain him for dread of his wrath, and lifted up his sword to slay him; and therewith Merlin cast an enchantment on the knight, so that he fell to the earth in a great sleep. Then Merlin took up King Arthur and set him on his horse. "Alas!" said Arthur, "what hast thou done, Merlin? hast thou slain this good knight by thy crafts?" "Care ye not," said Merlin; "he is wholer than ye be. He is only asleep, and will wake in three hours."

Right so the king and he departed, and went unto an hermit that was a good man and a great leech. So the hermit searched all his wounds and gave him good salves; so the king was there three days, and then were his wounds well amended that he might ride and go, and so departed. And as they rode Arthur said, "I have no sword." "No force," said Merlin; "hereby is a sword that shall be yours." So they rode till they came to a lake, the which was a fair water and broad, and in the midst of the lake Arthur was ware of an arm clothed in white samite, that held a fair sword in that hand. "So," said Merlin, "yonder is that sword that I spake of." With that they saw a damsel going upon the lake. "What damsel is that?" said Arthur. "That is the Lady of the Lake," said Merlin; "and within that lake is a rock, and therein is as fair a place as any on earth, and richly beseen, and this damsel will come to you anon, and then speak ye

fair to her and she will give thee that sword." Anon withal came the damsel unto Arthur and saluted him, and he her again. "Damsel," said Arthur, "what sword is that that yonder the arm holdeth above the waves? I would it were mine, for I have no sword." "Sir Arthur king," said the damsel, "that sword is mine, and if ye will give me a gift when I ask it you ye shall have it." "By my faith," said Arthur, "I will give ye what gift ye shall ask." "Well," said the damsel, "go you into yonder barge and row yourself to the sword, and take it and the scabbard with you, and I will ask my gift when I see my time." So Arthur and Merlin alighted, and tied their horses to two trees, and so they went into the ship, and when they came to the sword that the hand held, Arthur took it by the handles, and took it with him. And the arm and the hand went under the water.

Then they returned unto the land and rode forth. And Sir Arthur looked on the sword and liked it right well.

So they rode unto Caerleon, whereof his knights were passing glad. And when they heard of his adventures they marvelled that he would jeopard his person so alone. But all men of worship said it was a fine thing to be under such a chieftain as would put his person in adventure as other poor knights did.

CHAPTER IV

CARADOC BRIEFBRAS; OR, CARADOC WITH THE SHRUNKEN ARM

CARADOC was the son of Ysenne, the beautiful niece of Arthur. He was ignorant who his father was, till it was discovered in the following manner: When the youth was of proper years to receive the honors of knighthood, King Arthur held a grand court for the purpose of knighting him. On this occasion a strange knight presented himself, and challenged the knights of Arthur's court to exchange blow for blow with him. His proposal was this,—to

lay his neck on a block for any knight to strike, on condition that, if he survived the blow, the knight should submit in turn to the same experiment. Sir Kay, who was usually ready to accept all challenges, pronounced this wholly unreasonable, and declared that he would not accept it for all the wealth in the world. And when the knight offered his sword, with which the operation was to be performed, no person ventured to accept it, till Caradoc, growing angry at the disgrace which was thus incurred by the Round Table, threw aside his mantle and took it. "Do you do this as one of the best knights?" said the stranger. "No," he replied, "but as one of the most foolish." The stranger lays his head upon the block, receives a blow which sends it rolling from his shoulders, walks after it, picks it up, replaces it with great success, and says he will return when the court shall be assembled next year, and claim his turn. When the anniversary arrived both parties were punctual to their engagement. Great entreaties were used by the king and queen, and the whole court, in behalf of Caradoc, but the stranger was inflexible. The young knight laid his head upon the block, and more than once desired him to make an end of the business, and not keep him longer in so disagreeable a state of expectation. At last the stranger strikes him gently with the side of the sword, bids him rise, and reveals to him the fact that he is his father, the enchanter Eliaures, and that he gladly owns him for a son, having proved his courage, and fidelity to his word.

But the favor of enchanters is short-lived and uncertain. Eliaures fell under the influence of a wicked woman, who, to satisfy her pique against Caradoc, persuaded the enchanter to fasten on his arm a serpent, which remained there sucking at his flesh and blood, no human skill sufficing either to remove the reptile or alleviate the torments which Caradoc endured.

Caradoc was betrothed to Guimier, sister to his bosom friend Cador, and daughter to the king of Cornwall. As soon as they were informed of his deplorable condition they set out for Nantes, where Caradoc's castle was, that Guimier might attend upon him. When Caradoc heard of their coming his first emotion was that of joy and love. But soon he began to fear that the sight of his emaciated form and of his sufferings would disgust Guimier; and this apprehension became so strong that he departed secretly from Nantes, and hid himself in a hermitage. He was sought far and near by the knights of Arthur's court, and Cador made a vow never to desist from the quest till he should have found him. After long wandering, Cador discovered his friend in the hermitage, reduced almost to a skeleton and apparently near his death. All other means of relief having already been tried in vain, Cador at last prevailed on the enchanter Eliaures to disclose the only method which could avail for his rescue. A maiden must be found, his equal in birth and beauty, and loving him better than herself, so that she would expose herself to the same torment to deliver him. Two vessels were then to be provided, the one filled with sour wine and the other with milk. Caradoc must enter the first, so that the wine should reach his neck, and the maiden must get into the other, and, exposing her bosom upon the edge of the vessel, invite the serpent to forsake the withered flesh of his victim for this fresh and inviting food. The vessels were to be placed three feet apart, and as the serpent crossed from one to the other a knight was to cut him in two. If he failed in his blow, Caradoc would indeed be delivered, but it would only be to see his fair champion suffering the same cruel and hopeless torment. The sequel may be easily foreseen. Guimier willingly exposed herself to the perilous adventure, and Cador, with a lucky blow, killed the serpent. The arm, in which Caradoc had suffered so long, recovered its strength, but not its shape, in consequence of which he was called Caradoc Briefbras, Caradoc of the Shrunken Arm.

Caradoc and Guimier are the hero and heroine of the ballad of The Boy and the Mantle, which follows.

The Boy and the Mantle

In Carlisle dwelt King Arthur,
  A prince of passing might,
And there maintained his Table
  Beset with many a knight.

And there he kept his Christmas,
  With mirth and princely cheer,
When lo! a strange and cunning boy
  Before him did appear.

A kirtle and a mantle
  This boy had him upon,
With brooches, rings, and ouches,
  Full daintily bedone.

He had a sash of silk
  About his middle meet;
And thus with seemly curtesie
  He did King Arthur greet:

"God speed thee, brave King Arthur,
  Thus feasting in thy bower,
And Guenever, thy goodly queen,
  That fair and peerless flower.

"Ye gallant lords and lordlings,
  I wish you all take heed,
Lest what ye deem a blooming rose
  Should prove a cankered weed."

Then straightway from his bosom
  A little wand he drew;
And with it eke a mantle,
  Of wondrous shape and hue.

"Now have thou here, King Arthur,
  Have this here of me,
And give unto thy comely queen,
  All shapen as you see.

"No wife it shall become,
  That once hath been to blame."
Then every knight in Arthur's court
  Sly glancèd at his dame.

And first came Lady Guenever,
  The mantle she must try.
This dame she was new-fangled,[1]
  And of a roving eye.

When she had taken the mantle,
  And all with it was clad,
From top to toe it shivered down,
  As though with shears beshred.

One while it was too long,
  Another while too short,
And wrinkled on the shoulders,
  In most unseemly sort.

Now green, now red it seemed,
  Then all of sable hue;
"Beshrew me," quoth King Arthur,
  "I think thou be'st not true!"

Down she threw the mantle,
  No longer would she stay;
But, storming like a fury,
  To her chamber flung away.

She cursed the rascal weaver,
  That had the mantle wrought;
And doubly cursed the froward imp
  Who thither had it brought.

"I had rather live in deserts,
  Beneath the greenwood tree,
Than here, base king, among thy
    grooms,
  The sport of them and thee."

Sir Kay called forth his lady,
  And bade her to come near:
"Yet, dame, if thou be guilty,
  I pray thee now forbear."

This lady, pertly giggling,
  With forward step came on,
And boldly to the little boy
  With fearless face is gone.

When she had taken the mantle,
  With purpose for to wear,
It shrunk up to her shoulder,
  And left her back all bare.

Then every merry knight,
  That was in Arthur's court,
Gibed and laughed and flouted,
  To see that pleasant sport.

Down she threw the mantle,
  No longer bold or gay,
But, with a face all pale and wan,
  To her chamber slunk away.

Then forth came an old knight
  A-pattering o'er his creed,
And proffered to the little boy
  Five nobles to his meed:

"And all the time of Christmas
  Plum-porridge shall be thine,
If thou wilt let my lady fair
  Within the mantle shine."

A saint his lady seemed,
  With step demure and slow,
And gravely to the mantle
  With mincing face doth go.

When she the same had taken
  That was so fine and thin,
It shrivelled all about her,
  And showed her dainty skin.

Ah! little did her mincing,
  Or his long prayers bestead;
She had no more hung on her
  Than a tassel and a thread.

---

[1] New-fangled,—fond of novelty.

Down she threw the mantle,
  With terror and dismay,
And with a face of scarlet
  To her chamber hied away.

Sir Cradock called his lady,
  And bade her to come near;
"Come win this mantle, lady,
  And do me credit here:

"Come win this mantle, lady,
  For now it shall be thine,
If thou hast never done amiss,
  Since first I made thee mine."

The lady, gently blushing,
  With modest grace came on;
And now to try the wondrous charm
  Courageously is gone.

When she had ta'en the mantle,
  And put it on her back,
About the hem it seemed
  To wrinkle and to crack.

"Lie still," she cried, "O mantle!
  And shame me not for naught;
I'll freely own whate'er amiss
  Or blameful I have wrought.

"Once I kissed Sir Cradock
  Beneath the greenwood tree;
Once I kissed Sir Cradock's mouth,
  Before he married me."

When she had thus her shriven,
  And her worst fault had told,
The mantle soon became her,
  Right comely as it should.

Most rich and fair of color,
  Like gold it glittering shone,
And much the knight in Arthur's court
  Admired her every one.

The ballad goes on to tell of two more trials of a similar kind, made by means of a boar's head and a drinking-horn, in both of which the result was equally favorable with the first to Sir Cradock and his lady. It then concludes as follows:

Thus boar's head, horn, and mantle
  Were this fair couple's meed;
And all such constant lovers,
  God send them well to speed.

Percy's Reliques

CHAPTER V

SIR GAWAIN

SIR GAWAIN was nephew to King Arthur, by his sister Morgana, married to Lot, king of Orkney, who was by Arthur made king of Norway. Sir Gawain was one of the most famous knights of the Round Table, and is characterized by the romancers as the sage and courteous Gawain. To this Chaucer alludes in his "Squiere's Tale," in which the strange knight "saluteth" all the court:

"With so high reverence and observance,
As well in speeche as in countenance,
That Gawain, with his olde curtesie,
Though he were come agen out of faërie,
Ne coude him not amenden with a word."

Gawain's brothers were Agrivain, Gaheris, and Gareth.

SIR GAWAIN'S MARRIAGE

ONCE upon a time King Arthur held his court in merry Carlisle, when a damsel came before him and craved a boon. It was for vengeance upon a caitiff knight, who had made her lover captive and despoiled her of her lands. King Arthur commanded to bring him his sword, Excalibur, and to saddle his steed, and rode forth without delay to right the lady's wrong. Ere long he reached the castle of the grim baron, and challenged him to the conflict. But the castle stood on magic ground, and the spell was such that no knight could tread thereon but straight his courage fell and his strength decayed. King Arthur felt the charm, and before a blow was struck his sturdy limbs lost their strength, and his head grew faint. He was fain to yield himself prisoner to the churlish knight, who refused to release him except upon condition that he should return at the end of a year, and bring a true answer to the question, "What thing is it which women most desire?" or in default thereof surrender himself and his lands. King Arthur accepted the terms, and gave his oath to return at the time appointed. During the year the king rode east, and he rode west, and inquired of all whom he met what thing it is which all women most desire. Some told him riches; some pomp and state; some mirth; some flattery; and some a gallant knight. But in the diversity of answers he could find no sure dependence. The year was well nigh spent when, one day, as he rode thoughtfully through a forest, he saw sitting beneath a tree a lady of such hideous aspect that he turned away his eyes, and when she greeted him in seemly sort made no answer. "What wight art thou," the lady said, "that will not speak to me? It may chance that I may resolve thy doubts, though I be not fair of aspect." "If thou wilt do so," said King Arthur, "choose what reward thou wilt, thou grim lady, and it shall be given thee." "Swear me this upon thy faith," she said, and Arthur swore it. Then the lady told him the secret, and demanded her reward, which was that the king should find some fair and courtly knight to be her husband.

King Arthur hastened to the grim baron's castle and told him one by one all the answers which he had received from his various advisers, except the last, and not one was admitted as the true one. "Now yield thee, Arthur," the giant said, "for thou hast not paid thy ransom, and thou and thy lands are forfeited to me." Then King Arthur said:

"Yet hold thy hand, thou proud baron,
  I pray thee hold thy hand.
And give me leave to speak once more,
  In rescue of my land.
This morn, as I came over a moor,
  I saw a lady set,
Between an oak and a green holly,
  All clad in red scarlet.
She says *all women would have their will*
  This is their chief desire;
Now yield, as thou art a baron true,
  That I have paid my hire."

"It was my sister that told thee this," the churlish baron exclaimed. "Vengeance light on her! I will some

THE AGE OF CHIVALRY

time or other do her as ill a turn."

King Arthur rode homeward, but not light of heart; for he remembered the promise he was under to the loathly lady to give her one of his young and gallant knights for a husband. He told his grief to Sir Gawain, his nephew, and he replied, "Be not sad, my lord, for I will marry the loathly lady." King Arthur replied:

"Now nay, now nay, good Sir Gawaine,
My sister's son ye be;
The loathly lady's all too grim,
And all too foule for thee."

But Gawain persisted, and the king at last, with sorrow of heart, consented that Gawain should be his ransom. So, one day, the king and his knights rode to the forest, met the loathly lady, and brought her to the court. Sir Gawain stood the scoffs and jeers of his companions as he best might, and the marriage was solemnized, but not with the usual festivities. Chaucer tells us:

"There was no joye, ne feste at alle;
There n'as but hevinesse and mochel sorwe,
For prively he wed her on the morwe,
And all day after hid him as an owle,
So wo was him his wife loked so foule!"[1]

When night came, and they were alone together, Sir Gawain could not conceal his aversion; and the lady asked him why he sighed so heavily, and turned away his face. He candidly confessed it was on account of three things, her age, her ugliness, and her low degree. The lady, not at all offended, replied with excellent arguments to all his objections. She showed him that with age is discretion, with ugliness security

---

[1] N'as is not was, contracted; in modern phrase, there was not. Mochel sorwe is much sorrow: morwe is morrow.

from rivals, and that all true gentility depends, not upon the accident of birth, but upon the character of the individual.

Sir Gawain made no reply; but, turning his eyes on his bride, what was his amazement to perceive that she wore no longer the unseemly aspect that had so distressed him. She then told him that the form she had worn was not her true form, but a disguise imposed upon her by a wicked enchanter, and that she was condemned to wear it until two things should happen; one, that she should obtain some young and gallant knight to be her husband. This having been done, one half of the charm was removed. She was now at liberty to wear her true form for half the time, and she bade him choose whether he would have her fair by day and ugly by night, or the reverse. Sir Gawain would fain have had her look her best by night, when he alone should see her, and show her repulsive visage, if at all, to others. But she reminded him how much more pleasant it would be to her to wear her best looks in the throng of knights and ladies by day. Sir Gawain yielded, and gave up his will to hers. This alone was wanting to dissolve the charm. The lovely lady now with joy assured him that she should change no more; but as she now was so would she remain by night as well as by day.

"Sweet blushes stayned her rud-red cheek,
    Her eyen were black as sloe,
The ripening cherrye swelled her lippe,
    And all her neck was snow.
Sir Gawain kist that ladye faire
    Lying upon the sheete,
And swore, as he was a true knight,
    The spice was never so swete."

The dissolution of the charm which had held the lady also released her brother, the "grim baron," for he too had been implicated in it. He ceased to be a churlish oppressor, and became a gallant and generous knight as any at Arthur's court.

CHAPTER VI

LAUNCELOT OF THE LAKE

KING BAN, of Brittany, the faithful ally of Arthur, was attacked by his enemy Claudas, and, after a long war, saw himself reduced to the possession of a single fortress, where he was besieged by his enemy. In this extremity he determined to solicit the assistance of Arthur, and escaped in a dark night, with his wife Helen and his infant son Launcelot, leaving his castle in the hands of his seneschal, who immediately surrendered the place to Claudas. The flames of his burning citadel reached the eyes of the unfortunate monarch during his flight, and he expired with grief. The wretched Helen, leaving her child on the brink of a lake, flew to receive the last sighs of her husband, and on returning perceived the little Launcelot in the arms of a nymph, who, on the approach of the queen, threw herself into the lake with the child. This nymph was Viviane, mistress of the enchanter Merlin, better known by the name of the Lady of the Lake. Launcelot received his appellation from having been educated at the court of this enchantress, whose palace was situated in the midst, not of a real, but, like the appearance which deceives the African traveller, of an imaginary lake, whose deluding resemblance served as a barrier to her residence. Here she dwelt not alone, but in the midst of a numerous retinue, and a splendid court of knights and damsels.

The queen, after her double loss, retired to a convent, where she was joined by the widow of Bohort, for this good king had died of grief on hearing of the death of his brother Ban. His two sons, Lionel and Bohort, were rescued by a faithful knight, and arrived in the shape of greyhounds at the palace of the lake, where, having resumed their natural form, they were educated along with their cousin Launcelot.

The fairy, when her pupil had attained the age of eighteen, conveyed him to the court of Arthur, for the purpose of demanding his admission to the honor of knighthood; and at the first appearance of the youthful candidate the graces of his person, which were not inferior to his courage and skill in arms, made an instantaneous and indelible impression on the heart of Guenever, while her charms inspired him with an equally ardent and constant passion. The mutual attachment of these lovers exerted, from that time forth, an influence over the whole history of Arthur. For the sake of Guenever Launcelot achieved the conquest of Northumberland, defeated Gallehaut, king of the Marches, who afterwards became his most faithful friend and ally, exposed himself in numberless encounters, and brought hosts of prisoners to the feet of his sovereign.

After King Arthur was come from Rome into England all the knights of the Table Round resorted unto him, and made him many jousts and tournaments. And in especial Sir Launcelot of the Lake, in all tournaments and jousts and deeds of arms, both for life and death, passed all other knights, and was never overcome, except it were by treason or enchantment; and he increased marvellously in worship, wherefore Queen Guenever had him in great favor, above all other knights. And for certain he loved the queen again above all other ladies; and for her he did many deeds of arms, and saved her from peril through his noble chivalry. Thus Sir Launcelot rested him long with play and game, and then he thought to prove himself in strange adventures; so he bade his nephew, Sir Lionel, to make him ready,— "for we two will seek adventures." So they mounted on their horses, armed at all sights, and rode into a forest, and so into a deep plain. And the weather was hot about noon, and Sir Launcelot had great desire to sleep. Then Sir Lionel espied a great apple-tree that stood by a hedge; and he said: "Brother, yonder is a fair shadow,—there may we rest us and our horses." "It is well said," replied Sir Launcelot. So they there alighted, and Sir Launcelot laid him down, and his helm under his head, and soon was asleep passing fast. And Sir Lionel waked while he slept. And presently there came three knights riding as fast as ever they might ride, and there followed them but one knight. And Sir Lionel thought he never saw so great a knight before. So within a while this great knight overtook one of those knights, and smote him so that he fell to the earth. Then he rode to the second knight and smote him, and so he did to the third knight. Then he alighted down, and bound all the three knights fast with their own bridles. When Sir Lionel saw him do thus he thought to assay him, and made him ready, silently, not to awake Sir Launcelot, and rode after the strong knight, and bade him turn. And the other smote Sir Lionel so hard that horse and man fell to the earth; and then he alighted down, and bound Sir Lionel, and threw him across his own horse; and so he served them all four, and rode with them away to his own castle. And when he came there, he put them in a deep prison, in which were many more knights in great distress.

Now while Sir Launcelot lay under the apple-tree sleeping there came by him four queens of great estate. And that the heat should not grieve them, there rode four knights about them, and bare a cloth of green silk, on four spears, betwixt them and the sun. And the queens rode on four white mules.

Thus as they rode they heard by them a great horse grimly neigh. Then they were aware of a sleeping knight, that lay all armed under an apple-tree; and as the queens looked on his face they knew it was Sir Launcelot. Then they began to strive for that knight, and each one said she would have him for her love. "We will not strive," said Morgane le Fay, that was King Arthur's sister, "for I will put an enchantment upon him, that he shall not wake for six hours, and we will take him away to my castle; and then when he is surely within my hold I will take the enchantment from him, and then let him choose

which of us he will have for his love." So the enchantment was cast upon Sir Launcelot. And then they laid him upon his shield, and bare him so on horseback between two knights, and brought him unto the castle and laid him in a chamber, and at night they sent him his supper.

And on the morning came early those four queens, richly dight, and bade him good morning, and he them again. "Sir knight," they said, "thou must understand that thou art our prisoner; and we know thee well, that thou art Sir Launcelot of the Lake, King Ban's son, and that thou art the noblest knight living. And we know well that there can no lady have thy love but one, and that is Queen Guenever; and now thou shalt lose her forever, and she thee; and therefore it behooveth thee now to choose one of us. I am the Queen Morgane le Fay, and here is the queen of North Wales, and the queen of Eastland, and the queen of the Isles. Now choose one of us which thou wilt have, for if thou choose not in this prison thou shalt die." "This is a hard case," said Sir Launcelot, "that either I must die or else choose one of you; yet had I liever to die in this prison with worship than have to have one of you for my paramour, for ye be false enchantresses." "Well," said the queens, "is this your answer, that ye will refuse us?" "Yea, on my life it is," said Sir Launcelot. Then they departed, making great sorrow.

Then at noon came a damsel unto him with his dinner, and asked him, "What cheer?" "Truly, fair damsel," said Sir Launcelot, "never so ill." "Sir," said she, "if you will be ruled by me, I will help you out of this distress. If ye will promise me to help my father on Tuesday next, who hath made a tournament betwixt him and the king of North Wales; for the last Tuesday my father lost the field." "Fair maiden," said Sir Launcelot, "tell me what is your father's name, and then will I give you an answer." "Sir knight," she said, "my father is King Bagdemagus." "I know him well," said Sir Launcelot, "for a noble king and a good knight, and, by the faith of my body, I will be ready to do your father and you service at that day."

So she departed, and came on the next morning early and found him ready, and brought him out of twelve locks, and brought him to his own horse, and lightly he saddled him, and so rode forth.

And on the Tuesday next he came to a little wood where the tournament should be. And there were scaffolds and holds, that lords and ladies might look on, and give the prize. Then came into the field the king of North Wales, with eightscore helms, and King Bagdemagus came with fourscore helms. And then they couched their spears, and came together with a great dash, and there were overthrown at the first encounter twelve of King Bagdemagus's party and six of the king of North Wales's party, and King Bagdemagus's party had the worse.

With that came Sir Launcelot of the Lake, and thrust in with his spear in the thickest of the press; and he smote down five knights ere he held his hand; and he smote down the king of North Wales, and he brake his thigh in that fall. And then the knights of the king of North Wales would

joust no more; and so the gree was given to King Bagdemagus.

And Sir Launcelot rode forth with King Bagdemagus unto his castle; and there he had passing good cheer, both with the king and with his daughter. And on the morn he took his leave, and told the king he would go and seek his brother, Sir Lionel, that went from him when he slept. So he departed, and by adventure he came to the same forest where he was taken sleeping. And in the highway he met a damsel riding on a white palfrey, and they saluted each other. "Fair damsel," said Sir Launcelot, "know ye in this country any adventures?" "Sir knight," said the damsel, "here are adventures near at hand, if thou durst pursue them." "Why should I not prove adventures?" said Sir Launcelot, "since for that came I hither." "Sir," said she, "hereby dwelleth a knight that will not be overmatched for any man I know, except thou overmatch him. His name is Sir Turquine, and, as I understand, he is a deadly enemy of King Arthur, and he has in his prison good knights of Arthur's court three score and more, that he hath won with his own hands." "Damsel," said Launcelot, "I pray you bring me unto this knight." So she told him, "Hereby, within this mile, is his castle, and by it on the left hand is a ford for horses to drink of; and over that ford there groweth a fair tree, and on that tree hang many shields that good knights wielded aforetime, that are now prisoners: and on the tree hangeth a basin of copper and latten, and if thou strike upon that basin thou shalt hear tidings." And Sir Launcelot departed, and rode as the damsel had showed him, and shortly he came to the ford, and the tree where hung the shields and basin. And among the shields he saw Sir Lionel's and Sir Hector's shield, besides many others of knights that he knew.

Then Sir Launcelot struck on the basin with the butt of his spear; and long he did so, but he saw no man. And at length he was ware of a great knight that drove a horse before him, and across the horse there lay an armed knight bounden. And as they came near Sir Launcelot thought he should know the captive knight. Then Sir Launcelot saw that it was Sir Gaheris, Sir Gawain's brother, a knight of the Table Round. "Now, fair knight," said Sir Launcelot, "put that wounded knight off the horse, and let him rest awhile, and let us two prove our strength. For, as it is told me, thou hast done great despite and shame unto knights of the Round Table, therefore now defend thee." "If thou be of the Table Round," said Sir Turquine, "I defy thee and all thy fellowship." "That is overmuch said," said Sir Launcelot.

Then they put their spears in the rests, and came together with their horses as fast as they might run. And each smote the other in the middle of their shields, so that their horses fell under them, and the knights were both staggered; and as soon as they could clear their horses, they drew out their swords and came together eagerly, and each gave the other many strong strokes, for neither shield nor harness might withstand their strokes. So within a while both had grimly wounds, and bled grievously. Then at the last they were breathless both, and stood leaning upon their swords. "Now, fellow," said Sir Turquine, "thou art the stoutest man that ever I met with, and best breathed; and so be it thou be not the knight that I hate above all other knights, the knight that slew my brother, Sir Caradoc, I will gladly accord with thee; and for thy love I will deliver all the prisoners that I have."

"What knight is he that thou hatest so above others?" "Truly," said Sir Turquine, "his name is Sir Launcelot of the Lake." "I am Sir Launcelot of the Lake, King Ban's son of Benwick, and very knight of the Table Round; and now I defy thee do thy best." "Ah," said Sir Turquine, "Launcelot, thou art to me the most welcome that ever was knight; for we shall never part till the one of us be dead." And then they hurtled together like two wild bulls, rashing and lashing with their swords and shields, so that sometimes they fell, as it were, headlong. Thus they fought two hours and more, till the ground where they fought was all bepurpled with blood.

Then at the last Sir Turquine waxed sore faint, and gave somewhat aback, and bare his shield full low for weariness. That spied Sir Launcelot, and leapt then upon him fiercely as a lion, and took him by the beaver of his helmet, and drew him down on his knees. And he raised off his helm, and smote his neck in sunder.

And Sir Gaheris, when he saw Sir Turquine slain, said, "Fair lord, I pray you tell me your name, for this day I say ye are the best knight in the world, for ye have slain this day in my sight the mightiest man and the best knight except you that ever I saw." "Sir, my name is Sir Launcelot du Lac, that ought to help you of right for King Arthur's sake, and in especial for Sir Gawain's sake, your own dear brother. Now I pray you, that ye go into yonder castle, and set free all the prisoners ye find there, for I am sure ye shall find there many knights of the Table Round, and especially my brother Sir Lionel. I pray you greet them all from me, and tell them I bid them take there such stuff as they find; and tell my brother to go unto the court and abide me there, for by the feast of Pentecost I think to be there; but at this time I may not stop, for I have adventures on hand." So he departed, and Sir Gaheris rode into the castle, and took the keys from the porter, and hastily opened the prison door and let out all the prisoners. There was Sir Kay, Sir Brandeles, and Sir Galynde, Sir Bryan and Sir Alyduke, Sir Hector de Marys and Sir Lionel, and many more. And when they saw Sir Gaheris, they all thanked him, for they thought, because he was wounded, that he had slain Sir Turquine. "Not so," said Sir Gaheris; "it was Sir Launcelot that slew him, right worshipfully; I saw it with mine eyes."

Sir Launcelot rode till at nightfall he came to a fair castle, and therein he found an old gentlewoman, who lodged him with goodwill, and there he had good cheer for him and his horse. And when time was, his host brought him to a fair chamber over the gate to his bed. Then Sir Launcelot unarmed him, and set his harness by him, and went to bed, and anon he fell asleep. And soon after, there came one on horseback and knocked at the gate in great haste; and when Sir Launcelot heard this, he arose and looked out of the window, and saw by the moonlight three knights riding after that one man, and all three lashed on him with their swords, and that one knight turned on them knightly again and defended himself. "Truly," said Sir Launcelot, "yonder one knight will I help, for it is shame to see three knights on one." Then he took his harness and went out at the window by a sheet down to the four knights; and he said aloud, "Turn you knights unto me, and leave your fighting with that knight." Then the knights left Sir Kay, for it was he they were upon, and turned unto Sir Launcelot, and struck many great strokes at Sir Launcelot, and assailed him on every side. Then Sir Kay addressed him to help Sir Launcelot, but he said, "Nay, sir, I will none of your help; let me alone with them." So Sir Kay suffered him to do his will, and stood one side. And within six strokes, Sir Launcelot had stricken them down.

Then they all cried, "Sir knight, we yield us unto you." "As to that," said Sir Launcelot, "I will not take your yielding unto me. If so be ye will yield you unto Sir Kay the seneschal, I will save your lives, but else not." "Fair knight," then they said, "we will do as thou commandest us." "Then shall ye," said Sir Launcelot, "on Whitsunday next, go unto the court of King Arthur, and there shall ye yield you unto Queen Guenever, and say that Sir Kay sent you thither to be her prisoners." "Sir," they said, "it shall be done, by the faith of our bodies;" and then they swore, every knight upon his sword. And so Sir Launcelot suffered them to depart.

On the morn Sir Launcelot rose early and left Sir Kay sleeping; and Sir Launcelot took Sir Kay's armor and his shield, and armed him, and went to the stable and took his horse, and so he departed. Then soon after arose Sir Kay and missed Sir Launcelot.

And then he espied that he had taken his armor and his horse. "Now, by my faith, I know well," said Sir Kay, "that he will grieve some of King Arthur's knights, for they will deem that it is I, and will be bold to meet him. But by cause of his armor I am sure I shall ride in peace." Then Sir Kay thanked his host and departed.

Sir Launcelot rode in a deep forest, and there he 50 ▷ saw four knights under an oak, and they were of Arthur's court. There was Sir Sagramour le Desirus and Hector de Marys, and Sir Gawain and Sir Uwaine. As they spied Sir Launcelot, they judged by his arms it had been Sir Kay. "Now, by my faith," said Sir Sagramour, "I will prove Sir Kay's might;" and got his spear in his hand, and came toward Sir Launcelot. Therewith Sir Launcelot couched his spear against him, and smote Sir Sagramour so sore that horse and man fell both to the earth. Then said Sir Hector, "Now shall ye see what I may do with him." But he fared worse than Sir Sagramour, for Sir Launcelot's spear went through his shoulder and bare him from his horse to the ground. "By my faith," said Sir Uwaine, "yonder is a strong knight, and I fear he hath slain Sir Kay, and taken his armor." And therewith Sir Uwaine took his spear in hand, and rode toward Sir Launcelot; and Sir Launcelot met him on the plain and gave him such a buffet that he was staggered, and wist not where he was. "Now see I well," said Sir Gawain, "that I must encounter with that knight." Then he adjusted his shield, and took a good spear in his hand, and Sir Launcelot knew him well. Then they let run their horses with all their mights, and each knight smote the other in the middle of his shield. But Sir Gawain's spear broke, and Sir Launcelot charged so sore upon him that his horse fell over backward. Then Sir Launcelot rode away smiling with himself; and he said, "Good luck be with him that made this spear, for never came a better into my hand." Then the four knights went each to the other and comforted one another. "What say ye to this adventure," said Sir Gawain, "that one spear hath felled us all four?" "I dare lay my head it is Sir Launcelot," said Sir Hector; "I know it by his riding."

And Sir Launcelot rode through many strange countries, till, by fortune, he came to a fair castle; and as he passed beyond the castle, he thought he

heard two bells ring. And then he perceived how a falcon came flying over his head toward a high elm; and she had long lunys[1] about her feet, and she flew unto the elm to take her perch, and the lunys got entangled in a bough; and when she would have taken her flight, she hung by the legs fast, and Sir Launcelot saw how she hung and beheld the fair falcon entangled, and he was sorry for her. Then came a lady out of the castle and cried aloud, "O Launcelot, Launcelot, as thou art the flower of all knights, help me to get my hawk; for if my hawk be lost, my lord will slay me, he is so hasty." "What is your lord's name?" said Sir Launcelot. "His name is Sir Phelot, a knight that belongeth to the king of North Wales." "Well, fair lady, since ye know my name, and require me of knighthood to help you, I will do what I may to get your hawk; and yet, in truth, I am an ill climber and the tree is passing high and few boughs to help me." And therewith Sir Launcelot alighted and tied his horse to a tree, and prayed the lady to unarm him. And when he was unarmed, he put off his jerkin, and with might and force he clomb up to the falcon, and tied the lunys to a rotten bough, and threw the hawk down with it; and the lady got the hawk in her hand. Then suddenly there came out of the castle her husband all armed, and with his naked sword in his hand, and said, "O Knight Launcelot, now have I got thee as I would;" and stood at the boll of the tree to slay him. "Ah, lady!" said Sir Launcelot, "why have ye betrayed me?" "She hath done," said Sir Phelot, "but as I commanded her; and therefore there is none other way but thine hour is come, and thou must die." "That were shame unto thee," said Sir Launcelot; "thou an armed knight to slay a naked man by treason." "Thou gettest none other grace," said Sir Phelot, "and therefore help thyself if thou canst." "Alas!" said Sir Launcelot, "that ever a knight should die weaponless!" And therewith he turned his

[1]*Lunys*, the string with which the falcon is held.

eyes upward and downward; and over his head he saw a big bough leafless, and he brake it off from the trunk. And then he came lower, and watched how his own horse stood; and suddenly he leapt on the further side of his horse from the knight. Then Sir Phelot lashed at him eagerly, meaning to have slain him. But Sir Launcelot put away the stroke with the big bough, and smote Sir Phelot therewith on the side of the head, so that he fell down in a swoon to the ground. Then Sir Launcelot took his sword out of his hand and struck his head from the body. Then said the lady, "Alas! why hast thou slain my husband?" "I am not the cause," said Sir Launcelot, "for with falsehood ye would have slain me, and now it is fallen on yourselves." Thereupon Sir Launcelot got all his armor and put it upon him hastily for fear of more resort, for the knight's castle was so nigh. And as soon as he might, he took his horse and departed, and thanked God he had escaped that adventure.

And two days before the feast of Pentecost, Sir Launcelot came home; and the king and all the court were passing glad of his coming. And when Sir Gawain, Sir Uwaine, Sir Sagramour, and Sir Hector de Marys saw Sir Launcelot in Sir Kay's armor, then they wist well it was he that smote them down, all with one spear. Then there was laughing and merriment among them; and from time to time came all the knights that Sir Turquine had prisoners, and they all honored and worshipped Sir Launcelot. Then Sir Gaheris said, "I saw all the battle from the beginning to the end," and he told King Arthur all how it was. Then Sir Kay told the king how Sir Launcelot had rescued him, and how he "made the knights yield to me, and not to him." And there they were, all three, and confirmed it all. "And by my faith," said Sir Kay, "because Sir Launcelot took my harness and left me his, I rode in peace, and no man would have to do with me."

And so at that time Sir Launcelot had the greatest name of any knight of the world, and most was he honored of high and low.

CHAPTER VII

THE STORY OF LAUNCELOT—THE ADVENTURE OF THE CART

So it befell in the month of May, Queen Guenever called unto her knights of the Table Round, and she gave them warning that early upon the morrow she would ride on maying into the woods and fields beside Westminster. "And I warn you that there be none of you but that he be well horsed, and that ye be all clothed in green, either in silk, either in cloth, and I shall bring with me ten ladies, and every knight shall have a lady behind him, and every knight shall have a squire and two yeomen, and I will that ye all be well horsed." So they made them ready in the freshest manner, and these were the names of the knights: Sir Kay the seneschal, Sir Agrivain, Sir Brandeles, Sir Sagramour le Desirus, Sir Dodynas le Sauvage, Sir Ozanna le Cure Hardy, Sir Ladynas of the Forest Savage, Sir Perseant of Inde, Sir Ironside that was called the knight of the red lawns, and Sir Pelleas the lover; and these ten knights made them ready in the freshest manner to ride with the queen. And so upon the morn they took their horses, with the queen, and rode on maying in woods and meadows, as it pleased them, in great joy and delight; for the queen had cast to have been again with King Arthur at the furthest by ten of the clock, and so was that time her purpose. Then there was a knight, that knight Meleagans, and he was son unto King Bagdemagus, and this knight had at that time a castle, of the gift of King Arthur, within seven miles of Westminster; and this knight Sir Meleagans loved passing well Queen Guenever, and so had he done long and many years. And he had lain in a wait for to steal away the queen, but evermore he forbore, because of Sir Launcelot, for in no wise would he meddle with the queen if Sir Launcelot were in her company, or else if he were near at hand to her. And at that time was such a custom the queen rode never without a great fellowship of men of arms about her; and they were many good knights, and the most part were young men that would have worship, and they were called the queen's knights, and never in no battle, tournament, nor joust, they bare none of them no manner of acknowledging of their own arms, but plain white shields, and thereby they were called the queen's knights. And then when it happed any of them to be of great worship by his noble deeds, then at the next feast of Pentecost, if there were any slain or dead, as there was no year that these failed, but some were dead, then was there chosen in his stead the most men of worship that were called the queen's knights. And thus they came up all first, or they were renowned men of worship, both Sir Launcelot and the remnant of them.

But this knight, Sir Meleagans, had espied the queen well and her purpose, and how Sir Launcelot was not with her, and how she had no men of arms with her but the ten noble knights all arrayed in green for maying. Then he provided him a twenty men of arms and an hundred archers, for to destroy the queen and her knights, for he thought that time was the best season to take the queen. So as the queen had mayed and all her knights, all were bedashed with herbs, mosses, and flowers, in the best manner and freshest. Right so came out of a wood Sir Meleagans with an eightscore men well harnessed, as they should fight in a battle of arrest and bade the queen and her knights abide, for maugre their heads they should abide. "Traitor knight," said Queen Guenever, "what castest thou for to do? Wilt thou shame thyself? Bethink thee how thou art a king's son and knight of the Table Round, and thou to be about to dishonor the noble king that made thee knight; thou shamest all knighthood and thyself, and me. I let thee wit, me shalt thou never shame, for I had liever cut my throat in twain than thou shouldst dishonor me." "As for all this language," said Sir Meleagans, "be it as it may, for wit you well, madam, I have loved you many a year, and never or now could I get you at such an advantage as I do now, and therefore I will take you as I find you." Then spake all the ten noble knights at once, and said: "Sir

Meleagans, wit thou well ye are about to jeopard your worship to dishonor, and also ye cast to jeopard our persons; howbeit we be unarmed, ye have us at great avail for it seemeth by you that ye have laid watch upon us; but rather than ye should put the queen to shame, and us all, we had as lief to depart from our lives, for if we other ways did we should be ashamed forever." Then Sir Meleagans said, "Dress you as well as you can, and keep the queen." Then all the ten knights of the Table Round drew their swords, and. the other let run at them with their spears, and the ten knights manly abode them, and smote away their spears, that no spear did them none harm. Then they lashed together with swords, and anon Sir Kay, Sir Sagramour, Sir Agrivain, Sir Dodynas, Sir Ladynas, and Sir Ozanna were smitten to the earth with grimly wounds. Then Sir Brandeles, and Sir Perseant, Sir Ironside, and Sir Pelleas fought long, and they were sorely wounded; for these ten knights or ever they were laid to the ground slew forty men of the boldest and best of them. So when the queen saw her knights thus dolefully wounded, and needs must be slain at the last, then for pity and sorrow she cried, "Sir Meleagans, slay not my noble knights, and I will go with thee upon this covenant, that thou save them, and suffer them not to be no more hurt, with this, that they be led with me wheresoever thou leadest me; for I will rather slay myself than I will go with thee, unless that these my noble knights may be in my presence." "Madam," said Meleagans, "for your sake they shall be led with you into mine own caste, with that ye will be ruled and ride with me." Then the queen prayed the four knights to leave their fighting, and she and they would not part. "Madam," said Sir Pelleas, "we will do as ye do, for as for me I take no force of my life nor death." For Sir Pelleas gave such buffets that none armor might hold him.

Then by the queen's commandment they left battle, and dressed the wounded knights on horseback, some sitting, some overthwart their horses, that it was pity to behold them. And then Sir Meleagans charged the queen and all her knights that none of all her fellowship should depart from her; for full sore he dreaded Sir Launcelot du Lac, lest he should have any knowledging. All this espied the queen and privily she called unto her a child of her chamber, that was swiftly horsed, to whom she said, "Go thou, when thou seest thy time, and bear this ring to Sir Launcelot du Lac, and pray him, as he loveth me, that he will see me, and rescue me if ever he will have joy of me; and spare thou not thy horse," said the queen, "neither for water nor for land." So the child espied his time, and lightly he took his horse with the spurs, and departed as fast as he might. And when Sir Meleagans saw him so flee he understood that it was by the queen's commandment for to warn Sir Launcelot. Then they that were best horsed chased him, and shot at him, but from them all the child went suddenly; and then Sir Meleagans said unto the queen, "Madam, ye are about to betray me, but I shall ordain for Sir Launcelot that he shall not come lightly to you." And then he rode with her and them all to his castle in all the haste that he might. And by the way Sir Meleagans laid in an ambushment the best archers that he might get in his country, to the number of thirty, to await upon Sir Launcelot, charging them that if they saw such a manner of knight come by the way upon a white horse, that in any wise they slay his horse, but in no manner of wise have not ado with him bodily, for he was over-hard to be overcome. So this was done, and they were come to his castle, but in no wise the queen would never let none of the ten knights and her ladies out of her sight, but always they were in her presence. So when the child was departed from the fellowship of Sir Meleagans, within awhile he came to Westminster. And anon he found Sir Launcelot. And when he had told him his message, and delivered him the queen's ring, "Alas!" said Sir Launcelot, "now am I shamed forever, unless that I may rescue that noble lady from dishonor." Then eagerly he asked his armor, and ever the child told Sir Launcelot how the ten knights fought marvellously, and how Sir Pelleas, and Sir Ironside, and Sir Brandeles, and Sir Perseant of Inde fought strongly, but as for Sir Pelleas there might none withstand him, and how they all fought till at last they were laid to the earth, and then the queen made appointment for to save their lives, and go with Sir Meleagans. "Alas!" said Sir Launcelot, "that most noble lady that she should be so destroyed! I had liever," said Sir Launcelot, "than all France that I had been there well armed." So when Launcelot was armed and upon his horse, he prayed the child of the queen's chamber to warn Sir Lavaine how suddenly he was departed, and for what cause,—"and pray him, as he loveth me, that he will hie him after me, and that he stint not until he come to the castle where Sir Meleagans abideth or dwelleth, for there," said Launcelot, "shall he hear of me if I am a man living, and rescue the queen and her ten knights, the which he traitorously hath taken, and that shall I prove upon his head, and all them that hold with him."

Then Sir Launcelot rode as fast as he might, and he took the water at Westminster, and made his horse to swim over Thames at Lambeth. And then within a while he came to the place where the ten knights had fought with Sir Meleagans, and then Sir Launcelot followed that track until he came to a wood, and there was a straight way, and there the thirty archers bade Sir Launcelot turn again, and follow no longer that track. "What commandment have ye thereto," said Sir Launcelot, "to cause me, that am a knight of the Round Table, to leave my right way?" "This way shalt thou leave, or else thou shalt go it on thy foot, for wit thou well thy horse shall be slain." "That is little mastery," said Launcelot, "to slay my horse, but as for myself, when my horse is slain, I give right nought for you, not if ye were five hundred more." So then they shot Sir Launcelot's horse, and smote him with many arrows. And then Sir Launcelot avoided his horse and went on foot; but there were so many ditches and hedges betwixt them and him that he might meddle with none of them. "Alas, for shame," said Sir Launcelot, "that ever one knight should betray another knight, but it is an old saw, 'A good man is never in danger but when he is in danger of a coward.'" Then Sir Launcelot went a while, and then he was foul cumbered of his armor, his shield, and his spear, and all that belonged to him. Wit ye well he was sore annoyed, and full loth he was to leave anything that belonged to him, for he dreaded sore the treason of Sir Meleagans. And then by fortune there came by a cart that came thither for to fetch wood.

Now at this time carts were but little used save for carrying offal or such like, and for conveying criminals to execution. But Sir Launcelot took no thought save of rescuing the queen. "Say me, carter," said he, "what shall I give thee for to suffer me to leap into the cart, and that thou shalt bring me unto a castle within this two mile?" "Thou shalt not come within my cart," said the carter, "for I am sent for to fetch wood for my lord Sir Meleagans." "With him would I speak." "Thou shalt not go with me," said the carter. Then Sir Launcelot lept to him, and gave him such a buffet that he fell to the earth stark dead. Then the other carter, his fellow, thought to have gone the same way, and then he cried, "Fair lord, save my life, and I shall bring you where you will."

So then Sir Launcelot placed himself in the cart, and only lamented that with much jolting he made but little progress. Then it happened Sir Gawain passed by, and seeing an armed knight travelling in that unusual way, he drew near to see who it might be. Then Sir Launcelot told him how the queen had been carried off, and how, in hastening to her rescue, his horse had been disabled, and he had been compelled to avail himself of the cart rather than give up his enterprise. Then Sir Gawain said, "Surely it is unworthy of a knight to travel in such sort!" but Sir Launcelot heeded him not.

At nighfall they arrived at a castle, and the lady thereof came out at the head of her damsels to welcome Sir Gawain. But to admit his companion, whom she supposed to be a criminal, or at least a prisoner, it pleased her not; however, to oblige Sir Gawain, she consented. At supper Sir Launcelot came near being consigned to the kitchen, and was only admitted to the lady's table at the earnest solicitation of Sir Gawain. Neither would the damsels prepare a bed for him. He seized the first he found unoccupied, and was left undisturbed.

Next morning he saw from the turrets of the castle a train accompanying a lady, whom he imagined to be the queen. Sir Gawain thought it might be so, and became equally eager to depart. The lady of the castle supplied Sir Launcelot with a horse, and they traversed the plain at full speed. They learned from some travellers whom they met that there were two roads which led to the castle of Sir Meleagans. Here therefore the friends separated. Sir Launcelot found his way beset with obstacles, which he encountered successfully, but not without much loss of time. As evening approached he was met by a young and sportive damsel, who gayly proposed to him a supper at her castle. The knight, who was hungry and weary, accepted the offer, though with no very good grace. He followed the lady to her castle, and ate voraciously of her supper, but was quite impenetrable to all her amorous advances. Suddenly the scene changed, and he was assailed by six furious ruffians, whom he dealt with so vigorously that most of them were speedily disabled, when again there was a change, and he found himself alone with his fair hostess, who informed him that she was none other than his guardian fairy, who had but subjected him to tests of his courage and fidelity. The next day the fairy brought him on his road, and before parting gave him a ring, which she told him would by its changes of color disclose to him all enchantments, and enable him to subdue them.

Sir Launcelot pursued his journey, being but little troubled save by the taunts of travellers, who all seemed to have learned by some means his disgraceful drive in the cart. One, more insolent than the rest, had the audacity to interrupt him during dinner, and even to risk a battle in support of his pleasantry. Launcelot, after an easy victory, only doomed him to be carted in his turn.

At night he was received at another castle, with great apparent hospitality, but found himself in the morning in a dungeon and loaded with chains. Consulting his ring, and finding that this was an enchantment, he burst his chains, seized his armor in spite of the visionary monsters who attempted to defend it, broke open the gates of the tower, and continued his journey. At length his progress was checked by a wide and rapid torrent, which could only be passed on a narrow bridge, on which a false step would prove his destruction. Launcelot, leading his horse by the bridle, and making him swim by his side, passed over the bridge, and was attacked, as soon as he reached the bank, by a lion and a leopard, both of which he slew, and then, exhausted and bleeding, seated himself on the grass, and endeavored to bind up his wounds, when he was accosted by Brademagus, the father of Meleagans, whose castle was then in sight, and at no great distance. The king, no less courteous than his son was haughty and insolent, after complimenting Sir Launcelot on the valor and skill he had displayed in the perils of the bridge and the wild beasts, offered him his assistance, and informed him that the queen was safe in his castle, but could only be rescued by encountering Meleagans. Launcelot demanded the battle for the next day, and accordingly it took place, at the foot of the tower, and under the eyes of the fair captive. Launcelot was enfeebled by his wounds, and fought not with his usual spirit, and the contest for a time was doubtful; till Guenever exclaimed, "Ah, Launcelot! my knight, truly have I been told that thou art no longer worthy of me!" These words instantly revived the drooping knight; he resumed at once his usual superiority, and soon laid at his feet his haughty adversary.

He was on the point of sacrificing him to his resentment when Guenever, moved by the entreaties of Brademagus, ordered him to withhold the blow, and he obeyed. The castle and its prisoners were now at his disposal. Launcelot hastened to the apartment of the queen, threw himself at her feet, and was about to kiss her hand, when she exclaimed, "Ah, Launcelot! why do I see thee again, yet feel thee to be no longer worthy of me, after having been disgracefully drawn about the country in a —" She had not time to finish the phrase, for her lover suddenly started from her, and bitterly lamenting that he had incurred the displeasure of his sovereign lady, rushed out of the castle, threw his sword and his shield to the right and left, ran furiously into the woods, and disappeared.

It seems that the story of the abominable cart, which haunted Launcelot at every step, had reached the ears of Sir Kay, who had told it to the queen, as a proof that her knight must have been dishonored. But Guenever had full leisure to repent the haste with which she had given credit to the tale. Three days elapsed, during which Launcelot wandered without knowing where he went, till at last he began to reflect that his mistress had doubtless been deceived by misrepresentation, and that it was his duty to set her right. He therefore returned, compelled Meleagans to release his prisoners, and, taking the road by which he expected the arrival of Sir Gawain, had the satisfaction of meeting him the next day; after which the whole company proceeded gayly towards Camelot.

CHAPTER VIII

THE STORY OF LAUNCELOT—THE LADY OF SHALOTT

KING ARTHUR proclaimed a solemn tournament to be held at Winchester. The king, not less impatient than his knights for this festival, set off some days before to superintend the preparations, leaving the queen with her court at Camelot. Sir Launcelot, under pretence of indisposition, remained behind also. His intention was to attend the tournament in disguise; and having communicated his project to Guenever, he mounted his horse, set off without any attendant, and, counterfeiting the feebleness of age, took the most unfrequented road to Winchester, and passed unnoticed as an old knight who was going to be a spectator of the sports. Even Arthur and Gawain, who happened to behold him from the windows of a castle under which he passed, were the dupes of his disguise. But an accident betrayed him. His horse happened to stumble, and the hero, forgetting for a moment his assumed character, recovered the animal with a strength and agility so peculiar to himself, that they instantly recognized the inimitable Launcelot. They suffered him, however, to proceed on his journey without interruption, convinced that his extraordinary feats of arms must discover him at the approaching festival.

In the evening Launcelot was magnificently entertained as a stranger knight at the neighboring castle of Shalott. The lord of this castle had a daughter of exquisite beauty, and two sons lately received into the order of knighthood, one of whom was at that time ill in bed, and thereby prevented from attending the tournament, for which both brothers had long made preparations. Launcelot offered to attend the other, if he were permitted to borrow the armor of the invalid, and the lord of Shalott, without knowing the name of his guest, being satisfied from his appearance that his son could not have a better assistant in arms, most thankfully accepted the offer. In the meantime the young lady, who had been much struck by the first appearance of the stranger knight, continued to survey him with increased attention, and before the conclusion of supper, became so deeply enamored of him, that, after frequent changes of color, and other symptoms which Sir Launcelot could not possibly mistake, she was obliged to retire to her chamber, and seek relief in tears. Sir Launcelot hastened to convey to her, by means of her brother, the information that his heart was already disposed of, but that it would be his pride and pleasure to act as her knight at the approaching tournament. The lady, obliged to be satisfied with that courtesy, presented him her scarf to be worn at the tournament.

Launcelot set off in the morning with the young knight, who, on their approaching Winchester, carried him to the castle of a lady, sister to the lord of Shalott, by whom they were hospitably entertained. The next day they put on their armor, which was perfectly plain, and without any device, as was usual to youths during the first year of knighthood, their shields being only painted red, as some color was necessary to enable them to be recognized by their attendants. Launcelot wore on his crest the scarf of the maid of Shalott, and, thus equipped, proceeded to the tournament, where the knights were divided into two companies, the one commanded by Sir Gallehaut, the

other by King Arthur. Having surveyed the combat for a short time from without the lists, and observed that Sir Gallehaut's party began to give way, they joined the press and attacked the royal knights, the young man choosing such adversaries as were suited to his strength, while his companion selected the principal champions of the Round Table, and successively overthrew Gawain, Bohort, and Lionel. The astonishment of the spectators was extreme, for it was thought that no one but Launcelot could possess such invincible force; yet the favor on his crest seemed to preclude the possibility of his being thus disguised, for Launcelot had never been known to wear the badge of any but his sovereign lady. At length Sir Hector, Launcelot's brother, engaged him, and, after a dreadful combat, wounded him dangerously in the head, but was himself completely stunned by a blow on the helmet, and felled to the ground; after which the conqueror rode off at full speed, attended by his companion.

They returned to the castle of Shalott, where Launcelot was attended with the greatest care by the good earl, by his two sons, and, above all, by his fair daughter, whose medical skill probably much hastened the period of his recovery. His health was almost completely restored, when Sir Hector, Sir Bohort, and Sir Lionel, who, after the return of the court to Camelot, had undertaken the quest of their relation, discovered him walking on the walls of the castle. Their meeting was very joyful; they passed three days in the castle amidst constant festivities, and bantered each other on the events of the tournament. Launcelot, though he began by vowing vengeance against the author of his wound, yet ended by declaring that he felt rewarded for the pain by the pride he took in witnessing his brother's extraordinary prowess. He then dismissed them with a message to the queen, promising to follow immediately, it being necessary that he should first take a formal leave of his kind hosts, as well as of the fair maid of Shalott.

The young lady, after vainly attempting to detain him by her tears and solicitations, saw him depart without leaving her any ground for hope.

It was early summer when the tournament took place; but some months had passed since Launcelot's departure, and winter was now near at hand. The health and strength of the Lady of Shalott had gradually sunk, and she felt that she could not live apart from the object of her affections. She left the castle, and, descending to the river's brink, placed herself in a boat, which she loosed from its moorings, and suffered to bear her down the current toward Camelot.

One morning, as Arthur and Sir Lionel looked from the window of the tower, the walls of which were washed by a river, they descried a boat richly ornamented, and covered with an awning of cloth of gold, which appeared to be floating down the stream without any human guidance. It struck the shore while they watched it, and they hastened down to examine it. Beneath the awning they discovered the dead body of a beautiful woman, in whose features Sir Lionel easily recognized the lovely maid of Shalott. Pursuing their search, they discovered a purse richly embroidered with gold and jewels, and within the purse a letter, which Arthur opened, and found addressed to himself and all the knights of the Round Table, stating that Launcelot of the Lake, the most accomplished of knights and most beautiful of men, but at the same time the most cruel and inflexible, had by his rigor produced the death of the wretched maiden, whose love was no less invincible than his cruelty.

The king immediately gave orders for the interment of the lady with all the honors suited to her rank, at the same time explaining to the knights the history of her affection for Launcelot, which moved the compassion and regret of all.

Tennyson has chosen the story of the Lady of Shalott for the subject of a poem:

"There she weaves by night and day
A magic web with colors gay.
She has heard a whisper say

A curse is on her if she stay
    To look down to Camelot.
She knows not what the curse may be,
    And so she weaveth steadily,
    And little other care hath she,
        The Lady of Shalott.

"And moving thro' a mirror clear
That hangs before her all the year,
Shadows of the world appear.
There she sees the highway near
    Winding down to Camelot:
There the river eddy whirls,
And there the surly village churls,
And the red cloaks of market girls
    Pass onward from Shalott.

"Sometimes a troop of damsels glad,
An abbot on an ambling pad,
Sometimes a curly shepherd lad,
Or long-haired page in crimson clad
    Goes by to towered Camelot.
And sometimes thro' the mirror blue
The knights come riding two and two:
She has no loyal knight and true,
    The Lady of Shalott.

"But in her web she still delights
To weave the mirror's magic sights,
For often thro' the silent nights
A funeral, with plumes and lights
    And music, went to Camelot:
Or when the moon was overhead
Came two young lovers lately wed;
'I am half sick of shadows,' said
    The Lady of Shalott."

The poem goes on as the story: the lady sees Launcelot, he rides away, and she afterward dies and floats down the river in a boat to Camelot. The poem ends as follows:

"Under tower and balcony,
By garden wall and gallery,
A gleaming shape she floated by
Dead-pale between the houses high,

Silent unto Camelot.
Out upon the wharves they came,
Knight and burgher, lord and dame,
And round the prow they read her name,
    The Lady of Shalott.

"Who is this? and what is here?
And in the lighted palace near
Died the sound of royal cheer;
And they crossed themselves for fear

All the knights at Camelot:
But Launcelot mused a little space;
He said 'She has a lovely face;
God in his mercy lend her grace,
    The Lady of Shalott.' "

The story of "Elaine, the fair, Elaine, the lovable, Elaine, the lily-maid of Astolat," one of the earliest of the "Idylls of the King," is of course the same tale as the Lady of Shalott.

CHAPTER IX

THE STORY OF LAUNCELOT— QUEEN GUENEVER'S PERIL

I T happened at this time that Queen Guenever was thrown into great peril of her life. A certain squire who was in her immediate service, having some cause of animosity to Sir Gawain, determined to destroy him by poison at a public entertainment. For this purpose he concealed the poison in an apple of fine appearance, which he placed on the top of several others, and put the dish before the queen, hoping that, as Sir Gawain was the knight of greatest dignity, she would present the apple to him. But it happened that a Scottish knight of high distinction, who arrived on that day, was seated next to the queen, and to him, as a stranger, she presented the apple, which he had no sooner eaten than he was seized with dreadful pain, and fell senseless. The whole court was of course thrown into confusion; the knights rose from table, darting looks of indignation at the wretched queen, whose tears and protesta-

tions were unable to remove their suspicions. In spite of all that could be done the knight died, and nothing remained but to order a magnificent funeral and monument for him, which was done.

Some time after, Sir Mador, brother of the murdered knight, arrived at Arthur's court in quest of him. While hunting in the forest he by chance came to the spot where the monument was erected, read the inscription, and returned to court determined on immediate and signal vengeance. He rode into the hall, loudly accused the queen of treason, and insisted on her being given up to punishment, unless she should find, by a certain day, a knight hardy enough to risk his life in support of her innocence. Arthur, powerful as he was, did not dare to deny the appeal, but was compelled, with a heavy heart, to accept it, and Mador sternly took his departure, leaving the royal couple plunged in terror and anxiety.

During all this time Launcelot was absent, and no one knew where he was. He had fled in anger from his fair mistress, upon being reproached by her with his passion for the Lady of Shalott, which she had hastily inferred from his wearing her scarf at the tournament. He took up his abode with a hermit in the forest, and resolved to think no more of the cruel beauty, whose conduct he thought must flow from a wish to get rid of him. Yet calm reflection had somewhat cooled his indignation, and he had begun to wish, though hardly able to hope, for a reconciliation, when the news of Sir Mador's challenge fortunately reached his ears. The intelligence revived his spirits, and he began to prepare with the utmost cheerfulness for a contest which, if successful, would insure him at once the affection of his mistress and the gratitude of his sovereign.

The sad fate of the Lady of Shalott had ere this completely acquitted Launcelot in the queen's mind of all suspicion of his fidelity, and she lamented most grievously her foolish quarrel with him, which now, at her time of need, deprived her of her most efficient champion.

As the day appointed by Sir Mador was fast approaching, it became necessary that she should procure a champion for her defence; and she successively adjured Sir Hector, Sir Lionel, Sir Bohort, and Sir Gawain to undertake the battle. She fell on her knees before them, called heaven to witness her innocence of the crime alleged against her, but was sternly answered by all that they could not fight to maintain the innocence of one whose act, and the fatal consequences of it, they had seen with their own eyes. She retired, therefore, dejected and disconsolate; but the sight of the fatal pile on which, if guilty, she was doomed to be burned, exciting her to fresh effort, she again repaired to Sir Bohort, threw herself at his feet, and, piteously calling on him for mercy, fell into a swoon. The brave knight was not proof against this. He raised her up, and hastily promised that he would undertake her cause, if no other or better champion should present himself. He then summoned his friends, and told them his resolution; and as a mortal combat with Sir Mador was a most fearful enterprise, they agreed to accompany him in the morning to the hermitage in the forest, where he proposed to

receive absolution from the hermit, and to make his peace with heaven, before he entered the lists. As they approached the hermitage, they espied a knight riding in the forest, whom they at once recognized as Sir Launcelot. Overjoyed at the meeting, they quickly, in answer to his questions, confirmed the news of the queen's imminent danger, and received his instructions to return to court, to comfort her as well as they could, but to say nothing of his intention of undertaking her defence, which he meant to do in the character of an unknown adventurer.

On their return to the castle they found that mass was finished, and had scarcely time to speak to the queen before they were summoned into the hall to dinner. A general gloom was spread over the countenances of all the guests. Arthur himself was unable to conceal his dejection, and the wretched Guenever, motionless and bathed in tears, sat in trembling expectation of Sir Mador's appearance. Nor was it long ere he stalked into the hall, and with a voice of thunder, rendered more impressive by the general silence, demanded instant justice on the guilty party. Arthur replied with dignity, that little of the day was yet spent, and that perhaps a champion might yet be found capable of satisfying his thirst for battle. Sir Bohort now rose from table, and, shortly returning in complete armor, resumed his place, after receiving the embraces and thanks of the king, who now began to resume some degree of confidence. Sir Mador, growing impatient, again repeated his denunciations of vengeance, and insisted that the combat should no longer be postponed.

In the height of the debate there came riding into the hall a knight mounted on a black steed, and clad in black armor, with his visor down, and lance in hand. "Sir," said the king, "is it your will to alight and partake of our cheer?" "Nay, sir," he replied; "I come to save a lady's life. The queen hath ill bestowed her favors, and honored many a knight, that in her hour of need she should have none to take her part. Thou that darest accuse her of treachery stand forth, for today shalt thou need all thy might."

Sir Mador, though surprised, was not appalled by the stern challenge and formidable appearance of his antagonist, but prepared for the encounter. At the first shock both were unhorsed. They then drew their swords, and commenced a combat which lasted from noon till evening, when Sir Mador, whose strength began to fail, was felled to the ground by Launcelot, and compelled to sue for mercy. The victor, whose arm was already raised to terminate the life of his opponent, instantly dropped his sword, courteously lifted up the fainting Sir Mador, frankly confessing that he had never before encountered so formidable an enemy. The other, with similar courtesy, solemnly renounced all further projects of vengeance for his brother's death; and the two knights, now become fast friends, embraced each other with the greatest cordiality. In the meantime Arthur, having recognized Sir Launcelot, whose helmet was now unlaced, rushed down into the lists, followed by all his knights, to welcome and thank his deliverer. Guenever swooned with joy, and the place of combat suddenly exhibited a scene of the most tumultuous delight.

The general satisfaction was still further increased by the discovery of the real culprit. Having accidentally incurred some suspicion, he confessed his crime, and was publicly punished in the presence of Sir Mador.

The court now returned to the castle, which, with the title of "La Joyeuse Garde" bestowed upon it in memory of the happy event, was conferred on Sir Launcelot by Arthur, as a memorial of his gratitude.

So far of the Story of Sir Launcelot. Let us turn now to the Story of Sir Tristram of Lyonesse.

CHAPTER X

THE STORY OF TRISTRAM OF LYONESSE

M ELIADUS was king of Leonois, or Lyonesse, a country famous in the annals of romance, which adjoined the kingdom of Cornwall, but has now disappeared from the map, having been, it is said, overwhelmed by the ocean. Meliadus was married to Isabella, sister of Mark, king of Cornwall. A fairy fell in love with him, and drew him away by enchantment while he was engaged in hunting. His queen set out in quest of him, but was taken ill on her journey, and died, leaving an infant son, whom, from the melancholy circumstances of his birth, she called Tristram.

Gouvernail, the queen's squire, who had accompanied her, took charge of the child, and restored him to his father, who had at length burst the enchantments of the fairy, and returned home.

Meliadus, after seven years, married again, and the new queen, being jealous of the influence of Tristram with his father, laid plots for his life, which were discovered by Gouvernail, who, in consequence, fled with the boy to the court of the king of France, where Tristram was kindly received, and grew up improving in every gallant and knightly accomplishment, adding to his skill in arms the arts of music and of chess. In particular, he devoted himself to the chase and to all woodland sports, so that he became distinguished above all other chevaliers of the court for his knowledge of all that relates to hunting. <u>No wonder that Belinda, the king's daughter, fell in love with him</u>; but as he did not return her passion, she, in a sudden impulse of anger, excited her father against him, and he was banished from the kingdom. The princess soon repented of her act, and in despair destroyed herself, having first written a most tender letter to Tristram, sending him at the same time a beautiful and sagacious dog, of which she was very fond, desiring him to keep it as a memorial of her. Meliadus was now dead, and as his queen, Tristram's stepmother, held the throne, Gouvernail was afraid to carry his pupil to his native country, and took him to Cornwall, to his uncle Mark, who gave him a kind reception.

King Mark resided at the castle of Tintadiel, already mentioned in the history of Uther and Igaerne. In this court Tristram became distinguished in all the exercises incumbent on a knight; nor was it long before he had an opportunity of practically employing his valor and skill. Moraunt, a celebrated champion, brother to the queen of Ireland, arrived at the court, to demand tribute of King Mark. The knights of Cornwall are in ill repute, in romance, for their cowardice, and they exhibited it on this occasion. King Mark could find no champion who dared to encounter the Irish knight, till his nephew Tristram, who had not yet received the honors of knighthood, craved to be admitted to the order, offering at the same time to fight the battle of Cornwall against the Irish champion. King Mark assented with reluctance; Tristram received the accolade, which conferred knighthood upon him; and the place and time were assigned for the encounter.

Without attempting to give the details of this famous combat, the first and one of the most glorious of Tristram's exploits, we shall only say that the young knight, though severely wounded, cleft the head of Moraunt, leaving a portion of his sword in the wound. Moraunt, half dead with his wound and the disgrace of his defeat, hastened to hide himself in his ship, sailed away with all speed for Ireland, and died soon after arriving in his own country.

The kingdom of Cornwall was thus delivered from its tribute. Tristram, weakened by loss of blood, fell senseless. His friends flew to his assistance. They dressed his wounds, which in general healed readily; but the lance of Moraunt was poisoned, and one wound which it made yielded to no remedies, but grew worse day by day. The surgeons could do no more. Tristram asked permission of his uncle to depart, and seek for aid in the kingdom of Loegria (England). With his consent he embarked, and, after tossing for many days on the sea, was driven by the winds to the coast of Ireland. He landed, full of joy and gratitude that he had escaped the peril of the sea; took his rote,[1] and began to play. It was a summer evening, and the king of Ireland and his daughter, the beautiful Isoude, were at a window which overlooked the sea. The strange harper was sent for, and conveyed to the palace, where, finding that he was in Ireland, whose champion he had lately slain, he concealed his name, and called himself Tramtris. The queen undertook his cure, and by a medicated bath gradually restored him to health. His skill in music and in games occasioned his being frequently called to court, and <u>he became instructor of the Princess Isoude in minstrelsy and poetry</u>, who profited so well under his care, that she soon had no equal in the kingdom, except her instructor.

64 ▷

At this time a tournament was held, at which many knights of the Round Table, and others, were present. On the first day a Saracen prince, named Palamedes, obtained the advantage over all. They brought him to the court, and gave him a feast, at which Tristram, just recovering from his wound, was present. The fair Isoude appeared on this occasion in all her charms. Palamedes could not behold them without emotion, and made no effort to conceal his love. Tristram perceived it, and the pain he felt from jealousy taught him how dear the fair Isoude had already become to him.

Next day the tournament was renewed. Tristram, still feeble from his wound, rose during the night, took his arms, and concealed them in a forest near the place of the contest, and, after it had begun, mingled with the combatants. He overthrew all that encountered him, in particular Palamedes, whom he brought to the ground with a stroke of his lance, and then fought him hand to hand, bearing off the prize

---

[1]A musical instrument.

of the tourney. But his exertions caused his wound to reopen; he bled fast, and in this sad state, yet in triumph, they bore him to the palace. The fair Isoude devoted herself to his relief with an interest which grew more vivid day by day; and her skilful care soon restored him to health.

It happened one day that a damsel of the court, entering the closet where Tristram's arms were deposited, perceived that a part of the sword had been broken off. It occurred to her that the missing portion was like that which was left in the skull of Moraunt, the Irish champion. She imparted her thought to the queen, who compared the fragment taken from her brother's wound with the sword of Tristram, and was satisfied that it was part of the same, and that the weapon of Tristram was that which reft her brother's life. She laid her griefs and resentment before the king, who satisfied himself with his own eyes of the truth of her suspicions. Tristram was cited before the whole court, and reproached with having dared to present himself before them after having slain their kinsman. He acknowledged that he had fought with Moraunt to settle the claim for tribute, and said that it was by force of winds and waves alone that he was thrown on their coast. The queen demanded vengeance for the death of her brother; the fair Isoude trembled and grew pale, but a murmur rose from all the assembly that the life of one so handsome and so brave should not be taken for such a cause, and generosity finally triumphed over resentment in the mind of the king. Tristram was dismissed in safety, but commanded to leave the kingdom without delay, and never to return thither under pain of death. Tristram went back, with restored health, to Cornwall.

King Mark made his nephew give him a minute recital of his adventures. Tristram told him all minutely; but when he came to speak of the fair Isoude, he described her charms with a warmth and energy such as none but a lover could display. King Mark was fascinated with the description, and, choosing a favorable time, demanded a boon[1] of his nephew, who readily

---

[1]"Good faith was the very corner-stone of chivalry. Whenever a knight's word was pledged (it mattered not how rashly), it was to be redeemed at any price. Hence the sacred obligation of the

granted it. The king made him swear upon the holy reliques that he would fulfil his commands. Then Mark directed him to go to Ireland, and obtain for him the fair Isoude to be queen of Cornwall.

Tristram believed it was certain death for him to return to Ireland; and how could he act as ambassador for his uncle in such a cause? Yet, bound by his oath, he hesitated not for an instant. He only took the precaution to change his armor. He embarked for Ireland; but a tempest drove him to the coast of England, near Camelot, where King Arthur was holding his court, attended by the knights of the Round Table, and many others, the most illustrious in the world.

Tristram kept himself unknown. He took part in many jousts; he fought many combats, in which he covered himself with glory. One day he saw among those recently arrived the king of Ireland, father of the fair Isoude. This prince, accused of treason against his liege sovereign, Arthur, came to Camelot to free himself of the charge. Blanor, one of the most redoubtable warriors of the Round Table, was his accuser, and Argius, the king, had neither youthful vigor nor strength to encounter him. He must therefore seek a champion to sustain his innocence. But the knights of the Round Table were not at liberty to fight against one another, unless in a quarrel of their own. Argius heard of the great renown of the unknown knight; he also was witness of his exploits. He sought him, and conjured him to adopt his defence, and on his oath declared that he was innocent of the crime of which he was accused. Tristram readily consented, and made himself known to the king, who on his part promised to reward his exertions, if successful, with whatever gift he might ask.

Tristram fought with Blanor, and overthrew him, and held his life in his power. The fallen warrior called on him to use his right of conquest, and strike the fatal blow. "God forbid," said Tristram, "that I should take the life of so brave a knight!" He raised him up and restored him to his friends. The judges of the field decided that the king of Ireland was acquitted of the charge against him, and they led Tristram in triumph to his tent. King Argius, full of gratitude, conjured Tristram to accompany him to his kingdom. They departed together, and arrived in Ireland, and the queen, forgetting her resentment for her brother's death, exhibited to the preserver of her husband's life nothing but gratitude and good-will.

How happy a moment for Isoude, who knew that her father had promised his deliverer whatever boon he might ask. But the unhappy Tristram gazed on her with despair, at the thought of the cruel oath which bound him. His magnanimous soul subdued the force of his love. He revealed the oath which he had taken, and with trembling voice demanded the fair Isoude for his uncle.

Argius consented and soon all was prepared for the departure of Isoude. Brengwain, her favorite maid-of-honor, was to accompany her. On the day of departure the queen took aside this devoted attendant, and told her that she had observed that her daughter and Tristram were attached to one another, and that to avert the bad effects of this inclination she had procured from a powerful fairy a potent philter (love-draught), which she directed Brengwain to administer to Isoude and to King Mark on the evening of their marriage.

Isoude and Tristram embarked together. A favorable wind filled the sails and promised them a fortunate voyage. The lovers gazed upon one another; and could not repress their sighs. Love seemed to light up all his fires on their lips, as in their hearts. The day was warm; they suffered from thirst. Isoude first complained. Tristram descried the bottle containing the love-draught, which Brengwain had been so imprudent as to leave in sight. He took it, gave some of it to the charming Isoude, and drank the remainder himself. The dog Houdain licked the cup. The ship arrived in Cornwall, and Isoude was married to King Mark. The old monarch was delighted with his bride, and his gratitude to Tristram was unbounded. He loaded him with honors, and made him chamberlain of his palace, thus giving him access to the queen at all times.

boon granted by a knight to his suppliant. Instances without number occur in romance, in which a knight, by rashly granting an indefinite boon, was obliged to do or suffer something extremely to his prejudice. But it is not in romance alone that we find some singular instances of adherence to an indefinite promise. The history of the times presents authentic transactions equally embarrassing and absurd."— *Scott*, note of Sir Tristram.

In the midst of the festivities of the court which followed the royal marriage, an unknown minstrel one day presented himself, bearing a harp of peculiar construction. He excited the curiosity of King Mark by refusing to play upon it till he should grant him a boon. The king having promised to grant his request, the minstrel, who was none other than the Saracen knight, Sir Palamedes, the lover of the fair Isoude, sung to the harp a lay, in which he demanded Isoude as the promised gift. King Mark could not by the laws of knighthood withhold the boon. The lady was mounted on her horse and led away by her triumphant lover. Tristram, it is needless to say, was absent at the time, and did not return until their departure. When he heard what had taken place, he seized his rote, and hastened to the shore, where Isoude and her new master had already embarked. Tristram played upon his rote, and the sound reached the ears of Isoude, who became so deeply affected that Sir Palamedes was induced to return with her to land, that they might see the unknown musician. Tristram watched his opportunity, seized the lady's horse by the bridle, and plunged with her into the forest, tauntingly informing his rival that "what he had got by the harp he had lost by the rote." Palamedes pursued, and a combat was about to commence, the result of which must have been fatal to one or other of these gallant knights; but Isoude stepped between them, and, addressing Palamedes, said, "You tell me that you love me; you will not then deny me the request I am about to make?" "Lady," he replied, "I will perform your bidding." "Leave, then," said she, "this contest, and repair to King Arthur's court, and salute Queen Guenever for me; tell her that there are in the world but two ladies, herself and I, and two lovers, hers and mine; and come thou not in future in any place where I am." Palamedes burst into tears. "Ah, lady," said he, "I will obey you; but I beseech you that you will not forever steel your heart against me." "Palamedes," she replied, "may I never taste of joy again if I ever quit my first love." Palamedes then went his way. The lovers remained a week in concealment, after which Tristram restored Isoude to her husband, advising him in future to reward minstrels in some other way.

The king showed much gratitude to Tristram, but

in the bottom of his heart he cherished bitter jealousy of him. One day Tristram and Isoude were alone together in her private chamber. A base and cowardly knight of the court, named Andret, spied them through a keyhole. They sat at a table of chess, but were not attending to the game. Andret brought the king, having first raised his suspicions, and placed him so as to watch their motions. The king saw enough to confirm his suspicions, and he burst into the apartment with his sword drawn, and had nearly slain Tristram before he was put on his guard. But Tristram avoided the blow, drew his sword, and drove before him the cowardly monarch, chasing him through all the apartments of the palace, giving him frequent blows with the flat of his sword, while he cried in vain to his knights to save him. They were not inclined, or did not dare to interpose in his behalf.

A proof of the great popularity of the tale of Sir Tristram is the fact that the Italian poets, Boiardo and Ariosto, have founded upon it the idea of the two enchanted fountains, which produced the opposite effects of love and hatred. Boiardo thus describes the fountain of hatred:

> "Fair was that fountain, sculptured all of gold,
> With alabaster sculptured, rich and rare;
> And in its basin clear thou might'st behold
> The flowery marge reflected fresh and fair.
> Sage Merlin framed the font,—so legends bear,—
> When on fair Isoude doated Tristram brave,
> That the good errant knight, arriving there,
> Might quaff oblivion in the enchanted wave,
> And leave his luckless love, and 'scape his timeless
>   grave.

> "But ne'er the warrior's evil fate allowed
> His steps that fountain's charmed verge to gain,
> Though restless, roving on adventure proud,
> He traversed oft the land and oft the main."

CHAPTER XI

TRISTRAM AND ISOUDE

AFTER this affair Tristram was banished from the kingdom, and Isoude shut up in a tower which stood on the bank of a river. Tristram could not resolve to depart without some further communication with his beloved; so he concealed himself in the forest, till at last he contrived to attract her attention by means of twigs, which he curiously peeled and sent down the stream under her window. By this means many secret interviews were obtained. Tristram dwelt in the forest, sustaining himself by game, which the dog Houdain ran down for him; for this faithful animal was unequalled in the chase, and knew so well his master's wish for concealment that in the pursuit of his game he never barked. At length Tristram departed, but left Houdain with Isoude, as a remembrance of him.

Sir Tristram wandered through various countries, achieving the most perilous enterprises, and covering himself with glory, yet unhappy at the separation from his beloved Isoude. At length King Mark's territory was invaded by a neighboring chieftain, and he was forced to summon his nephew to his aid. Tristram obeyed the call, put himself at the head of his uncle's vassals, and drove the enemy out of the country. Mark was full of gratitude, and Tristram, restored to favor and to the society of his beloved Isoude, seemed at the summit of happiness. But a sad reverse was at hand.

Tristram had brought with him a friend named Pheredin, son of the king of Brittany. This young knight saw Queen Isoude, and could not resist her charms. Knowing the love of his friend for the queen, and that that love was returned, Pheredin concealed his own, until his health failed, and he feared he was drawing near his end. He then wrote to the beautiful queen that he was dying for love of her.

The gente Isoude, in a moment of pity for the friend of Tristram, returned him an answer so kind and compassionate that it restored him to life. A few days afterward Tristram found this letter. The most terrible jealousy took possession of his soul; he would have slain Pheredin, who with difficulty made his escape. Then Tristram mounted his horse, and rode to the forest, where for ten days he took no rest nor food. At length he was found by a damsel lying almost dead by the brink of a fountain. She recognized him, and tried in vain to rouse his attention. At last, recollecting his love for music, she went and got her harp, and played thereon. Tristram was roused from his reverie; tears flowed; he breathed more freely; he took the harp from the maiden, and sung this lay, with a voice broken with sobs:

"Sweet I sang in former days,
Kind love perfected my lays:
Now my art alone displays
The woe that on my being preys.

"Charming love, delicious power,
Worshipped from my earliest hour,
Thou who life on all dost shower,
Love! my life thou dost devour.

"In death's hour I beg of thee,
Isoude, dearest enemy,
Thou who erst couldst kinder be,
When I'm gone, forget not me.

"On my gravestone passers by
Oft will read, as low I lie,
'Never wight in love could vie
With Tristram, yet she let him die.'"

Tristram, having finished his lay, wrote it off and gave it to the damsel, conjuring her to present it to the queen.

Meanwhile Queen Isoude was inconsolable at the absence of Tristram. She discovered that it was caused by the fatal letter which she had written to Pheredin. Innocent, but in despair at the sad effects of her letter, she wrote another to Pheredin, charging him never to see her again. The unhappy lover obeyed this cruel decree. He plunged into the forest, and died of grief and love in a hermit's cell.

Isoude passed her days in lamenting the absence and unknown fate of Tristram. One day her jealous husband, having entered her chamber unperceived, overheard her singing the following lay:

"My voice to piteous wail is bent,
My harp to notes of languishment;
Ah, love! delightsome days be meant
For happier wights, with hearts content.

"Ah, Tristram! far away from me,
Art thou from restless anguish free?
Ah! could'st thou so one moment be
From her who so much loveth thee?"

The king, hearing these words, burst forth in a rage; but Isoude was too wretched to fear his violence. "You have heard me," she said; "I confess it all. I love Tristram, and always shall love him. Without doubt he is dead, and died for me. I no longer wish to live. The blow that shall finish my misery will be most welcome."

The king was moved at the distress of the fair Isoude, and perhaps the idea of Tristram's death tended to allay his wrath. He left the queen in charge of her women, commanding them to take especial care lest her despair should lead her to do harm to herself.

Tristram, meanwhile, distracted as he was, rendered a most important service to the shepherds by slaying a gigantic robber named Taullas, who was in the habit of plundering their flocks and rifling their cottages. The shepherds, in their gratitude to Tristram, bore him in triumph to King Mark to have him bestow on him a suitable reward. No wonder Mark failed to recognize in the half-clad wild man before him his nephew Tristram; but grateful for the service the unknown had rendered, he ordered him to be well taken care of, and gave him in charge to the queen and her women. Under such care Tristram rapidly recovered his serenity and his health, so that the romancer tells us he became handsomer than ever. King Mark's jealousy revived with Tristram's health and good looks, and, in spite of his debt of gratitude so lately increased, he again banished him from the court.

Sir Tristram left Cornwall, and proceeded into the land of Loegria (England) in quest of adventures. One day he entered a wide forest. The sound of a little bell showed him that some inhabitant was near. He followed the sound, and found a hermit, who informed him that he was in the forest of Arnantes, belonging to the fairy Viviane, the Lady of the Lake, who, smitten with love for King Arthur, had found means to entice him to this forest, where by enchantments she held him a prisoner, having deprived him of all memory of who and what he was. The hermit informed him that all the knights of the Round Table were out in search of the king, and that he (Tristram) was now in the scene of the most grand and important adventures.

This was enough to animate Tristram in the search. He had not wandered far before he encountered a knight of Arthur's court, who proved to be Sir Kay the seneschal, who demanded of him whence he came. Tristram answering, "From Cornwall," Sir Kay did not let slip the opportunity of a joke at the expense of the Cornish knight. Tristram chose to leave him in his error, and even confirmed him in it; for meeting some other knights, Tristram declined to joust with them. They spent the night together at an abbey, where Tristram submitted patiently to all their jokes. The seneschal gave the word to his companions that they should set out early next day, and intercept the Cornish knight on his way, and enjoy the amusement of seeing his fright when they should insist on

running a tilt with him. Tristram next morning found himself alone; he put on his armor, and set out to continue his quest. He soon saw before him the seneschal and the three knights, who barred the way, and insisted on a joust. Tristram excused himself a long time; at last he reluctantly took his stand. He encountered them, one after the other, and overthrew them all four, man and horse, and then rode off, bidding them not to forget their friend, the knight of Cornwall.

Tristram had not ridden far when he met a damsel, who cried out, "Ah, my lord! hasten forward, and prevent a horrid treason!" Tristram flew to her assistance, and soon reached a spot where he beheld a knight, whom three others had borne to the ground, and were unlacing his helmet in order to cut off his head.

Tristram flew to the rescue, and slew with one stroke of his lance one of the assailants. The knight, recovering his feet, sacrificed another to his vengeance, and the third made his escape. The rescued knight then raised the visor of his helmet, and a long white beard fell down upon his breast. The majesty and venerable air of this knight made Tristram suspect that it was none other than Arthur himself, and the prince confirmed his conjecture. Tristram would have knelt before him, but Arthur received him in his arms, and inquired his name and country; but Tristram declined to disclose them, on the plea that he was now on a quest requiring secrecy. At this moment the damsel who had brought Tristram to the rescue darted forward, and, seizing the king's hand, drew from his finger a ring, the gift of the fairy, and by that act dissolved the enchantment. Arthur, having recovered his reason and his memory, offered to Tristram to attach him to his court, and to confer honors an dignities upon him; but Tristram declined all, and only consented to accompany him till he should see him safe in the hands of his knights. Soon after, Hector de Marys rode up, and saluted the king, who on his part introduced him to Tristram as one of the bravest of his knights. Tristram took leave of the king and his faithful follower, and continued his quest.

We cannot follow Tristram through all the adventures which filled this epoch of his history. Suffice it to say, he fulfilled on all occasions the duty of a true knight, rescuing the oppressed, redressing wrongs, abolishing evil customs, and suppressing injustice, thus by constant action endeavoring to lighten the pains of absence from her he loved. In the meantime Isoude, separated from her dear Tristram, passed her days in languor and regret. At length she could no longer resist the desire to hear some news of her lover. She wrote a letter, and sent it by one of her damsels, niece of her faithful Brengwain. One day Tristram, weary with his exertions, had dismounted and laid himself down by the side of a fountain and fallen asleep. The damsel of Queen Isoude arrived at the same fountain, and recognized Passebreul, the horse of Tristram, and presently perceived his master, asleep. He was thin and pale, showing evident marks of the pain he suffered in separation from his beloved. She awaked him, and gave him the letter which she bore, and Tristram enjoyed the pleasure, so sweet to a lover, of hearing from and talking about the object of his affections. He prayed the damsel postpone her return till after the magnificent tournament which Arthur had proclaimed should have taken place, and conducted her to the castle of Persides, a brave and loyal knight, who received her with great consideration.

Tristram conducted the damsel of Queen Isoude to the tournament and had her placed in the balcony among the ladies of the queen. He then joined the tourney. Nothing could exceed his strength and valor. Launcelot admired him, and by a secret presentiment declined to dispute the honor of the day with a knight so gallant and so skilful. Arthur descended from the balcony to greet the conqueror; but the modest and devoted Tristram, content with having borne off the prize in the sight of the messenger of Isoude, made his escape with her, and disappeared.

The next day the tourney recommenced. Tristram assumed different armor, that he might not be known; but he was soon detected by the terrible blows that he gave. Arthur and Guenever had no doubt that it was the same knight who had borne off the prize of the day before. Arthur's gallant spirit was roused. After Launcelot of the Lake and Sir Gawain, he was accounted the best knight of the Round Table. He went privately and armed himself, and came into the tourney in undistinguished armor. He ran a joust with Tristram, whom he shook in his seat; but Tristram, who did not know him, threw him out of the saddle. Arthur recovered himself and, content with having made proof of the stranger knight, bade Launcelot finish the adventure, and vindicate the honor of the Round Table. Sir Launcelot, at the bidding of the monarch, assailed Tristram, whose lance was already broken in former encounters. But the law of this sort of combat was, that the knight, after having broken his lance, must fight with his sword, and must not refuse to meet with his shield the lance of his antagonist. Tristram met Launcelot's charge upon his shield, which that terrible lance could not fail to pierce. It inflicted a wound upon Tristram's side, and breaking, left the iron in the wound. But Tristram also with his sword smote so vigorously on Launcelot's casque that he cleft it, and wounded his head. The wound was not deep, but the blood flowed into his eyes, and blinded him for a moment, and Tristram, who thought himself mortally wounded, retired from the field. Launcelot declared to the king that he had never received such a blow in his life before.

Tristram hastened to Gouvernail, his squire, who drew forth the iron, bound up the wound, and gave him immediate ease. Tristram, after the tournament, kept retired in his tent, but Arthur, with the consent of the knights of the Round Table, decreed him the honors of the second day. But it was no longer a secret that the victor of the two days was the same individual, and Gouvernail, being questioned, confirmed the suspicions of Launcelot and Arthur, that it was no other than Sir Tristram of Lyonesse, the nephew of the king of Cornwall.

King Arthur, who desired to reward his distinguished valor, and knew that his uncle Mark had ungratefully banished him, would have eagerly availed himself of the opportunity to attach Tristram to his court,—all the knights of the Round Table declaring with acclamation that it would be impossible to find a more worthy companion. But Tristram had already departed in search of adventures, and the damsel of Queen Isoude returned to her mistress.

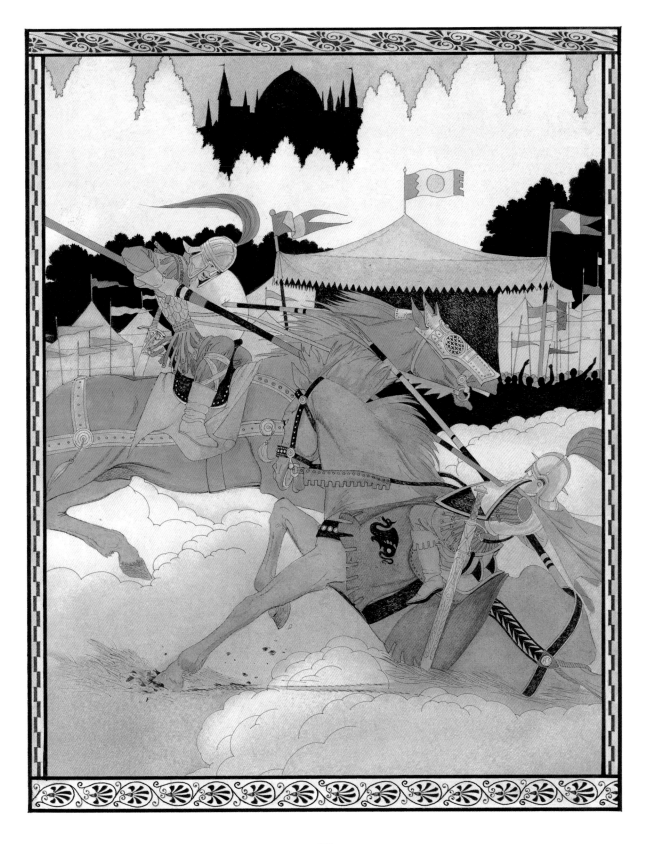

CHAPTER XII

THE STORY OF SIR TRISTRAM OF LYONESSE

SIR TRISTRAM rode through a forest, and saw ten men fighting, and one man did battle against nine. So he rode to the knights and cried to them, bidding them cease their battle, for they did themselves great shame, so many knights to fight against one. Then answered the master of the knights (his name was Sir Breuse sans Pitié, who was at that time the most villainous knight living): "Sir knight, what have ye to do to meddle with us? If ye be wise, depart on your way as you came, for this knight shall not escape us." "That were pity," said Sir Tristram, "that so good a knight should be slain so cowardly; therefore I warn you I will succor him with all my puissance."

Then Sir Tristram alighted off his horse, because they were on foot, that they should not slay his horse. And he smote on the right hand and on the left so

vigorously, that well-nigh at every stroke he struck down a knight. At last they fled, with Breuse sans Pitié, into the tower, and shut Sir Tristram without the gate. Then Sir Tristram returned back to the rescued knight, and found him sitting under a tree, sore wounded. "Fair knight," said he, "how is it with you?" "Sir knight," said Sir Palamedes, for he it was, "I thank you for your great goodness, for ye have rescued me from death." "What is your name?" said Sir Tristram. He said, "My name is Sir Palamedes." "Say ye so?" said Sir Tristram; "now know that thou art the man in the world that I most hate; therefore make thee ready, for I will do battle with thee." "What is your name?" said Sir Palamedes. "My name is Sir Tristram, your mortal enemy." "It may be so," said Sir Palamedes; "but you have done overmuch for me this day, that I should fight with you. Moreover, it will be no honor for you to have to do with me, for you are fresh and I am wounded. Therefore, if you will needs have to do with me, assign me a day, and I shall meet you without fail." "You say well," said Sir Tristram; "now I assign you to meet me in the meadow by the river of Camelot, where Merlin set the monument." So they were agreed. Then they departed, and took their ways diverse. Sir Tristram passed through a great forest into a plain, till he came to a priory, and there he reposed him with a good man six days. Then departed Sir Tristram, and rode straight into Camelot to the monument of Merlin, and there he looked about him for Sir Palamedes. And he perceived a seemly knight, who came riding against him all in white, with a covered shield. When he came nigh, Sir Tristram said aloud, "Welcome, Sir knight, and well and truly have you kept your promise." Then they made ready their shields and spears, and came together with all the might of their horses, so fiercely, that both the horses and the knights fell to the earth. And as soon as they might, they quitted their horses, and struck together with bright swords as men of might, and each wounded the other wonderfully sore, so that the blood ran out upon the grass. Thus they fought for the space of four hours, and never one would speak to the other one word. Then at last spake the white knight, and said, "Sir, thou fightest wonderful well, as ever I saw knight; therefore, if it please you, tell me your name." "Why dost thou ask my name?" said Sir Tristram; "art thou not Sir Palamedes?" "No, fair knight," said he, "I am Sir Launcelot of the Lake." "Alas!" said Sir Tristram, "what have I done? for you are the man of the world that I love best." "Fair knight," said Sir Launcelot, "tell me your name." "Truly," said he, "my name is Sir Tristram de Lyonesse." "Alas! alas!" said Sir Launcelot, "what adventure has befallen me!" And therewith Sir Launcelot kneeled down, and yielded him up his sword; and Sir Tristram kneeled down, and yielded him up his sword; and so either gave other the degree. And then they both went to the stone, and sat them down upon it, and took off their helms, and each kissed the other a hundred times. And then anon they rode toward Camelot, and on the way they met with Sir Gawain and Sir Gaheris, that had made promise to Arthur never to come again to the court till they had brought Sir Tristram with them.

"Return again," said Sir Launcelot, "for your quest is done; for I have met with Sir Tristram. Lo, here he is in his own person. Then was Sir Gawain glad, and said to Sir Tristram, "Ye are welcome." With this came King Arthur, and when he wist there was Sir Tristram, he ran unto him, and took him by the hand, and said, "Sir Tristram, ye are as welcome as any knight that ever came to this court." Then Sir Tristram told the king how he came thither for to have had to do with Sir Palamedes, and how he had rescued him from Sir Breuse sans Pitié and the nine knights. Then King Arthur took Sir Tristram by the hand, and went to the Table Round, and Queen Guenever came, and many ladies with her, and all the ladies said with one voice "Welcome, Sir Tristram." "Welcome," said the knights. "Welcome," said Arthur, "for one of the best knights, and the gentlest of the world, and the man of most worship; for of all manner of hunting thou bearest the prize, and of all measures of blowing thou art the beginning, and of all the terms of hunting and hawking ye are the inventor, and of all instruments of music ye are the best skilled; therefore, gentle knight," said Arthur, "ye are welcome to this court." And then King Arthur made Sir Tristram knight of the Table Round with great nobley and feasting as can be thought.

The Round Table had been made by the famous enchanter Merlin, and on it he had exerted all his skill and craft. Of the seats which surrounded it he had constructed thirteen, in memory of the thirteen Apostles. Twelve of these seats only could be occupied, and they only by knights of the highest fame; the thirteenth represented the seat of the traitor Judas. It remained always empty. It was called the *perilous seat* ever since a rash and haughty Saracen knight had dared to place himself in it, when the earth opened and swallowed him up.

A magic power wrote upon each seat the name of the knight who was entitled to sit in it. No one could succeed to a vacant seat unless he surpassed in valor and glorious deeds the knight who had occupied it before him; without this qualification he would be violently repelled by a hidden force. Thus proof was made of all those who presented themselves to replace any companions of the order who had fallen.

One of the principal seats, that of Moraunt of Ireland, had been vacant ten years, and his name still remained over it ever since the time when that distinguished champion fell beneath the sword of Sir Tristram. Arthur now took Tristram by the hand and led him to that seat. Immediately the most melodious sounds were heard, and exquisite perfumes filled the place; the name of Moraunt disappeared, and that of Tristram blazed forth in light. The rare modesty of Tristram had now to be subjected to a severe task; for the clerks charged with the duty of preserving the annals of the Round Table attended, and he was required by the law of his order to declare what feats of arms he had accomplished to entitle him to take that seat. This ceremony being ended, Tristram received the congratulations of all his companions. Sir Launcelot and Guenever took occasion to speak to him of the fair Isoude, and to express their wish that some happy chance might bring her to the kingdom of Loegria.

While Tristram was thus honored and caressed at the court of King Arthur, the most gloomy and malignant jealousy harassed the soul of Mark. He could not

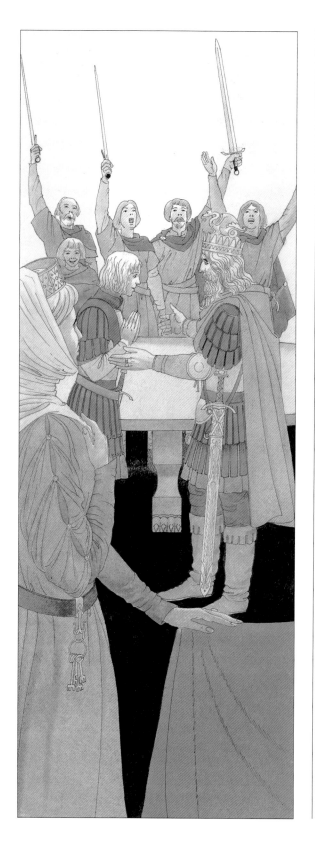

look upon Isoude without remembering that she loved Tristram, and the good fortune of his nephew goaded him to thoughts of vengeance. He at last resolved to go disguised into the kingdom of Loegria, attack Tristram by stealth, and put him to death. He took with him two knights, brought up in his court, who he thought were devoted to him; and, not willing to leave Isoude behind, named two of her maidens to attend her, together with her faithful Brengwain, and made them accompany him.

Having arrived in the neighborhood of Camelot, Mark imparted his plan to his two knights, but they rejected it with horror; nay, more, they declared that they would no longer remain in his service; and left him, giving him reason to suppose that they should repair to the court to accuse him before Arthur. It was necessary for Mark to meet and rebut their accusation; so, leaving Isoude in an abbey, he pursued his way alone to Camelot.

Mark had not ridden far when he encountered a party of knights of Arthur's court, and would have avoided them, for he knew their habit of challenging to a joust every stranger knight whom they met. But it was too late. They had seen his armor, and recognized him as a Cornish knight, and at once resolved to have some sport with him. It happened they had with them, Daguenet, King Arthur's fool, who, though deformed and weak of body, was not wanting in courage. The knights as Mark approached laid their plan that Daguenet should personate Sir Launcelot of the Lake, and challenge the Cornish knight. They equipped him in armor belonging to one of their number who was ill, and sent him forward to the cross-road to defy the strange knight. Mark, who saw that his antagonist was by no means formidable in appearance, was not disinclined to the combat; but when the dwarf rode towards him, calling out that he was Sir Launcelot of the Lake, his fears prevailed, he put spurs to his horse, and rode away at full speed, pursued by the shouts and laughter of the party.

Meanwhile, Isoude, remaining at the abbey with her faithful Brengwain, found her only amusement in walking occasionally in a forest adjoining the abbey. There, on the brink of a fountain girdled with trees, she thought of her love, and sometimes joined her voice and, her harp in lays reviving the memory of its pains or pleasures. One day the caitiff knight, Breuse the Pitiless, heard her voice, concealed himself, and drew near. She sang:

"Sweet silence, shadowy bower, and verdant lair,
　Ye court my troubled spirit to repose,
Whilst I, such dear remembrance rises there,
　Awaken every echo with my woes.

"Within these woods, by Nature's hand arrayed,
　A fountain springs, and feeds a thousand flowers;
Ah! how my groans do all its murmurs aid!
　How my sad eyes do swell it with their showers!

"What doth my knight the while? to him is given
　A double meed; in love and arms' emprise,
Him the Round Table elevates to heaven!
　Tristram! ah me! he hears not Isoude's cries."

Breuse the Pitiless, who, like most other caitiffs, had felt the weight of Tristram's arm, and hated him accordingly, at hearing his name breathed forth by the beautiful songstress, impelled by a double impulse, rushed forth from his concealment and laid hands on his victim. Isoude fainted, and Brengwain filled the air with her shrieks. Breuse carried Isoude to the place where he had left his horse; but the animal had got away from his bridle, and was at some distance. He was obliged to lay down his fair burden, and go in pursuit of his horse. Just then a knight came up, drawn by the cries of Brengwain, and demanded the cause of her distress. She could not speak, but pointed to her mistress lying insensible on the ground.

Breuse had by this time returned, and the cries of Brengwain, renewed at seeing him, sufficiently showed the stranger the cause of the distress. Tristram spurred his horse towards Breuse, who, not unprepared, ran to the encounter. Breuse was unhorsed, and lay motionless, pretending to be dead; but when the stranger knight left him to attend to the distressed damsels, he mounted his horse, and made his escape.

The knight now approached Isoude, gently raised her head, drew aside the golden hair which covered her countenance, gazed thereon for an instant, uttered a cry, and fell back insensible. Brengwain

came; her caress soon restored her mistress to life, and they then turned their attention to the fallen warrior. They raised his visor, and discovered the countenance of Sir Tristram. Isoude threw herself on the body of her lover, and bedewed his face with her tears. Their warmth revived the knight, and Tristram, on awaking, found himself in the arms of his dear Isoude.

It was the law of the Round Table that each knight after his admission should pass the next ten days in quest of adventures, during which time his companions might meet him in disguised armor, and try their strength with him. Tristram had now been out seven days, and in that time had encountered many of the best knights of the Round Table, and acquitted himself with honor. During the remaining three days Isoude remained at the abbey, under his protection, and then set out with her maidens, escorted by Sir Tristram, to rejoin King Mark at the court of Camelot.

This happy journey was one of the brightest epochs in the lives of Tristram and Isoude. He celebrated it by a lay upon the harp in a peculiar measure, to which the French give the name of *Triolet*:

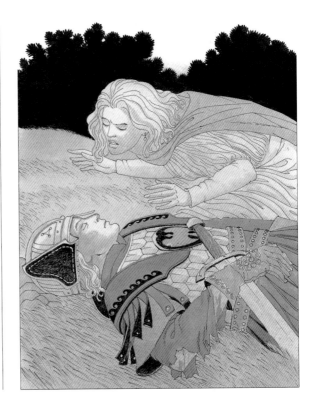

"With fair Isoude, and with love,
Ah! how sweet the life I lead!
How blest forever thus to rove,
With fair Isoude, and with love!
As she wills, I live and move,
And cloudless days to days succeed:
With fair Isoude, and with love,
Ah! how sweet the life I lead!

"Journeying on from break of day,
Feel you not fatigued, my fair?
Yon green turf invites to play;
Journeying on from day to day,
Ah! let us to that shade away,
Were it but to slumber there!
Journeying on from break of day,
Feel you not fatigued, my fair?"

They arrived at Camelot, where Sir Launcelot received them most cordially. Isoude was introduced to King Arthur and Queen Guenever, who welcomed her as a sister. As King Mark was held in arrest under the accusation of the two Cornish knights, Queen Isoude could not rejoin her husband, and Sir Launcelot placed his castle of La Joyeuse Garde at the disposal of his friends, who there took up their abode.

King Mark, who found himself obliged to confess the truth of the charge against him, or to clear himself by combat with his accusers, preferred the former, and King Arthur, as his crime had not been perpetrated, remitted the penalty, only enjoining upon him, under pain of his signal displeasure, to lay aside all thoughts of vengeance against his nephew. In the presence of the king and his court, all parties were formally reconciled; Mark and his queen departed for their home, and Tristram remained at Arthur's court.

CHAPTER XIII

END OF THE STORY OF SIR TRISTRAM OF LYONESSE

WHILE Sir Tristram and the fair Isoude abode yet at La Joyeuse Garde, Sir Tristram rode forth one day, without armor, having no weapon but his spear and his sword. And as he rode he came to a place where he saw two knights in battle, and one of them had gotten the better, and the other lay overthrown. The knight who had the better was Sir Palamedes. When Sir Palamedes knew Sir Tristram, he cried out, "Sir Tristram, now we be met, and ere we depart we will redress our old wrongs." "As for that," said Sir Tristram, "there never yet was Christian man that might make his boast that I ever fled from him, and thou that art a Saracen shalt never say that of me." And therewith Sir Tristram made his horse to run, and with all his might came straight upon Sir Palamedes, and broke his spear upon him. Then he

drew his sword and struck at Sir Palamedes six great strokes, upon his helm. Sir Palamedes saw that Sir Tristram had not his armor on, and he marvelled at his rashness and his great folly; and said to himself, "If I meet and slay him I am ashamed wheresoever I go." Then Sir Tristram cried out and said, "Thou coward knight, why wilt thou not do battle with me? for have thou no doubt I shall endure all thy malice." "Ah, Sir Tristram!" said Sir Palamedes, "thou knowest I may not fight with thee for shame; for thou art here naked, and I am armed; now I require that thou answer me a question that I shall ask you." "Tell me what it is," said Sir Tristram. "I put the case," said Sir Palamedes, "that you were well armed, and I naked as ye be; what would you do to me now, by your true knighthood?" "Ah!" said Sir Tristram, "now I understand thee well, Sir Palamedes; and, as

76

God me bless, what I shall say shall not be said for fear that I have of thee. But if it were so, thou shouldest depart from me, for I would not have to do with thee." "No more will I with thee," said Sir Palamedes, "and therefore ride forth on thy way." "As for that, I may choose," said Sir Tristram, "either to ride or to abide. But, Sir Palamedes, I marvel at one thing,—that thou art so good a knight, yet that thou wilt not be christened." "As for that," said Sir Palamedes, "I may not yet be christened, for a vow which I made many years ago; yet in my heart I believe in our Saviour and his mild mother Mary; but I have yet one battle to do, and when that is done I will be christened, with a good will." "By my head," said Sir Tristram, "as for that one battle, thou shalt seek it no longer; for yonder is a knight, whom you have smitten down. Now help me to be clothed in his armor, and I will soon fulfil thy vow." "As ye will," said Sir Palamedes, "so shall it be." So they rode both unto that knight that sat on a bank; and Sir Tristram saluted him, and he full wealdy saluted him again. "Sir," said Sir Tristram, "I pray you to lend me your whole armor; for I am unarmed, and I must do battle

with this knight." "Sir," said the hurt knight, "you shall have it, with a right good will." Then Sir Tristram unarmed Sir Galleron, for that was the name of the hurt knight, and he as well as he could helped to arm Sir Tristram. Then Sir Tristram mounted upon his own horse, and in his hand he took Sir Galleron's spear. Thereupon Sir Palamedes was ready, and so they came hurtling together, and each smote the other in the midst of their shields. Sir Palamedes' spear broke, and Sir Tristram smote down the horse. Then Sir Palamedes leapt from his horse, and drew out his sword. That saw Sir Tristram, and therewith he alighted and tied his horse to a tree. Then they came together as two wild beasts, lashing the one on the other, and so fought more than two hours; and often Sir Tristram smote such strokes at Sir Palamedes that he made him to kneel, and Sir Palamedes broke away Sir Tristram's shield, and wounded him. Then Sir Tristram was wroth out of measure, and he rushed to Sir Palamedes and wounded him passing sore through the shoulder, and by fortune smote Sir Palamedes' sword out of his hand. And if Sir Palamedes had stooped for his sword, Sir Tristram had slain him. Then Sir Palamedes stood and beheld his sword with a full sorrowful heart. "Now," said Sir Tristram, "I have thee at a vantage, as thou hadst me today; but it shall never be said, in court, or among good knights, that Sir Tristram did slay any knight that was weaponless: therefore take thou thy sword, and let us fight this battle to the end." Then spoke Sir Palamedes to Sir Tristram: "I have no wish to fight this battle any more. The offence that I have done unto you is not so great but that, if it please you, we may be friends. All that I have offended is for the love of the queen, La Belle Isoude, and I dare maintain that she is peerless among ladies; and for that offence ye have given me many grievous and sad strokes, and some I have given you again. Wherefore I require you, my lord Sir Tristram, forgive me all that I have offended you, and this day have me unto the next church; and first I will be clean confessed, and after that see you that I be truly baptized, and then we will ride together unto the court of my lord, King Arthur, so that we may be there at the feast of Pentecost." "Now take your horse," said Sir Tristram, "and as you have said, so shall it be done." So they took their horses, and Sir Galleron rode with them. When they came to the church of Carlisle, the bishop commanded to fill a great vessel with water; and when he had hallowed it, he then confessed Sir Palamedes clean, and christened him; and Sir Tristram and Sir Galleron were his godfathers. Then soon after they departed, and rode toward Camelot, where the noble King Arthur and Queen Guenever were keeping a court royal. And the king and all the court were glad that Sir Palamedes was christened. Then Sir Tristram returned again to La Joyeuse Garde, and Sir Palamedes went his way.

Not long after these events Sir Gawain returned from Brittany, and related to King Arthur the adventure which befell him in the forest of Brécéliande,—how Merlin had there spoken to him, and enjoined him to charge the king to go without delay upon the quest of the Holy Greal. While King Arthur deliberated, Tristram determined to enter upon the quest, and the more readily, as it was well known to him that this holy adventure would, if achieved, procure him the pardon of all his sins. He immediately departed for the kingdom of Brittany, hoping there to obtain from Merlin counsel as to the proper course to pursue to insure success.

On arriving in Brittany Tristram found King Hoel engaged in a war with a rebellious vassal, and hard pressed by his enemy. His best knights had fallen in a late battle, and he knew not where to turn for assistance. Tristram volunteered his aid. It was accepted; and the army of Hoel, led by Tristram, and inspired by his example, gained a complete victory. The king, penetrated by the most lively sentiments of gratitude, and having informed himself of Tristram's birth, offered him his daughter in marriage. The princess was beautiful and accomplished, and bore the same name with the Queen of Cornwall; but this one is designated by the Romancers as Isoude of the White Hands, to distinguish her from Isoude the Fair.

How can we describe the conflict that agitated the heart of Tristram? He adored the first Isoude, but his love for her was hopeless, and not unaccompanied by remorse. Moreover, the sacred quest on which he had now entered demanded of him perfect purity of life. It seemed as if a happy destiny had provided for him, in the charming princess Isoude of the White Hands, the best security for all his good resolutions. This last reflection determined him. They were married, and passed some months in tranquil happiness at the court of King Hoel. The pleasure which Tristram felt in his wife's society increased day by day. An inward grace seemed to stir within him from the moment when he took the oath to go on the quest of the Holy Greal; it seemed even to triumph over the power of the magic love-potion.

The war, which had been quelled for a time, now burst out anew. Tristram, as usual, was foremost in every danger. The enemy was worsted in successive conflicts, and at last shut himself up in his principal city. Tristram led on the attack of the city. As he mounted a ladder to scale the walls, he was struck on the head by a fragment of rock, which the besieged threw down upon him. It bore him to the ground, where he lay insensible.

As soon as he recovered consciousness, he demanded to be carried to his wife. The princess, skilled in the art of surgery, would not suffer any one but herself to touch her beloved husband. Her fair hands bound up his wounds; Tristram kissed them with gratitude, which began to grow into love. At first the devoted cares of Isoude seemed to meet with great success; but after awhile these flattering appearances vanished, and, in spite of all her care, the malady grew more serious day by day.

In this perplexity, an old squire of Tristram's reminded his master that the princess of Ireland, afterward queen of Cornwall, had once cured him under circumstances quite as discouraging. He called Isoude of the White Hands to him, told her of his former cure, added that he believed that the Queen Isoude could heal him, and that he felt sure that she would come to his relief if sent for.

Isoude of the White Hands consented that Gesnes, a trusty man and skilful navigator, should be sent to Cornwall. Tristram called him, and, giving him a ring, "Take this," he said, "to the Queen of Cornwall. Tell her that Tristram, near to death, demands her aid. If you succeed in bringing her with you, place white sails to your vessel on your return, that we may know of your success when the vessel first heaves in sight. But if Queen Isoude refuses, put on black sails; they will be the presage of my impending death."

Gesnes performed his mission successfully. King Mark happened to be absent from his capital, and the queen readily consented to return with the bark to Brittany. Gesnes clothed his vessel in the whitest of sails, and sped his way back to Brittany.

Meantime the wound of Tristram grew more desperate day by day. His strength, quite prostrated, no longer permitted him to be carried to the seaside daily, as had been his custom from the first moment when it was possible for the bark to be on the way homeward. He called a young damsel, and gave her in charge to keep watch in the direction of Cornwall, and to come and tell him the color of the sails of the first vessel she should see approaching.

When Isoude of the White Hands consented that the queen of Cornwall should be sent for, she had not known all the reasons which she had for fearing the influence which renewed intercourse with that princess might have on her own happiness. She had now learned more, and felt the danger more keenly. She thought, if she could only keep the knowledge of the queen's arrival from her husband, she might

employ in his service any resources which her skill could supply, and still avert the dangers which she apprehended. When the vessel was seen approaching, with its white sails sparkling in the sun, the damsel, by command of her mistress, carried word to Tristram that the sails were black.

Tristram, penetrated with inexpressible grief, breathed a profound sigh, turned away his face, and said, "Alas, my beloved! we shall never see one another again!" Then he commended himself to God, and breathed his last.

The death of Tristram was the first intelligence which the queen of Cornwall heard on landing. She was conducted almost senseless into the chamber of Tristram, and expired holding him in her arms.

Tristram, before his death, had requested that his body should be sent to Cornwall, and that his sword, with a letter he had written, should be delivered to King Mark. The remains of Tristram and Isoude were embarked in a vessel, along with the sword, which was presented to the king of Cornwall. He was melted with tenderness when he saw the weapon which slew Moraunt of Ireland,—which had so often saved his life, and redeemed the honor of his kingdom. In the letter Tristram begged pardon of his uncle, and related the story of the amorous draught.

Mark ordered the lovers to be buried in his own chapel. From the tomb of Tristram there sprung a vine, which went along the walls, and descended into the grave of the queen. It was cut down three times, but each time sprung up again more vigorous than before, and this wonderful plant has ever since shaded the tombs of Tristram and Isoude. 80 ▷

Spenser introduces Sir Tristram in his Faery Queene. In Book VI., Canto ii., Sir Calidore encounters in the forest a young hunter, whom he thus describes:

> "Him steadfastly he marked, and saw to be
> A goodly youth of amiable grace,
> Yet but a slender slip, that scarce did see
> Yet seventeen yeares; but tall and faire of face,
> That sure he deemed him borne of noble race.
> All in a woodman's jacket he was clad
> Of Lincoln greene, belayed with silver lace;

And on his head an hood with aglets[1] sprad,
And by his side his hunter's horne he hanging had.

"Buskins he wore of costliest cordawayne,
Pinckt upon gold, and paled part per part,[2]
As then the guize was for each gentle swayne,
In his right hand he held a trembling dart,
Whose fellow he before had sent apart;
And in his left he held a sharp bore-speare,
With which he wont to launch the salvage heart
Of many a lyon, and of many a beare,
That first unto his hand in chase did happen neare."

Tristram is often alluded to by the Romancers as the great authority and model in all matters relating to the chase. In the Faery Queene, Tristram, in answer to the inquiries of Sir Calidore, informs him of his name and parentage, and concludes:

"All which my days I have not lewdly spent,
Nor spilt the blossom of my tender years
In idlesse; but, as was convenient,
Have trained been with many noble feres
In gentle thewes, and such like seemly leers;[3]
'Mongst which my most delight hath always been
To hunt the salvage chace, amongst my peers,
Of all that rangeth in the forest green
Of which none is to me unknown that yet was seen.

"Ne is there hawk which mantleth on her perch,
Whether high towering or accosting low,
But I the measure of her flight do search,
And all her prey, and all her diet know.
Such be our joys, which in these forests grow.
. . . .

---

[1]*Aglets*, points or tags.

[2]*Pinckt upon gold*, etc., adorned with golden points, or eyelets, and regularly intersected with stripes. *Paled* (in heraldry), striped.

[3]*Feres*, companions; *thewes*, labors; *leers*, learning.

CHAPTER XIV

THE STORY OF PERCEVAL

"—Sir Percivale,
Whom Arthur and his knighthood called the Pure."

Tennyson

THE father and two elder brothers of Perceval had fallen in battle or tournaments, and hence, as the last hope of his family, his mother retired with him into a solitary region, where he was brought up in total ignorance of arms and chivalry. He was allowed no weapon but "a lyttel Scots spere," which was the only thing of all "her lordes faire gere" that his mother carried to the wood with her. In the use of this he became so skilful that he could kill with it not only the animals of the chase for her table, but even birds on the wing. At length, however, Perceval was roused to a desire of military renown by seeing in the forest five knights who were in complete armor. He said to his mother, "Mother, what are those yonder?" "They are angels, my son," said she. "By my faith, I will go and become an angel with them." And Perceval went to the road and met them. "Tell me, good lad," said one of them, "sawest thou a knight pass this way either today or yesterday?" "I know not," said he, "what a knight is." "Such an one as I am," said the knight. "If thou wilt tell me what I ask thee, I will tell thee what thou askest me." "Gladly will I do so, said Sir Owain, for that was the knight's name. "What is this?" demanded Perceval, touching the saddle. "It is a saddle," said Owain. Then he asked about all the accoutrements which he saw upon the men and the horses, and about the arms, and what they were for, and how they were used. And Sir Owain showed him all those things fully. And Perceval in return gave him such information as he had.

Then Perceval returned to his mother, and said to her, "Mother, those were not angels, but honorable knights." Then his mother swooned away. And Perceval went to the place where they kept the horses that carried firewood and provisions for the castle, and he took a bony, piebald horse, which seemed to him the strongest of them. And he pressed a pack into the form of a saddle, and with twisted twigs he imitated the trappings which he had seen upon the horses. When he came again to his mother the countess had recovered from her swoon. "My son," said she, "desirest thou to ride forth?" "Yes, with thy leave," said he. "Go forward then," she said, "to the court of Arthur, where there are the best and the noblest and the most bountiful of men, and tell him thou art Perceval, the son of Pelenore, and ask of him to bestow knighthood on thee. And whenever thou seest a church, repeat there thy paternoster; and if thou see meat and drink, and hast need of them, thou mayest take them. If thou hear an outcry of one in distress, proceed toward it, especially if it be the cry of a woman, and render her what service thou canst. If thou see a fair jewel, win it, for thus shalt thou acquire fame; yet freely give it to another, for thus thou shalt obtain praise. If thou see a fair woman, pay court to her, for thus thou wilt obtain love."

After this discourse Perceval mounted the horse, and, taking a number of sharp-pointed sticks in his hand, he rode forth. And he rode far in the woody wilderness without food or drink. At last he came to an opening in the wood, where he saw a tent, and as he thought it might be a church he said his paternoster to it. And he went toward it; and the door of the tent was open. And Perceval dismounted and entered the tent. In the tent he found a maiden sitting, with a golden frontlet on her forehead and a gold ring on her hand. And Perceval said, "Maiden, I salute you, for my mother told me whenever I met a lady I must respectfully salute her." Perceiving in one corner of the tent some food, two flasks full of wine, and some boar's flesh roasted, he said, "My mother told me, whenever I saw meat and drink to take it." And he ate greedily, for he was very hungry. "Sir, thou hadst best go quickly from here, for fear that my friends should come, and evil should befall you." But Perceval said, "My mother told me wheresoever I saw a fair jewel to take it," and he took the gold ring from her finger, and put it on his own; and he gave the maiden his own ring in exchange for hers; then he mounted his horse and rode away.

Perceval journeyed on till he arrived at Arthur's court. And it so happened that just at that time an uncourteous knight had offered Queen Guenever a gross insult. For when her page was serving the queen with a golden goblet, this knight struck the arm of the page and dashed the wine in the queen's face and over her stomacher. Then he said, "If any have boldness to avenge this insult to Guenever, let him follow me to the meadow." So the knight took his horse and rode to the meadow, carrying away the golden goblet. And all the household hung down their heads, and no one offered to follow the knight to take vengeance upon him. For it seemed to them that no one would have ventured on so daring an outrage unless he possessed such powers, through magic or charms, that none could be able to punish him. Just then, behold, Perceval entered the hall upon the bony, piebald horse, with his uncouth trappings. In the centre of the hall stood Kay the seneschal. "Tell me, tall man," said Perceval, "is that Arthur yonder?" "What wouldst thou with Arthur?" asked Kay. "My mother told me to go to Arthur and receive knighthood from him." "By my faith," said he, "thou art all too meanly equipped with horse and with arms." Then all the household began to jeer and laugh at him. But there was a certain damsel who had been a whole year at Arthur's court, and had never been known to smile. And the king's fool[1] had said that this damsel would not smile till she had seen him who would be the flower of chivalry. Now this damsel came up to Perceval and told him, smiling, that, if he lived, he would be one of the bravest and best of knights. "Truly," said Kay, "thou art ill taught to remain a year at Arthur's court, with choice of society, and smile on no one, and now before the face of Arthur and all his knights to call such a man as this

---

[1] A fool was a common appendage of the courts of those days when this romance was written. A fool was the ornament held in next estimation to a dwarf. He wore a white dress with a yellow bonnet, and carried a bell or bauble in his hand. Though called a fool, his words were often weighed and remembered as if there were a sort of oracular meaning in them.

the flower of knighthood;" and he gave her a box on the ear, that she fell senseless to the ground. Then said Kay to Perceval, "Go after the knight who went hence to the meadow, overthrow him and recover the golden goblet, and possess thyself of his horse and arms, and thou shalt have knighthood." "I will do so, tall man," said Perceval. So he turned his horse's head toward the meadow. And when he came there, the knight was riding up and down, proud of his strength and valor and noble mien. "Tell me," said the knight, "didst thou see any one coming after me from the court?" "The tall man that was there," said Perceval, "told me to come and overthrow thee, and to take from thee the goblet and thy horse and armor for myself." "Silence!" said the knight; "go back to the court, and tell Arthur either to come himself, or to send some other to fight with me; and unless he do so quickly, I will not wait for him." "By my faith," said Perceval, "choose thou whether it shall be willingly or unwillingly, for I will have the horse and the arms and the goblet." Upon this the knight ran at him furiously, and struck him a violent blow with the shaft of his spear, between the neck and the shoulder. "Ha, ha, lad!" said Perceval, "my mother's servants were not used to play with me in this wise; so thus will I play with thee." And he threw at him one of his sharp-pointed sticks, and it struck him in the eye, and came out at the back of his head, so that he fell down lifeless.

But at the court of Arthur, Sir Owain said to Kay, "Verily, thou wert ill advised when thou didst send that madman after the knight. For one of two things must befall him. He must either be overthrown or slain. If he is overthrown by the knight, he will be counted by him to be an honorable person of the court, and an eternal disgrace will it be to Arthur and his warriors. And if he is slain, the disgrace will be the same, and moreover his sin will be upon him; therefore will I go to see what has befallen him." So Sir Owain went to the meadow, and he found Perceval dragging the man about. "What art thou doing thus?" said Sir Owain. "This iron coat," said Perceval, "will never come from off him; not by my efforts, at any rate." And Sir Owain unfastened his armor and his clothes. "Here, my good soul," said he, "is a horse and armor better than thine. Take them joyfully, and come with me to Arthur to receive the order of knighthood, for thou dost merit it. And Owain helped Perceval to put it on, and taught him how to put his foot in the stirrup, and use the spur; for Perceval had never used stirrup nor spur, but rode without saddle, and urged on his horse with a stick. Then Owain would have had him return to the court to receive the praise that was his due; but Perceval said, "I will not come to the court till I have encountered the tall man that is there, to revenge the injury he did to the maiden. But take thou the goblet to Queen Guenever, and tell King Arthur that, wherever I am, I will be his vassal, and will do him what profit and service I can." And Sir Owain went back to the court, and related all these things to Arthur and Guenever, and to all the household.

And Perceval rode forward. And as he proceeded, behold a knight met him. "Whence comest thou?" said the knight. "I come from Arthur's court," said Perceval. "Art thou one of his men?" asked he. "Yes, by my faith," he answered. "A good service, truly, is that of Arthur." "Wherefore sayest thou so?" said Perceval. "I will tell thee," said he. "I have always been Arthur's enemy, and all such of his men as I have ever encountered I have slain." And without further parlance they fought, and it was not long before Perceval brought him to the ground, over his horse's crupper. Then the knight besought his mercy. "Mercy thou shalt have," said Perceval, "if thou wilt make oath to me that thou wilt go to Arthur's court and tell him that it was I that overthrew thee, for the honor of his service; and say that I will never come to the court until I have avenged the insult offered to the maiden." The knight pledged him his faith of this, and proceeded to the court of Arthur and said as he had promised, and conveyed the threat to Sir Kay.

And Perceval rode forward. And within that week he encountered sixteen knights, and overthrew them all shamefully. And they all went to Arthur's court, taking with them the same message which the first knight had conveyed from Perceval, and the same threat which he had sent to Sir Kay. And thereupon Sir Kay was reproved by Arthur; and Sir Kay was greatly grieved thereat.

And Perceval rode forward. And he came to a lake, on the side of which was a fair castle, and on the border of the lake he saw a hoary-headed man sitting upon a velvet cushion, and his attendants were fishing in the lake. When the hoary-headed man beheld Perceval approaching, he arose and went into the castle. Perceval rode to the castle, and the door was open, and he entered the hall. And the hoary-headed man received Perceval courteously, and asked him to sit by him on the cushion. When it was time, the tables were set, and they went to meat. And when they had finished their meat, the hoary-headed man asked Perceval if he knew how to fight with the sword. "I know not," said Perceval, "but were I to be taught, doubtless I should." "Whoever can play well with the cudgel and shield will also be able to fight with a sword." And the man had two sons; the one had yellow hair and the other auburn. "Arise, youths," said the old man, "and play with the cudgel and the shield." And so did they. "Tell me, my son," said the man, "which of the youths thinkest thou plays best?" "I think," said Perceval, "that the yellow-haired youth could draw blood if he chose." "Arise thou, then, and take the cudgel and the shield from the hand of the youth with the auburn hair, and draw blood from the yellow-haired youth if thou canst." So Perceval arose, and he lifted up his arm, and struck him such a mighty blow that he cut his forehead open from one side to the other. "Ah, my life," said the old man, "come, now, and sit down, for thou wilt become the best fighter with the sword of any in this island; and I am thy uncle, thy mother's brother; I am called King Pecheur.[1] Thou shalt remain with me a space, in order to learn the manners and customs of different countries, and courtesy and noble bearing. And this do thou remember: if thou seest aught to cause thy wonder, ask not the meaning of it; if no one has the courtesy to inform thee, the reproach will not fall upon thee, but upon me that am thy teacher." While Perceval and his uncle discoursed together, Perceval beheld two youths enter the hall, bearing a golden cup and a spear of mighty size, with blood dropping from its point to the ground. And when all the company saw this, they began to weep and lament. But for all that, the man did not break off his discourse with Perceval. And as he did not tell him the meaning of what he saw, he

---

[1] The word means both *fisher* and *sinner*.

forbore to ask him concerning it. Now the cup that Perceval saw was the Sangreal, and the spear the sacred spear; and afterwards King Pecheur removed with those sacred relics into a far country.

.   .   .   .

One evening Perceval entered a valley, and came to a hermit's cell; and the hermit welcomed him gladly, and there he spent the night. And in the morning he arose, and when he went forth, behold! a shower of snow had fallen in the night, and a hawk had killed a wild-fowl in front of the cell. And the noise of the horse had scared the hawk away, and a raven alighted on the bird. And Perceval stood and compared the blackness of the raven and the whiteness of the snow and the redness of the blood to the hair of the lady that best he loved, which was blacker than jet, and to her skin, which was whiter than the snow, and to the two red spots upon her cheeks, which were redder than the blood upon the snow.

Now Arthur and his household were in search of Perceval, and by chance they came that way. "Know ye," said Arthur, "who is the knight with the long spear that stands by the brook up yonder?" "Lord," said one of them, "I will go and learn who he is." So the youth came to the place where Perceval was, and asked him what he did thus, and who he was. But Perceval was so intent upon his thought that he gave him no answer. Then the youth thrust at Perceval with his lance; and Perceval turned upon him and struck him to the ground. And when the youth returned to the king, and told how rudely he had been treated, Sir Kay said, "I will go myself." And when he greeted Perceval, and got no answer, he spoke to him rudely and angrily. And Perceval thrust at him with his lance, and cast him down so that he broke his arm and his shoulder-blade. And while he lay thus stunned, his horse returned back at a wild and prancing pace.

Then said Sir Gawain, surnamed the Golden-Tongued, because he was the most courteous knight in Arthur's court: "It is not fitting that any should disturb an honorable knight from his thought unadvisedly; for either he is pondering some damage that he has sustained, or he is thinking of the lady he best loves. If it seem well to thee, lord, I will go and see if this knight has changed from his thought, and if he has, I will ask him courteously to come and visit thee."

And Perceval was resting on the shaft of his spear, pondering the same thought, and Sir Gawain came to him, and said, "If I thought it would be as agreeable to thee as it would be to me, I would converse with thee. I have also a message from Arthur unto thee, to pray thee to come and visit him. And two men have been before on this errand." "That is true," said Perceval, "and uncourteously they came. They attacked me, and I was annoyed thereat." Then he told him the thought that occupied his mind, and Gawain said, "This was not an ungentle thought, and I should marvel if it were pleasant for thee to be drawn from it." Then said Perceval, "Tell me, is Sir Kay in Arthur's court?" "He is," said Gawain; "and truly he is the knight who fought with thee last." "Verily," said Perceval, "I am not sorry to have thus avenged the insult to the smiling maiden." Then Perceval told him his name, and said, "Who art thou?" And he replied, "I am Gawain." "I am right glad to meet thee," said Perceval, "for I have everywhere heard of thy prowess and uprightness; and I solicit thy fellowship." "Thou shalt have it, by my faith; and grant me thine," said he. "Gladly will I do so," answered Perceval.

So they went together to Arthur, and saluted him. "Behold, lord," said Gawain, "him whom thou hast sought so long." "Welcome unto thee, chieftain," said Arthur. And hereupon there came the queen and her handmaidens, and Perceval saluted them. And they were rejoiced to see him, and bade him welcome. And Arthur did him great honor and respect, and they returned toward Caerleon.

Chapter XV

The Quest of the Sangreal

"—The cup itself from which our Lord
Drank at the last sad supper with His own.
This from the blessed land of Aromat,
After the day of darkness, when the dead
Went wandering over Moriah—the good saint,
Arimathean Joseph, journeying, brought
To Glastonbury, where the winter thorn
Blossoms at Christmas, mindful of our Lord,
And there awhile abode; and if a man
Could touch or see it, he was healed at once,
By faith, of all his ills. But then the times
Grew to such evil that the holy cup
Was caught away to Heaven, and disappeared."

Tennyson

THE Sangreal was the cup from which our Saviour drank at his last supper. He was supposed to have given it to Joseph of Arimathea, who carried it to Europe, together with the spear with which the soldier pierced the Saviour's side. From generation to generation one of the descendants of Joseph of Arimathea had been devoted to the guardianship of these precious relics; but on the sole condition of leading a life of purity in thought, word, and deed. For a long time the Sangreal was visible to all pilgrims, and its presence conferred blessings upon the land in which it was preserved. But at length one of those holy men to whom its guardianship had descended so far forgot the obligation of his sacred office as to look with unhallowed eye upon a young female pilgrim whose robe was accidentally loosened as she knelt before him. The sacred lance instantly punished his frailty, spontaneously falling upon him, and inflicting a deep wound. The marvellous wound could by no means

be healed, and the guardian of the Sangreal was ever after called "Le Roi Pecheur,"—the Sinner King. The Sangreal withdrew its visible presence from the crowds who came to worship, and an iron age succeeded to the happiness which its presence had diffused among the tribes of Britain.

We have told in the history of Merlin how that great prophet and enchanter sent a message to King Arthur by Sir Gawain, directing him to undertake the recovery of the Sangreal, informing him at the same time that the knight who should accomplish that sacred quest was already born, and of a suitable age to enter upon it. Sir Gawain delivered his message, and the king was anxiously revolving in his mind how best to achieve the enterprise, when, at the vigil of Pentecost, all the fellowship of the Round Table being met together at Camelot, as they sat at meat, suddenly there was heard a clap of thunder, and then a bright light burst forth, and every knight, as he looked on his fellow, saw him, in seeming, fairer than ever before. All the hall was filled with sweet odors, and every knight had such meat and drink as he best loved. Then there entered into the hall the Holy Greal, covered with white samite, so that none could see it, and it passed through the hall suddenly and disappeared. During this time no one spoke a word, but when they had recovered breath to speak, King Arthur said, "Certainly we ought greatly to thank the Lord for what He hath showed us this day." Then Sir Gawain rose up, and made a vow that for twelve months and a day he would seek the Sangreal, and not return till he had seen it, if so he might speed. When they of the Round Table heard Sir Gawain say so, they arose, the most part of them, and vowed the same. When King Arthur heard this he was greatly displeased, for he knew well that they might not gainsay their vows. "Alas!" said he to Sir Gawain, "you have nigh slain me with the vow and promise that ye have made, for ye have bereft me of the fairest fellowship that ever was seen together in any realm of the world; for when they shall depart hence, I am sure that all shall never meet more in this world."

SIR GALAHAD

A T that time there entered the hall a good old man, and with him he brought a young knight, and these words he said: "Peace be with you, fair lords." Then the old man said unto King Arthur, "Sir, I bring you here a young knight that is of kings' lineage, and of the kindred of Joseph of Arimathea, being the son of Dame Elaine, the daughter of King Pelles, king of the foreign country." Now the name of the young knight was Sir Galahad, and he was the son of Sir Launcelot du Lac; but he had dwelt with his mother, at the court of King Pelles, his grandfather, till now he was old enough to bear arms, and his mother had sent him in the charge of a holy hermit to King Arthur's court. Then Sir Launcelot beheld his son, and had great joy of him. And Sir Bohort told his fellows, "Upon my life, this young knight shall come to great worship." The noise was great in all the court, so that it came to the queen. And she said, "I would fain see him, for he must needs be a noble knight, for so is his father." And the queen and her

ladies all said that he resembled much unto his father; and he was seemly and demure as a dove, with all manner of good features, that in the whole world men might not find his match. And King Arthur said, "God make him a good man, for beauty faileth him not, as any that liveth."

Then the hermit led the young knight to the Siege Perilous; and he lifted up the cloth, and found there letters that said, "This is the seat of Sir Galahad, the good knight;" and he made him sit in that seat. And all the knights of the Round Table marvelled greatly at Sir Galahad, seeing him sit securely in that seat, and said, "This is he by whom the Sangreal shall be achieved, for there never sat one before in that seat without being mischieved."

On the next day the king said, "Now, at this quest of the Sangreal shall all ye of the Round Table depart, and never shall I see you again all together; therefore I will that ye all repair to the meadow of Camelot, for to joust and tourney yet once more before ye depart." But all the meaning of the king was to see Sir Galahad proved. So then were they all assembled in the meadow. Then Sir Galahad, by request of the king and queen, put on his harness and his helm, but shield would he take none for any prayer of the king. And the queen was in a tower, with all her ladies, to behold that tournament. Then Sir Galahad rode into the midst of the meadow; and there he began to break spears marvellously, so that all men had wonder of him, for he surmounted all knights that encountered with him, except two, Sir Launcelot and Sir Perceval. Then the king, at the queen's request, made him to alight, and presented him to the queen; and she said, "Never two men resembled one another more than he and Sir Launcelot, and therefore it is no marvel that he is like him in prowess."

Then the king and the queen went to the minister, and the knights followed them. And after the service was done, they put on their helms and departed, and there was great sorrow. They rode through the streets of Camelot, and there was weeping of the rich and poor; and the king turned away, and might not speak for weeping. And so they departed, and every knight took the way that him best liked.

Sir Galahad rode forth without shield, and rode four days, and found no adventure. And on the fourth

day he came to a white abbey; and there he was received with great reverence, and led to a chamber. He met there two knights, King Bagdemagus and Sir Uwaine, and they made of him great solace. "Sirs," said Sir Galahad, "what adventure brought you hither?" "Sir," said they, "it is told us that within this place is a shield which no man may bear unless he be worthy; and if one unworthy should attempt to bear it, it shall surely do him a mischief." Then King Bagdemagus said, "I fear not to bear it, and that shall ye see tomorrow."

So on the morrow they arose, and heard mass; then King Bagdemagus asked where the adventurous shield was. Anon a monk led him behind an altar, where the shield hung, as white as snow; but in the midst there was a red cross. Then King Bagdemagus took the shield, and bare it out of the minster; and he said to Sir Galahad, "If it please you, abide here till ye know how I shall speed."

Then King Bagdemagus and his squire rode forth; and when they had ridden a mile or two, they saw a goodly knight come towards them, in white armor, horse and all; and he came as fast as his horse might run, with his spear in the rest; and King Bagdemagus directed his spear against him, and broke it upon the white knight, but the other struck him so hard that he broke the mails, and thrust him through the right shoulder, for the shield covered him not, and so he bare him from his horse. Then the white knight turned his horse and rode away.

Then the squire went to King Bagdemagus, and asked him whether he were sore wounded or not. "I am sore wounded," said he, "and full hardly shall I escape death." Then the squire set him on his horse, and brought him to an abbey; and there he was taken down softly, and unarmed, and laid in a bed, and his wound was looked to, for he lay there long, and hardly escaped with his life. And the squire brought the shield back to the abbey.

The next day Sir Galahad took the shield, and within a while he came to the hermitage, where he met the white knight, and each saluted the other courteously. "Sir," said Sir Galahad, "can you tell me the marvel of the shield?" "Sir," said the white knight, "that shield belonged of old to the gentle knight, Joseph of Arimathea; and when he came to die, he said, 'Never shall man bear this shield about

his neck but he shall repent it, unto the time that Sir Galahad, the good knight, bear it, the last of my lineage, the which shall do many marvellous deeds.' " And then the white knight vanished away.

SIR GAWAIN

AFTER Sir Gawain departed, he rode many days, both toward and forward, and at last he came to the abbey where Sir Galahad took the white shield. And they told Sir Gawain of the marvellous adventure that Sir Galahad had done. "Truly," said Sir Gawain, "I am not happy that I took not the way that he went, for, if I may meet with him, I will not part from him lightly, that I may partake with him all the marvellous adventures which he shall achieve." "Sir," said one of the monks, "he will not be of your fellowship." "Why?" said Sir Gawain. "Sir," said he, "because ye be sinful, and he is blissful." Then said the monk, "Sir Gawain, thou must do penance for thy sins." "Sir, what penance shall I do?" "Such as I will show," said the good man. "Nay," said Sir Gawain, "I will do no penance, for we knights adventurous often suffer great woe and pain." "Well," said the good man; and he held his peace. And Sir Gawain departed.

Now it happened, not long after this, that Sir Gawain and Sir Hector rode together, and they came to a castle where was a great tournament. And Sir Gawain and Sir Hector joined themselves to the party that seemed the weaker, and they drove before them the other party. Then suddenly came into the lists a knight, bearing a white shield with a red cross, and by adventure he came by Sir Gawain, and he smote him so hard that he cave his helm and wounded his head, so that Sir Gawain fell to the earth. When Sir Hector saw that, he knew that the knight with the white shield was Sir Galahad, and he thought it no wisdom to abide with him, and also for natural love, that he was his uncle. Then Sir Galahad retired privily, so that none knew where he had gone. And Sir Hector raised up Sir Gawain, and said, "Sir, me seemeth your quest is done." "It is done," said Sir Gawain; "I shall seek no further." Then Gawain was borne into the castle, and unarmed, and laid in a rich bed, and a leech found to search his wound. And Sir Gawain and Sir Hector abode together, for Sir Hector would not away until Sir Gawain were whole.

Now Sir Galahad, after that the white knight had vanished away, rode till he came to a waste forest, and there he met with Sir Launcelot and Sir Perceval, but they knew him not, for he was new disguised. Right so, Sir Launcelot his father dressed his spear, and brake it upon Sir Galahad, and Sir Galahad smote him so again, that he smote down horse and man. And then he drew his sword, and dressed him to Sir Perceval, and smote him so on the helm that it rove to the coif of steel, and had not the sword swerved Sir Perceval had been slain, and with the stroke he fell out of his saddle. This joust was done before the hermitage where a recluse dwelled. And when she saw Sir Galahad ride, she said, "God be with thee, best knight of the world. Ah, certes," she said all aloud, that Launcelot and Perceval might hear it, "and yonder two knights had known thee as well as I do, they would not have encountered with thee." When Sir Galahad heard her say so he was sore adread to be known: therewith he smote his horse with his spurs, and rode at a great pace away from

them. Then perceived they both that he was Sir Galahad, and up they got on their horses, and rode fast after him, but in a while he was out of their sight. And then they turned again with heavy cheer. "Let us spere some tidings," said Sir Perceval, "at yonder recluse." "Do as ye list," said Sir Launcelot. When Sir Perceval came to the recluse, she knew him well enough, and Sir Launcelot both.

But Sir Launcelot rode overthwart and endlong in a wild forest, and held no path, but as wild adventure led him. And at the last he came to a stony cross, which departed two ways in waste land, and by the cross was a stone that was of marble, but it was so dark that Sir Launcelot might not wit what it was. Then Sir Launcelot looked by him, and saw an old chapel, and there he thought to have found people. And Sir Launcelot tied his horse to a tree, and there he did off his shield, and hung it upon a tree. And then he went to the chapel door, and found it waste and broken. And within he found a fair altar full richly arrayed with cloth of clean silk, and there stood a fair, clean candlestick which bare six great candles, and the candlestick was of silver. And when Sir Launcelot saw this light, he had great will for to enter into the chapel, but he could find no place where he might enter: then was he passing heavy and dismayed. And he returned and came again to his horse, and took off his saddle and his bridle, and let him pasture; and unlaced his helm, and ungirded his sword, and laid him down to sleep upon his shield before the cross. 90 ▷

And as he lay, half waking and half sleeping, he saw come by him two palfreys, both fair and white, which bare a litter, on which lay a sick knight. And when he was nigh the cross, he there abode still. And Sir Launcelot heard him say, "O sweet Lord, when shall the sorrow leave me, and when shall the holy vessel come by me whereby I shall be healed?" And thus a great while complained the knight, and Sir Launcelot heard it. Then Sir Launcelot saw the candlestick, with the lighted tapers, come before the cross, but he could see nobody that brought it. Also there came a salver of silver and the holy vessel of the Sangreal; and therewith the sick knight sat him upright, and held up both his hands, and said, "Fair, sweet Lord, which is here within the holy vessel, take

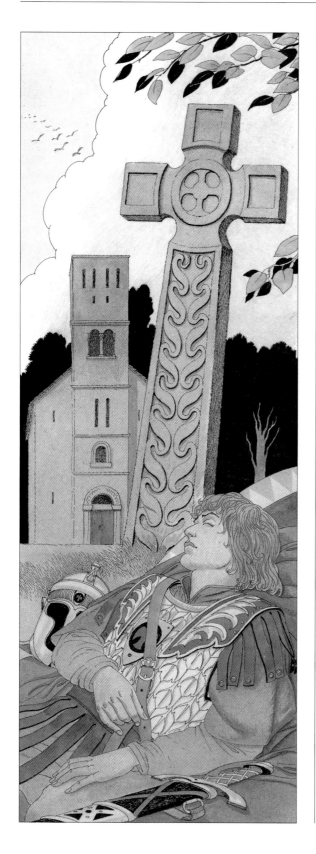

heed to me, that I may be whole of this great malady." And therewith, upon his hands and upon his knees, he went so nigh that he touched the holy vessel and kissed it. And anon he was whole. Then the holy vessel went into the chapel again, with the candle-stick and the light, so that Sir Launcelot wist not what became of it.

Then the sick knight rose up and kissed the cross; and anon his squire brought him his arms, and asked his lord how he did. "I thank God right heartily," said he, "for, through the holy vessel, I am healed. But I have great marvel of this sleeping knight, who hath had neither grace nor power to awake during the time that the holy vessel hath been here present." "I dare it right well say," said the squire, "that this same knight is stained with some manner of deadly sin, whereof he was never confessed." So they departed.

Then anon Sir Launcelot waked, and set himself upright, and bethought him of what he had seen, and whether it were dreams or not. And he was passing heavy, and wist not what to do. And he said: "My sin and my wretchedness hath brought me into great dishonor. For when I sought worldly adventures and worldly desires, I ever achieved them, and had the better in every place, and never was I discomfited in any quarrel, were it right or wrong. And now I take upon me the adventure of holy things, I see and understand that mine old sin hindereth me, so that I had no power to stir nor to speak when the holy blood appeared before me." So thus he sorrowed till it was day, and heard the fowls of the air sing. Then was he somewhat comforted.

Then he departed from the cross into the forest. And there he found a hermitage, and a hermit there-in, who was going to mass. So when mass was done, Sir Launcelot called the hermit to him, and prayed him for charity to hear his confession. "With a good will," said the good man. And then he told that good man all his life, and how he had loved a queen unmeasurably many years. "And all my great deeds of arms that I have done, I did the most part for the queen's sake, and for her sake would I do battle, were it right or wrong, and never did I battle all only for God's sake, but for to win worship, and to cause me to be better beloved; and little or naught I thanked God for it. I pray you counsel me."

"I will counsel you," said the hermit, "if ye will insure me that ye will never come in that queen's fellowship as much as ye may forbear." And then Sir Launcelot promised the hermit, by his faith, that he would no more come in her company. "Look that your heart and your mouth accord," said the good man, "and I shall insure ye that ye shall have more worship than ever ye had."

Then the good man enjoined Sir Launcelot such penance as he might do, and he assoiled Sir Launcelot, and made him abide with him all that day. And Sir Launcelot repented him greatly.

SIR PERCEVAL

SIR PERCEVAL departed, and rode till the hour of noon; and he met in a valley about twenty men of arms. And when they saw Sir Perceval, they asked him whence he was; and he answered, "Of the court of King Arthur." Then they cried all at once, "Slay him." But Sir Perceval smote the first to the earth, and his horse upon him. Then seven of the knights smote upon his shield all at once, and the remnant slew his horse, so that he fell to the earth. So had they slain him or taken him, had not the good knight Sir Galahad, with the red cross, come there by adventure. And when he saw all the knights upon one, he cried out, "Save me that knight's life." Then he rode toward the twenty men of arms as fast as his horse might drive, with his spear in the rest, and smote the foremost horse and man to the earth. And when his spear was broken, he set his hand to his sword, and smote on the right hand and on the left, that it was marvel to see; and at every stroke he smote down one, or put him to rebuke, so that they would fight no more, but fled to a thick forest, and Sir Galahad followed them. And when Sir Perceval saw him chase them so, he made great sorrow that his horse was slain. And he wist well it was Sir Galahad. Then he cried aloud, "Ah, fair knight, abide, and suffer me to do thanks unto thee; for right well have ye done for me." But Sir Galahad rode so fast, that at last he passed out of his sight. When Sir Perceval saw that he would not turn, he said, "Now am I a very wretch, and most unhappy above all other knights." So in this sorrow he abode all that day till it was night; and then he was faint, and laid him down and slept till midnight; and then he awaked, and saw before him a woman, who said unto him, "Sir Perceval, what dost thou here?" He answered, "I do neither good, nor great ill." "If thou wilt promise me," said she, "that thou wilt fulfil my will when I summon thee, I will lend thee my own horse, which shall bear thee whither thou wilt." Sir Perceval was glad of her proffer, and insured her to fulfil all her desire. "Then abide me here, and I will go fetch you a horse." And so she soon came again, and brought a horse with her that was inky black. When Perceval beheld that horse, he marvelled, it was so great and so well apparelled. And he leapt upon him, and took no heed of himself. And he thrust him with his spurs, and within an hour and less he bare him four days' journey thence, until he came to a rough water, which roared, and his horse would have bare him into it. And when Sir Perceval came nigh the brim, and saw the water so boisterous, he doubted to overpass it. And then he made the sign of the cross on his forehead. When the fiend felt him so charged, he shook off Sir Perceval, and went into the water crying and roaring; and it seemed unto him that the water burned. Then Sir Perceval perceived it was a fiend that would have brought him unto his perdition. Then he commended himself unto God, and prayed our Lord to keep him from all such temptations; and so he prayed all that night till it was day. Then he saw that he was in a wild place, that was closed with the sea nigh all about. And Sir Perceval looked forth over the sea, and saw a ship come sailing toward him; and it came and stood still under the rock. And when Sir Perceval saw this, he hied him thither, and found the ship covered with silk; and therein was a lady of great beauty, and clothed so richly that none might be better.

And when she saw Sir Perceval she saluted him, and Sir Perceval returned her salutation. Then he asked her of her country and her lineage. And she said, "I am a gentlewoman that am disinherited, and was once the richest woman of the world." "Damsel," said Sir Perceval, "who hath disinherited you? for I have great pity of you." "Sir," said she, "my enemy is a great and powerful lord, and aforetime he made much of me, so that of his favor and of my beauty I had a little pride more than I ought to have had. Also I said a word that pleased him not. So he drove me from his company and from mine heritage. Therefore I know no good knight nor good man but I get him on my side if I may. And, for that I know that thou art a good knight, I beseech thee to help me."

Then Sir Perceval promised her all the help that he might, and she thanked him.

And at that time the weather was hot and she called to her a gentlewoman, and bade her bring forth a pavilion. And she did so, and pitched it upon the gravel. "Sir," said she, "now may ye rest you in this heat of the day." Then he thanked her, and she put off his helm and his shield, and there he slept a great while. Then he awoke, and asked her if she had any meat, and she said yea, and so there was set upon the table all manner of meats that he could think on. Also he drank there the strongest wine that ever he drank, and therewith he was a little chafed more than he ought to be. With that he beheld the lady, and he thought she was the fairest creature that ever he saw. And then Sir Perceval proffered her love, and prayed her that she would be his. Then she refused him in a manner, for the cause he should be the more ardent on her, and ever he ceased not to pray her of love. And when she saw him well enchafed, then she said, "Sir Perceval, wit ye well I shall not give ye my love unless you swear from henceforth you will be my true servant, and do no thing but that I shall command you. Will you insure me this, as ye be a true knight?" "Yea," said he, "fair lady, by the faith of my body." And as he said this, by adventure and grace, he saw his sword lie on the ground naked, in whose pommel was a red cross, and the sign of the crucifix thereon. Then he made the sign of the cross upon his forehead, and therewith the pavilion shrivelled up, and changed into a smoke and a black cloud. And the damsel cried aloud, and hasted into the ship, and so she went with the wind roaring and yelling that it seemed all the water burned after her. Then Sir Perceval made great sorrow, and called himself a wretch, saying, "How nigh was I lost." Then he took his arms, and departed thence.

CHAPTER XVI

THE END OF THE QUEST

SIR BOHORT

WHEN Sir Bohort departed from Camelot he met with a religious man, riding upon an ass; and Sir Bohort saluted him. "What are ye?" said the good man. "Sir," said Sir Bohort, "I am a knight that fain would be counselled in the quest of the Sangreal." So rode they both together till they came to a hermitage; and there he prayed Sir Bohort to dwell that night with him. So he alighted, and put away his armor, and prayed him that he might be confessed. And they went both into the chapel, and there he was clean confessed. And they ate bread and drank water together. "Now," said the good man, "I pray thee that thou eat none other till thou sit at the table where the Sangreal shall be." "Sir," said Sir Bohort, "but how know ye that I shall sit there?" "Yea," said the good man, "that I know well; but there shall be few of your fellows with you." Then said Sir Bohort, "I agree me thereto." And the goodman, when he had heard his confession, found him in so pure a life and so stable that he marvelled thereof.

On the morrow, as soon as the day appeared, Sir Bohort departed thence, and rode into a forest unto the hour of midday. And there befell him a marvellous adventure. For he met, at the parting of two ways, two knights that led Sir Lionel, his brother, all naked, bound upon a strong hackney, and his hands bound before his breast; and each of them held in his hand thorns wherewith they went beating him, so that he was all bloody before and behind; but he said never a word, but, as he was great of heart, he suffered all that they did to him as though he had felt none anguish. Sir Bohort prepared to rescue his brother. But he looked on the other side of him, and saw a knight dragging along a fair gentlewoman, who cried out, "Saint Mary! succor your maid!" And when she saw Sir Bohort, she called to him and said, "By the faith that ye owe to knighthood, help me!" When Sir Bohort heard her say thus, he had such sorrow that he wist not what to do. "For if I let my brother be he must be slain, and that would I not for all the earth; and if I help not the maid I am shamed forever." Then lift he up his eyes and said, weeping, "Fair Lord, whose liegeman I am, keep Sir Lionel, my brother, that none of these knights slay him, and for pity of you, and our Lady's sake, I shall succor this maid."

Then he cried out to the knight, "Sir knight, lay your hand off that maid, or else ye be but dead." Then the knight set down the maid, and took his shield, and drew out his sword. And Sir Bohort smote

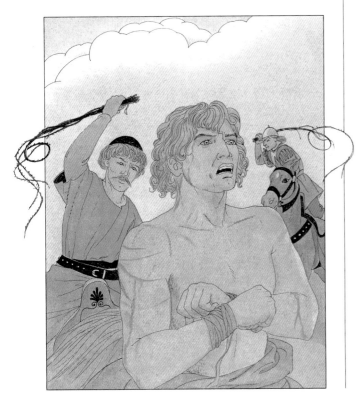

him so hard that it went through his shield and habergeon, on the left shoulder, and he fell down to the earth. Then came Sir Bohort to the maid, "Ye be delivered of this knight this time." "Now," said she, "I pray you lead me there where this knight took me." "I shall gladly do it," said Sir Bohort. So he took the horse of the wounded knight and set the gentlewoman upon it, and brought her there where she desired to be. And there he found twelve knights seeking after her; and when she told them how Sir Bohort had delivered her, they made great joy, and besought him to come to her father, a great lord, and he should be right welcome. "Truly," said Sir Bohort, "that may not be; for I have a great adventure to do." So he commended them to God and departed.

Then Sir Bohort rode after Sir Lionel, his brother, by the trace of their horses. Thus he rode, seeking, a great while. Then he overtook a man clothed in a religious clothing, who said, "Sir knight, what seek ye?" "Sir," said Sir Bohort, "I seek my brother, that I saw within a little space beaten of two knights." "Ah, Sir Bohort, trouble not thyself to seek for him, for truly he is dead." Then he showed him a new-slain body, lying in a thick bush; and it seemed him that it was the body of Sir Lionel. And then he made such sorrow that he fell to the ground in a swoon, and lay there long. And when he came to himself again he said, "Fair brother, since the fellowship of you and me is sundered, shall I never have joy again; and now He that I have taken for my master He be my help!" And when he had said thus, he took up the body in his arms, and put it upon the horse. And then he said to the man, "Canst thou tell me the way to some chapel, where I may bury this body?" "Come on," said the man, "here is one fast by." And so they rode till they saw a fair tower, and beside it a chapel. Then they alighted both, and put the body into a tomb of marble.

Then Sir Bohort commended the good man unto God, and departed. And he rode all that day, and harbored with an old lady. And on the morrow he rode unto the castle in a valley, and there he met with a yeoman. "Tell me," said Sir Bohort, "knowest thou of any adventure?" "Sir," said he, "here shall be, under this castle, a great and marvellous tournament." Then Sir Bohort thought to be there, if he might meet with any of the fellowship that were in quest of the Sangreal; so he turned to a hermitage that was on the border of the forest. And when he was come thither, he found there Sir Lionel his brother, who sat all armed at the entry of the chapel door. And when Sir Bohort saw him, he had great joy, and he alighted off his horse, and said, "Fair brother, when came ye hither?" As soon as Sir Lionel saw him, he said, "Ah, Sir Bohort, make ye no false show, for, as for you, I might have been slain, for ye left me in peril of death to go succor a gentlewoman; and for that misdeed I now insure you but death, for ye have right well deserved it." When Sir Bohort perceived his brother's wrath, he kneeled down to the earth and cried him mercy, holding up both his hands, and prayed him to forgive him. "Nay," said Sir Lionel, "thou shalt have but death for it, if I have the upper hand; therefore leap upon thy horse and keep thyself; and if thou do not, I will ran upon thee there, as thou standest on foot, and so the shame shall be mine, and the harm thine, but of that I reck not." When Sir Bohort saw that he must fight with his brother or else die, he wist not what to do. Then his heart counselled him not so to do, inasmuch as Sir Lionel was his elder brother, wherefore he ought to bear him reverence. Yet kneeled he down before Sir Lionel's horses feet, and said, "Fair brother, have mercy upon me, and slay me not." But Sir Lionel cared not, for the fiend had brought him in such a will that he should slay him. When he saw that Sir Bohort would not rise to give him battle, he rushed over him, so that he smote him with his horse's feet to the earth, and hurt him sore, that he swooned of distress. When Sir Lionel saw this, he alighted from his horse for to have smitten off his head; and so he took him by the helm, and would have rent it from his head. But it happened that Sir Colgrevance, a knight of the Round Table, came at that time thither, as it was our Lord's will; and then he beheld how Sir Lionel would have slain his brother, and he knew Sir Bohort, whom he loved right well. Then leapt he down from his horse, and took Sir Lionel by the shoulders, and drew him strongly back from Sir Bohort, and said, 'Sir Lionel, will ye slay your brother?" "Why," said Sir Lionel, "will ye slay me? If ye interfere in this, I will slay you, and him after." Then he ran upon Sir Bohort, and would have smitten him; but Sir Colgrevance ran between

them, and said, "If ye persist to do so any more, we two shall meddle together." Then Sir Lionel defied him, and gave him a great stroke through the helm. Then he drew his sword, for he was a passing good knight, and defended himself right manfully. So long endured the battle, that Sir Bohort rose up all anguishly, and beheld Sir Colgrevance, the good knight, fight with his brother for his quarrel. Then was he full sorry and heavy, and thought that, if Sir Colgrevance slew him that was his brother, he should never have joy, and if his brother slew Sir Colgrevance, the shame should ever be his.

Then would he have risen for to have parted them, but he had not so much strength to stand on his feet; so he staid so long that Sir Colgrevance had the worse, for Sir Lionel was of great chivalry and right hardy. Then cried Sir Colgrevance, "Ah, Sir Bohort, why come ye not to bring me out of peril of death, wherein I have put me to succor you?" With that, Sir Lionel smote off his helm, and bore him to the earth. And when he had slain Sir Colgrevance, he ran upon his brother as a fiendly man, and gave him such a stroke that he made him stoop. And he that was full of humility prayed him, "For God's sake leave this battle, for if it befell, fair brother, that I slew you, or ye me, we should be dead of that sin." "Pray ye not me for mercy," said Sir Lionel. Then Sir Bohort, all weeping, drew his sword, and said, "Now God have mercy upon me, though I defend my life against my brother." With that Sir Bohort lifted up his sword, and would have stricken his brother. Then heard he a voice that said, "Flee, Sir Bohort, and touch him not." Right so alighted a cloud between them, in the likeness of a fire, and a marvellous flame, so that they both fell to the earth, and lay there a great while in a swoon. And when they came to themselves, Sir Bohort saw that his brother had no harm; and he was right glad, for he dread sore that God had taken vengeance upon him. Then Sir Lionel said to his brother, "Brother, forgive me, for God's sake, all that I have trespassed against you." And Sir Bohort answered, "God forgive it thee, and I do."

With that Sir Bohort heard a voice say, "Sir Bohort, take thy way anon, right to the sea, for Sir Perceval abideth thee there." So Sir Bohort departed, and rode the nearest way to the sea. And at last he came to an abbey that was nigh the sea. That night he rested him there, and in his sleep there came a voice unto him and bade him go to the sea-shore. He started up, and made the sign of the cross on his forehead, and armed himself, and made ready his horse and mounted him, and at a broken wall he rode out, and came to the sea-shore. And there he found a ship, covered all with white samite. And he entered into the ship; but it was anon so dark that he might see no man, and he laid him down and slept till it was day. Then he awaked, and saw in the middle of the ship a knight all armed, save his helm. And then he knew it was Sir Perceval de Galis, and each made of other right great joy. Then said Sir Perceval, "We lack nothing now but the good knight Sir Galahad."

OF SIR LAUNCELOT AGAIN

IT befell upon a night Sir Launcelot arrived before a castle, which was rich and fair. And there was a postern that opened toward the sea, and was open without any keeping, save two lions kept the entry; and the moon shined clear. Anon Sir Launcelot heard a voice that said, "Launcelot, enter into the castle, where thou shalt see a great part of thy desire." So he went unto the gate, and saw the two lions; then he set hands to his sword, and drew it. Then there came suddenly as it were a stroke upon the arm, so sore that the sword fell out of his hand, and he heard a voice that said, "O man of evil faith, wherefore believest thou more in thy armor than in thy Maker?" Then said Sir Launcelot, "Fair Lord, I thank thee of thy great mercy, that thou reprovest me of my misdeed; now see I well that thou holdest me for thy servant." Then he made a cross on his forehead, and came to the lions; and they made semblance to do him harm, but he passed them without hurt, and entered into the castle, and he found no gate nor door but it was open. But at the last he found a chamber whereof the door was shut; and he set his hand thereto, to have opened it, but he might not. Then he listened, and heard a voice which sung so sweetly that it seemed none earthly thing; and the voice said, "Joy and honor be to the Father of heaven." Then Sir Launcelot kneeled down before the chamber, for well he wist that there was the Sangreal in that chamber. Then said he, "Fair sweet Lord, if ever I did anything that pleased thee for thy pity show me something of that which I seek." And with that he saw the chamber door open, and there came out a great clearness, that the house was as bright as though all the torches of the world had been there. So he came to the chamber door, and would have entered; and anon a voice said unto him, "Stay, Sir Launcelot, and enter not." And he withdrew him back, and was right heavy in his mind. Then looked 96 ▷ he in the midst of the chamber, and saw a table of silver, and the holy vessel, covered with red samite, and many angels about it; whereof one held a candle of wax burning, and another held a cross, and the ornaments of the altar. Then, for very wonder and thankfulness, Sir Launcelot forgot himself, and he stepped forward and entered the chamber. And suddenly a breath that seemed intermixed with fire smote him so sore in the visage, that therewith he fell to the ground, and had no power to rise. Then felt he many hands about him, which took him up, and bare him out of the chamber, without any amending of his swoon, and left him there, seeming dead to all the people. So on the morrow, when it was fair daylight, and they within were arisen, they found Sir Launcelot lying before the chamber door. And they looked upon him and felt his pulse, to know if there were any life in him. And they found life in him, but he might neither stand nor stir any member that he had. So they took him and bare him into a chamber, and laid him upon a bed, far from all folk, and there he lay many days. Then the one said he was alive, and others said nay. But said an old man, "He is as full of life as the mightiest of you all, and therefore I counsel you that he be well kept till God bring him back again." And after twenty-four days he opened his eyes; and when he saw folk, he made great sorrow, and said, "Why have ye wakened me? for I was better at ease than I am now." "What have ye seen?" said they about him. "I have seen," said he, "great marvels that no tongue can tell, and more than any heart can think." Then they said, "Sir, the quest of the Sangreal is achieved right now in you, and never shall ye see more of it than ye have seen." "I thank God," said Sir Launcelot, "of His great mercy, for

that I have seen, for it sufficeth me." Then he rose up and clothed himself; and when he was so arrayed, they marvelled all, for they knew it was Sir Launcelot, the good knight. And, after four days, he took his leave of the lord of the castle, and of all the fellowship that were there, and thanked them for their great labor and care of him. Then he departed, and turned to Camelot, where he found King Arthur and Queen Guenever; but many of the knights of the Round Table were slain and destroyed, more than half. Then all the court was passing glad of Sir Launcelot; and he told the king all his adventures that had befallen him since he departed.

SIR GALAHAD

N ow, when Sir Galahad had rescued Perceval from the twenty knights, he rode into a vast forest, wherein he abode many days. Then he took his way to the sea, and it befell him that he was benighted in a hermitage. And the good man was glad when he saw he was a knight-errant. And when they were at rest, there came a gentlewoman knocking at the door; and the good man came to the door to wit what she would. Then she said, "I would speak with the knight which is with you." Then Galahad went to her, and asked her what she would. "Sir Galahad," said she, "I will that ye arm you, and mount upon your horse, and follow me; for I will show you the highest adventure that ever knight saw." Then Galahad armed himself and commended himself to God, and bade the damsel go before, and he would follow where she led.

So she rode as fast as her palfrey might bear her, till she came to the sea; and there they found the ship where Sir Bohort and Sir Perceval were, who cried from the ship, "Sir Galahad, you are welcome; we have awaited you long." And when he heard them, he asked the damsel who they were. "Sir," said she, "leave your horse here, and I shall leave mine, and we will join ourselves to their company." So they entered into the ship, and the two knights received them both with great joy. For they knew the damsel, that she was Sir Perceval's sister. Then the wind arose and drove them through the sea all that day and the next,

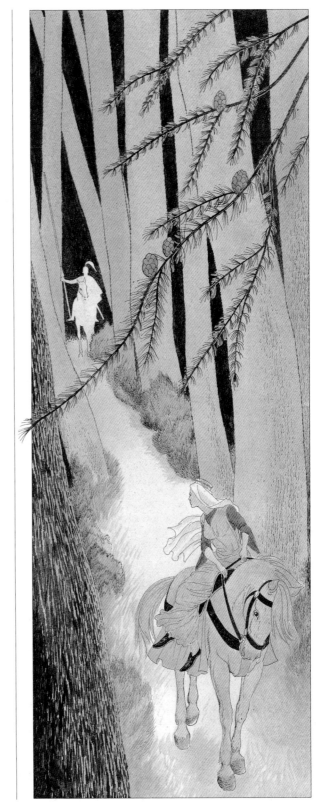

till the ship arrived between two rocks, passing great and marvellous; but there they might not land, for there was a whirlpool; but there was another ship, and upon it they might go without danger. "Go we thither," said the gentlewoman, "and there shall we see adventures, for such is our Lord's will." Then Sir Galahad blessed him, and entered therein, and then next the gentlewoman, and then Sir Bohort and Sir Perceval. And when they came on board, they found there the table of silver, and the Sangreal, which was covered with red samite. And they made great reverence thereto, and Sir Galahad prayed a long time to our Lord, that at what time he should ask to pass out of this world, he should do so; and a voice said to him, "Galahad, thou shalt have thy request; and when thou askest the death of thy body thou shalt have it, and then shalt thou find the life of thy soul."

And anon the wind drove them across the sea, till they came to the city of Sarras. Then they took out of the ship the table of silver, and he took it to Sir Perceval and Sir Bohort to go before, and Sir Galahad came behind, and right so they came to the city, and at the gate of the city they saw an old man, crooked. Then Sir Galahad called him and bade him help bear this heavy thing. "Truly," said the old man, "it is ten years ago that I might not go save with crutches." "Care thou not," said Sir Galahad, "but arise up and show thy good will." And so he assayed and found himself as whole as ever he was. Then ran he to the table and took one part against Sir Galahad. And anon arose there a great noise in the city, that a cripple was made whole by knights marvellous that entered into the city. Then anon after, the three knights went to the water, and brought up into the palace Sir Perceval's sister. And when the king of the city, which was cleped Estorause, saw the fellowship, he asked them of whence they were, and what thing it was they had brought upon the table of silver. And they told him the truth of the Sangreal, and the power which God had set there. Then the king was a tyrant, and was come of the line of Paynims, and took them and put them in prison in a deep hole.

But as soon as they were there, our Lord sent them the Sangreal, through whose grace they were always filled while that they were in prison. So at the year's end it befell that this king Estorause lay sick, and felt that he should die. Then he sent for the three knights, and they came afore him, and he cried them mercy of that he had done to them, and they forgave it him goodly, and he died anon. When the king was dead, all the city was dismayed, and wist not who might be their king. Right so they were in council, there came a voice among them, and bade them choose the youngest knight of them three to be their king, "for he shall well maintain you and all yours." So they made Sir Galahad king by all the assent of the whole city, and else they would have slain him. And when he was come to behold the land, he had made about the table of silver a chest of gold and of precious stones that covered the holy vessel, and every day early the three fellows would come afore it and make their prayers. Now at the year's end, and the next day after Sir Galahad had borne the crown of gold, he rose up early, and his fellows, and came to the palace, and saw before them the holy vessel, and a man kneeling on his knees, in likeness of a bishop, that had about him a great fellowship of angels, as it had been Jesus Christ himself. And then he arose and began a mass of Our Lady. And when he came to the sacrament of the mass, and had done, anon he called Sir Galahad, and said to him, "Come forth, the servant of Jesus Christ, and thou shalt see that thou hast much desired to see." And then he began to tremble right hard, when the deadly flesh began to behold the spiritual things. Then he held up his hands toward heaven, and said, "Lord, I thank thee, for now I see that that hath been my desire many a day. Now, blessed Lord, would I not longer live; if it might please thee, Lord." And therewith the good man took our Lord's body betwixt his hands, and proffered it to Sir Galahad, and he received it right gladly and meekly. "Now, wottest thou what I am?" said the good man. "Nay," said Sir Galahad. "I am Joseph of Arimathea, which our Lord hath sent here to bear thee fellowship. And wottest thou wherefore that he hath sent me more than any other? For thou hast resembled me in two things, in that thou hast seen the marvels of the Sangreal, and in that thou hast been a clean maiden as I have been and am." And when he had said these words Sir Galahad went to Sir Perceval and kissed him, and commended him to God. And so he went to Sir Bohort and kissed him, and commended

him to God, and said, "Fair lord, salute me to my lord
Sir Launcelot, my father, and as soon as ye see him
bid him remember of this unstable world." And
therewith he kneeled down before the table and
made his prayers, and then suddenly his soul departed to Jesus Christ, and a great multitude of angels
bare his soul up to heaven, that the two fellows might
well behold it. Also the two fellows saw come from
heaven a hand, but they saw not the body; and then
it came right to the vessel and took it and the spear,
and so bare it up to heaven. Sithen there was never
man so hardy to say that he had seen the Sangreal.

When Sir Perceval and Sir Bohort saw Sir
Galahad dead they made as much sorrow as ever did
two men; and if they had not been good men they
might lightly have fallen into despair. And the people
of the country and of the city were right heavy. And
then he was buried. And as soon as he was buried Sir
Perceval yielded him to a hermitage out of the city,
and took a religious clothing; and Sir Bohort was
always with him, but never changed he his secular
clothing, for that he purposed to go again into the
realm of Loegria. Thus a year and two months lived
Sir Perceval in the hermitage a full holy life, and then
he passed out of this world. And Sir Bohort let bury
him by his sister and by Sir Galahad.

And when Sir Bohort saw that he was in so far
countries as in the parts of Babylon, he departed from
Sarras, and armed him, and came to the sea, and
entered into a ship, and so it befell him in good adventure he came into the realm of Loegria. And he rode so
fast till he came to Camelot, where the king was. And
then was there great joy made of him in the court, for
they wend all he had been dead, forasmuch as he had
been so long out of the country. And when they had
eaten, the king made great clerks to come afore him,
that they should chronicle of the high adventures of the
good knights. Then Sir Bohort told him of the adventures of the Sangreal, such as had befallen him and his
three fellows, that was Sir Launcelot, Sir Perceval, and
Sir Galahad. Then Sir Launcelot told the adventures
of the Sangreal that he had seen. All this was made in
great books, and put in almeries in Salisbury. And anon
Sir Bohort said to Sir Launcelot, "Galahad, your own
son, saluted you by me, and after you King Arthur, and
all the court, and so did Sir Perceval; for I buried them

with mine own hands in the city of Sarras. Also, Sir Launcelot, Galahad prayeth you to remember of this uncertain world, as ye behight him when ye were together more than half a year." "This is true," said Sir Launcelot; "now I trust to God his prayer shall avail me." Then Sir Launcelot took Sir Bohort in his arms, and said, "Gentle cousin, ye are right welcome to me, and all that ever I may do for you and for yours, ye shall find my poor body ready at all times whiles the spirit is in it, and that I promise you faithfully, and never to fail. And wit ye well, gentle cousin Sir Bohort, that ye and I will never part in sunder whilst our lives may last." "Sir," said he, "I will as ye will."

Thus endeth the history of the Sangreal, which is a story chronicled as one of the truest and holiest that is in this world.

Tennyson has among his shorter poems one on Sir Galahad, which we add as being the conception of this purest of knights held by the poet who has loved best of all English poets the old stories of the Knights of the Round Table:

Sir Galahad

"My good blade carves the casques
  of men,
  My tough lance thrusteth sure,
My strength is as the strength of ten,
  Because my heart is pure.
The shattering trumpet shrilleth high,
  The hard brands shiver on the steel,
The splintered spear-shafts crack and
  fly,
  The horse and rider reel:
They reel, they roll in clanging lists,
  And when the tide of combat stands,
Perfume and flowers fall in showers,
  That lightly rain from ladies' hands.

"How sweet are looks that ladies bend
  On whom their favors fall!
For them I battle to the end,
  To save from shame and thrall:
But all my heart is drawn above,
  My knees are bound in crypt and
    shrine:
I never felt the kiss of love,
  Nor maiden's hand in mine.
More bounteous aspects on me beam,
  Me mightier transports move and
    thrill;
So keep I fair thro' faith and prayer,
  A virgin heart in work and will.

"When down the stormy crescent goes,
  A light before me swims,

Between dark stems the forest glows,
  I hear a noise of hymns:
Then by some secret shrine I ride;
  I hear a voice, but none are there;
The stalls are void, the doors are wide,
  The tapers burning fair.
Fair gleams the snowy altar-cloth,
  The silver vessels sparkle clean,
The shrill bell rings, the censer swings,
  And solemn chants resound between.

"Sometimes on lonely mountain meres
  I find a magic bark,
I leap on board; no helmsman steers:
  I float till all is dark.
A gentle sound, an awful light!
  Three angels bear the holy Grail:
With folded feet, in stoles of white,
  On sleeping wings they sail.
Ah, blessed vision! blood of God!
  My spirit beats her mortal bars,
As down dark tides the glory slides
  And star-like mingles with the stars.

"When on my goodly charger borne
  Thro' dreaming towns I go,
The cock crows ere the Christmas morn,
  The streets are dumb with snow.
The tempest crackles on the leads,
  And, ringing, springs from brand
    and mail;
But o'er the dark a glory spreads

And gilds the driving hail.
I leave the plain, I climb the height;
  No branchy thicket shelter yields;
But blessed forms in whisking storms
  Fly o'er waste fens and windy fields.

"A maiden knight—to me is given
  Such hope, I know not fear;
I yearn to breathe the airs of heaven
  That often meet me here.
I muse on joy that will not cease,
  Pure spaces clothed in living beams,
Pure lilies of eternal peace,
  Whose odors haunt my dreams;
And stricken by an angel's hand,
  This mortal armour that I wear,
This weight and rise, this heart and eyes,
  Are touched, are turned to finest air.

"The clouds are broken in the sky,
  And thro' the mountain-walls
A rolling organ-harmony
  Swells up, and shakes and falls.
Then move the trees, the copses nod,
  Wings flutter, voices hover clear:
O just and faithful knight of God!
  Ride on! the prize is near!
So pass I hostel, hall, and grange;
  By hedge and ford, by park and
    pale,
All armed I ride, whate'er betide,
  Until I find the holy Grail."

CHAPTER XVII

SIR AGRIVAIN'S TREASON

So after the quest of the Sangreal was fulfilled, and all the knights that were left alive were come again to the Table Round, there was great joy in the court, and in especial King Arthur and Queen Guenever made great joy of the remnant that were come home, and passing glad were the king and the queen of Sir Launcelot and of Sir Bohort, for they had been passing long away in the quest of the Sangreal.

Then Sir Launcelot began to resort unto Queen Guenever again, and forgot the promise that he made in the quest; so that many in the court spoke of it, and in especial Sir Agrivain, Sir Gawain's brother, for he was ever open-mouthed. So it happened Sir Gawain and all his brothers were in King Arthur's chamber, and then Sir Agrivain said thus openly, "I marvel that we all are not ashamed to see and to know so noble a knight as King Arthur so to be shamed by the conduct of Sir Launcelot and the queen." Then spoke Sir Gawain, and said, "Brother, Sir Agrivain, I pray you and charge you move not such matters any more before me, for be ye assured I will not be of your counsel." "Neither will we," said Sir Gaheris and Sir Gareth. "Then will I," said Sir Modred. "I doubt you not," said Sir Gawain, "for to all mischief ever were ye prone; yet I would that ye left all this, for I know what will come of it." "Fall of it what fall may," said Sir Agrivain, "I will disclose it to the king." With that came to them King Arthur. "Now, brothers, hold your peace," said Sir Gawain. "We will not," said Sir Agrivain. Then said Sir Gawain, "I will not hear your tales, nor be of your counsel." "No more will I," said Sir Gareth and Sir Gaheris, and therewith they departed, making great sorrow.

Then Sir Agrivain told the king all that was said in the court of the conduct of Sir Launcelot and the queen, and it grieved the king very much. But he would not believe it to be true without proof. So Sir Agrivain laid a plot to entrap Sir Launcelot and the queen, intending to take them together unawares. Sir Agrivain and Sir Modred led a party for this purpose, but Sir Launcelot escaped from them, having slain Sir Agrivain and wounded Sir Modred. Then Sir Launcelot hastened to his friends, and told them what had happened, and withdrew with them to the forest; but he left spies to bring him tidings of whatever might be done.

So Sir Launcelot escaped, but the queen remained in the king's power, and Arthur could no longer doubt of her guilt. And the law was such in those days that they who committed such crimes, of what estate or condition soever they were, must be burned to death, and so it was ordained for Queen Guenever. Then said King Arthur to Sir Gawain, "I pray you make you ready, in your best armor, with your brethren, Sir Gaheris and Sir Gareth, to bring my queen to the fire, there to receive her death." "Nay, my most noble lord," said Sir Gawain, "that will I never do; for know thou well, my heart will never serve me to see her die, and it shall never be said that I was of your counsel in her death." Then the king commanded Sir Gaheris and Sir Gareth to be there, and they said, "We will be there, as ye command us, sire, but in peaceable wise, and bear no armor upon us."

So the queen was led forth, and her ghostly father was brought to her to shrive her, and there was weeping and wailing of many lords and ladies. And one went and told Sir Launcelot that the queen was led forth to her death. Then Sir Launcelot and the knights that were with him fell upon the troop that guarded the queen, and dispersed them, and slew all who withstood them. And in the confusion Sir Gareth and Sir Gaheris were slain, for they were unarmed and defenceless. And Sir Launcelot carried away the queen to his castle of La Joyeuse Garde. 102 ▷

Then there came one to Sir Gawain and told him how that Sir Launcelot had slain the knights and carried away the queen. "O Lord, defend my brethren!" said Sir Gawain. "Truly," said the man, "Sir Gareth and Sir Gaheris are slain." "Alas!" said Sir Gawain, "now is my joy gone." And then he fell down and swooned, and long he lay there as he had been dead.

When he arose out of his swoon Sir Gawain ran to the king, crying, "O King Arthur, mine uncle, my brothers are slain." Then the king wept and he both. "My king, my lord, and mine uncle," said Sir Gawain, "bear witness now that I make you a promise that I shall hold by my knighthood, that from this day I will never fail Sir Launcelot until the one of us have slain the other. I will seek Sir Launcelot throughout seven kings' realms, but I shall slay him or he shall slay me." "Ye shall not need to seek him," said the king, "for, as I hear, Sir Launcelot will abide me and you in the Joyeuse Garde; and much people draweth unto him, as I hear say." "That may I believe," said Gawain, "but, my lord, summon your friends, and I will summon mine." "It shall be done," said the king. So then the king sent letters and writs throughout all England, both in the length and breadth, to summon all his knights. And unto Arthur drew many knights, dukes, and earls, so that he had a great host. Thereof heard Sir Launcelot, and collected all whom he could; and many good knights held with him, both for his sake and for the queen's sake. But King Arthur's host was too great for Sir Launcelot to abide him in the field; and he was full loath to do battle against the king. So Sir Launcelot drew him to his strong caste, with all manner of provisions. Then came King Arthur and Sir Gawain, and laid siege all about La Joyeuse Garde, both the town and the castle; but in no wise would Sir Launcelot ride out of his castle neither suffer any of his knights to issue out, until many weeks were past.

Then it befell upon a day in harvest-time Sir Launcelot looked over the wall, and spake aloud to King Arthur and Sir Gawain, "My lords both, all is vain that ye do at this siege, for here ye shall win no worship, but only dishonor; for if I list to come out, and my good knights, I shall soon make an end of this war." "Come forth," said Arthur, "if thou darest, and I promise thee I shall meet thee in the midst of the field." "God forbid me," said Sir Launcelot, "that I should encounter with the most noble king that made me knight." "Fie upon thy fair language," said the king, "for know thou well that I am thy mortal foe,

and ever will be to my dying day." And Sir Gawain said, "What cause hadst thou to slay my brother, Sir Gaheris, who bore no arms against thee, and Sir Gareth, whom thou madest knight, and who loved thee more than all my kin? Therefore know thou well I shall make war to thee all the while that I may live."

When Sir Bohort, Sir Hector de Marys, and Sir Lionel heard this outcry they called to them Sir Palamedes, and Sir Saffire his brother, and Sir Lawayne, with many more, and all went to Sir Launcelot. And they said, "My lord, Sir Launcelot, we pray you, if you will have our service, keep us no longer within these walls, for know well all your fair speech and forbearance will not avail you." "Alas!" said Sir Launcelot, ."to ride forth and to do battle I am full loath." Then he spake again unto the king and Sir Gawain, and willed them to keep out of the battle; but they despised his words. So then Sir Launcelot's fellowship came out of the castle in full good array. And always Sir Launcelot charged all his knights, in any wise, to save King Arthur and Sir Gawain.

Then came forth Sir Gawain from the king's host, and offered combat, and Sir Lionel encountered with him, and there Sir Gawain smote Sir Lionel through the body, that he fell to the earth as if dead. Then there began a great conflict, and much people were slain; but ever Sir Launcelot did what he might to save the people in King Arthur's party, and ever King Arthur followed Sir Launcelot to slay him; but Sir Launcelot suffered him, and would not strike again. Then Sir Bohort encountered with King Arthur, and smote him down; and he alighted and drew his sword, and said to Sir Launcelot, "Shall I make an end of this war?" for he meant to have slain King Arthur. "Not so," said Sir Launcelot, "touch him no more, for I will never see that most noble king that made me knight either slain or shamed;" and therewith Sir Launcelot alighted off his horse and took up the king, and horsed him again, and said thus: "My lord Arthur, for God's love, cease this strife." And King Arthur looked upon Sir Launcelot, and his tears burst from his eyes, thinking on the great courtesy that was in Sir Launcelot more than in any other man; and therewith the king rode his way. Then anon both parties withdrew to repose them, and buried the dead.

But the war continued, and it was noised abroad through all Christendom, and at last it was told afore the pope; and he, considering the great goodness of King Arthur, and of Sir Launcelot, called unto him a noble clerk, which was the bishop of Rochester, who was then in his dominions, and sent him to King Arthur, charging him that he take his queen, dame Guenever, unto him again, and make peace with Sir Launcelot.

So, by means of this bishop, peace was made for the space of one year; and King Arthur received back the queen, and Sir Launcelot departed from the kingdom with all his knights, and went to his own country. So they shipped at Cardiff, and sailed unto Benwick, which some men call Bayonne. And all the people of those lands came to Sir Launcelot, and received him home right joyfully. And Sir Launcelot stablished and garnished all his towns and castles, and he greatly advanced all his noble knights, Sir Lionel and Sir Bohort, and Sir Hector de Marys, Sir Blanor, Sir Lawayne, and many others, and made them lords of lands and castles; till he left himself no more than any one of them.

But when the year was passed, King Arthur and Sir Gawain came with a great host, and landed upon Sir Launcelot's lands, and burnt and wasted all that they might overrun. Then spake Sir Bohort and said, "My lord, Sir Launcelot, give us leave to meet them in the field, and we shall make them rue the time that ever they came to this country." Then said Sir Launcelot, "I am full loath to ride out with my knights for shedding of Christian blood; so we will yet awhile keep our walls, and I will send a messenger unto my lord Arthur, to propose a treaty; for better is peace than always war." So Sir Launcelot sent forth a damsel, and a dwarf with her, requiring King Arthur to leave his warring upon his lands; and so she started on a palfrey, and the dwarf ran by her side. And when she came to the pavilion of King Arthur, she alighted, and there met her a gentle knight, Sir

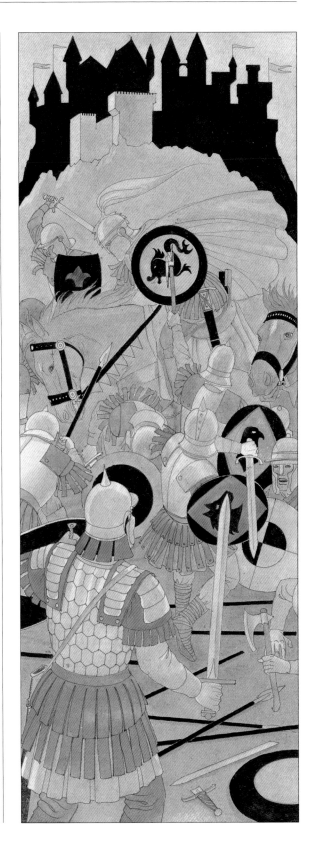

Lucan the butler, and said, "Fair damsel, come ye from Sir Launcelot du Lac?" "Yea, sir," she said, "I come hither to speak with the king." "Alas!" said Sir Lucan, "my lord Arthur would be reconciled to Sir Launcelot, but Sir Gawain will not suffer him." And with this Sir Lucan led the damsel to the king, where he sat with Sir Gawain, to hear what she would say. So when she had told her tale, the tears ran out of the king's eyes; and all the lords were forward to advise the king to be accorded with Sir Launcelot, save only Sir Gawain; and he said, "My lord, mine uncle, what will ye do? Will you now turn back, now you are so far advanced upon your journey? If ye do, all the world will speak shame of you." "Nay," said King Arthur, "I will do as ye advise me; but do thou give the damsel her answer, for I may not speak to her for pity.

Then said Sir Gawain, "Damsel, say ye to Sir Launcelot, that it is waste labor to sue to mine uncle for peace, and say that I, Sir Gawain, send him word that I promise him, by the faith I owe unto God and to knighthood, I shall never leave him till he have slain me or I him." So the damsel returned; and when Sir Launcelot had heard this answer, the tears ran down his cheeks.

Then it befell on a day Sir Gawain came before the gates, armed at all points, and cried with a loud voice, "Where art thou now, thou false traitor, Sir Launcelot? Why hidest thou thyself within holes and walls like a coward? Look out now, thou traitor knight, and I will avenge upon thy body the death of my three brethren." All this language heard Sir Launcelot, and the knights which were about him; and they said to him, "Sir Launcelot, now must ye defend you like a knight, or else be shamed for ever, for you have slept overlong and suffered overmuch." Then Sir Launcelot spoke on high unto King Arthur, and said, "My lord Arthur, now I have forborne long, and suffered you and Sir Gawain to do what ye would, and now must I needs defend myself, inasmuch as Sir Gawain hath appealed me of treason." Then Sir Launcelot armed him and mounted upon his horse, and the noble knights came out of the city, and the host without stood all apart; and so the covenant was made that no man should come near the two knights, nor deal with them, till one were dead or yielded.

Then Sir Gawain and Sir Launcelot departed a great way in sunder, and then they came together with all their horses' might as they might run, and either smote the other in the midst of their shields, but the knights were so strong, and their spears so big, that their horses might not endure their buffets, and so the horses fell to the earth. And then they avoided their horses, and dressed their shields afore them. Then they stood together, and gave many sad strokes on divers places of their bodies, that the blood burst out on many sides and places. Then had Sir Gawain such a grace and gift that an holy man had given to him, that every day in the year, from morning till high noon, his might increased those three hours, as much as thrice his strength, and that caused Sir Gawain to win great honor. And for his sake King Arthur made an ordinance that all manner of battles for any quarrels that should be done before King Arthur should begin at Underne,[1] and all was done for Sir Gawain's love, that by likelihood if that Sir Gawain were on the one part he should have the better in battle, whilst his strength endured three hours, but there were few knights that time living that knew this advantage that Sir Gawain had, but King Arthur only. Thus Sir Launcelot fought with Sir Gawain, and when Sir Launcelot felt his might evermore increase, Sir Launcelot wondered and dread him sore to be ashamed. For Sir Launcelot thought when he felt Sir Gawain double his strength, that he had been a fiend, and no earthly man; wherefore Sir Launcelot traced and traversed, and covered himself with his shield, and kept his might and his braid during three hours; and that while Sir Gawain gave him many sad brunts and many sad strokes, that all the knights that beheld Sir Launcelot marvelled how he might endure him, but full little understood they that travail that Sir Launcelot had for to endure him. And then when it was past noon Sir Gawain had no more but his own might. Then Sir Launcelot felt him so come down; then he stretched him up, and stood near Sir Gawain, and said thus: "My lord Sir Gawain, now I fear ye have done; now my lord Sir Gawain, I must do my part, for many great and grievous strokes I have endured you this day with great pain." Then Sir Launcelot doubled his strokes, and gave Sir Gawain such a buffet on the helmet that he fell down on his

---

[1]Underne. The third hour in the day, nine o'clock.

side, and Sir Launcelot withdrew from him. "Why turnest thou thee?" said Sir Gawain; "now turn again, false traitor knight, and slay me; for an thou leave me thus, when I am whole, I shall do battle with thee again." "I shall endure you, sir, by God's grace, but wit thou well, Sir Gawain, I will never smite a felled knight." And so Sir Launcelot went into the city, and Sir Gawain was borne into one of King Arthur's pavilions, and leeches were brought to him, and he was searched and salved with soft ointments.

And then Sir Launcelot said, "Now have good day, my lord the king, for, wit you well, ye win no worship at these walls; and if I would my knights out bring, there should many a man die. Therefore, my lord Arthur, remember you of old kindness, and however I fare, Jesus be your guide in all places."

Thus the siege endured, and Sir Gawain lay helpless near a month; and when he was near recovered, came tidings unto King Arthur that made him return with all his host to England.

CHAPTER XVIII

MORTE D'ARTHUR

"And now the whole ROUND TABLE is dissolved,
Which was an image of the mighty world,
And I, the last, go forth companionless;
And the days darken round me, and the years
Among new men, strange faces, other minds."

Tennyson

SIR MODRED was left ruler of all England, and he caused letters to be written, as if from beyond sea, that King Arthur was slain in battle. So he called a Parliament, and made himself be crowned king; and he took the queen, Guenever, and said plainly that he would wed her, but she escaped from him, and took refuge in the Tower of London. And Sir Modred went and laid siege about the Tower of London, and made great assaults thereat, but all might not avail him. Then came word to Sir Modred that King Arthur had raised the siege of Sir Launcelot, and was coming home. Then Sir Modred summoned all the barony of the land; and much people drew unto Sir Modred, and said they would abide with him for better and for worse; and he drew a great host to Dover, for there he heard say that King Arthur would arrive.

And as Sir Modred was at Dover with his host, came King Arthur, with a great number of ships and galleys, and there was Sir Modred awaiting upon the landing. Then was there launching of great boats and small, full of noble men of arms, and there was much slaughter of gentle knights on both parts. But King Arthur was so courageous, there might no manner of knights prevent him to land, and his knights fiercely followed him; and so they landed, and put Sir Modred aback so that he fled, and all his people. And when the battle was done, King Arthur commanded to bury his people that were dead. And then was noble Sir Gawain found, in a great boat, lying more than half dead. And King Arthur went to him, and made sorrow out of measure. "Mine uncle," said Sir Gawain, "know thou well my death-day is come, and all is through mine own hastiness and wilfulness, for I am smitten upon the old wound which Sir Launcelot gave me, of the which I feel I must die. And had Sir Launcelot been with you as of old, this war had never begun, and of all this I am the cause." Then Sir Gawain prayed the king to send for Sir Launcelot, and to cherish him above all other knights.

And so, at the hour of noon, Sir Gawain yielded up his spirit, and then the king bade inter him in a chapel within Dover Castle; and there all men may see the skull of him, and the same wound is seen that Sir Launcelot gave him in battle.

Then was it told the king that Sir Modred had pitched his camp upon Barrendown; and the king rode thither, and there was a great battle betwixt them, and King Arthur's party stood best, and Sir Modred and his party fled unto Canterbury.

And there was a day assigned betwixt King Arthur and Sir Modred that they should meet upon a down beside Salisbury, and not far from the seaside, to do battle yet again. And at night, as the king slept, he dreamed a wonderful dream. It seemed him verily that there came Sir Gawain unto him, with a number of fair ladies with him. And when King Arthur saw him, he said, "Welcome, my sister's son; I weened thou hadst been dead; and now I see thee alive, great is my joy. But, O fair nephew, what be these ladies that hither be come with you?" "Sir," said Sir Gawain, "all these be ladies for whom I have fought when I was a living man; and because I did battle for them in righteous quarrel, they have given me grace to bring me hither unto you, to warn you of your death, if ye fight tomorrow with Sir Modred. Therefore take ye treaty, and proffer you largely for a month's delay; for within a month shall come Sir Launcelot and all his noble knights, and rescue you worshipfully, and slay Sir Modred and all that hold with him." And then Sir Gawain and all the ladies vanished. And anon the king called to fetch his noble lords and wise bishops unto him. And when they were come, the king told them his vision, and what Sir Gawain had told him. Then the king sent Sir Lucan the butler, and Sir Bedivere, with two bishops, and charged them in any wise to take a treaty for a month and a day with Sir Modred. So they departed, and came to Sir Modred; and so, at the last, Sir Modred was agreed to have Cornwall and Kent, during Arthur's life, and all England after his death.

Then was it agreed that King Arthur and Sir Modred should meet betwixt both their hosts, and each of them should bring fourteen persons, and then and there they should sign the treaty. And when King Arthur and his knights were prepared to go forth, he warned all his host, "If so be ye see any sword drawn, look ye come on fiercely, and slay whomsoever withstandeth, for I in no wise trust that traitor, Sir Modred." In likewise Sir Modred warned his host. So they met, and were agreed and accorded thoroughly. And wine was brought, and they drank. Right then came an adder out of a little heath-bush, and stung a knight on the foot. And when the knight felt him sting, he looked down and saw the adder, and then he drew his sword to slay the adder, and thought of no other harm. And when the host on both sides saw that sword drawn, they blew trumpets and horns, and shouted greatly. And King Arthur took his horse, and rode to his party, saying, "Alas, this unhappy day!" And Sir Modred did in like wise. And never was there a more doleful battle in Christian land. And ever King Arthur rode throughout the battle, and did full nobly, as a worthy king should, and Sir Modred that day did his devoir, and put himself in great peril. And thus they fought all the long day, till the most of all the noble knights lay dead upon the ground. Then the king looked about him, and saw of all his host were left alive but two knights, Sir Lucan the butler, and Sir Bedivere his brother, and they were full sore wounded.

Then King Arthur saw where Sir Modred leaned upon his sword among a great heap of dead men. "Now give me my spear," said Arthur unto Sir Lucan, "for yonder I espy the traitor that hath wrought all this woe." "Sir, let him be," said Sir Lucan; "for if ye pass this unhappy day ye shall be right well revenged upon him. Remember what the sprite of Sir Gawain told you, and leave off now, for ye have won the field; and if ye leave off now this evil day of destiny is past." "Betide me life, betide me death," said King Arthur, 108 ▷ "he shall not now escape my hands." Then the king took his spear in both hands, and ran toward Sir Modred, crying, "Traitor, now is thy death-day come." And there King Arthur smote Sir Modred under the shield, with a thrust of his spear through the body. And when Sir Modred felt that he had his deathwound, with the might that he had he smote King Arthur, with his sword holden in both his hands, on the side of the head, that the sword pierced the helmet and the brain-pan; and then Sir Modred fell stark dead upon the earth. And the noble Arthur fell in a swoon to the earth. And Sir Lucan the butler and

Sir Bedivere raised him up, and gently led him betwixt them both to a little chapel not far from the seaside, and when the king was there he thought him well eased. Then heard they people cry in the field. And Sir Lucan went to see what that cry betokened; and he saw by the moonlight that pillers[1] and robbers were come to rob the dead. And he returned, and said to the king, "By my rede, it is best that we bring you to some town." "I would it were so," said the king. And when the king tried to go he fainted. Then Sir Lucan took up the king on the one part, and Sir Bedivere on the other part; and in the lifting Sir Lucan fell in a swoon to the earth, for he was grievously wounded. And then the noble knight's heart burst. And when the king awoke he beheld Sir Lucan, how he lay foaming at the mouth, and speechless. "Alas!" said the king, "this is to me a full heavy sight, to see this noble duke so die for my sake; for he would have holpen me that had more need of help than I, and he would not complain, his heart was so set to help me." Then Sir Bedivere wept for his brother. "Leave this mourning and weeping," said the king, "for wit thou well, if I might live myself, the death of Sir Lucan would grieve me evermore; but my time hieth fast. Therefore," said Arthur unto Sir Bedivere, "take thou Excalibur, my good sword, and go with it to yonder waterside; and when thou comest there I charge thee throw my sword in that water, and come again and tell me what thou there seest." "My lord," said Sir Bedivere, "your commandment shall be done." So Sir Bedivere departed, and by the way he beheld that noble sword, that the pommel and the haft were all of precious stones; and then he said to himself, "If I throw this rich sword into the water no good shall come thereof, but only harm and loss." And then Sir Bedivere hid Excalibur under a tree. And so, as soon as he might, he came again unto the king. "What sawest thou there?" said the king. "Sir," he said, "I saw nothing." "Alas! thou hast deceived me," said the king. "Go thou lightly again, and as thou love me, spare not to throw it in." Then Sir Bedivere went again, and took the sword in his hand to throw it; but again it beseemed him but sin and shame to throw away that noble sword, and he hid it

---

[1]Plunderers: the word is not now used.

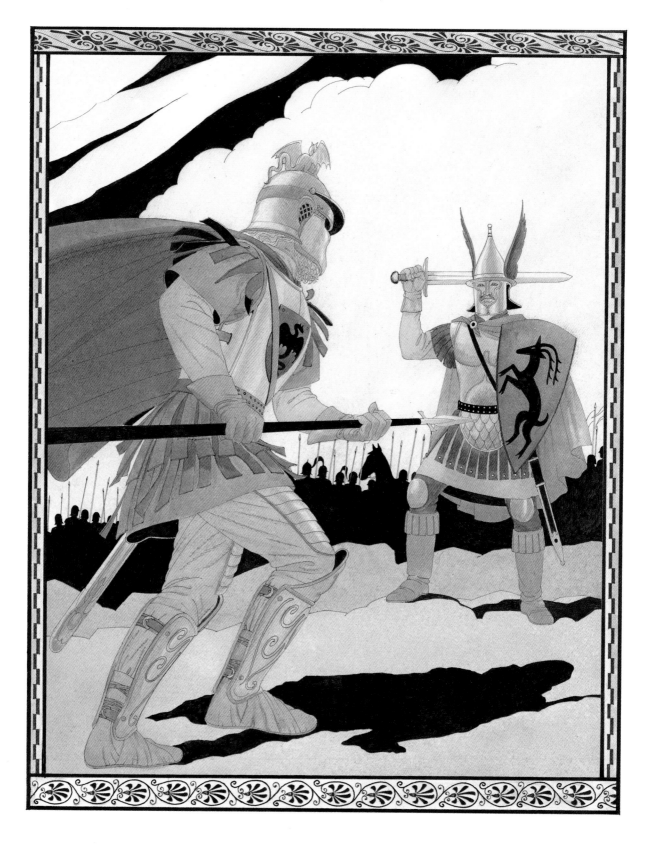

away again, and returned, and told the king he had done his commandment. "What sawest thou there?" said the king. "Sir," he said, "I saw nothing but waters deep and waves wan." "Ah, traitor untrue!" said King Arthur, "now hast thou betrayed me twice. And yet thou art named a noble knight, and hast been lief and dear to me. But now go again, and do as I bid thee, for thy long tarrying putteth me in jeopardy of my life." Then Sir Bedivere went to the sword, and lightly took it up, and went to the waterside, and he bound the girdle about the hilt, and then he threw the sword as far into the water as he might. And there came an arm and a hand out of the water and met it, and caught it, and shook it thrice and brandished it, and then vanished away the hand with the sword in the water.

Then Sir Bedivere came again to the king, and told him what he saw. "Help me hence," said the king, "for I fear I have tarried too long." Then Sir Bedivere took the king on his back, and so went with him to that water-side; and when they came there, even fast by the bark there rode a little barge with many fair ladies in it, and among them was a queen; and all had black hoods, and they wept and shrieked when they saw King Arthur.

"Now put me in the barge," said the king. And there received him three queens with great mourning, and in one of their laps King Arthur laid his head. And the queen said, "Ah, dear brother, why have ye tarried so long? Alas! this wound on your head hath caught overmuch cold." And then they rowed from the land, and Sir Bedivere beheld them go from him. Then he cried: "Ah, my lord Arthur, will ye leave me here alone among mine enemies?" "Comfort thyself," said the king, "for in me is no further help; for I will to the Isle of Avalon, to heal me of my grievous wound." And as soon as Sir Bedivere had lost sight of the barge he wept and wailed; then he took the forest, and went all that night, and in the morning he was ware of a chapel and a hermitage.

Then went Sir Bedivere thither; and when he came into the chapel he saw where lay an hermit on the ground, near a tomb that was newly graven. "Sir," said Sir Bedivere, "what man is there buried that ye pray so near unto?" "Fair son," said the hermit, "I know not verily. But this night there came a number of ladies, and brought hither one dead, and prayed me to bury him." "Alas!" said Sir Bedivere, "that was my lord, King Arthur." Then Sir Bedivere swooned; and when he awoke he prayed the hermit he might abide with him, to live with fasting and prayers. "Ye are welcome," said the hermit. So there bode Sir Bedivere with the hermit; and he put on poor clothes, and served the hermit full lowly in fasting and in prayers.

Thus of Arthur I find never more written in books that he authorized, nor more of the very certainty of his death; but thus was he led away in a ship, wherein were three queens; the one was King Arthur's sister, Queen Morgane le Fay; the other was Viviane, the Lady of the Lake; and the third was the queen of North Galis. And this tale Sir Bedivere, knight of the Table Round, made to be written. Yet some men say that King Arthur is not dead, but hid away into another place, and men say that he shall come again and reign over England. But many say that there is written on his tomb this verse:

"Hic jacet Arthurus, Rex quondam, Rexque futurus."
Here Arthur lies, king once and king to be.

And when Queen Guenever understood that King Arthur was slain, and all the noble knights with him, she stole away, and five ladies with her; and so she went to Almesbury, and made herself a nun, and ware white clothes and black, and took great penance as ever did sinful lady, and lived in fasting, prayers, and alms-deeds. And there she was abbess and ruler of the nuns.

109

Now turn we from her, and speak of Sir Launcelot of the Lake.

When Sir Launcelot heard in his country that Sir Modred was crowned king of England and made war against his own uncle, King Arthur, then was Sir Launcelot wroth out of measure, and said to his kinsmen: "Alas, that double traitor, Sir Modred! now it repenteth me that ever he escaped out of my hands." Then Sir Launcelot and his fellows made ready in all haste, with ships and galleys, to pass into England; and so he passed over till he came to Dover, and there he landed with a great army. Then Sir Launcelot was told that King Arthur was slain. "Alas!" said Sir Launcelot, "this is the heaviest tidings that ever came to me." Then he called the kings, dukes, barons, and knights, and said thus: "My fair lords, I thank you all for coming into this country with me, but we came too late, and that shall repent me while I live. But since it is so," said Sir Launcelot, "I will myself ride and seek my lady, Queen Guenever, for I have heard say she hath fled into the west; therefore ye shall abide me here fifteen days, and if I come not within that time, then take your ships and your host and depart into your country."

So Sir Launcelot departed and rode westerly, and there he sought many days; and at last he came to a nunnery, and was seen of Queen Guenever as he walked in the cloister; and when she saw him, she swooned away. And when she might speak, she bade him to be called to her. And when Sir Launcelot was brought to her, she said: "Sir Launcelot, I require thee and beseech thee, for all the love that ever was betwixt us, that thou never see me more, but return to thy kingdom and take thee a wife, and live with her with joy and bliss; and pray for me to my Lord, that I may get my soul's health." "Nay, madam," said Sir Launcelot, "wit you well that I shall never do; but the same destiny that ye have taken you to will I take me unto, for to please and serve God." And so they parted, with tears and much lamentation; and the ladies bare the queen to her chamber and Sir Launcelot took his horse and rode away, weeping.

And at last Sir Launcelot was ware of a hermitage and a chapel, and then he heard a little bell ring to mass; and thither he rode and alighted, and tied his horse to the gate, and heard mass. And he that sang the mass was the hermit with whom Sir Bedivere had taken up his abode; and Sir Bedivere knew Sir Launcelot, and they spake together after mass. But when Sir Bedivere had told his tale, Sir Launcelot's heart almost burst for sorrow. Then he kneeled down, and prayed the hermit to shrive him, and besought that he might be his brother. Then the hermit said, "I will gladly;" and then he put a habit upon Sir Launcelot, and there he served God day and night, with prayers and fastings.

And the great host abode at Dover till the end of the fifteen days set by Sir Launcelot, and then Sir Bohort made them to go home again to their own country; and Sir Bohort, Sir Hector de Marys, Sir Blanor, and many others, took on them to ride through all England to seek Sir Launcelot. So Sir Bohort by fortune rode until he came to the same chapel where Sir Launcelot was; and when he saw Sir Launcelot in that manner of clothing, he prayed the hermit that he might be in that same. And so there was a habit put upon him, and there he lived in prayers and fasting. And within half a year came others of the knights, their fellows, and took such a habit as Sir Launcelot and Sir Bohort had. Thus they endured in great penance six years.

And upon a night there came a vision to Sir Launcelot, and charged him to haste him toward Almesbury, and "by the time thou come there, thou shalt find Queen Guenever dead." Then Sir Launcelot rose up early, and told the hermit thereof. Then said the hermit, "It were well that ye disobey not this vision. And Sir Launcelot took his seven companions with him, and on foot they went from Glastonbury to Almesbury, which is more than thirty miles. And when they were come to Almesbury, they found that Queen Guenever died but half an hour before. Then Sir Launcelot saw her visage, but he wept not greatly, but sighed. And so he did fill the observance of the service himself, both the "dirige" at night, and at morn he sang mass. And there was prepared an horse-bier, and Sir Launcelot and his fellows followed the bier on foot from Almesbury until they came to Glastonbury; and she was wrapped in cered clothes, and laid in a coffin of marble. And when she was put in the earth, Sir Launcelot swooned, and lay long as one dead.

And Sir Launcelot never after ate but little meat, nor drank; but continually mourned. And within six weeks Sir Launcelot fell sick; and he sent for the hermit and all his true fellows, and said, "Sir hermit, I pray you give me all my rights that a Christian man ought to have." "It shall not need," said the hermit and all his fellows; "it is but heaviness of your blood, and tomorrow morn you shall be well." "My fair lords," said Sir Launcelot, "my careful body will into the earth; I have warning more than now I will say; therefore give me my rights." So when he was houseled and aneled, and had all that a Christian man ought to have, he prayed the hermit that his fellows might bear his body to Joyous Garde. (Some men say it was Alnwick, and some say it was Bamborough.) "It repenteth me sore," said Sir Launcelot, "but I made a vow aforetime that in Joyous Garde I would be buried." Then there was weeping and wringing of hands among his fellows. And that night Sir Launcelot died; and when Sir Bohort and his fellows came to his bedside the next morning, they found him stark dead; and he lay as if he had smiled, and the sweetest savor all about him that ever they knew.

And they put Sir Launcelot into the same horse-bier that Queen Guenever was laid in, and the hermit and they all together went with the body till they came to Joyous Garde. And there they laid his corpse in the body of the quire, and sang and read many psalms and prayers over him. And ever his visage was laid open and naked, that all folks might behold him. And right thus, as they were at their service, there came Sir Hector de Marys, that had seven years sought Sir Launcelot his brother, through all England, Scotland and Wales. And when Sir Hector heard such sounds in the chapel of Joyous Garde, he alighted and came into the quire. And all they knew Sir Hector. Then went Sir Bohort, and told him how there lay Sir Launcelot his brother, dead. Then Sir Hector threw his shield, his sword, and helm from

him. And when he beheld Sir Launcelot's visage, it were hard for any tongue to tell the doleful complaints he made for his brother. "Ah, Sir Launcelot!" he said, "there thou liest. And now I dare to say thou wert never matched of none earthly knight's hand. And thou wert the courteousest knight that ever bare shield; and thou wert the truest friend to thy lover that ever bestrode horse; and thou were the truest lover, of a sinful man, that ever loved woman; and thou wert the kindest man that ever struck with sword. And thou wert the goodliest person that ever came among press of knights. And thou wert the meekest man, and the gentlest, that ever ate in hall among ladies. And thou wert the sternest knight to thy mortal foe that ever put spear in the rest." Then there was weeping and dolor out of measure. Thus they kept Sir Launcelot's corpse fifteen days, and then they buried it with great devotion.

Then they went back with the hermit to his hermitage. And Sir Bedivere was there ever still hermit to his life's end. And Sir Bohort, Sir Hector, Sir Blanor and Sir Bleoberis went into the Holy Land. And these four knights did many battles upon the miscreants, the Turks; and there they died upon a Good Friday, as it pleased God.

Thus endeth this noble and joyous book, entitled La Morte d'Arthur; notwithstanding it treateth of the birth, life and acts of the said King Arthur, and of his noble Knights of the Round Table, their marvellous enquests and adventures, the achieving of the Sangreal, and in the end, la Morte d'Arthur, with the dolorous death and departing out of this world of them all. Which book was reduced into English by Sir Thomas Mallory, Knight, and divided into twenty-one books, chaptered and imprinted and finished in the Abbey Westmestre, the last day of July, the year of our Lord MCCCCLXXXV.

Caxton me fieri fecit.

PART TWO

THE MABINOGEON

CHAPTER XIX

THE BRITONS

THE earliest inhabitants of Britain are supposed to have been a branch of that great family known in history by the designation of Celts. Cambria, which is a frequent name for Wales, is thought to be derived from Cymri, the name which the Welsh traditions apply to an immigrant people who entered the island from the adjacent continent. This name is thought to be identical with those of Cimmerians and Cimbri, under which the Greek and Roman historians describe a barbarous people, who spread themselves from the north of the Euxine over the whole of Northwestern Europe.

The origin of the names *Wales* and *Welsh* has been much canvassed. Some writers make them a derivation from Gael or Gaul, which names are said to signify "woodlanders;" others observe that *Walsh*, in the Northern languages, signifies *a stranger*, and that the aboriginal Britons were so called by those who at a later era invaded the island and possessed the greater part of it, the Saxons and Angles.

The Romans held Britain from the invasion of Julius Cæsar till their voluntary withdrawal from the island, A.D. 420,—that is, about five hundred years. In that time there must have been a wide diffusion of their arts and institutions among the natives. The remains of roads, cities, and fortifications show that they did much to develop and improve the country, while those of their villas and castles prove that many of the settlers possessed wealth and taste for the ornamental arts. Yet the Roman sway was sustained chiefly by force, and never extended over the entire island. The northern portion, now Scotland, remained independent, and the western portion, constituting Wales and Cornwall, was only nominally subjected.

Neither did the later invading hordes succeed in subduing the remoter sections of the island. For ages after the arrival of the Saxons under Hengist and Horsa, A.D. 449, the whole western coast of Britain was possessed by the aboriginal habitants, engaged in constant warfare with the invaders.

It has, therefore, been a favorite boast of the people of Wales and Cornwall, that the original British stock flourishes in its unmixed purity only among them. We see this notion flashing out in poetry occasionally, as when Gray, in "The Bard," prophetically describing Queen Elizabeth, who was of the Tudor, a Welsh race, says:

"Her eye proclaims her of the Briton line";

and, contrasting the princes of the Tudor with those of the Norman race, he exclaims:

"All hail, ye genuine kings, Britannia's issue, hail!"

THE WELSH LANGUAGE AND LITERATURE

THE Welsh language is one of the oldest in Europe. It possesses poems the origin of which is referred with probability to the sixth century. The language of some of these is so antiquated, that the best scholars differ about the interpretation of many passages; but, generally speaking, the body of poetry which the Welsh possess, from the year 1000 downwards, is intelligible to those who are acquainted with the modern language.

Till within the last half-century these compositions remained buried in the libraries of colleges or of individuals, and so difficult of access that no successful attempt was made to give them to the world. This reproach was removed, after ineffectual appeals to the patriotism of the gentry of Wales, by Owen Jones, a furrier of London, who at his own expense collected and published the chief productions of Welsh literature, under the title of the Myvyrian Archæology of Wales. In this task he was assisted by Dr. Owen and other Welsh scholars.

After the cessation of Jones's exertions, the old apathy returned, and continued till within a few years. Dr. Owen exerted himself to obtain support for the publication of the Mabinogeon, or Prose Tales of the Welsh, but died without accomplishing his purpose, which has since been carried into execution by Lady Charlotte Guest. The legends which fill the remainder of this volume are taken from this work, of which we have already spoken more fully in the introductory chapter to the First Part.

THE WELSH BARDS

THE authors to whom the oldest Welsh poems are attributed are Aneurin, who is supposed to have lived A.D. 500 and 550, and Taliesin, Llywarch Hen (Llywarch the Aged), and Myrddin or Merlin, who were a few years later. The authenticity of the poems which bear their names has been assailed, and it is still an open question how many and which of them are authentic, though it is hardly to be doubted that some are so. The poem of Aneurin, entitled the "Gododin," bears very strong marks of authenticity. Aneurin was one of the Northern Britons of Strath-Clyde, who have left to that part of the district they inhabited the name of Cumberland, or Land of the Cymri. In this poem he laments the defeat of his countrymen by the Saxons at the battle of Cattraeth, in consequence of having partaken too freely of the mead before joining in combat. The bard himself and two of his fellow-warriors were all who escaped from the field. A portion of this poem has been translated by Gray, of which the following is an extract:

"To Cattraeth's vale, in glittering row,
Twice two hundred warriors go;
Every warrior's marily neck
Chains of regal honor deck,
Wreathed in many a golden link;
From the golden cup they drink
Nectar that the bees produce,
Or the grape's exalted juice.
Flushed with mirth and hope they burn,
But none to Cattraeth's vale return,
Save Aëron brave, and Conan strong,
Bursting through the bloody throng,
And I, the meanest of them all,
That live to weep, and sing their fall."

The works of Taliesin are of much more questionable authenticity. There is a story of the adventures of Taliesin so strongly marked with mythical traits as to cast suspicion on the writings attributed to him. This story will be found in the subsequent pages.

THE TRIADS

THE Triads are a peculiar species of poetical composition, of which the Welsh bards have left numerous examples. They are enumerations of a triad of persons, or events, or observations, strung together in one short sentence. This form of composition, originally invented, in all likelihood, to assist the memory, has been raised by the Welsh to a degree of elegance of which it hardly at first sight appears susceptible. The Triads are of all ages, some of them probably as old as anything in the language. Short as they are individually, the collection in the Myvyrian Archæology occupies more than one hundred and seventy pages of double columns. We will give some specimens, beginning with personal triads, and giving the first place to one of King Arthur's own composition:

"I have three heroes in battle;
Mael the tall, and Llyr, with his army,
And Caradoc, the pillar of Wales."

"The three principal bards of the island of Britain:
Merlin Ambrose
Merlin the son of Morfyn, called also Merlin the Wild,
And Taliesin, the chief of the bards."

"The three golden-tongued knights of the Court of Arthur:
Gawain, son of Gwyar,
Drydvas, son of Tryphin,
And Eliwlod, son of Madag, ap Uther."

"The three honorable feasts of the island of Britain:
The feast of Caswallaun, after repelling Julius Caesar from this isle,
The feast of Aurelius Ambrosius, after he had conquered the Saxons;
And the feast of King Arthur, at Caerleon upon Usk."

"Guenever, the daughter of Laodegan the giant,
Bad when little, worse when great."

Next follow some moral triads:

"Hast thou heard what Dremhidydd sung,
An ancient watchman on the castle walls?
A refusal is better than a promise unperformed."

"Hast thou heard what Llenleawg sung,
The noble chief wearing the golden torques?
The grave is better than a life of want."

"Hast thou heard what Garselit sung,
The Irishman whom it is safe to follow?
Sin is bad, if long pursued."

"Hast thou heard what Avaon sung,
The son of Taliesin, of the recording verse?
The cheek will not conceal the anguish of the heart."

"Didst thou hear what Llywarch sung,
The intrepid and brave old man?
Greet kindly, though there be no acquaintance."

CHAPTER XX

THE LADY OF THE FOUNTAIN

KYNON'S ADVENTURE

KING ARTHUR was at Caerleon upon Usk; and one day he sat in his chamber, and with him were Owain the son of Urien, and Kynon the son of Clydno, and Kay the son of Kyner, and Guenever and her hand-maidens at needlework by the window. In the centre of the chamber King Arthur sat, upon a seat of green rushes[1] over which was spread a covering of flame-colored satin, and a cushion of red satin was under his elbow.

Then Arthur spoke. "If I thought you would not disparage me," said he, "I would sleep while I wait for my repast; and you can entertain one another with relating tales, and can obtain a flagon of mead and some meat from Kay." And the king went to sleep. And Kynon the son of Clydno asked Kay for that which Arthur had promised them. "I too will have the good tale which he promised me," said Kay. "Nay," answered Kynon; "fairer will it be for thee to fulfil Arthur's behest in the first place, and then we will tell thee the best tale that we know." So Kay went to the kitchen and to the mead-cellar, and returned, bearing a flagon of mead, and a golden goblet, and a handful of skewers, upon which were broiled collops of meat. Then they ate the collops, and began to drink the mead. "Now," said Kay, "it is time for you to give me my story." "Kynon," said Owain, "do thou pay to Kay the tale that is his due." "I will do so," answered Kynon.

"I was the only son of my mother and father, and I was exceedingly aspiring, and my daring was very great. I thought there was no enterprise in the world too mighty for me; and after I had achieved all the adventures that were in my own country, I equipped myself, and set forth to journey through deserts and distant regions. And at length it chanced that I came to the fairest valley in the world, wherein were trees all of equal growth; and a river ran through the valley, and a path was by the side of the river. And I followed the path until midday, and continued my journey along the remainder of the valley until the evening; and at the extremity of a plain I came to a large and lustrous castle, at the foot of which was a torrent. And I approached the castle, and there I beheld two youths with yellow curling hair, each with a frontlet of gold upon his head, and clad in a garment of yellow satin; and they had gold clasps upon their insteps. In the hand of each of them was an ivory bow, strung with the sinews of the stag, and their arrows and their shafts were of the bone of the whale, and were winged with peacocks' feathers. The shafts also had golden heads. And they had daggers with blades of gold, and with hilts of the bone of the whale. And they were shooting at a mark.

"And a little way from them I saw a man in the prime of life, with his beard newly shorn, clad in a robe and mantle of yellow satin, and round the top of his mantle was a band of gold lace. On his feet were shoes of variegated leather,[2] fastened by two bosses of gold. When I saw him I went towards him and saluted him; and such was his courtesy, that he no sooner received my greeting than he returned it. And he went with me towards the castle. Now there were no dwellers in the castle, except those who were in one hall. And there I saw four and twenty damsels, embroidering satin at a window. And this I tell thee, Kay, that the least fair of them was fairer than the fairest maid thou didst ever behold in the island of Britain; and the least lovely of them was more lovely than Guenever, the wife of Arthur, when she appeared loveliest, at the feast of Easter. They rose up at my coming, and six of them took my horse, and divested me of my armor, and six others took my arms, and washed them in a vessel till they were perfectly bright. And the third six spread cloths upon the tables, and prepared meat. And the fourth six took off

---

[1]The use of green rushes in apartments was by no means peculiar to the court of Caerleon upon Usk. Our ancestors had a great predilection for them, and they seem to have constituted an essential article, not only of comfort but of luxury. The custom of strewing the floor with rushes, it is well known, existed in England during the Middle Ages, and also in France.

[2]*Cordwal* is the word in the original, and from the manner in which it is used it is evidently intended for the French Cordouan or Cordovan leather, which derived its name from Cordova, where it was manufactured. From this comes also our English word *cordwainer*.

my soiled garments, and placed others upon me, namely, an under vest and a doublet of fine linen, and a robe and a surcoat, and a mantle of yellow satin, with a broad gold band upon the mantle. And they placed cushions both beneath and around me, with coverings of red linen. And I sat down. Now the six maidens who had taken my horse unharnessed him as well as if they had been the best squires in the island of Britain.

"Then behold they brought bowls of silver, wherein was water to wash, and towels of linen, some green and some white; and I washed. And in a little while the man sat down at the table. And I sat next to him, and below me sat all the maidens, except those who waited on us. And the table was of silver, and the cloths upon the table were of linen. And no vessel was served upon the table that was not either of gold or of silver or of buffalo-horn. And our meat was brought to us. And verily, Kay, I saw there every sort of meat and every sort of liquor that I ever saw elsewhere; but the meat and the liquor were better served there than I ever saw them in any other place.

"Until the repast was half over, neither the man nor any one of the damsels spoke a single word to me; but when the man perceived that it would be more agreeable for me to converse than to eat any more, he began to inquire of me who I was. Then I told the man who I was, and what was the cause of my journey, and said that I was seeking whether any one was superior to me, or whether I could gain the mastery over all. The man looked upon me, and he smiled and said, 'If I did not fear to do thee a mischief, I would show thee that which thou seekest.' Then I desired him to speak freely. And he said: 'Sleep here tonight, and in the morning arise early, and take the road upwards through the valley, until thou reachest the wood. A little way within the wood thou wilt come to a large sheltered glade, with a mound in the centre. And thou wilt see a black man of great stature on the top of the mound. He has but one foot, and one eye in the middle of his forehead. He is the wood-ward of that wood. And thou wilt see a thousand wild animals grazing around him. Inquire of him the way out of the glade, and he will reply to thee briefly, and will point out the road by which thou shalt find that which thou art in quest of.'

"And long seemed that night to me. And the next morning I arose and equipped myself, and mounted my horse, and proceeded straight through the valley to the wood, and at length I arrived at the glade. And the black man was there, sitting upon the top of the mound; and I was three times more astonished at the number of wild animals that I beheld, than the man had said I should be. Then I inquired of him the way, and he asked me roughly whither I would go. And when I had told him who I was, and what I sought, 'Take,' said he, 'that path that leads toward the head of the glade, and there thou wilt find an open space like to a large valley, and in the midst of it a tall tree. Under this tree is a fountain, and by the side of the fountain a marble slab, and on the marble slab a silver bowl, attached by a chain of silver, that it may not be carried away. Take the bowl, and throw a bowlful of water on the slab. And if thou dost not find trouble in that adventure, thou needest not seek it during the rest of thy life.'

"So I journeyed on until I reached the summit of the steep. And there I found everything as the black man had described it to me. And I went up to the tree, and beneath it I saw the fountain, and by its side the marble slab, and the silver bowl fastened by the chain. Then I took the bowl, and cast a bowlful of water upon the slab. And immediately I heard a mighty peal of thunder, so that heaven and earth seemed to tremble with its fury. And after the thunder came a shower; and of a truth I tell thee, Kay, that it was such a shower as neither man nor beast could endure and live. I turned my horse's flank toward the shower, and placed the beak of my shield over his head and neck, while I held the upper part of it over my own neck. And thus I withstood the shower. And presently the sky became clear, and with that, behold, the birds lighted upon the tree, and sang. And truly, Kay, I never heard any melody equal to that, either before or since. And when I was most charmed with listening to the birds, lo! a chiding voice was heard of one approaching me, and saying, 'O knight, what has brought thee hither? What evil have I done to thee, that thou shouldst act towards me and my possessions as thou hast this day? Dost thou not know that the shower today has left in my dominions neither man nor beast alive that was exposed to it?' And thereupon, behold, a knight on a black horse appeared, clothed in jet-black velvet, and with a tabard of black linen about him. And we charged each other, and, as the onset was furious, it was not long before I was overthrown. Then the knight passed the shaft of his lance through the bridle-rein of my horse, and rode off with the two horses, leaving me where I was. And he did not even bestow so much notice upon me as to imprison me, nor did he despoil me of my arms. So I returned along the road by which I had come. And when I reached the glade where the black man was, I confess to thee, Kay, it is a marvel that I did not melt down into a liquid pool, through the shame I felt at the black man's derision. And that night I came to the same castle where I had spent the night preceding. And I was more agreeably entertained that night than I had been the night before. And I conversed freely with the inmates of the castle; and none of them alluded to my expedition to the fountain, neither did I mention it to any. And I remained there that night. When I arose on the morrow I found ready saddled a dark bay palfrey, with nostrils as red as scarlet. And after putting on my armor, and leaving there my blessing, I returned to my own court. And that horse I still possess, and he is in the stable yonder. And I declare that I would not part with him for the best palfrey in the island of Britain.

"Now, of a truth, Kay, no man ever before confessed to an adventure so much to his own discredit; and verily it seems strange to me that neither before nor since have I heard of any person who knew of this adventure, and that the subject of it should exist within King Arthur's dominions without any other person lighting upon it."

CHAPTER XXI

THE LADY OF THE FOUNTAIN, CONTINUED

OWAIN'S ADVENTURE[1]

So quoth Owain, "Now, would it not be well to go and endeavor to discover that place?"

"By the hand of my friend," said Kay, "often dost thou utter that with thy tongue which thou wouldest not make good with thy deeds."

"In very truth," said Guenever, "it were better thou were hanged, Kay, than to use such uncourteous speech towards a man like Owain."

"By the hand of my friend, good lady," said Kay; "thy praise of Owain is not greater than mine."

With that Arthur awoke, and asked if he had not been sleeping a little.

"Yes, lord," answered Owain, "thou hast slept awhile."

"Is it time for us to go to meat?"

"It is, lord," said Owain.

Then the horn for washing was sounded, and the king and all his household sat down to eat. And when the meal was ended, Owain withdrew to his lodging, and made ready his horse and his arms.

---

[1]Amongst all the characters of early British history none is more interesting or occupies a more conspicuous place, than the hero of this tale. Urien, his father, was prince of Rheged, a district comprising the present Cumberland and part of the adjacent country. His valor and the consideration in which he was held are a frequent theme of Bardic song, and form the subject of several very spirited odes by Taliesin. Among the Triads there is one relating to him; it is thus translated:

"Three knights of Battle were in the court of Arthur: Cadwr the Earl of Cornwall, Launcelot du Lac, and Owain the son of Urien. And this was their characteristic,—that they would not retreat from battle, neither for spear, nor for arrow, nor for sword. And Arthur never had shame in battle the day he saw their faces there. And they were called the Knights of Battle."

On the morrow with the dawn of day he put on his armor, and mounted his charger, and travelled through distant lands, and over desert mountains. And at length he arrived at the valley which Kynon had described to him, and he was certain that it was the same that he sought. And journeying along the valley, by the side of the river, he followed its course till he came to the plain, and within sight of the castle. When he approached the castle, he saw the youths shooting with their bows, in the place where Kynon had seen them, and the yellow man, to whom the castle belonged, standing hard by. And no sooner had Owain saluted the yellow man, than he was saluted by him in return.

And he went forward towards the castle, and there he saw the chamber; and when he had entered the chamber, he beheld the maidens working at satin embroidery, in chains of gold. And their beauty and their comeliness seemed to Owain far greater than Kynon had represented to him. And they arose to wait upon Owain, as they had done to Kynon. And the meal which they set before him gave even more satisfaction to Owain than it had done to Kynon.

About the middle of the repast the yellow man asked Owain the object of his journey. And Owain made it known to him, and said, "I am in quest of the knight who guards the fountain." Upon this the yellow man smiled, and said that he was as loath to point out that adventure to him as he had been to Kynon. However, he described the whole to Owain, and they retired to rest.

The next morning Owain found his horse made ready for him by the damsels, and he set forward and came to the glade where the black man was. And the stature of the black man seemed more wonderful to Owain than it had done to Kynon; and Owain asked of him his road, and he showed it to him. And Owain followed the road till he came to the green tree; and he beheld the fountain, and the slab beside the fountain, and the bowl upon it. And Owain took the bowl and threw a bowlful of water upon the slab. And, lo! the thunder was heard, and after the thunder came the shower, more violent than Kynon had described, and after the shower the sky became bright. And immediately the birds came and settled upon the tree and sang. And when their song was most pleasing to

Owain, he beheld a knight coming towards him through the valley; and he prepared to receive him, and encountered him violently. Having broken both their lances, they drew their swords and fought blade to blade. Then Owain struck the knight a blow through his helmet, head-piece, and visor, and through the skin, and the flesh, and the bone, until it wounded the very brain. Then the black knight felt that he had received a mortal wound, upon which he turned his horse's head and fled. And Owain pursued him, and followed close upon him, although he was not near enough to strike him with his sword. Then Owain descried a vast and resplendent castle; and they came to the castle gate. And the black knight was allowed to enter, and the portcullis was let fall upon Owain; and it struck his horse behind the saddle, and cut him in two, and carried away the rowels of the spurs that were upon Owain's heels. And the portcullis descended to the floor. And the rowels of the spurs and part of the horse were without, and Owain with the other part of the horse remained between the two gates, and the inner gate was closed, so that Owain could not go thence; and Owain was in a perplexing situation. And while he was in this state, he could see through an aperture in the gate a street facing him, with a row of houses on each side. And he beheld a maiden, with yellow, curling hair, and a frontlet of gold upon her head; and she was clad in a dress of yellow satin, and on her feet were shoes of variegated leather. And she approached the gate, and desired that it should be opened. "Heaven knows, lady," said Owain, "it is no more possible for me to open to thee from hence, than it is for thee to set me free." And he told her his name, and who he was. "Truly," said the damsel, "it is very sad that thou canst not be released; and every woman ought to succor thee, for I know there is no one more faithful in the service of ladies than thou. Therefore," quoth she, "whatever is in my power to do for thy release, I will do it. Take this ring, and put it on thy finger, with the stone inside thy hand, and close thy hand upon the stone. And as long as thou concealest it, it will conceal thee. When they come forth to fetch thee, they will be much grieved that they cannot find thee. And I will await thee on the horseblock yonder, and thou wilt be able to see me, though I cannot see thee.

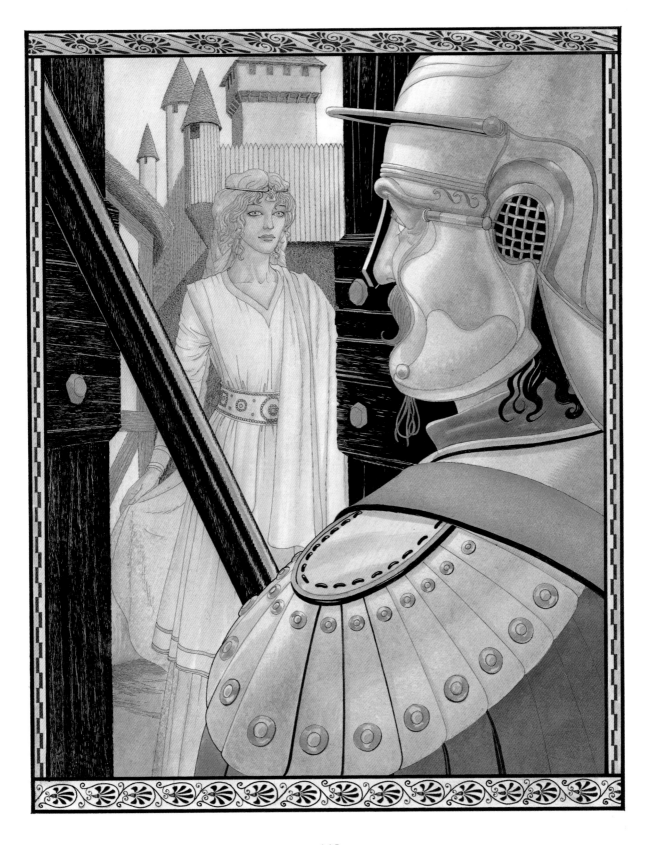

Therefore come and place thy hand upon my shoulder, that I may know that thou art near me. And by the way that I go hence, do thou accompany me."

Then the maiden went away from Owain, and he did all that she had told him. And the people of the castle came to seek Owain to put him to death; and when they found nothing but the half of his horse, they were sorely grieved.

And Owain vanished from among them, and went to the maiden, and placed his hand upon her shoulder; whereupon she set off, and Owain followed her, until they came to the door of a large and beautiful chamber, and the maiden opened it, and they went in. And Owain looked around the chamber, and behold there was not a single nail in it that was not painted with gorgeous colors, and there was not a single panel that had not sundry images in gold portrayed upon it.

The maiden kindled a fire, and took water in a silver bowl, and gave Owain water to wash. Then she placed before him a silver table, inlaid with gold; upon which was a cloth of yellow linen, and she brought him food. And, of a truth, Owain never saw any kind of meat that was not there in abundance, but it was better cooked there than he had ever found it in any other place. And there was not one vessel from which he was served that was not of gold or of silver. And Owain ate and drank until late in the afternoon, when, lo! they heard a mighty clamor in the castle, and Owain asked the maiden what it was. "They are administering extreme unction," said she, "to the nobleman who owns the castle." And she prepared a couch for Owain which was meet for Arthur himself, and Owain went to sleep.

And a little after daybreak he heard an exceeding loud clamor and wailing, and asked the maiden what was the cause of it. "They are bearing to the church the body of the nobleman who owned the castle."

And Owain rose up, and clothed himself, and opened a window of the chamber, and looked towards the castle; and he could see neither the bounds nor the extent of the hosts that filled the streets. And they were fully armed; and a vast number of women were with them, both on horseback and on foot, and all the ecclesiastics in the city singing. In the midst of the throng he beheld the bier, over which was a veil of white linen; and wax tapers were burning beside and around it; and none that supported the bier was lower in rank than a powerful baron.

Never did Owain see an assemblage so gorgeous with silk[1] and satin. And, following the train, he beheld a lady with yellow hair falling over her shoulders, and stained with blood; and about her a dress of yellow satin, which was torn. Upon her feet were shoes of variegated leather. And it was a marvel that the ends of her fingers were not bruised from the violence with which she smote her hands together. Truly she would have been the fairest lady Owain ever saw had she been in her usual guise. And her cry was louder than the shout of the men or the clamor of the trumpets. No sooner had he beheld the lady than he became inflamed with her love, so that it took entire possession of him.

Then he inquired of the maiden who the lady was. "Heaven knows," replied the maiden, "she is the fairest, and the most chaste, and the most liberal, and the most noble of women. She is my mistress, and she is called the Countess of the Fountain, the wife of him whom thou didst slay yesterday." "Verily," said Owain, "she is the woman that I love best." "Verily," said the maiden, "she shall also love thee, not a little."

Then the maiden prepared a repast for Owain, and truly he thought he had never before so good a meal, nor was he ever so well served. Then she left him, and went towards the castle. When she came there she found nothing but mourning and sorrow; and the Countess in her chamber could not bear the sight of any one through grief. Luned, for that was the name of the maiden, saluted her, but the Countess answered her not. And the maiden bent down towards her, and said, "What aileth thee that

---

[1]Before the sixth century all the silk used by Europeans had been brought to them by the Seres, the ancestors of the present Boukharians, whence it derived its Latin name of Serica. In 551 the silkworm was brought by two monks to Constantinople; but the manufacture of silk was continued to the Greek empire till the year 1130, when Roger, king of Sicily, returning from a crusade, collected some manufacturers from Athens and Corinth, and established them at Palermo, whence the trade was gradually disseminated over Italy. The varieties of silk stuffs known at this time were velvet, satin (which was called *samite*), and taffety (called *cendal* or *sendall*), all of which were occasionally stitched with gold and silver.

thou answerest no one today?" "Luned," said the Countess, "what change hath befallen thee that thou hast not come to visit me in my grief? It was wrong in thee, and I so sorely afflicted." "Truly," said Luned, "I thought thy good sense was greater than I find it to be. Is it well for thee to mourn after that good man, or for anything else that thou canst not have?" "I declare to heaven," said the Countess, "that in the whole world there is not a man equal to him." "Not so," said Luned, "for an ugly man would be as good as, or better than he." "I declare to heaven," said the Countess, "that were it not repugnant to me to put to death one whom I have brought up I would have thee executed for making such comparison to me. As it is, I will banish thee." "I am glad," said Luned, "that thou hast no other cause to do so than that I would have been of service to thee, where thou didst not know what was to thine advantage. Henceforth evil betide whichever of us shall make the first advance towards reconciliation to the other, whether I should seek an invitation from thee, or thou of thine own accord shouldst send to invite me."

With that Luned went forth; and the Countess arose and followed her to the door of the chamber, and began coughing loudly. And when Luned looked back the Countess beckoned to her, and she returned to the Countess. "In truth," said the Countess, "evil is thy disposition; but if thou knowest what is to my advantage, declare it to me." "I will do so," said she.

"Thou knowest that, except by warfare and arms, it is impossible for thee to preserve thy possessions; delay not, therefore, to seek some one who can defend them." "And how can I do that?" said the Countess. "I will tell thee," said Luned; "unless thou canst defend the fountain thou canst not maintain thy dominions; and no one can defend the fountain except it be a knight of Arthur's household. I will go to Arthur's court, and ill betide me if I return not thence with a warrior who can guard the fountain as well as, or even better, than he who defended it formerly." "That will be hard to perform," said the Countess. "Go, however, and make proof of that which thou hast promised."

Luned set out under the pretence of going to Arthur's court; but she went back to the mansion where she had left Owain, and she tarried there as long as it might have taken her to travel to the court of King Arthur and back. And at the end of that time she apparelled herself, and went to visit the Countess. And the Countess was much rejoiced when she saw her, and inquired what news she brought from the court. "I bring thee the best of news," said Luned, "for I have compassed the object of my mission. When wilt thou that I should present to thee the chieftain who has come with me thither?" "Bring him here to visit me tomorrow," said the Countess, "and I will cause the town to be assembled by that time."

And Luned returned home. And the next day, at noon, Owain arrayed himself in a coat and a surcoat, and a mantle of yellow satin, upon which was a broad band of gold lace; and on his feet were high shoes of variegated leather, which

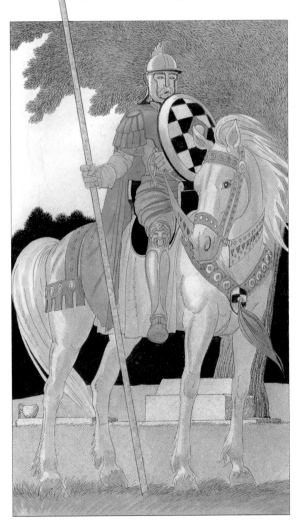

were fastened by golden clasps, in the form of lions. And they proceeded to the chamber of the Countess.

Right glad was the Countess of their coming. And she gazed steadfastly upon Owain, and said, "Luned, this knight has not the look of a traveller." "What harm is there in that, lady?" said Luned. "I am certain," said the Countess, "that no other man than this chased the soul from the body of my lord." "So much the better for thee, lady," said Luned, "for had he not been stronger than thy lord, he could not have deprived him of life. There is no remedy for that which is past, be it as it may." "Go back to thine abode," said the Countess, "and I will take counsel."

The next day the Countess caused all her subjects to assemble, and showed them that her earldom was left defenceless, and that it could not be protected but with horse and arms, and military skill. "Therefore," said she, "this is what I offer for your choice: either let one of you take me, or give your consent for me to take a husband from elsewhere, to defend my dominions."

So they came to the determination that it was better that she should have permission to marry some one from elsewhere; and thereupon she sent for the bishops and archbishops, to celebrate her nuptials with Owain. And the men of the earldom did Owain homage.

And Owain defended the fountain with lance and ◁121 sword. And this is the manner in which he defended it. Whensoever a knight came there, he overthrew him, and sold him for his full worth. And what he thus gained he divided among his barons and his knights, and no man in the whole world could be more beloved than he was by his subjects. And it was thus for the space of three years.[1]

---

[1]There exists an ancient poem, printed among those of Taliesin, called the Elegy of Owain ap Urien, and containing several very beautiful and spirited passages. It commences:

"The soul of Owain ap Urien,
May its Lord consider its exigencies!
Reged's chief the green turf covers."

In the course of this Elegy, the bard, alluding to the incessant warfare with which this chieftain harassed his Saxon foes, exclaims:

"Could England sleep with the light upon her eyes!"

CHAPTER XXII

THE LADY OF THE FOUNTAIN, CONTINUED

GAWAIN'S ADVENTURE

IT befell that, as Gawain went forth one day with King Arthur, he perceived him to be very sad and sorrowful. And Gawain was much grieved to see Arthur in this state, and he questioned him, saying, "O my lord, what has befallen thee?" "In sooth, Gawain," said Arthur, "I am grieved concerning Owain, whom I have lost these three years; and I shall certainly die if the fourth year pass without my seeing him. Now I am sure that it is through the tale which Kynon, the son of Clydno, related, that I have lost Owain." "There is no need for thee," said Gawain, "to summon to arms thy whole dominions on this account, for thou thyself, and the men of thy household, will be able to avenge Owain if he be slain, or to set him free if he be in prison; and, if alive, to bring him back with thee." And it was settled according to what Gawain had said.

Then Arthur and the men of his household prepared to go and seek Owain. And Kynon, the son of Clydno, acted as their guide. And Arthur came to the castle where Kynon had been before. And when he came there, the youths were shooting in the same place, and the yellow man was standing hard by. When the yellow man saw Arthur, he greeted him, and invited him to the castle. And Arthur accepted his invitation, and they entered the castle together. And great as was the number of his retinue, their presence was scarcely observed in the castle, so vast was its extent. And the maidens rose up to wait on them. And the service of the maidens appeared to them all to excel any attendance they had ever met with; and even the pages, who had charge of the horses, were no worse served that night than Arthur himself would have been in his own palace.

The next morning Arthur set out thence, with Kynon for his guide, and came to the place where the black man was. And the stature of the black man was more surprising to Arthur than it had been represented to him. And they came to the top of the wooded steep, and traversed the valley, till they reached the green tree, where they saw the fountain and the bowl and the slab. And upon that Kay came to Arthur, and spoke to him. "My lord," said he, "I know the meaning of all this, and my request is that thou wilt permit me to throw the water on the slab, and to receive the first adventure that may befall." And Arthur gave him leave.

Then Kay threw a bowlful of water upon the slab, and immediately there came the thunder, and after the thunder the shower. And such a thunder-storm they had never known before. After the shower had ceased, the sky became clear, and on looking at the tree, they beheld it completely leafless. Then the birds descended upon the tree. And the song of the birds was far sweeter than any strain they had ever heard before. Then they beheld a knight, on a coal-black horse, clothed in black satin, coming rapidly towards them. And Kay met him and encountered him, and it was not long before Kay was overthrown. And the knight withdrew. And Arthur and his host encamped for the night.

And when they arose in the morning, they perceived the signal of combat upon the lance of the knight. Then, one by one, all the household of Arthur went forth to combat the knight, until there was not one that was not overthrown by him, except Arthur and Gawain. And Arthur armed himself to encounter the knight. "O my lord," said Gawain, "permit me to fight with him first." And Arthur permitted him. And he went forth to meet the knight, having over himself and his horse a satin robe of honor, which had been sent him by the daughter of the earl of Rhangyr, and in this dress he was not known by any of the host. And they charged each other, and fought all that day until the evening. And neither of them was able to unhorse the other. And so it was the next day; they broke their lances in the shock, but neither of them could obtain the mastery.

And the third day they fought with exceeding strong lances. And they were incensed with rage, and fought furiously, even until noon. And they gave each other such a shock, that the girths of their horses were broken, so that they fell over their horses' cruppers to the ground. And they rose up speedily and drew their swords, and resumed the combat. And all they that witnessed their encounter felt assured that they had never before seen two men so valiant or so powerful. And had it been midnight, it would have been light, from the fire that flashed from their weapons. And the knight gave Gawain a blow that turned his helmet from off his face, so that the knight saw that it was Gawain. Then Owain said, "My lord Gawain, I did not know thee for my cousin, owing to the robe of honor that enveloped thee; take my sword and my arms." Said Gawain, "Thou, Owain, art the victor; take thou my sword." And with that Arthur saw that they were conversing, and advanced toward them. "My lord Arthur," said Gawain, "here is Owain who has vanquished me, and will not take my arms." "My lord," said Owain, "it is he that has vanquished me, and he will not take my sword." "Give me your swords," said Arthur, "and then neither of you has vanquished the other." Then Owain put his arms around Arthur's neck, and they embraced. And all the host hurried forward, to see Owain, and to embrace him. And there was nigh being a loss of life, so great was the press.

And they retired that night, and the next day Arthur prepared to depart. "My lord," said Owain, "this is not well of thee. For I have been absent from thee these three years, and during all that time, up to this very day, I have been preparing a banquet for thee, knowing that thou wouldst come to seek me. Tarry with me, therefore, until thou and thy attendants have recovered the fatigues of the journey, and have been anointed."

And they all proceeded to the castle of the Countess of the Fountain and the banquet which had been three years preparing was consumed in three months. Never had they a more delicious or agreeable banquet. And Arthur prepared to depart. Then he sent an embassy to the Countess to beseech her to permit Owain to go with him for the space of three months, that he might show him to the nobles and the fair dames of the island of Britain. And the Countess gave her consent, although it was very painful to her. So Owain came with Arthur to the island of Britain. And when he was once more amongst his kindred and friends, he remained three years, instead of three months, with them.

THE ADVENTURE OF THE LION

AND as Owain one day sat at meat, in the city of Caerleon upon Usk, behold a damsel entered the hall, upon a bay horse,[1] with a curling mane, and covered with foam; and the bridle, and as much as was seen of the saddle, were of gold. And the damsel was arrayed in a dress of yellow satin. And she came up to Owain, and took the ring from off his hand. "Thus," said she, "shall be treated the deceiver, the traitor, the faithless, the disgraced, and the beardless." And she turned her horse's head, and departed.

Then his adventure came to Owain's remembrance, and he was sorrowful. And having finished eating, he went to his own abode, and made preparations that night. And the next day he arose, but did not go to the court, nor did he return to the Countess of the Fountain, but wandered to the distant parts of the earth and to uncultivated mountains. And he remained there until all his apparel was worn out and his body was wasted away, and his hair was grown long. And he went about with the wild beasts, and fed with them, until they became familiar with him. But at length he became so weak that he could no longer bear them company. Then he descended from the mountains to the valley, and came to a park, that was the fairest in the world, and belonged to a charitable lady.

One day the lady and her attendants went forth to walk by a lake that was in the middle of the park. And they saw the form of a man lying as if dead. And they were terrified. Nevertheless they went near him, and touched him, and they saw that there was life in him. And the lady returned to the castle, and took a flask full of precious ointment and gave it to one of her maidens. "Go with this," said she, "and take with thee yonder horse, and clothing, and place them near the man we saw just now, and anoint him with this balsam near his heart; and if there is life in him he will revive, through the efficiency of this balsam. Then watch what he will do."

And the maiden departed from her, and went and poured of the balsam upon Owain, and left the horse and the garments hard by, and went a little way off

---

[1]The custom of riding into a hall while the lord and his guests sat at meals might be illustrated by numerous passages of ancient romance and history. But a quotation from Chaucer's beautiful and half-told tale of Cambuscan is sufficient:

"And so befell that after the thridde cours,
While that this king sat thus in his nobley,
Herking his minstralles thir thinges play,
Beforne him at his bord deliciously,
In at the halle door all sodenly
Ther came a knight upon a stede of bras,
And in his hond a brod mirrour of glas,
Upon his thombe he had of gold a ring,
And by his side a naked sword hanging;
And up he rideth to the highe bord.
In all the halle ne was ther spoke a word,
For mervaille of this knight; him to behold
Full besily they waiten, young and old."

and hid herself to watch him. In a short time she saw him begin to move; and he rose up and looked at his person, and became ashamed of the unseemliness of his appearance. Then he perceived the horse and the garments that were near him. And he clothed himself, and with difficulty mounted the horse. Then the damsel discovered herself to him, and saluted him. And he and the maiden proceeded to the castle, and the maiden conducted him to a pleasant chamber, and kindled a fire, and left him.

And he stayed at the castle three months, till he was restored to his former guise, and became even more comely than he had ever been before. And Owain rendered signal service to the lady in a controversy with a powerful neighbor, so that he made ample requital to her for her hospitality; and he took his departure.

And as he journeyed he heard a loud yelling in a wood. And it was repeated a second and a third time. And Owain went towards the spot, and beheld a huge craggy mound, in the middle of the wood, on the side of which was a gray rock. And there was a cleft in the rock, and a serpent was within the cleft. And near the rock stood a black lion, and every time the lion sought to go thence the serpent darted towards him to attack him. And Owain unsheathed his sword, and ◁125 drew near to the rock; and as the serpent sprung out he struck him with his sword and cut him in two. And he dried his sword, and went on his way as before. But behold the lion followed him, and played about him, as though it had been a greyhound that he had reared.

They proceeded thus throughout the day, until the evening. And when it was time for Owain to take his rest he dismounted, and turned his horse loose in a flat and wooded meadow. And he struck fire, and when the fire was kindled the lion brought him fuel enough to last for three nights. And the lion disappeared. And presently the lion returned, bearing a fine large roebuck. And he threw it down before Owain, who went towards the fire with it.

And Owain took the roebuck and skinned it, and placed collops of its flesh upon skewers round the fire. The rest of the buck he gave to the lion to devour. While he was so employed he heard a deep groan near him, and a second, and a third. And the place whence the groans proceeded was a cave in the rock;

and Owain went near, and called out to know who it was that groaned so piteously. And a voice answered, "I am Luned, the handmaiden of the Countess of the Fountain." "And what dost thou here?" said he. "I am imprisoned," said she, "on account of the knight who came from Arthur's court and married the Countess. And he stayed a short time with her, but he afterwards departed for the court of Arthur, and has not returned since. And two of the Countess's pages traduced him, and called him a deceiver. And because I said I would vouch for it he would come before long and maintain his cause against both of them they imprisoned me in this cave, and said that I should be put to death unless he came to deliver me by a certain day; and that is no further off than tomorrow, and I have no one to send to seek him for me. His name is Owain, the son of Urien." "And art thou certain that if that knight knew all this he would come to thy rescue?" "I am most certain of it," said she.

When the collops were cooked, Owain divided them into two parts, between himself and the maiden, and then Owain laid himself down to sleep; and never did sentinel keep stricter watch over his lord than the lion that night over Owain.

And the next day there came two pages with a great troop of attendants to take Luned from her cell, and put her to death. And Owain asked them what charge they had against her. And they told him of the compact that was between them; as the maiden had done the night before. "And," said they, "Owain has failed her, therefore we are taking her to be burnt." "Truly," said Owain, "he is a good knight, and if he knew that the maiden was in such peril, I marvel that he came not to her rescue. But if you will accept me in his stead, I will do battle with you." "We will," said the youths.

And they attacked Owain, and he was hard beset by them. And with that, the lion came to Owain's assistance, and they two got the better of the young men. And they said to him, "Chieftain, it was not agreed that we should fight save with thyself alone, and it is harder for us to contend with yonder animal than with thee." And Owain put the lion in the place where Luned had been imprisoned, and blocked up the door with stones. And he went to fight with the young men as before. But Owain had not his usual strength, and the two youths pressed hard upon him.

And the lion roared incessantly at seeing Owain in trouble. And he burst through the wall, until he found his way out, and rushed upon the young men and instantly slew them. So Luned was saved from being burned.

Then Owain returned with Luned to the castle of the Lady of the Fountain. And when he went thence, he took the Countess with him to Arthur's court, and she was his wife as long as she lived.

CHAPTER XXIII

GERAINT, THE SON OF ERBIN

ARTHUR was accustomed to hold his court at Caerleon upon Usk. And there he held it seven Easters and five Christmases. And once upon a time he held his court there at Whitsuntide. For Caerleon was the place most easy of access in his dominions, both by sea and by land. And there were assembled nine crowned kings, who were his tributaries, and like-wise earls and barons. For they were his invited guests at all the high festivals, unless they were prevented by any great hinderance. And when he was at Caerleon holding his court, thirteen churches were set apart for mass. And thus they were appointed: one church for Arthur and his kings, and his guests; and the second for Guenever and her ladies; and the third for the steward of the household and the suitors; and the fourth for the Franks and the other officers; and the other nine churches were for the nine masters of the household, and chiefly for Gawain, for he, from the eminence of his warlike fame, and from the nobleness of his birth, was the most exalted of the nine. And there was no other arrangement respecting the churches than that which we have here mentioned.

And on Whit-Tuesday, as the king sat at the banquet, lo, there entered a tall, fair-headed youth, clad in a coat and surcoat of satin, and a golden-hilted sword

about his neck, and low shoes of leather upon his feet. And he came and stood before Arthur. "Hail to thee, lord," said he. "Heaven prosper thee," he answered, "and be thou welcome." "Dost thou bring any new tidings?" "I do, lord," he said. "I am one of thy foresters, lord, in the forest of Dean, and my name is Madoc, son of Turgadarn. In the forest I saw a stag, the like of which beheld I never yet." "What is there about him," asked Arthur, "that thou never yet didst see his like?" "He is of pure white, lord, and he does not herd with any other animal, through stateliness and pride, so royal is his bearing. And I come to seek thy counsel, lord, and to know thy will concerning him. "It seems best to me," said Arthur, "to go and hunt him tomorrow at break of day, and to cause general notice thereof to be given tonight, in all quarters of the court." And Arryfuerys was Arthur's chief huntsman, and Arelivri his chief page. And all received notice; and thus it was arranged.

Then Guenever said to Arthur, "Wilt thou permit me, lord, to go tomorrow to see and hear the hunt of the stag of which the young man spoke?" "I will gladly," said Arthur. And Gawain said to Arthur, "Lord, if it seem well to thee, permit that into whose hunt soever the stag shall come, that one, be he a knight or one on foot, may cut off his head, and give it to whom he pleases, whether to his own lady-love, or to the lady of his friend." "I grant it gladly," said Arthur, "and let the steward of the household be chastised, if all things are not ready tomorrow for the chase."

And they passed the night with songs and diversions and discourse, and ample entertainment. And when it was time for them all to go to sleep, they went. And when the next day came, they arose. And Arthur called the attendants who guarded his couch. And there were four pages whose names were Cadyrnerth, the son of Gandwy, and Ambreu, the son of Bedwor, and Amhar, the son of Arthur, and Goreu, the son of Custennin. And these men came to Arthur and saluted him, and arrayed him in his garments. And Arthur wondered that Guenever did not awake, and the attendants wished to awaken her. "Disturb her not," said Arthur, "for she had rather sleep than go to see the hunting."

Then Arthur went forth, and he heard two horns sounding, one from near the lodging of the chief huntsman, and the other from near that of the chief page. And the whole assembly of the multitudes came to Arthur, and they took the road to the forest.

And after Arthur had gone forth from the palace, Guenever awoke, and called to her maidens, and apparelled herself.

"Maidens," said she, "I had leave last night to go and see the hunt. Go one of you to the stable, and order hither a horse such as a woman may ride." And one of them went, and she found but two horses in the stable; and Guenever and one of her maidens mounted them, and went through the Usk, and followed the track of the men and the horses. And as they rode thus, they heard a loud and rushing sound; and they looked behind them, and beheld a knight upon a hunter foal of mighty size. And the rider was a fair-haired youth, bare-legged, and of princely mien; and a golden-hilted sword was at his side, and a robe and a surcoat of satin were upon him, and two low shoes of leather were upon his feet; and around him was a scarf of blue purple, at each corner of which was a golden apple. And his horse stepped stately and swift and proud; and he overtook Guenever, and saluted her. "Heaven prosper thee, Geraint," said she; "and why didst thou not go with thy lord to hunt?"

"Because I knew not when he went," said he. "I marvel too," said she, "how he could go, unknown to me. But thou, O young man, art the most agreeable companion I could have in the whole kingdom; and it may be I shall be more amused with the hunting than they; for we shall hear the horns when they sound, and we shall hear the dogs when they are let loose and begin to cry."

So they went to the edge of the forest, and there they stood. "From this place," said she, "we shall hear when the dogs are let loose." And thereupon they heard a loud noise; and they looked towards the spot whence it came, and they beheld a dwarf riding upon a horse, stately and foaming and prancing and strong and spirited. And in the hand of the dwarf was a whip. And near the dwarf they saw a lady upon a beautiful white horse, of steady and stately pace; and she was clothed in a garment of gold brocade. And near her was a knight upon a war-horse of large size, with heavy and bright armor both upon himself and upon his horse. And truly they never before saw a knight, or a horse, or armor, of such remarkable size.

"Geraint," said Guenever, "knowest thou the name of that tall knight yonder?" "I know him not," said he, "and the strange armor that he wears prevents my either seeing his face or his features." "Go, maiden," said Guenever, "and ask the dwarf who that knight is." Then the maiden went up to the dwarf; and she inquired of the dwarf who the knight was. "I will not tell thee," he answered. "Since thou art so churlish," said she, "I will ask him, myself." "Thou shalt not ask him, by my faith," said he. "Wherefore not?" said she. "Because thou art not of honor sufficient to befit thee to speak to my lord." Then the maiden turned her horse's head towards the knight, upon which the dwarf struck her with the whip that was in his hand across the face and the eyes, so that the blood flowed forth. And the maiden returned to Guenever, complaining of the hurt she had received. "Very rudely has the dwarf treated thee," said Geraint, and he put his hand upon the hilt of his sword. But he took counsel with himself, and considered that it would be no vengeance for him to slay the dwarf, and to be attacked unarmed by the armed knight; so he refrained.

"Lady," said he, "I will follow him, with thy permission, and at last he will come to some inhabited place, where I may have arms, either as a loan or for a pledge, so that I may encounter the knight." "Go," said she, "and do not attack him until thou hast good arms; and I shall be very anxious concerning thee, until I hear tidings of thee." "If I am alive," said he, "thou shalt hear tidings of me by tomorrow afternoon;" and with that he departed.

And the road they took was below the palace of Caerleon, and across the ford of the Usk; and they went along a fair and even and lofty ridge of ground, until they came to a town, and at the extremity of the town they saw a fortress and a castle. And as the knight passed through the town, all the people arose and saluted him, and bade him welcome. And when Geraint came into the town, he looked at every house to see if he knew any of those whom he saw. But he knew none, and none knew him, to do him the kindness to let him have arms, either as a loan or for a pledge. And every house he saw was full of men and arms and horses. And they were polishing shields, and burnishing swords, and washing armor, and shoeing horses. And the knight and the lady and the dwarf rode up to the castle, that was in the town, and every one was glad in the castle. And from the battlements and the gates they risked their necks, through their eagerness to greet them, and to show their joy.

Geraint stood there to see whether the knight would remain in the castle; and when he was certain that he would do so, he looked around him. And at a little distance from the town he saw an old palace in ruins, wherein was a hall that was falling to decay. And as he knew not any one in the town, he went towards the old palace. And when he came near to the palace, he saw a hoary-headed man, standing by it, in tattered garments. And Geraint gazed steadfastly upon him. Then the hoary-headed man said to him, "Young man, wherefore art thou thoughtful?" "I am thoughtful," said he, "because I know not where to pass the night." "Wilt thou come forward this way, chieftain," said he, "and thou shalt have of the best that can be procured for thee." So Geraint went forward. And the hoary-headed man led the way into the hall. And in the hall he dismounted, and he left there his horse. Then he went on to the upper chamber with the hoary-headed man. And in the chamber he beheld an old woman, sitting on a cushion, with old, worn-out garments upon her; yet it seemed to him that she must have been comely when in the bloom of youth. And beside her was a maiden, upon whom were a vest and a veil, that were old, and beginning to be worn out. And truly he never saw a maiden more full of comeliness and grace and beauty than she. And the hoary-headed man said to the maiden, "There is no attendant for the horse of this youth but thyself." "I will render the best service I am able," said she, "both to him and to his horse." And the maiden disarrayed the youth, and then she furnished his horse with straw and with corn; and then she returned to the chamber. And the hoary-headed man said to the maiden, "Go to the town, and bring hither the best that thou canst find, both of food and of liquor." "I will gladly, lord," said she. And to the town went the maiden. And they conversed together while the maiden was at the town. And behold, the maiden came back, and a youth with her, bearing on his back a costrel full of good purchased mead, and a quarter of a young bullock. And in the hands of the maiden was a quantity of white bread, and she had some manchet bread in her veil, and she came into the chamber. "I could not obtain better than this," said she, "nor with better should I have been trusted." "It is good enough," said Geraint. And they caused the meat to be boiled; and when their food was ready, they sat down. And it was in this wise. Geraint sat between the hoary-headed man and his wife, and the maiden served them. And they ate and drank.

And when they had finished eating, Geraint talked with the hoary-headed man, and he asked him in the first place to whom belonged the palace that he was in. "Truly," said he, "it was I that built it, and to me also belonged the city and the castle which thou sawest." "Alas!" said Geraint, "how is it that thou hast lost them now?" "I lost a great earldom as well as these," said he, "and this is how I lost them. I had a nephew, the son of my brother, and I took care of his possessions; but he was impatient to enter upon them, so he made war upon me, and wrested from me not only his own, but also my estates, except this castle." "Good sir," said Geraint, "wilt thou tell me wherefore came the knight and the lady and the dwarf just now into the town, and what is the prepa-

ration which I saw, and the putting of arms in order?" "I will do so," said he. "The preparations are for the game that is to be held tomorrow by the young earl, which will be on this wise. In the midst of a meadow which is here, two forks will be set up, and upon the two forks a silver rod, and upon the silver rod a sparrow-hawk, and for the sparrow-hawk there will be a tournament. And to the tournament will go all the array thou didst see in the city, of men and of horses and of arms. And with each man will go the lady he loves best; and no man can joust for the sparrow-hawk, except the lady he loves best be with him. And the knight that thou sawest has gained the sparrow-hawk these two years; and if he gains it the third year, he will be called the Knight of the Sparrow-hawk from that time forth." "Sir," said Geraint, "what is thy counsel to me concerning this knight, on account of the insult which the maiden of Guenever received from the dwarf?" And Geraint told the hoary-headed man what the insult was that the maiden had received. "It is not easy to counsel thee, inasmuch as thou hast neither dame nor maiden belonging to thee, for whom thou canst joust. Yet I have arms here, which thou couldst have, and there is my horse also, if he seem to thee better than thine own." "Ah, sir," said he, "Heaven reward thee! But my own horse, to which I am accustomed, together with thine arms, will suffice me. And if when the appointed time shall come tomorrow, thou wilt permit me, sir, to challenge for yonder maiden that is thy daughter, I will engage, if I escape from the tournament, to love the maiden as long as I live." "Gladly will I permit thee," said the hoary-headed man; "and since thou dost thus resolve, it is necessary that thy horse and arms should be ready tomorrow at break of day. For then the Knight of the Sparrow-hawk will make proclamation, and ask the lady he loves best to take the sparrow-hawk; and if any deny it to her, by force will he defend her claim. And therefore," said the hoary-headed man, "it is needful for thee to be there at daybreak, and we three will be with thee." And thus was it settled.

And at night they went to sleep. And before the dawn they arose and arrayed themselves; and by the time that it was day, they were all four in the meadow. And there was the Knight of the Sparrow-hawk making the proclamation and asking his lady-love to take the sparrow-hawk. "Take it not," said Geraint, "for here is a maiden who is fairer, and more noble, and more comely, and who has a better claim to it than thou." Then said the knight, "If thou maintainest the sparrow-hawk to be due to her, come forward and do battle with me." And Geraint went forward to the top of the meadow, having upon himself and upon his horse armor which was heavy and rusty, and of uncouth shape. Then they encountered each other, and they broke a set of lances; and they broke a second set, and a third. And when the earl and his company saw the Knight of the Sparrow-hawk gaining the mastery, there was shouting and joy and mirth amongst them; and the hoary-headed man and his wife and his daughter were sorrowful. And the hoary-headed man served Geraint with lances as often as he broke them, and the dwarf served the Knight of the Sparrow-hawk. Then the hoary-headed man said to Geraint, "O chieftain, since no other will hold with thee, behold, here is the lance which was in my hand on the day when I received the honor of knighthood, and from that time to this I never broke it, and it has an excellent point." Then Geraint took the lance, thanking the hoary-headed man. And thereupon the dwarf also brought a lance to his lord. "Behold, here is a lance for thee, not less good than his," said the dwarf. "And bethink thee that no knight ever withstood thee so long as this one has done." "I declare to heaven," said Geraint, "that unless death takes me quickly hence, he shall fare never the better for thy service." And Geraint pricked his horse towards him from afar, and, warning him, he rushed upon him, and gave him a blow so severe, and furious, and fierce, upon the face of his shield, that he cleft it in two, and broke his armor, and burst his girths, so that both he and his saddle were borne to the ground over the horse's crupper. And Geraint dismounted quickly. And he was wroth, and he drew his sword, and rushed fiercely upon him. Then the knight also arose, and drew his sword against Geraint. And they fought on foot with their swords until their arms struck sparks of fire like stars from one another; and thus they continued fighting until the blood and sweat obscured the light from their eyes. At length Geraint called to him all his strength,

and struck the knight upon the crown of his head, so that he broke all his head-armour, and cut through all the flesh and the skin, even to the skull, until he wounded the bone.

Then the knight fell upon his knees, and cast his sword from his hand, and besought mercy from Geraint. "Of a truth," said he, "I relinquish my over-daring and my pride, and crave thy mercy; and unless I have time to commit myself to heaven for my sins, and to talk with a priest, thy mercy will avail me little." "I will grant thee grace upon this condition," said Geraint; "that thou go to Guenever, the wife of Arthur, to do her satisfaction for the insult which her maiden received from thy dwarf. Dismount not from the time thou goest hence until thou comest into the presence of Guenever, to make her what atonement shall be adjudged at the court of Arthur." "This will I do gladly; and who art thou?" "I am Geraint, the son of Erbin; and declare thou also who thou art." "I am Edeyrn, the son of Nudd." Then he threw himself upon his horse, and went forward to Arthur's court; and the lady he loved best went before him, and the dwarf, with much lamentation.

Then came the young earl and his hosts to Geraint, and saluted him, and bade him to his castle. "I may not go," said Geraint; "but where I was last night, there will I be tonight also." "Since thou wilt none of my inviting, thou shalt have abundance of all that I can command for thee; and I will order ointment for thee, to recover thee from thy fatigues, and from the weariness that is upon thee." "Heaven reward thee," said Geraint, "and I will go to my lodging." And thus went Geraint and Earl Ynywl, and his wife and his daughter. And when they reached the old mansion, the household servants and attendants of the young earl had arrived, and had arranged all the apartments, dressing them with straw and with fire; and in a short time the ointment was ready, and Geraint came there, and they washed his head. Then came the young earl, with forty honorable knights from among his attendants, and those who were bidden to the tournament. And Geraint came from the anointing. And the earl asked him to go to the hall to eat. "Where is the Earl Ynywl," said Geraint, "and his wife and his daughter?" "They are in the chamber yonder," said the earl's chamberlain, "arraying themselves in garments which the earl has caused to be brought for them." "Let not the damsel array herself," said he, "except in her vest and her veil, until she come to the court of Arthur, to be clad by Guenever in such garments as she may choose." So the maiden did not array herself.

Then they all entered the hall, and they washed, and sat down to meat. And thus were they seated. On one side of Geraint sat the young earl, and Earl Ynywl beyond him, and on the other side of Geraint was the maiden and her mother. And after these all sat according to their precedence in honor. And they ate. And they were served abundantly, and they received a profusion of divers kinds of gifts. Then they conversed together. And the young earl invited Geraint to visit him next day. "I will not, by heaven," said Geraint. "To the court of Arthur will I go with this maiden tomorrow. And it is enough for me, as long as Earl Ynywl is in poverty and trouble; and I go chiefly to seek to add to his maintenance." "Ah, chieftain," said the young earl, "it is not by my fault that Earl Ynywl is without his possessions." "By my faith," said Geraint, "he shall not remain without them, unless death quickly takes me hence." "O chieftain," said he, "with regard to the disagreement between me and Ynywl, I will gladly abide by thy counsel, and agree to what thou mayest judge right between us." "I but ask thee," said Geraint, to restore to him what is his and what he should have received from the time he lost his possessions even until this day." "That will I do, gladly, for thee," answered he. "Then," said Geraint, "whosoever is here who owes homage to Ynywl, let him come forward, and perform it on the spot. " And all the men did so; and by that treaty they abided. And his castle and his town, and all his possessions, were restored to Ynywl. And he received back all that he had lost, even to the smallest jewel.

Then spoke Earl Ynywl to Geraint. "Chieftain," said he, "behold the maiden for whom thou didst challenge at the tournament; I bestow her upon thee." "She shall go with me," said Geraint, "to the court of Arthur, and Arthur and Guenever, they shall dispose of her as they will." And the next day they proceeded to Arthur's court. So far concerning Geraint.

CHAPTER XXIV

GERAINT, THE SON OF ERBIN, CONTINUED

Now this is how Arthur hunted the stag. The men and the dogs were divided into hunting-parties, and the dogs were let loose upon the stag.

And the last dog that was let loose was the favorite dog of Arthur, Cavall was his name. And he left all the other dogs behind him, and turned the stag. And at the second turn the stag came toward the hunting-party of Arthur. And Arthur set upon him, and before he could be slain by any other Arthur cut off his head. Then they sounded the death-horn for slaying, and they all gathered round.

Then came Kadyriath to Arthur, and spoke to him. "Lord," said he, "behold, yonder is Guenever, and none with her save only one maiden." "Command Gildas, the son of Caw, and all the scholars of the court," said Arthur, "to attend Guenever to the palace." And they did so.

Then they all set forth, holding converse together concerning the head of the stag, to whom it should be given. One wished that it should be given to the lady best beloved by him and another to the lady whom he loved best. And so they came to the palace. And when Arthur and Guenever heard them disputing about the head of the stag, Guenever said to Arthur, "My lord, this is my counsel concerning the stag's head; let it not upon it than its own color." "Knowest thou his name?" said she. "I do," said he; "he tells me that he is Edeyrn, the son of Nudd." Then she replied, "I know him not."

So Guenever went to the gate to meet him, and he entered. And Guenever was sorry when she saw the condition he was in, even though he was accompanied by the churlish dwarf. Then Edeyrn saluted Guenever. "Heaven protect thee," said she. "Lady," said he, "Geraint, the son of Erbin, thy best and most valiant servant, greets thee." "Did he meet with thee?" she asked. "Yes," said he, "and it was not to my advantage; and that was not his fault, but mine, lady. And Geraint greets thee well; and in greeting thee he compelled me to come hither to do thy pleasure for the insult which thy maiden received from the dwarf." "Now where did he overtake thee?" "At the place where we were jousting and contending for the sparrow-hawk, in the town which is now called Cardiff. And it was for the avouchment of the love of the maiden, the daughter of Earl Ynywl, that Geraint jousted at the tournament. And thereupon we encountered each other, and he left me, lady, as thou seest." "Sir," said she, "when thinkest thou that Geraint will be here?" "Tomorrow, lady, I think he will be here with the maiden."

Then Arthur came to them. And he saluted Arthur, and Arthur gazed a long time upon him, and was amazed to see him thus. And thinking that he knew him, he inquired of him, "Art thou Edeyrn, the son of Nudd?" "I am, lord," said he, "and I have met with much trouble and received wounds insupportable." Then he told Arthur all his adventure. "Well," said Arthur, "from what I hear it behooves Guenever to be merciful towards thee." "The mercy which thou desirest, lord," said she, "will I grant to him, since it is as insulting to thee that an insult should be offered to me as to thyself." "Thus will it be best to do," said Arthur; "let this man have medical care until it be known whether he may live. And if he live he shall do such satisfaction as shall be judged best by the men of the court. And if he die too much will be the death of such a youth as Edeyrn for an insult to a maiden." "This pleases me," said Guenever. And Arthur caused Morgan Tud to be called to him. He was chief physician. "Take with thee Edeyrn, the son of Nudd, and cause a chamber to be prepared for him, and let him

be given away until Geraint, the son of Erbin, shall return from the errand he is upon." And Guenever told Arthur what that errand was. "Right gladly shall it be so," said Arthur. And Guenever caused a watch to be set upon the ramparts for Geraint's coming. And after midday they beheld an unshapely little man upon a horse, and after him a dame or a damsel, also on horseback, and after her a knight of large stature, bowed down, and hanging his head low and sorrowfully, and clad in broken and worthless armor.

And before they came near to the gate one of the watch went to Guenever, and told her what kind of people they saw, and what aspect they bore. "I know not who they are," said he. "But I know," said Guenever; "this is the knight whom Geraint pursued, and methinks he comes not here by his own free will. But Geraint has overtaken him, and avenged the insult to the maiden to the uttermost." And thereupon, behold, a porter came to the spot where Guenever was. "Lady," said he, "at the gate there is a knight, and I saw never a man of so pitiful an aspect to look upon as he. Miserable and broken is the armor that he wears, and the hue of blood is more conspicuous have the aid of medicine as thou wouldst do unto myself if I were wounded; and let none into his chamber to molest him, but thyself and thy disciples, to administer to him remedies." "I will do so gladly, lord," said Morgan Tud. Then said the steward of the household, "Whither is it right, lord, to order the maiden?" "To Guenever and her handmaidens," said he. And the steward of the household so ordered her.

The next day came Geraint towards the court; and there was a watch set on the ramparts by Guenever, lest he should arrive unawares. And one of the watch came to Guenever. "Lady," said he, "methinks that I see Geraint, and a maiden with him. He is on horseback, but he has his walking gear upon him, and the maiden appears to be in white, seeming to be clad in a garment of linen." "Assemble all the women," said Guenever, "and come to meet Geraint, to welcome him and wish him joy." And Guenever went to meet Geraint and the maiden. And when Geraint came to the place where Guenever was he saluted her. "Heaven prosper thee," said she, "and welcome to thee." "Lady," said he, "I earnestly desired to obtain thee satisfaction, according to thy will; and, behold here is the maiden through whom thou hadst thy revenge." "Verily," said Guenever, "the welcome of heaven be unto her; and it is fitting that we should receive her joyfully." Then they went in and dismounted. And Geraint came to where Arthur was, and saluted him. "Heaven protect thee," said Arthur, "and the welcome of heaven be unto thee. And inasmuch as thou hast vanquished Edeyrn, the son of Nudd, thou hast had a prosperous career." "Not upon me be the blame," said Geraint; "it was through the arrogance of Edeyrn, the son of Nudd, himself, that we were not friends." "Now," said Arthur, "where is the maiden for whom I heard thou didst give challenge?" "She is gone with Guenever to her chamber." Then went Arthur to see the maiden. And Arthur, and all his companions, and his whole court, were glad concerning the maiden. And certain were they all that, had her array been suitable to her beauty, they had never seen a maid fairer than she. And Arthur gave away the maiden to Geraint. And the usual bond made between two persons was made between Geraint and the maiden, and the choicest of all Guenever's apparel was given to the maiden; and

thus arrayed, she appeared comely and graceful to all who beheld her. And that day and the night were spent in abundance of minstrelsy, and ample gifts of liquor, and a multitude of games. And when it was time for them to go to sleep they went. And in the chamber where the couch of Arthur and Guenever was the couch of Geraint and Enid was prepared. And from that time she became his wife. And the next day Arthur satisfied all the claimants upon Geraint with bountiful gifts. And the maiden took up her abode in the palace, and she had many companions both men and women, and there was no maiden more esteemed than she in the island of Britain.

Then spake Guenever. "Rightly did I judge," said she, "concerning the head of the stag, that it should not be given to any until Geraint's return; and behold, here is a fit occasion for bestowing it. Let it be given to Enid, the daughter of Ynywl, the most illustrious maiden. And I do not believe any will begrudge it her, for between her and every one there exists nothing but love and friendship." Much applauded was this by them all, and by Arthur also. And the head of the stag was given to Enid. And thereupon her fame increased, and her friends became more in number than before. And Geraint from that time forth loved the hunt, and the tournament, and hard encounters; and he came victorious from them all. And a year, and a second, and a third, he proceeded thus, until his fame had flown over the face of the kingdom.

And, once upon a time, Arthur was holding his court at Caerleon upon Usk; and behold, there came to him ambassadors, wise and prudent, full of knowledge and eloquent of speech, and they saluted Arthur. "Heaven prosper you!" said Arthur; "and whence do you come?" "We come, lord," said they, "from Cornwall, and we are ambassadors from Erbin, the son of Custennin, thy uncle, and our mission is unto thee. And he greets thee well, as an uncle should greet his nephew, and as a vassal should greet his lord. And he represents unto thee that he waxes heavy and feeble, and is advancing in years. And the neighboring chiefs, knowing this, grow insolent towards him, and covet his land and possessions. And he earnestly beseeches thee, lord, to permit Geraint his son to return to him, to protect his possessions, and to become acquainted with his boundaries. And unto him he represents that it were better for him to spend the flower of his youth and the prime of his age in preserving his own boundaries, than in tournaments which are productive of no profit, although he obtains glory in them."

"Well," said Arthur, "go and divest yourselves of your accoutrements, and take food, and refresh yourselves after your fatigues; and before you go from hence you shall have an answer." And they went to eat. And Arthur considered that it would go hard with him to let Geraint depart from him, and from his court; neither did he think it fair that his cousin should be restrained from going to protect his dominions and his boundaries, seeing that his father was unable to do so. No less was the grief and regret of Guenever, and all her women, and all her damsels, through fear that the maiden would leave them. And that day and that night was spent in abundance of feasting. And Arthur told Geraint the cause of the mission, and of the coming of the ambassadors to him out of Cornwall. "Truly," said Geraint, "be it to my advantage or disadvantage, lord, I will do according to thy will concerning this embassy." "Behold," said Arthur, "though it grieves me to part with thee, it is my counsel that thou go to dwell in thine own dominions, and to defend thy boundaries, and take with thee to accompany thee as many as thou wilt of those thou lovest best among my faithful ones, and among thy friends, and among thy companions in arms." "Heaven reward thee! and this will I do," said Geraint. "What discourse," said Guenever, "do I hear between you? Is it of those who are to conduct Geraint to his country?" "It is," said Arthur. "Then it is needful for me to consider," said she, "concerning companions and a provision for the lady that is with me." "Thou wilt do well," said Arthur.

And that night they went to sleep. And the next day the ambassadors were permitted to depart, and they were told that Geraint should follow them. And on the third day Geraint set forth, and many went with him,—Gawain, the son of Gwyar, and Riogoned, the son of the king of Ireland, and Ondyaw, the son of the duke of Burgundy, Gwilim, the son of the ruler of the Franks, Howel, the son of the earl of Brittany, Perceval, the son of Evrawk,

Gwyr, a judge in the court of Arthur, Bedwyr, the son of Bedrawd, Kai, the son of Kyner, Odyar, the Frank, and Edeyrn, the son of Nudd. Said Geraint, "I think I shall have enough of knighthood with me." And they set forth. And never was there seen a fairer host journeying towards the Severn. And on the other side of the Severn were the nobles of Erbin, the son of Custennin, and his foster-father at their head, to welcome Geraint with gladness; and many of the women of the court, with his mother, came to receive Enid, the daughter of Ynywl, his wife. And there was great rejoicing and gladness throughout the whole court, and through all the country, concerning Geraint, because of the greatness of their love to him, and of the greatness of the fame which he had gained since he went from amongst them, and because he was come to take possession of his dominions, and to preserve his boundaries. And they came to the court. And in the court they had ample entertainment, and a multitude of gifts, and abundance of liquor, and a sufficiency of service, and a variety of games. And to do honor to Geraint, all the chief men of the country were invited that night to visit him. And they passed that day and that night in the utmost enjoyment. And at dawn next day Erbin arose, and summoned to him Geraint, and the noble persons who had borne him company. And he said to Geraint: "I am a feeble and an aged man, and whilst I was able to maintain the dominion for thee and for myself, I did so. But thou art young, and in the flower of thy vigor and of thy youth. Henceforth do thou preserve thy possessions." "Truly," said Geraint, "with my consent thou shalt not give the power over thy dominions at this time into my hands, thou shalt not take me from Arthur's court." "Into thy hands will I give them," said Erbin, "and this day shalt thou receive the homage of thy subjects."

Then said Gawain, "It were better for thee to satisfy those who have boons to ask, today, and tomorrow thou canst receive the homage of thy dominions." So all that had boons to ask were summoned into one place. And Kadyriath came to them to know what were the requests. And every one asked that which he desired. And the followers of Arthur began to make gifts, and immediately the men of Cornwall came, and gave also. And they were not long in giving, so eager was every one to bestow gifts. And of those who came

136 ▷

to ask gifts, none departed unsatisfied. And that day and that night were spent in the utmost enjoyment.

And the next day at dawn Erbin desired Geraint to send messengers to the men to ask them whether it was displeasing to them that he should come to receive their homage, and whether they had anything to object to him. Then Geraint sent ambassadors to the men of Cornwall to ask them this. And they all said that it would be the fulness of joy and honor to them for Geraint to come and receive their homage. So he received the homage of such as were there. And the day after, the followers of Arthur intended to go away. "It is too soon for you to go away yet," said he; "stay with me until I have finished receiving the homage of my chief men, who have agreed to come to me." And they remained with him until he had done so. Then they set forth towards the court of Arthur. And Geraint went to bear them company, and Enid also, as far as Diganwy; there they parted. And Ondyaw, the son of the duke of Burgundy, said to Geraint, "Go, now, and visit the uttermost parts of thy dominions and see well to the boundaries of thy territories; and if thou hast any trouble respecting them, send unto thy companions." "Heaven reward thee!" said Geraint; "and this will I do." And Geraint journeyed to the uttermost parts of his dominions.

And experienced guides, and the chief men of his country, went with him. And the furthermost point that they showed him he kept possession of.

CHAPTER XXV

GERAINT, THE SON OF ERBIN, CONTINUED

GERAINT, as he had been used to do when he was at Arthur's court, frequented tournaments. And he became acquainted with valiant and mighty men, until he had gained as much fame there as he had formerly done elsewhere. And he enriched his court, and his companions, and his nobles, with the best horses and the best arms, and with the best and most valuable jewels, and he ceased not until his fame had flown over the face of the whole kingdom. When he knew that it was thus, he began to love ease and pleasure, for there was no one who was worth his opposing. And he loved his wife, and liked to continue in the palace, with minstrelsy and diversions. So he began to shut himself up in the chamber of his wife, and he took no delight in anything besides, insomuch that he gave up the friendship of his nobles, together with his hunting and his amusements, and lost the hearts of all the host in his court. And there was murmuring and scoffing concerning him among the inhabitants of the palace, on account of his relinquishing so completely their companionship for the love of his wife. These tidings came to Erbin. And when Erbin had heard these things, he spoke unto Enid, and inquired of her whether it was she that had caused Geraint to act thus, and to forsake his people and his hosts. "Not I, by my confession unto heaven," said she; "there is nothing more hateful unto me than this." And she knew not what she should do, for, although it was hard for her to own this to Geraint, yet was it not more easy for her to listen to what she heard, without warning Geraint concerning it. And she was very sorrowful.

One morning in the summer-time they were upon their couch, and Geraint lay upon the edge of it. And Enid was without sleep in the apartment, which had windows of glass;[1] and the sun shone upon the couch.

And the clothes had slipped from off his arms and his breast, and he was asleep. Then she gazed upon the marvellous beauty of his appearance, and she said, "Alas! and am I the cause that these arms and this breast have lost their glory, and the warlike fame which they once so richly enjoyed?" As she said this the tears dropped from her eyes, and they fell upon his breast. And the tears she shed, and the words she had spoken, awoke him. And another thing contributed to awaken him, and that was the idea that it was not in thinking of him that she spoke thus, but that it was because she loved some other man more than him, and that she wished for other society. Thereupon Geraint was troubled in his mind, and he called his squire; and when he came to him, "Go quickly," said he, "and prepare my horse and my arms, and make them ready. And do thou arise," said he to Enid, "and apparel thyself; and cause thy horse to be accoutred, and clothe thee in the worst riding-dress that thou hast in thy possession. And evil betide me," said he, "if thou returnest here until thou

knowest whether I have lost my strength so completely as thou didst say. And if it be so, it will then be easy for thee to seek the society thou didst wish for of him of whom thou wast thinking." So she arose, and clothed herself in her meanest garments. "I know nothing, lord," said she, "of thy meaning." "Neither wilt thou know at this time," said he.

Then Geraint went to see Erbin. "Sir," said he, "I am going upon a quest, and I am not certain when I may come back. Take heed, therefore, unto thy possessions until my return." "I will do so," said he; "but it is strange to me that thou shouldst go so suddenly. And who will proceed with thee, since thou art not strong enough to traverse the land of Loegyr alone?" "But one person only will go with me." "Heaven counsel thee, my son," said Erbin, "and may many attach themselves to thee in Loegyr." Then went Geraint to the place where his horse was, and it was equipped with foreign armor, heavy and shining. And he desired Enid to mount her horse, and to ride forward, and to keep a long way before him. "And whatever thou mayest see, and whatever thou mayest hear concerning me," said he, "do thou not turn back. And unless I speak unto thee, say not thou one word either." So they set forward. And he did not choose the pleasantest and most frequented road, but that which was the wildest and most beset by thieves and robbers and venomous animals.

And they came to a high-road, which they followed till they saw a vast forest; and they saw four armed horsemen come forth from the forest. When the armed men saw them, they said one to another, "Here is a good occasion for us to capture two horses and armor, and a lady likewise; for this we shall have no difficulty in doing against yonder single knight, who hangs his head so pensively and heavily." Enid heard this discourse, and she knew not what she should do through fear of Geraint, who had told her to be silent. "The vengeance of heaven be upon me," said she, "if I would not rather receive my death from his hand than from the hand of any other; and though he should slay me, yet will I speak to him, lest I should have the misery to witness his death." So she waited for Geraint until he came near to her. "Lord," said she, "didst thou hear the words of those men concerning thee?" Then he lifted up his eyes, and

---

[1] The terms of admiration in which the older writers invariably speak of *glass windows* would be sufficient proof, if other evidence were wanting, how rare an article of luxury they were in the houses of our ancestors. They were first introduced in ecclesiastical architecture, to which they were for a long time confined. Glass is said not to have been employed in domestic architecture before the fourteenth century.

looked at her angrily. "Thou hadst only," said he, "to hold thy peace, as I bade thee. I wish but for silence, and not for warning. And though thou shouldst desire to see my defeat and my death by the hands of those men, yet I do feel no dread." Then the foremost of them couched his lance, and rushed upon Geraint. And he received him, and that not feebly. But he let the thrust go by him, while he struck the horseman upon the centre of the shield, in such a manner that his shield was split, and his armor broken, so that a cubit's length of the shaft of Geraint's lance passed through his body, and sent him to the earth, the length of the lance over his horse's crupper. Then the second horseman attacked him furiously, being wroth at the death of his companion. But with one thrust Geraint overthrew him also, and killed him as he had done the other. Then the third set upon him, and he killed him in like manner. And thus also he slew the fourth. Sad and sorrowful was the maiden as she saw all this. Geraint dismounted his horse, and took the arms of the men he had slain, and placed them upon their saddles, and tied together the reins of their horses; and he mounted his horse again. "Behold what thou must do," said he; "take the four horses, and drive them before thee, and proceed forward as I bade thee just now. And say not one word unto me, unless I speak first unto thee. And I declare unto heaven," said he, "if thou doest not thus, it will be to thy cost." "I will do as far as I can, lord," said she, "according to thy desire."

So the maiden went forward, keeping in advance of Geraint, as he had desired her; and it grieved him as much as his wrath would permit to see a maiden so illustrious as she having so much trouble with the care of the horses. Then they reached a wood, and it was both deep and vast, and in the wood night overtook them. "Ah, maiden," said he, "it is vain to attempt proceeding forward." "Well, lord," said she, "whatever thou wishest we will do." "It will be best for us," he answered, "to rest and wait for the day in order to pursue our journey." "That will we, gladly," said she. And they did so. Having dismounted himself, he took her down from her horse. "I cannot by any means refrain from sleep through weariness," said he; "do thou therefore watch the horses and sleep not." "I will, lord," said she. Then he went to sleep in his armor, and thus passed the night, which

was not long at that season. And when she saw the dawn of day appear she looked around her to see if he were waking, and thereupon he awoke. Then he arose, and said unto her, "Take the horses and ride on, and keep straight on as thou didst yesterday." And they left the wood, and they came to an open country, with meadows on one hand, and mowers mowing the meadows. And there was a river before them, and the horses bent down and drank of the water. And they went up out of the river by a lofty steep; and there they met a slender stripling with a satchel about his neck, and they saw there was something in the satchel, but they knew not what it was. And he had a small blue pitcher in his hand, and a bowl on the mouth of the pitcher. And the youth saluted Geraint. "Heaven prosper thee!" said Geraint; "and whence dost thou come?" "I come," said he, "from the city that lies before thee. My lord," he added, "will it be displeasing to thee if I ask whence thou comest also?" "By no means; through yonder wood did I come." "Thou camest not through the wood today." "No," he replied; "we were in the wood last night." "I warrant," said the youth, "that thy condition there last night was not the most pleasant, and that thou hadst neither meat nor drink." "No, by my faith," said he. "Wilt thou follow my counsel," said the youth, "and take thy meal from me?" "What sort of meal?" he inquired. "The breakfast which is sent for yonder mowers, nothing less than bread and meat and wine; and if thou wilt, sir, they shall have none of it." "I will," said he, "and heaven reward thee for it."

So Geraint alighted, and the youth took the maiden from off her horse. Then they washed, and took their repast. And the youth cut the bread in slices, and gave them drink, and served them withal. And when they had finished the youth arose and said to Geraint, "My lord, with thy permission, I will now go and fetch some food for the mowers." "Go first to the town," said Geraint, "and take a lodging for me in the best place thou knowest, and the most commodious one for the horses; and take thou whichever horse and arms thou choosest in payment for thy service and thy gift." "Heaven reward thee, lord!" said the youth; "and this would be ample to repay services much greater than those I have rendered unto thee."

And to the town went the youth, and he took the best and most pleasant lodgings that he knew; and after that he went to the palace, having the horse and armor with him, and proceeded to the place where the earl was, and told him all his adventure. "I go now, lord," said he, "to meet the knight, and to conduct him to his lodging." "Go, gladly," said the earl, "and right joyfully shall he be received here, if he so come." And the youth went to meet Geraint, and told him that he would be received gladly by the earl in his own palace; but he would go only to his lodgings. And he had a goodly chamber, in which was plenty of straw and drapery, and a spacious and commodious place he had for the horses; and the youth prepared for them plenty of provender. After they had disarrayed themselves, Geraint spoke thus to Enid: "Go," said he, "to the other side of the chamber, and come not to this side of the house; and thou mayst call to thee the woman of the house if thou wilt." "I will do, lord," said she, "as thou sayest." Thereupon the man of the house came to Geraint, and welcomed him. And after they had eaten and drank Geraint went to sleep, and so did Enid also.

In the evening, behold, the earl came to visit Geraint, and his twelve honorable knights with him. And Geraint rose up and welcomed him. Then they all sat down according to their precedence in honor. And the earl conversed with Geraint, and inquired of him the object of his journey. "I have none," he replied, "but to seek adventures and to follow my own inclination." Then the earl cast his eye upon Enid, and he looked at her steadfastly. And he thought he had never seen a maiden fairer or more comely than she. And he set all his thoughts and his affections upon her. Then he asked of Geraint, "Have I thy permission to go and converse with yonder maiden, for I see that she is apart from thee?" "Thou hast it gladly," said he. So the earl went to the place where the maiden was, and spake with her. "Ah! maiden," said he, "it cannot be pleasant to thee to journey with yonder man." "It is not unpleasant to me," said she. "Thou hast neither youths nor maidens to serve thee," said he. "Truly," she replied, "it is more pleasant for me to follow yonder man than to be served by youths and maidens." "I will give thee good counsel," said he; "all my earldom will I place in thy possession if thou wilt dwell with me." "That will I not, by heaven," she said; "yonder man was the first to whom my faith was pledged, and shall I prove inconstant to him?" "Thou art in the wrong," said the earl; "if I slay the man yonder I can keep thee with me as long as I choose; and when thou no longer pleasest me I can turn thee away. But if thou goest with me by thy own good-will, I protest that our union shall continue as long as I shall remain alive." Then she pondered those words of his, and she considered that it was advisable to encourage him in his request. "Behold then, chieftain, this is most expedient for thee to do to save me from all reproach; come here tomorrow and take me away as though I knew nothing thereof." "I will do so," said he. So he arose and took his leave and went forth with his attendants. And she told not then to Geraint any of the conversation which she had had with the earl lest it should rouse his anger, and cause him uneasiness and care.

And at the usual hour they went to sleep. And at the beginning of the night Enid slept a little; and at midnight she arose, and placed all Geraint's armor together, so that it might be ready to put on. And

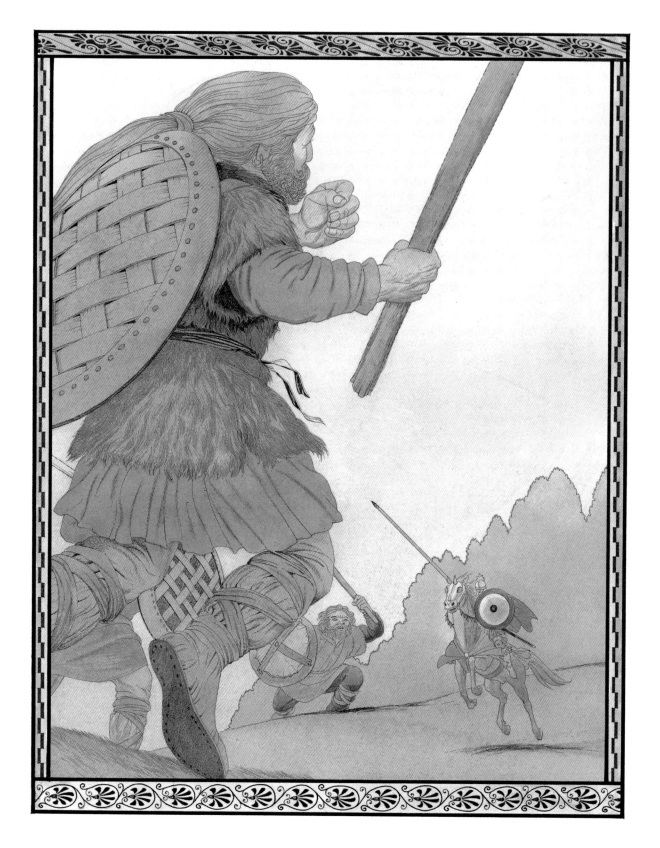

though fearful of her errand, she came to the side of Geraint's bed; and she spoke to him softly and gently, saying, "My lord, arise, and clothe thyself, for these were the words of the earl to me, and his intention concerning me." So she told Geraint all that had passed. And although he was wroth with her, he took warning, and clothed himself. And she lighted a candle that he might have light to do so. "Leave there the candle," said he, "and desire the man of the house to come here." Then she went, and the man of the house came to him. "Dost thou know how much I owe thee?" asked Geraint. "I think thou owest but little." "Take the three horses, and the three suits of armor." "Heaven reward thee, Lord," said he, "but I spent not the value of one suit of armor upon thee." "For that reason," said he, "thou wilt be the richer. And now, wilt thou come to guide me out of the town?" "I will, gladly," said he; "and in which direction dost thou intend to go?" "I wish to leave the town by a different way from that by which I entered it." So the man of the lodgings accompanied him as far as he desired. Then he bade the maiden to go on before him, and she did so, and went straight forward, and his host returned home.

And Geraint and the maiden went forward along the high-road. And as they journeyed thus, they heard an exceeding loud wailing near to them. "Stay thou here," said he, "and I will go and see what is the cause of this wailing." "I will," said she. Then he went forward into an open glade that was near the road. And in the glade he saw two horses, one having a man's saddle, and the other a woman's saddle upon it. And behold there was a knight lying dead in his armor, and a young damsel in a riding-dress standing over him lamenting. "Ah, lady," said Geraint, "what hath befallen thee?" "Behold," she answered, "I journeyed here with my beloved husband, when lo! three giants came upon us, and without any cause in the world, they slew him." "which way went they hence?" said Geraint. "Yonder by the high-road," she replied. So he returned to Enid. "Go," said he, "to the lady that is below yonder, and await me there till I come." She was sad when he ordered her to do thus, but nevertheless she went to the damsel, whom it was ruth to hear, and she felt certain that Geraint would never return.

Meanwhile Geraint followed the giants, and overtook them. And each of them was greater in stature than three other men, and a huge club was on the shoulder of each. Then he rushed upon one of them, and thrust his lance through his body. And having drawn it forth again, he pierced another of them through likewise. But the third turned upon him, and struck him with his club so that he split his shield and crushed his shoulder. But Geraint drew his sword, and gave the giant a blow on the crown of his head, so severe, and fierce, and violent, that his head and his neck were split down to his shoulders, and he fell dead. So Geraint left him thus, and returned to Enid. And when he reached the place where she was, he fell down lifeless from his horse. Piercing and loud and thrilling was the cry that Enid uttered. And she came and stood over him where he had fallen. And at the sound of her cries came the earl of Limours, and they who journeyed with him, whom her lamentations brought out of their road. And the earl said to Enid, "Alas, lady, what hath befallen thee?" "Ah, good sir," said she, "the only man I have loved, or ever shall love, is slain." Then he said to the other, "And what is the cause of thy grief?" "They have slain my beloved husband also," said she. "And who was it that slew them?" "Some giants," he answered, "slew my best-beloved, and the other knight went in pursuit of them, and came back in the state thou seest." The earl caused the knight that was dead to be buried, but he thought that there still remained some life in Geraint; and to see if he yet would live, he had him carried with him in the hollow of his shield, and upon a bier. And the two damsels went to the court; and when they arrived there, Geraint was placed upon a little couch in front of the table that was in the hall. Then they all took off their travelling-gear, and the earl besought Enid to do the same, and to clothe herself in other garments. "I will not, by heaven," said she. "Ah, lady," said he, "be not so sorrowful for this matter." "It were hard to persuade me to be otherwise," said she. "I will act towards thee in such wise that thou needest not be sorrowful, whether yonder knight live or die. Behold, a good earldom, together with myself, will I bestow upon thee; be therefore happy and joyful." "I declare to heaven," said she, "that henceforth I shall never be joyful while I live."

"Come," said he, "and eat." "No, by heaven, I will not." "But by heaven, thou shalt," said he. So he took her with him to the table against her will, and many times desired her to eat. "I call heaven to witness," said she, "that I will not eat until the man that is upon yonder bier shall eat likewise." "Thou canst not fulfil that," said the earl; "yonder man is dead already." "I will prove that I can," said she. Then he offered her a goblet of liquor. "Drink this goblet," he said, "and it will cause thee to change thy mind." "Evil betide me," she answered, "if I drink aught until he drink also." "Truly," said the earl, "it is of no more avail for me to be gentle with thee than ungentle." And he gave her a box in the ear. Thereupon she raised a loud and piercing shriek, and her lamentations were much greater than they had been before; for she considered in her mind that, had Geraint been alive, he durst not have struck her thus. But behold, at the sound of her cry, Geraint revived from his swoon, and he sat up on the bier; and finding his sword in the hollow of his shield, he rushed to the place where the earl was, and struck him a fiercely-wounding, severely-venomous, and sternly-smiting blow upon the crown of his head, so that he clove him in twain, until his sword was staid by the table. Then all left the board and fled away. And this was not so much through fear of the living, as through the dread they felt at seeing the dead man rise up to slay them. And Geraint looked upon Enid, and he was grieved for two causes; one was to see that Enid had lost her color and her wonted aspect; and the other, to know that she was in the right. "Lady," said he, "knowest thou where our horses are?" "I know, lord, where thy horse is," she replied, "but I know not where is the other. Thy horse is in the house yonder." So he went to the house, and brought forth his horse, and mounted him, and took up Enid, and placed her upon the horse with him. And he rode forward. And their road lay between two hedges; and the night was gaining on the day. And lo! they saw behind them the shafts of spears betwixt them and the sky, and they heard the tramping of horses, and the noise of a host approaching. "I hear something following us," said he, "and I will put thee on the other side of the hedge." And thus he did. And thereupon, behold, a knight pricked towards him, and couched his lance. When Enid saw this, she cried out, saying, "O chieftain, whoever thou art, what renown wilt thou gain by slaying a dead man?" "O heaven!" said he, "is it Geraint?" "Yes, in truth," said she; "and who art thou?" "I am Gwiffert Petit," said he, "thy husband's ally, coming to thy assistance, for I heard that thou wast in trouble. Come with me to the court of a son-in-law of my sister, which is near here, and thou shalt have the best medical assistance in the kingdom." "I will do so gladly," said Geraint. And Enid was placed upon the horse of one of Gwiffert's squires, and they went forward to the baron's palace. And they were received there with gladness, and they met with hospitality and attention. The next morning they went to seek physicians; and it was not long before they came, and they attended Geraint until he was perfectly well. And while Geraint was under medical care, Gwiffert caused his armor to be repaired, until it was as good as it had ever been. And they remained there a month and a fortnight. Then they separated, and Geraint went towards his own dominions, and thenceforth he reigned prosperously, and his warlike fame and splendor lasted with renown and honor both to him and to Enid,[1] from that time forward.

---

[1]Throughout the broad and varied regions of romance, it would be difficult to find a character of greater simplicity and truth than that of Enid, the daughter of Earl Ynywl. Conspicuous for her beauty and noble bearing, we are at a loss whether more to admire the patience with which she bore all the hardships she was destined to undergo, or the constancy and affection which finally achieved the triumph she so richly deserved.

The character of Enid is admirably sustained through the whole tale; and as it is more natural, because less overstrained, so perhaps it is even more touching, than that of Griselda, over which, however, Chaucer has thrown a charm that leads us to forget the improbabilty of her story.

CHAPTER XXVI

PWYLL, PRINCE OF DYVED

ONCE upon a time Pwyll was at Narberth, his chief palace, where a feast had been prepared for him, and with him was a great host of men. And after the first meal Pwyll arose to walk; and he went to the top of a mound that was above the palace, and was called Gorsedd Arberth. "Lord," said one of the court, "it is peculiar to the mound that whosoever sits upon it cannot go thence without either receiving wounds or blows, or else seeing a wonder." "I fear not to receive wounds or blows," said Pwyll; "but as to the wonder, gladly would I see it. I will therefore go and sit upon the mound."

And upon the mound he sat. And while he sat there, they saw a lady on a pure white horse of large size, with a garment of shining gold around her, coming along the highway that led from the mound. "My men," said Pwyll, "is there any among you who knows yonder lady?" "There is not, lord," said they. "Go one of you and meet her, that we may know who she is." And one of them arose, and as he came upon the road to meet her, she passed by; and he followed as fast as he could being on foot, and the greater was his speed, the further was she from him. And when he saw that it profited him nothing to follow her, he returned to Pwyll, and said unto him, "Lord, it is idle for any one in the world to follow her on foot." "Verily," said Pwyll, "go unto the palace, and take the fleetest horse that thou seest, and go after her."

And he took a horse and went forward. And he came to an open, level plain, and put spurs to his horse; and the more he urged his horse, the further was she from him. And he returned to the palace where Pwyll was, and said, "Lord, it will avail nothing for any one to follow yonder lady. I know of

no horse in these realms swifter than this, and it availed me not to pursue her." "Of a truth," said Pwyll, "there must be some illusion here; let us go towards the palace." So to the palace they went, and spent the day.

And the next day they amused themselves until it was time to go to meat. And when meat was ended, Pwyll said, "Where are the hosts that went yesterday to the top of the mound?" "Behold, lord, we are here," said they. "Let us go," said he, "to the mound, and sit there. And do thou," said he to the page who tended his horse, "saddle my horse well, and hasten with him to the road, and bring also my spurs with thee." And the youth did thus. And they went and sat upon the mound; and ere they had been there but a short time, they beheld the lady coming by the same road, and in the same manner, and at the same pace. "Young man," said Pwyll, "I see the lady coming; give me my horse." And before he had mounted his horse she passed him. And he turned after her and followed her. And he let his horse go bounding play-fully, and thought that he should soon come up with her. But he came no nearer to her than at first. Then he urged his horse to his utmost speed, yet he found that it availed not. Then said Pwyll, "O maiden, for the sake of him whom thou best lovest, stay for me." "I will stay gladly," said she; "and it were better for thy horse hadst thou asked it long since." So the maiden stopped; and she threw back that part of her headdress which covered her face. Then he thought that the beauty of all the maidens and all the ladies that he had ever seen was as nothing compared to her beauty. "Lady," he said, "wilt thou tell me aught concerning thy purpose?" "I will tell thee," said she; "my chief quest was to see thee." "Truly," said Pwyll,

144 ▷

go with him to the palace of Heveydd. And he came to the palace, and there was great joy concerning him, with much concourse of people, and great rejoicing, and vast preparations for his coming. And the whole court was placed under his orders.

And the hall was garnished, and they went to meat, and thus did they sit: Heveydd was on one side of Pwyll, and Rhiannon on the other; and all the rest according to their rank. And they ate and feasted, and talked one with another. And at the beginning of the carousal after the meat, there entered a tall, auburn-haired youth, of royal bearing, clothed in a garment of satin. And when he came into the hall, he saluted Pwyll and his companions. "The greeting of heaven be unto thee," said Pwyll; "come thou and sit down." "Nay," said he, "a suitor am I, and I will do my errand." "Do so, willingly," said Pwyll. "Lord," said he, "my errand is unto thee, and it is to crave a boon of thee that I come." "What boon soever thou mayest ask of me, so far as I am able, thou shalt have." "Ah!" said Rhiannon, "wherefore didst thou give that answer?" "Has he not given it before the presence of these nobles?" asked the youth. "My soul," said Pwyll, "what is the boon thou askest?" "The lady whom best I love is to be thy bride this night; I come to ask her of thee, with the feast and the banquet that are in this place." And Pwyll was silent, because of the promise which he had given. "Be silent as long as thou wilt," said Rhiannon, "never did man make worse use of his wits than thou hast done." "Lady," said he, "I knew not who he was." "Behold, this is the man to whom they would have given me against my will," said she; "and he is Gawl, the son of Clud, a man of great power and wealth, and because of the word thou hast spoken, bestow me upon him, lest shame befall thee." "Lady," said he, "I understand not thy answer; never can I do as thou sayest." "Bestow me upon him," said she, "and I will cause that I shall never be his." "By what means will that be?" asked Pwyll. Then she told him the thought that was in her mind. And they talked long together. Then Gawl said, "Lord, it is meet that I have an answer to my request." "As much of that thou hast asked as it is in my power to give, thou shalt have," replied Pwyll. "My soul," said Rhiannon unto Gawl, "as for the feast and the banquet that are here, I have bestowed

"this is to me the most pleasing quest on which thou couldst have come; and wilt thou tell me who thou art?" "I will tell thee, lord," said she. "I am Rhiannon, the daughter of Heveydd, and they sought to give me to a husband against my will. But no husband would I have, and that because of my love for thee; neither will I yet have one, unless thou reject me; and hither have I come to hear thy answer." "By heaven," said Pwyll, "behold this is my answer. If I might choose among all the ladies and damsels in the world, thee would I choose." "Verily," said she, "if thou art thus minded, make a pledge to meet me ere I am given to another." "The sooner I may do so, the more pleasing will it be to me," said Pwyll; "and wheresoever thou wilt, there will I meet with thee." "I will that thou meet me this day twelvemonth at the palace of Heveydd." "Gladly," said he, "will I keep this tryst." So they parted, and he went back to his hosts, and to them of his household. And whatsoever questions they asked him respecting the damsel, he always turned the discourse upon other matters.

And when a year from that time was gone, he caused a hundred knights to equip themselves, and to them upon the men of Lyyed, and the household and the warriors that are with us. These can I not suffer to be given to any. In a year from tonight, a banquet shall be prepared for thee in this palace, that I may become thy bride."

So Gawl went forth to his possessions, and Pwyll went also back to Dyved. And they both spent that year until it was the time for the feast at the palace of Heveydd. Then Gawl, the son of Clud, set out to the feast that was prepared for him; and he came to the palace, and was received there with rejoicing. Pwyll, also, the chief of Dyved, came to the orchard with a hundred knights, as Rhiannon had commanded him. And Pwyll was clad in coarse and ragged garments, and wore large, clumsy old shoes upon his feet. And when he knew that the carousal after the meat had begun, he went toward the hall; and when he came into the hall he saluted Gawl, the son of Clud, and his company, both men and women. "Heaven prosper thee," said Gawl, "and friendly greeting be unto thee!" "Lord," said he, "may heaven reward thee! I have an errand unto thee." "Welcome be thine errand, and if thou ask of me that which is right, thou shalt have it gladly." "It is fitting," answered he; "I crave but from want, and the boon I ask is to have this small bag that thou seest filled with meat." "A request within reason is this," said he, "and gladly shalt thou have it. Bring him food." A great number of attendants arose and began to fill the bag; but for all they put into it, it was no fuller than at first. "My soul," said Gawl, "will thy bag ever be full?" "It will not, I declare to heaven," said he, "for all that may be put into it, unless one possessed of lands, and domains, and treasure, shall arise and tread down with both his feet the food that is within the bag, and shall say, 'Enough has been put therein.'" Then said Rhiannon unto Gawl, the son of Clud, "Rise up quickly." "I will willingly arise," said he. So he rose up, and put his two feet into the bag. And Pwyll turned up the sides of the bag, so that Gawl was over his head in it. And he shut it up quickly, and slipped a knot upon the thongs, and blew his horn. And thereupon, behold, his knights came down upon the palace. And they seized all the host that had come with Gawl, and cast them into his own prison. And Pwyll threw off his rags, and his old shoes, and his

◁145 tattered array. And as they came in every one of Pwyll's knights struck a blow upon the bag, and asked, "what is here?" "A badger," said they. And in this manner they played, each of them striking the bag, either with his foot or with a staff. And thus played they with the bag. And then was the game of Badger in the Bag first played.

"Lord," said the man in the bag, "if thou wouldst but hear me, I merit not to be slain in a bag." Said Heveydd, "Lord, he speaks truth; it were fitting that thou listen to him, for he deserves not this." "Verily," said Pwyll, "I will do thy counsel concerning him." "Behold, this is my counsel then," said Rhiannon. "Thou art now in a position in which it behooves thee to satisfy suitors and minstrels. Let him give unto them in thy stead, and take a pledge from him that he will never seek to revenge that which has been done to him. And this will be punishment enough." "I will do this gladly," said the man in the bag. "And gladly will I accept it," said Pwyll, "since it is the counsel of Heveydd and Rhiannon. Seek thyself sureties." "We will be for him," said Heveydd, "until his men be free to answer for him." And upon this he was let out of the bag, and his liegemen were liberated. "Verily, lord," said Gawl, "I am greatly hurt, and I have many bruises. With thy leave I will go forth. I will leave nobles in my stead to answer for me in all that thou shalt require." "Willingly," said Pwyll, "mayest thou do thus." So Gawl went to his own possessions.

And the hall was set in order for Pwyll and the men of his host, and for them also of the palace, and they went to the tables and sat down. And as they had sat at that time twelve-month, so sat they that night. And they ate and feasted, and spent the night in mirth and tranquillity. And the time came that they should sleep, and Pwyll and Rhiannon went to their chamber.

And next morning at break of day, "My lord," said Rhiannon, "arise and begin to give thy gifts unto the minstrels. Refuse no one today that may claim thy bounty." "Thus shall it be gladly," said Pwyll, "both today and every day while the feast shall last." So Pwyll arose, and he caused silence to be proclaimed, and desired all the suitors and minstrels to show and to point out what gifts they desired. And this being done, the feast went on, and he denied no one while it lasted. And when the feast was ended, Pwyll said unto Heveydd, "My lord, with thy permission, I will set out for Dyved tomorrow." "Certainly," said Heveydd; "may heaven prosper thee! Fix also a time when Rhiannon shall follow thee." "By heaven," said Pwyll, "we will go hence together." "Willest thou this, lord?" said Heveydd. "Yes, lord," answered Pwyll.

And the next day they set forward towards Dyved, and journeyed to the palace of Narberth, where a feast was made ready for them. And there came to them great numbers of the chief men and the most noble ladies of the land, and of these there were none to whom Rhiannon did not give some rich gift, either a bracelet, or a ring, or a precious stone. And they ruled the land prosperously that year and the next.

CHAPTER XXVII

BRANWEN, THE DAUGHTER OF LLYR

BENDIGEID VRAN, the son of Llyr, was the crowned king of this island, and he was exalted from the crown of London. And one afternoon he was at Harlech, in Ardudwy, at his court; and he sat upon the rock of Harlech, looking over the sea. And with him were his brother, Manawyddan, the son of Llyr, and his brothers by his mother's side, Nissyen and Evnissyen, and many nobles likewise, as was fitting to see around a king. His two brothers by the mother's side were sons of

Euroswydd, and one of these youths was a good youth, and of gentle nature, and would make peace between his kindred, and cause his family to be friends when their wrath was at the highest, and this one was Nissyen; but the other would cause strife between his two brothers when they were most at peace. And as they sat thus they beheld thirteen ships coming from the south of Ireland, and making towards them; and they came with a swift motion, the wind being behind them; and they neared them rapidly. "I see ships afar," said the king, "coming swiftly towards the land. Command the men of the court that they equip themselves, and go and learn their intent." So the men equipped themselves, and went down towards them. And when they saw the ships near, certain were they that they had never seen ships better furnished. Beautiful flags of satin were upon them. And, behold, one of the ships outstripped the others, and they saw a shield lifted up above the side of the ship, and the point of the shield was upwards, in token of peace. And the men drew near, that they might hold converse. Then they put out boats, and came toward the land. And they saluted the king. Now the king could hear them from the place where he was upon the rock above their heads. "Heaven prosper you," said he, "and be ye welcome! To whom do those ships belong, and who is the chief amongst you?" "Lord," said they, "Matholch, king of Ireland, is here, and these ships belong to him." "Wherefore comes he?" asked the king, "and will he come to the land?" "He is a suitor unto thee, lord," said they, "and he will not land unless he have his boon." "And what may that be?" inquired the king. "He desires to ally himself, lord, with thee," said they, "and he comes to ask Branwen, the daughter of Llyr, that, if it seem well to thee, the Island of the Mighty[1] may be leagued with Ireland, and both become more powerful." "Verily," said he, "let him come to land, and we will take counsel thereupon." And this answer was brought to Matholch. "I will go willingly," said he. So he landed, and they received him joyfully; and great was the throng in the palace that night between his hosts and those of the court; and next day they took counsel, and they resolved to bestow Branwen upon Matholch. Now she was one of the three chief ladies of this island, and she was the fairest damsel in the world.

And they fixed upon Aberfraw as the place where she should become his bride. And they went thence, and towards Aberfraw the hosts proceeded, Matholch and his host in their ships, Bendigeid Vran and his host by land, until they came to Aberfraw. And at Aberfraw they began the feast, and sat down. And thus sat they: the king of the Island of the Mighty and Manawyddan, the son of Llyr, on one side, and Matholch on the other side, and Branwen, the daughter of Llyr, beside him. And they were not within a house, but under tents. No house could ever contain Bendigeid Vran. And they began the banquet, and caroused and discoursed. And when it was more pleasing to them to sleep than to carouse, they went to rest, and Branwen became Matholch's bride.

And the next day they arose, and all they of the court, and the officers began to equip, and to range the horses and the attendants, and they ranged them in order as far as the sea.

And, behold, one day Evnissyen, the quarrelsome man, of whom it is spoken above, came by chance into the place where the horses of Matholch were, and asked whose horses they might be. "They are the horses of Matholch, king of Ireland, who is married to Branwen, thy sister; his horses are they." "And is it thus they have done with a maiden such as she, and moreover my sister, bestowing her, without my consent? They could

---

[1]The Island of the Mighty is one of the many names bestowed upon Britain by the Welsh.

have offered me no greater insult than this," said he. And thereupon he rushed under the horses, and cut off their lips at the teeth, and their ears close to their heads, and their tails close to their backs; and he disfigured the horses, and rendered them useless.

And they came with these tidings unto Matholch, saying that the horses were disfigured and injured, so that not one of them could ever be of any use again. "Verily, lord," said one, "it was an insult unto thee, and as such was it meant." "Of a truth, it is a marvel to me that, if they desire to insult me, they should have given me a maiden of such high rank, and so much beloved by their kindred, as they have done." "Lord," said another, "thou seest that thus it is, and there is nothing for thee to do but to go to thy ships." And thereupon towards his ships he set out.

And tidings came to Bendigeid Vran that Matholch was quitting the court without asking leave, and messengers were sent to him to inquire wherefore he did so. And the messengers that went were Iddic, the son of Anarawd, and Heveyd Hir. And these overtook him, and asked of him what he designed to do, and wherefore he went forth. "Of a truth," said he, "if I had known I had not come hither. I have been altogether insulted; no one had ever worse treatment than I have had here." "Truly, lord, it was not the will of any that are of the court," said they, "nor of any that are of the council, that thou shouldst have received this insult; and as thou hast been insulted the dishonor is greater unto Bendigeid Vran than unto thee." "Verily," said he, "I think so. Nevertheless he cannot recall the insult." These men returned with that answer to the place where Bendigeid Vran was, and they told him what reply Matholch had given them. "Truly," said he, "there are no means by which we may prevent his going away at enmity with us that we will not take." "Well, lord," said they, "send after him another embassy." "I will do so," said he. "Arise, Manawyddan, son of Llyr, and Heveyd Hir, and go after him, and tell him that he shall have a sound horse for every one that has been injured. And besides that, as an atonement for the insult, he shall have a staff of silver as large and as tall as himself, and a plate of gold of the breadth of his face. And show unto him who it was that did this, and that it was done against my will; but that he who did it is my

brother, and therefore it would be hard for me to put him to death. And let him come and meet me," said he, "and we will make peace in any way he may desire."

The embassy went after Matholch, and told him all these sayings in a friendly manner; and he listened thereunto. "Men," said he, "I will take counsel." So to the council he went. And in the council they considered that, if they should refuse this, they were likely to have more shame rather than to obtain so great an atonement. They resolved, therefore, to accept it, and they returned to the court in peace.

Then the pavilions and tents were set in order after the fashion of a ball; and they went to meat, and as they had sat at the beginning of the feast so sat they there. And Matholch and Bendigeid Vran began to discourse; and, behold, it seemed to Bendigeid Vran, while they talked, that Matholch was not so cheerful as he had been before. And he thought that the chieftain might be sad because of the smallness of the atonement which he had for the wrong that had been done him. "O man," said Bendigeid Vran, "thou dost not discourse tonight so cheerfully as thou wast wont. And if it be because of the smallness of the atonement thou shalt add thereunto whatsoever thou mayest choose, and tomorrow I will pay thee for the horses." "Lord," said he, "Heaven reward thee!" "And I will enhance the atonement," said Bendigeid Vran, "for I will give thee a caldron, the property of which is that if one of thy men be slain today, and be cast therein, tomorrow he will be as well as ever he was at the best, except that he will not regain his speech." And thereupon he gave him great thanks, and very joyful was he for that cause.

That night they continued to discourse as much as they would, and had minstrelsy and carousing; and when it was more pleasant to them to sleep than to sit longer, they went to rest. And thus was the banquet carried on with joyousness; and when it was finished, Matholch journeyed towards Ireland, and Branwen with him; and they went from Aber Menei with thirteen ships, and came to Ireland. And in Ireland was there great joy because of their coming. And not one great man nor noble lady visited Branwen unto whom she gave not either a clasp or a ring, or a royal jewel to keep, such as it was honorable to be seen departing with. And in these things

she spent that year in much renown, and she passed her time pleasantly, enjoying honor and friendship. And in due time a son was born unto her, and the name that they gave him was Gwern, the son of Matholch, and they put the boy out to be nursed in a place where were the best men of Ireland.

And, behold, in the second year a great tumult arose in Ireland, on account of the insult which Matholch had received in Wales, and the payment made him for his horses. And his foster-brothers, and such as were nearest to him, blamed him openly for that matter. And he might have no peace by reason of the tumult, until they should revenge upon him this disgrace. And the vengeance which they took was to drive away Branwen from the same chamber with him, and to make her cook for the court; and they caused the butcher, after he had cut up the meat, to come to her and give her every day a blow on the ear; and such they made her punishment.

"Verily, lord," said his men to Matholch, "forbid now the ships and the ferry-boats, and the coracles, that they go not into Wales, and such as come over from Wales hither, imprison them, that they go not back for this thing to be known there." And he did so; and it was thus for no less than three years.

And Branwen reared a starling in the cover of the kneading-trough, and she taught it to speak, and she taught the bird what manner of man her brother was. And she wrote a letter of her woes, and the despite with which she was treated, and she bound the letter to the root of the bird's wing, and sent it toward Wales. And the bird came to that island; and one day it found Bendigeid Vran at Caer Seiont in Arvon, conferring there, and it alighted upon his shoulder, and ruffled its feathers, so that the letter was seen, and they knew that the bird had been reared in a domestic manner.

Then Bendigeid Vran took the letter and looked upon it. And when he had read the letter, he grieved exceedingly at the tidings of Branwen's woes. And immediately he began sending messengers to summon the island together. And he caused sevenscore and four of his chief men to come unto him, and he complained to them of the grief that his sister endured. So they took counsel. And in the council they resolved to go to Ireland, and to leave seven men as princes at home, and Caradoc,[1] the son of Bran, as the chief of them.

Bendigeid Vran, with the host of which we spoke, sailed towards Ireland; and it was not far across the sea, and he came to shoal water. Now the swineherds of Matholch were upon the seashore, and they came to Matholch. "Lord," said they, "greeting be unto thee." "Heaven protect you!" said he; "have you any news?" "Lord," said they, "we have marvellous news. A wood have we seen upon the sea, in a place where we never yet saw a single tree." "This is indeed a marvel," said he; "saw you aught else?" "We saw, lord," said they, "a vast mountain beside the wood, which moved, and there was a lofty ridge on the top of the mountain, and a lake on each side of the ridge. And the wood and the mountain, and all these things moved." "Verily," said he, "there is none who can know aught concerning this unless it be Branwen."

Messengers then went unto Branwen. "Lady," said they, "what thinkest thou that this is?" "The men of the Island of the Mighty, who have come hither on hearing of my ill-treatment and of my woes." "What is the forest that is seen upon the sea?" asked they. "The yards and the masts of ships," she answered. "Alas!" said they; "what is the mountain that is seen by the side of the ships?" "Bendigeid Vran, my brother," she replied, "coming to shoal water, and he is wading to the land." "What is the lofty ridge, with the lake on each side thereof?" "On

[1]Caractacus.

looking towards this island he is wroth, and his two eyes on each side of his nose are the two lakes on each side of the ridge."

The warriors and chief men of Ireland were brought together in haste, and they took counsel. "Lord," said the neighbors unto Matholch, "there is no other counsel than this alone. Thou shalt give the kingdom to Gwern, the son of Branwen his sister, as a compensation for the wrong and despite that have been done unto Branwen. And he will make peace with thee." And in the council it was resolved that this message should be sent to Bendigeid Vran, lest the country should be destroyed. And this peace was made. And Matholch caused a great house to be built for Bendigeid Vran, and his host. Thereupon came the hosts into the house. The men of the island of Ireland entered the house on the one side, and the men of the Island of the Mighty on the other. And as soon as they had sat down, there was concord between them; and the sovereignty was conferred upon the boy. When the peace was concluded, Bendigeid Vran called the boy unto him, and from Bendigeid Vran the boy went unto Manawyddan, and he was beloved by all that beheld him. And from Manawyddan the boy was called by Nissyen, the son of Euroswydd, and the boy went unto him lovingly. "Wherefore," said Evnissyen, "comes not my nephew, the son of my sister, unto me? Though he were not king of Ireland, yet willingly would I fondle the boy." "Cheerfully let him go to thee," said Bendigeid Vran; and the boy went unto him cheerfully. "By my confession to heaven," said Evnissyen in his heart, "unthought of is the slaughter that I will this instant commit."

Then he arose and took up the boy, and before any one in the house could seize hold of him he thrust the boy headlong into the blazing fire. And when Branwen saw her son burning in the fire, she strove to leap into the fire also, from the place where she sat between her two brothers. But Bendigeid Vran grasped her with one hand, and his shield with the other. Then they all hurried about the house, and never was there made so great a tumult by any host in one house as was made by them, as each man armed himself. And while they all sought their arms Bendigeid Vran supported Branwen between his shield and his shoulder. And they fought.

Then the Irish kindled a fire under the caldron of renovation, and they cast the dead bodies into the caldron until it was full; and the next day they came forth fighting men, as good as before, except that they were not able to speak. Then when Evnissyen saw the dead bodies of the men of the Island of the Mighty nowhere resuscitated, he said in his heart, "Alas! woe is me, that I should have been the cause of bringing the men of the Island of the Mighty into so great a strait. Evil betide me if I find not a deliverance therefrom." And he cast himself among the dead bodies of the Irish; and two unshod Irishmen came to him, and taking him to be one of the Irish, flung him into the caldron. And he stretched himself out in the caldron, so that he rent the caldron into four pieces, and burst his own heart also.

In consequence of this the men of the Island of the Mighty obtained such success as they had; but they were not victorious, for only seven men of them all escaped, and Bendigeid Vran himself was wounded in the foot with a poisoned dart. Now the men that escaped were Pryderi, Manawyddan, Taliesin, and four others.

And Bendigeid Vran commanded them that they should cut off his head. "And take you my head," said he, "and bear it even unto the White Mount in London, and bury it there with the face towards France. And so long as it lies there, no enemy shall ever land on the island." So they cut off his head, and these seven went forward therewith. And Branwen was the eighth with them. And they came to land on Aber Alaw, and they sat down to rest. And Branwen looked towards Ireland, and towards the Island of the Mighty, to see if she could descry them. "Alas!" said she, "woe is me that I was ever born; two islands have been destroyed because of me." Then she uttered a groan, and there broke her heart. And they made her a four-sided grave, and buried her upon the banks of the Maw.

Then the seven men journeyed forward, bearing the head with them; and as they went, behold, there met them a multitude of men and women. "Have you any tidings?" said Manawyddan. "We have none, said they, "save that Caswallawn,[1] the son of Beli, has

---

[1]Cassivellaunus.

conquered the Island of the Mighty, and is crowned king in London." "What has become," said they, "of Caradoc, the son of Bran, and the seven men who were left with him in this island?" "Caswallawn came upon them, and slew six of the men, and Caradoc's heart broke for grief thereof." And the seven men journeyed on towards London, and they buried the head in the White Mount, as Bendigeid Vran had directed them.[1]

---

[1]There is a Triad upon the story of the head buried under the White Tower of London, as a charm against invasion. Arthur, it seems, proudly disinterred the head, preferring to hold the island by his own strength alone.

CHAPTER XXVIII

MANAWYDDAN

PWYLL AND RHIANNON had a son, whom they named Pryderi. And when he was grown up, Pwyll, his father, died. And Pryderi married Kicva, the daughter of Gwynn Gloy.

Now Manawyddan returned from the war in Ireland, and he found that his cousin had seized all his possessions, and much grief and heaviness came upon him. "Alas! woe is me!" he exclaimed; "there is none save myself without a home and a resting-place." "Lord," said Pryderi, "be not so sorrowful. Thy cousin is king of the Island of the Mighty, and though he has done thee wrong, thou hast never been a claimant of land or possessions." "Yea," answered he; "but although this man is my cousin, it grieveth me to see any one in the place of my brother, Bendigeid Vran; neither can I be happy in the same dwelling with him." "Wilt thou follow the counsel of another?" said Pryderi. "I stand in need of counsel," he answered, "and what may that counsel be?" "Seven cantrevs belong unto me," said Pryderi, "wherein Rhiannon, my mother, dwells. I will bestow her upon thee, and the seven cantrevs with her; and though thou hadst no possessions but those cantrevs only, thou couldst not have any fairer than they. Do thou and Rhiannon enjoy them; and if thou desire any possessions thou wilt not despise these." "I do not, chieftain," said he. "Heaven reward thee for thy friendship! I will go with thee to seek Rhiannon, and to look at thy possessions. Thou wilt do well," he answered; "and I believe thou didst never hear a lady discourse

better than she, and when she was in her prime, none was ever fairer. Even now her aspect is not uncomely."

They set forth, and, however long the journey, they came at last to Dyved; and a feast was prepared for them by Rhiannon and Kicva. Then began Manawyddan and Rhiannon to sit and talk together; and his mind and his thoughts became warmed towards her, and he thought in his heart he had never beheld any lady more fulfilled of grace and beauty than she. "Pryderi," said he, "I will that it be as thou didst say." "What saying was that?" asked Rhiannon. "Lady," said Pryderi, "I did offer thee as a wife to Manawyddan, the son of Llyr." "By that will I gladly abide," said Rhiannon. "Right glad am I also," said Manawyddan; "may heaven reward him who hath shown unto me friendship so perfect as this."

And before the feast was over she became his bride. Said Pryderi, "Tarry ye here the rest of the feast, and I will go into England to tender my homage unto Caswallawn, the son of Beli." "Lord," said Rhiannon, "Caswallawn is in Kent; thou mayest therefore tarry at the feast, and wait until he shall be nearer." "We will wait," he answered. So they finished the feast. And they began to make the circuit of Dyved, and to hunt, and to take their pleasure. And as they went through the country, they had never seen lands more pleasant to live in, nor better hunting-grounds, nor greater plenty of honey and fish. And such was the friendship between these four, that they would not be parted from each other by night nor by day.

152

And in the midst of all this he went to Caswallawn at Oxford, and tendered his homage; and honorable was his reception there, and highly was he praised for offering his homage.

And after his return Pryderi and Manawyddan feasted and took their ease and pleasure. And they began a feast at Narberth, for it was the chief palace. And when they had ended the first meal, while those who served them ate, they arose and went forth, and proceeded to the Gorsedd, that is, the Mound of Narberth, and their retinue with them. And as they sat thus, behold a peal of thunder, and with the violence of the thunder-storm, lo! there came a fall of mist, so thick that not one of them could see the other. And after the mist it became light all around. And when they looked towards the place where they were wont to see cattle and herds and dwellings, they saw nothing now, neither house, nor beast, nor smoke, nor fire, nor man, nor dwelling, but the buildings of the court empty, and desert, and uninhabited, without either man or beast within them. And truly all their companions were lost to them, without their knowing aught of what had befallen them, save those four only.

"In the name of heaven," said Manawyddan, "where are they of the court, and all my host beside? Let us go and see."

So they came to the castle, and saw no man, and into the hall, and to the sleeping-place, and there was none; and in the mead-cellar and in the kitchen there was naught but desolation. Then they began to go through the land, and all the possessions that they had; and they visited the houses and dwellings, and found nothing but wild beasts. And when they had consumed their feast and all their provisions, they fed upon the prey they killed in hunting, and the honey of the wild swarms.

And one morning Pryderi and Manawyddan rose up to hunt, and they ranged their dogs and went forth. And some of the dogs ran before them, and came to a bush which was near at hand; but as soon as they were come to the bush, they hastily drew back, and returned to the men, their hair bristling up greatly. "Let us go near to the bush," said Pryderi, "and see what is in it." And as they came near, behold, a wild boar of a pure white color rose up from the bush. Then the dogs, being set on by the men, rushed towards him; but he left the bush, and fell back a little way from the men, and made a stand against the dogs, without retreating from them, until the men had come near. And when the men came up, he fell back a second time, and betook him to flight. Then they pursued the boar until they beheld a vast and lofty castle, all newly built, in a place where they had never before seen either stone or building. And the boar ran swiftly into the castle, and the dogs after him. Now when the boar and the dogs had gone into the castle, the men began to wonder at finding a castle in a place where they had never seen any building whatsoever. And from the top of the Gorsedd they looked and listened for the dogs. But so long as they were there, they heard not one of the dogs, nor aught concerning them.

"Lord," said Pryderi, "I will go into the castle to get tidings of the dogs." "Truly," he replied, "thou wouldst be unwise to go into this castle, which thou hast never seen till now. If thou wouldst follow my counsel, thou wouldst not enter therein. Whosoever has cast a spell over this land, has caused this castle to be here." "Of a truth," answered Pryderi, "I cannot thus give up my dogs." And for all the counsel that Manawyddan gave him, yet to the castle he went.

When he came within the castle neither man, nor beast, nor boar, nor dogs, nor house, nor dwelling, saw he within it. But in the centre of the castle floor he beheld a fountain with marble-work around it, and on the margin of the fountain a golden bowl upon a marble slab, and chains hanging from the air, to which he saw no end.

And he was greatly pleased with the beauty of the gold, and with the rich workmanship of the bowl; and he went up to the bowl, and laid hold of it. And when he had taken hold of it his hands stuck to the bowl, and his feet to the slab on which the bowl was placed; and all his joyousness forsook him, so that he could not utter a word. And thus he stood.

And Manawyddan waited for him till near the close of the day. And late in the evening, being certain that he should have no tidings of Pryden or the dogs, he went back to the palace. And as he entered Rhiannon looked at him. "Where," said she, "are thy companion and thy dogs?" "Behold," he answered, "the adventure that has befallen me." And he related it all unto her. "An evil companion hast thou been,"

said Rhiannon, "and a good companion hast thou lost." And with that word she went out, and proceeded towards the castle, according to the direction which he gave her. The gate of the castle she found open. She was nothing daunted, and she went in. And as she went in she perceived Pryden laying hold of the bowl, and she went towards him. "O my lord," said she, "what dost thou here?" And she took hold of the bowl with him; and as she did so her hands also became fast to the bowl, and her feet to the slab, and she was not able to utter a word. And with that, as it became night, lo! there came thunder upon them, and a fall of mist; and thereupon the castle vanished, and they with it.

When Kicva, the daughter of Gwynn Gloy, saw that there was no one in the palace but herself and Manawyddan, she sorrowed so that she cared not whether she lived or died. And Manawyddan saw this. "Thou art in the wrong," said he, "if through fear of me thou grievest thus. I call heaven to witness that thou hast never seen friendship more pure than that which I will bear thee, as long as heaven will that thou shouldst be thus. I declare to thee that, were I in the dawn of youth, I would keep my faith unto Pryderi, and unto thee also will I keep it. Be there no fear upon thee, therefore." "Heaven reward thee!" she said; "and that is what I deemed of thee." And the damsel thereupon took courage, and was glad.

"Truly, lady," said Manawyddan, "it is not fitting for us to stay here; we have lost our dogs, and cannot get food. Let us go into England; it is easier for us to find support there." "Gladly, lord," said she, "we will do so." And they set forth together to England.

"Lord," said she, "what craft wilt thou follow? Take up one that is seemly." "None other will I take," answered he, "but that of making shoes." "Lord," said she, "such a craft becomes not a man so nobly born as thou." "By that however will I abide," said he. "I know nothing thereof," said Kicva. "But I know," answered Manawyddan, "and I will teach thee to stitch. We will not attempt to dress the leather, but we will buy it ready dressed, and will make the shoes from it."

So they went into England, and went as far as Hereford; and they betook themselves to making shoes. And he began by buying the best cordwain that could be had in town, and none other would he buy. And he associated himself with the best goldsmith in the town, and caused him to make clasps for the shoes, and to gild the clasps; and he marked how it was done until he learned the method. And therefore is he called one of the three makers of gold shoes. And when they could be had from him not a shoe nor hose was bought from any of the cordwainers in the town. But when the cordwainers perceived that their gains were failing (for as Manawyddan shaped the work so Kicva stitched it), they came together and took counsel, and agreed that they would slay them. And he had warning thereof, and it was told him how the cordwainers had agreed to slay him.

"Lord," said Kicva, "wherefore should this be borne from these boors?" "Nay," said he, "we will go back unto Dyved." So towards Dyved they set forth.

Now Manawyddan, when he set out to return to Dyved, took with him a burden of wheat. And he proceeded towards Narberth, and there he dwelt. And never was he better pleased than when he saw Narberth again, and the lands where he had been wont to hunt with Pryderi and with Rhiannon. And he accustomed himself to fish and to hunt the deer in their covert. And then he began to prepare some ground, and he sowed a croft, and a second, and a third. And no wheat in the world ever sprang up better. And the three crofts prospered with perfect growth, and no man ever saw fairer wheat than it.

And thus passed the seasons of the year until the harvest came. And he went to look at one of his crofts, and, behold, it was ripe. "I will reap this tomorrow," said he. And that night he went back to Narberth, and on the morrow, in the gray dawn, he went to reap the croft; and when he came there he found nothing but the bare straw. Every one of the ears of the wheat was cut off from the stalk, and all the ears carried entirely away, and nothing but the straw left. And at this he marvelled greatly.

Then he went to look at another croft, and, behold, that also was ripe. "Verily," said he, "this will I reap tomorrow." And on the morrow he came with the intent to reap it; and when he came there he found nothing but the bare straw. "O gracious heaven!" he exclaimed, "I know that whomsoever has begun my ruin is completing it, and has also destroyed the country with me."

Then he went to look at the third croft; and when he came there, finer wheat had there never been seen, and this also was ripe. "Evil betide me," said he, "if I watch not here tonight. Whoever carried off the other corn will come in like manner to take this, and I will know who it is." And he told Kicva all that had befallen. "Verily," said she, "what thinkest thou to do?" "I will watch the croft tonight," said he. And he went to watch the croft. And at midnight he heard something stirring among the wheat; and he looked, and behold, the mightiest host of mice in the world, which could neither be numbered nor measured. And he knew not what it was until the mice had made their way into the croft, and each of them, climbing up the straw, and bending it down with its weight, had cut off one of the ears of wheat, and had carried it away, leaving there the stalk; and he saw not a single straw there that had not a mouse to it. And they all took their way, carrying the ears with them.

In wrath and anger did he rush upon the mice; but he could no more come up with them than if they had been gnats or birds of the air, except one only, which, though it was but sluggish, went so fast that a man on foot could scarce overtake it. And after this one he went, and he caught it, and put it in his glove, and tied up the opening of the glove with a string, and kept it with him, and returned to the palace. Then he came to the hall where Kicva was, and he lighted a fire, and hung the glove by the string upon a peg. "What hast thou there, lord?" said Kicva. "A thief," said he, "that I found robbing me." "What kind of a thief may it be, lord, that thou couldst put into thy glove?" said she. Then he told her how the mice came to the last of the fields in his sight. "And one of them was less nimble than the rest, and is now in my glove; tomorrow I will hang it." "My lord," said she, "this is marvellous; but yet it would be unseemly for a man of dignity like thee to be hanging such a reptile as this." "Woe betide me," said he, "if I would not hang them all, could I catch them, and such as I have I will hang." "Verily, lord," said she, "there is no reason that I should succor this reptile, except to prevent discredit unto thee. Do therefore, lord, as thou wilt."

Then he went to the Mound of Narberth, taking the mouse with him. And he set up two forks on the highest part of the mound. And while he was doing this, behold, he saw a scholar coming towards him, in old and poor and tattered garments. And it was now seven years since he had seen in that place either man or beast, except those four persons who had remained together until two of them were lost.

"My lord," said the scholar, "good day to thee." "Heaven prosper thee, and my greeting be unto thee! And whence dost thou come, scholar?" asked he. "I come, lord, from singing in England; and wherefore dost thou inquire?" "Because for the last seven years," answered he, "I have seen no man here save four secluded persons, and thyself this moment." "Truly, lord," said he, "I go through this land unto mine own. And what work art thou upon, lord?" "I am hanging a thief that I caught robbing me," said he. "What manner of thief is that?" asked the scholar. "I see a creature in thy hand like unto a mouse, and ill does it become a man of rank equal to thine to touch a reptile such as this. Let it go forth free." "I will not let it go free, by heaven," said he, "I caught it robbing me, and the doom of a thief will I inflict upon it, and I will hang it." "Lord," said he, "rather than see a man of rank equal to thine at such a work as this, I would give thee a pound, which I have received as alms, to let the reptile go forth free." "I will not let it go free," said he, "neither will I sell it." "As thou wilt, lord," he answered; "I care naught." And the scholar went his way.

And as he was placing the cross-beam upon the two forks, behold, a priest came towards him, upon a horse covered with trappings. "Good day to thee, lord," said he. "Heaven prosper thee!" said Manawyddan; "thy blessing." "The blessing of heaven be upon thee! And what, lord, art thou doing?" "I am hanging a thief that I caught robbing me," said he. "What manner of thief, lord?" asked he. "A creature," he answered, "in form of a mouse. It has been robbing me, and I am inflicting upon it the doom of a thief." "Lord," said he, "rather than see thee touch this reptile, I would purchase its freedom." "By my confession to heaven, neither will I sell it nor set it free." "It is true, lord, that it is worth nothing to buy; but rather than see thee defile thyself by touching such a reptile as this, I will give thee three pounds to let it go." "I will not, by heaven," said he, "take any price for it. As it ought, so shall it be hanged." And the priest went his way.

Then he noosed the string around the mouse's neck; and as he was about to draw it up, behold, he saw a bishop's retinue, with his sumpterhorses and his attendants. And the bishop himself came towards him. And he stayed his work. "Lord bishop," said he, "thy blessing." "Heaven's blessing be unto thee!" said he. "What work art thou upon?" "Hanging a thief that I caught robbing me," said he. "Is not that a mouse that I see in thy hand?" "Yes," answered he, "and she has robbed me." "Ah," said he, "since I have come at the doom of this reptile, I will ransom it of thee. I will give thee seven pounds for it, and that rather than see a man of rank equal to thine destroying so vile a reptile as this. Let it loose, and thou shalt have the money." "I declare to heaven that I will not let it loose." "If thou wilt not loose it for this, I will give thee four and twenty pounds of ready money to set it free." "I will not set it free, by heaven, for as much again," said he. "If thou wilt not set it free for this, I will give thee all the horses that thou seest in this plain, and the seven loads of baggage, and the seven horses that they are upon." "By heaven, I will not," he replied. "Since for this thou wilt not set it free, do so at what price soever thou wilt." "I will that Rhiannon and Pryderi be free," said he. "That thou shalt have," he answered. "Not yet will I loose the mouse, by heaven." "What then wouldst thou?" "That the charm and the illusion be removed from the seven cantrevs of Dyved." "This shalt thou have also; set therefore the mouse free." "I will not set it free, by heaven," said he, "till I know who the mouse may be." "She is my wife." "Wherefore came she to me?" "To despoil thee," he answered. "I am Lloyd, the son of Kilwed, and I cast the charm over the seven cantrevs of Dyved. And it was to avenge Gawl, the son of Clud, from the friendship that I had towards him, that I cast the charm. And upon Pryderi did I avenge Gawl, the son of Clud, for the game of Badger in the Bag, that Pwyll, the son of Auwyn, played upon him. And when it was known that thou wast come to dwell in the land, my household came and besought me to transform them into mice, that they might destroy thy corn. And they went the first and the second night, and destroyed thy two crops. And the third night came unto me my wife and the ladies of the court, and besought me to transform them. And I transformed them. Now she is not in her usual health. And had she been in her usual health, thou wouldst not have been able to overtake her; but since this has taken place, and she has been caught, I will restore to thee Pryderi and Rhiannon, and I will take the charm and illusion from off Dyved. Set her therefore free." "I will not set her free yet." "What wilt

thou more?" he asked. "I will that there be no more charm upon the seven cantrevs of Dyved, and that none shall be put upon it henceforth; moreover, that vengeance be never taken for this, either upon Pryderi or Rhiannon, or upon me." "All this shalt thou have. And truly thou hast done wisely in asking this. Upon thy head would have lit all this trouble." "Yea," said he, "for fear thereof was it that I required this." "Set now my wife at liberty." "I will not," said he, "until I see Pryderi and Rhiannon with me free." "Behold, here they come," he answered.

And thereupon behold Pryderi and Rhiannon. And he rose up to meet them, and greeted them, and sat down beside them. "Ah, chieftain, set now my wife at liberty," said the bishop. "Hast thou not received all thou didst ask?" "I will release her, gladly," said he. And thereupon he set her free.

Then he struck her with a magic wand, and she was changed back into a young woman, the fairest ever seen.

"Look round upon thy land," said he, "and thou wilt see it all tilled and peopled as it was in its best estate." And he rose up and looked forth. And when he looked he saw all the lands tilled, and full of herds and dwellings.

And thus ends this portion of the Mabinogi.

The following allusions to the preceding story are found in a letter of the poet Southey to John Rickman, Esq., dated June 6th, 1802:

"You will read the Mabinogeon, concerning which I ought to have talked to you. In the last, that most odd and Arabian-like story of the mouse, mention is made of a begging scholar, that helps to the date; but where did the Cymri get the imagination that could produce such a tale? That enchantment of the basin hanging by the chain from heaven is in the wildest spirit of the Arabian Nights. I am perfectly astonished that such fictions should exist in Welsh. They throw no light on the origin of romance, everything being utterly dissimilar to what we mean by that term, but they do open a new world of fiction; and if the date of their language be fixed about the twelfth or thirteenth century, I cannot but think the mythological substance is of far earlier date; very probably brought from the East by some of the first settlers or conquerors."

CHAPTER XXIX

KILWICH AND OLWEN

KILYDD, the son of Prince Kelyddon, desired a wife as a helpmate, and the wife that he chose was Goleudid, the daughter of Prince Anlawd. And after their union the people put up prayers that they might have an heir. And they had a son through the prayers of the people; and called his name Kilwich.

After this the boy's mother, Goleudid, the daughter of Prince Anlawd, fell sick. Then she called her husband to her, and said to him, "Of this sickness I shall die, and thou wilt take another wife. Now wives are the gift of the Lord, but it would be wrong for thee to harm thy son. Therefore I charge thee that thou take not a wife until thou see a briar with two blossoms upon my grave." And this he promised her. Then she besought him to dress her grave every year, that no weeds might grow thereon. So the queen died. Now the king sent an attendant every morning to see if anything were growing upon the grave. And at the end of the seventh year they neglected that which they had promised to the queen.

One day the king went to hunt; and he rode to the place of burial, to see the grave, and to know if it were time that he should take a wife; and the king saw the briar. And when he saw it, the king took counsel where he should find a wife. Said one of his counsellors, "I know a wife that will suit thee well; and she is the wife of King Doged." And they resolved to go to seek her; and they slew the king, and brought away his wife. And they conquered the king's lands. And he married the widow of King Doged, the sister of Yspadaden Penkawr.

And one day his stepmother said to Kilwich, "It were well for thee to have a wife." "I am not yet of an age to wed," answered the youth. Then said she unto him, "I declare to thee that it is thy destiny not to be suited with a wife until thou obtain Olwen, the daughter of Yspadaden Penkawr." And the youth blushed, and the love of the maiden diffused itself through all his frame, although he had never seen her. And his father inquired of him, "What has come over thee, my son, and what aileth thee?" "My stepmother has declared to me that I shall never have a wife until

I obtain Olwen, the daughter of Yspadaden Penkawr." "That will be easy for thee," answered his father. "Arthur is thy cousin. Go, therefore, unto Arthur to cut thy hair, and ask this of him as a boon."

And the youth pricked forth upon a steed with head dappled gray, four winters old, firm of limb, with shell-formed hoofs, having a bridle of linked gold on his head, and upon him a saddle of costly gold. And in the youth's hand were two spears of silver, sharp, well tempered, headed with steel, three ells in length, of an edge to wound the wind, and cause blood to flow, and swifter than the fall of the dew-drop from the blade of reed-grass, when the dew of June is at the heaviest. A goldhilted sword was upon his thigh, the blade of which was gilded, bearing a cross of inlaid gold of the hue of the lightning of heaven. His war-horn was of ivory. Before him were two brindled, white-breasted greyhounds, having strong collars of rubies about their necks, reaching from the shoulder to the ear. And the one that was upon the left side bounded across to the right side, and the one on the right to the left, and, like two sea-swallows, sported around him. And his courser cast up four sods, with his four hoofs, like four swallows in the air, about his head, now above, now below. About him was a four-cornered cloth of purple, and an apple of gold was at each corner, and every one of the apples was of the value of an hundred kine. And there was precious gold of the value of three hundred kine upon his shoes, and upon his stirrups, from his knee to the tip of his toe. And the blade of grass bent not beneath him, so light was his courser's tread, as he journeyed toward the gate of Arthur's palace.

Spoke the youth: "Is there a porter?" "There is; and if thou holdest not thy peace, small will be thy welcome. I am Arthur's porter every first day of January." "Open the portal." "I will not open it." "Wherefore not?" "The knife is in the meat, and the drink is in the horn, and there is revelry in Arthur's hall; and none may enter therein but the son of a king of a privileged country, or a craftsman bringing his craft. But there will be refreshment for thy dogs and for thy horse; and for thee there will be collops cooked and peppered, and luscious wine, and mirthful songs; and food for fifty men shall be brought unto thee in the guest-chamber, where the stranger and the sons of other countries eat, who come not into the precincts of the palace of Arthur. Thou wilt fare no worse there than thou wouldst with Arthur in the court. A lady shall smooth thy couch, and shall lull thee with songs; and early tomorrow morning, when the gate is open for the multitude that come hither today, for thee shall it be opened first, and thou mayest sit in the place that thou shalt choose in Arthur's hall, from the upper end to the lower." Said the youth: "That will I not do. If thou openest the gate, it is well. If thou dost not open it, I will bring disgrace upon thy lord, and evil report upon thee. And I will set up three shouts at this very gate, than which none were ever heard more deadly." "What clamor soever thou mayest make," said Glewlwyd the porter, "against the laws of Arthur's palace, shalt thou not enter therein, until I first go and speak with Arthur."

Then Glewlwyd went into the hall. And Arthur said to him, "Hast thou news from the gate?" "Half of my life is passed," said Glewlwyd, "and half of thine. I was heretofore in Kaer Se and Asse, in Sach and Salach, in Lotor and Potor, and I have been in India the Great and India the Lesser, and I have also been in Europe and Africa, and in the islands of Corsica, and I was present when thou didst conquer Greece in the East. Nine supreme sovereigns, handsome men, saw we there, but never did I behold a man of equal dignity with him who is now at the door of the portal." Then said Arthur, "If walking thou didst enter here, return thou running. It is unbecoming to keep such a man as thou sayest he is in the wind and the rain." Said Kay: "By the hand of my friend, if thou wouldst follow my counsel, thou wouldst not break through the laws of the court because of him." "Not so, blessed Kay," said Arthur; "it is an honor to us to be resorted to, and the greater our courtesy, the greater will be our renown and our fame and our glory."

And Glewlwyd came to the gate, and opened the gate before Kilwich; and although all dismounted upon the horse-block at the gate, yet did he not dismount, but he rode in upon his charger. Then said he, "Greeting be unto thee, sovereign ruler of this island, and be this greeting no less unto the lowest than unto the highest, and be it equally unto thy guests and thy warriors and thy chieftains; let all partake of it as completely as thyself. And complete be thy favor and thy fame and thy glory, throughout all this island." "Greeting unto thee also," said Arthur; "sit thou between two of my warriors, and thou shalt have minstrels before thee, and thou shalt enjoy the privileges of a king born to a throne, as long as thou remainest here. And when I dispense my presents to the visitors and strangers in this court, they shall be in thy hand at my commencing." Said the youth: "I came not here to consume meat and drink; but if I obtain the boon that I seek, I will requite it thee, and extol thee; but if I have it not I will bear forth thy dispraise to the four quarters of the world, as far as thy renown has extended." Then said Arthur, "Since thou wilt not remain here, chieftain, thou shalt receive the boon, whatsoever thy tongue may name, as far as the wind dries, and the rain moistens, and the sun revolves, and the sea encircles, and the earth extends; save only my ship Prydwen, and my mantle, and Caleburn, my

sword, and Rhongomyant, my lance, and Guenever, my wife. By the truth of heaven, thou shalt have it cheerfully, name what thou wilt." "I would that thou bless my hair," said he. "That shall be granted thee."

And Arthur took a golden comb, and scissors whereof the loops were of silver, and he combed his hair. And Arthur inquired of him who he was; "for my heart warms unto thee, and I know that thou art come of my blood. Tell me, therefore, who thou art." "I will tell thee," said the youth. "I am Kilwich, the son of Kilydd, the son of Prince Kelyddon, by Goleudid my mother, the daughter of Prince Anlawd." "That is true," said Arthur; "thou art my cousin. Whatsoever boon thou mayest ask, thou shalt receive, be it what it may that thy tongue shall name." "Pledge the truth of heaven and the faith of thy kingdom thereof." "I pledge it thee gladly." "I crave of thee, then, that thou obtain for me Olwen, the daughter of Yspadaden Penkawr, to wife; and this boon I likewise seek at the hands of thy warriors. I seek it from Kay and from Bedwyr; and from Gwynn, the son of Nudd, and Gadwy, the son of Geraint, and Prince Flewddur Flam, and Iona, king of France, and Sel, the son of Selgi, and Taliesin, the chief of the bards, and Geraint, the son of Erbin, Garanwyn, the son of Kay, and Amren, the son of Bedwyr, Ol, the son of Olwyd, Bedwin, the bishop, Guenever, the chief lady, and Guenhywach, her sister, Morved, the daughter of Urien, and Gwenlian Deg, the majestic maiden, Creiddylad,[1] the daughter of Lludd, the

---

[1]Creiddylad is no other than Shakespeare's Cordelia, whose father, King Lear, is by the Welsh authorities called indiscriminately Llyr or Llydd. All the old chroniclers give the story of her devotion to her aged parent, but none of them seems to have been aware that she is destined to remain with him till the day of doom, whilst Gwyn ap Nudd, the king of the fairies, and Gwythyr ap Greidiol, fight for her every first of May, and whichever of them may be fortunate enough to be the conqueror at that time will obtain her as his bride.

[2]The Welsh have a fable on the subject of the half-man, taken to be illustrative of the force of habit. In this allegory Arthur is supposed to be met by a sprite, who appears at first in a small and indistinct form, but who, on approaching nearer, increases in size, and, assuming the semblance of half a man, endeavors to provoke the king to wrestle. Despising his weakness, and considering that he should gain no credit by the encounter, Arthur refuses to do so, and delays the contest until at length the half-man (Habit) becomes so strong that it requires his utmost efforts to overcome him.

constant maiden, and Ewaedan, the daughter of Kynvelyn,[2] the half-man. "All these did Kilwich, the son of Kilydd, adjure to obtain his boon.

Then said Arthur, "O chieftain, I have never heard of the maiden of whom thou speakest, nor of her kindred, but I will gladly send messengers in search of her. Give me time to seek her." And the youth said, "I will willingly grant from this night to that at the end of the year to do so." Then Arthur sent messengers to every land within his dominions to seek for the maiden, and at the end of the year Arthur's messengers returned without having gained any knowledge or intelligence concerning Olwen more than on the first day. Then said Kilwich, "Every one has received his boon, and I yet lack mine. I will depart, and bear away thine honor with me." Then said Kay, "Rash chieftain! dost thou reproach Arthur? Go with us, and we will not part until thou dost either confess that the maiden exists not in the world, or until we obtain her." Thereupon Kay rose up. And Arthur called Bedwyr, who never shrank from any enterprise upon which Kay was bound. None were equal to him in swiftness throughout this island except Arthur alone; and although he was one-handed, three warriors could not shed blood faster than he on the field of battle.

And Arthur called to Kyndelig, the guide, "Go thou upon this expedition with the chieftain." For as good a guide was he in a land which he had never seen as he was in his own.

He called Gurhyr Gwalstat, because he knew all tongues.

He called Gawain, the son of Gwyar, because he never returned home without achieving the adventure of which he went in quest.

And Arthur called Meneu, the son of Teirgwed, in order that, if they went into a savage country, he might cast a charm and an illusion over them, so that none might see them whilst they could see every one.

They journeyed until they came to a vast open plain, wherein they saw a great castle, which was the fairest of the castles of the world. And when they came before the castle they beheld a vast flock of sheep. And upon the top of a mound there was a herdsman keeping the sheep. And a rug made of skins was upon him, and by his side was a shaggy mastiff, larger than a steed nine winters old.

Then said Kay, "Gurhyr Gwalstat, go thou and salute yonder man." "Kay," said he, "I engaged not to go further than thou thyself." "Let us go then together," answered Kay. Said Meneu, "Fear not to go thither, for I will cast a spell upon the dog so that he shall injure no one." And they went up to the mound whereon the herdsman was, and they said to him, "How dost thou fare, herdsman?" "Not less fair be it to you than to me." "Whose are the sheep that thou dost keep, and to whom does yonder castle belong?" "Stupid are ye, truly not to know that this is the castle of Yspadaden Penkawr. And ye also, who are ye?" "We are an embassy from Arthur, come to seek Olwen, the daughter of Yspadaden Penkawr." "O men! the mercy of heaven be upon you; do not that for all the world. None who ever came hither on this quest has returned alive." And the herdsman rose up. And as he rose Kilwich gave unto him a ring of gold. And he went home and gave the ring to his spouse to keep. And she took the ring when it was given her, and she said, "Whence came this ring, for thou art not wont to have good fortune?" "O wife, him to whom this ring belonged thou shalt see here this evening." "And who is he?" asked the woman. "Kilwich, the son of Kilydd, by Goleudid, the daughter of Prince Anlawd, who is come to seek Olwen as his wife." And when she heard that she had joy that her nephew, the son of her sister, was coming to her, and sorrow because she had never known any one depart alive who had come on that quest.

And the men went forward to the gate of the herdsman's dwelling. And when she heard their footsteps approaching she ran out with joy to meet them. And Kay snatched a billet out of the pile. And when she met them she sought to throw her arms about their necks. And Kay placed the log between her two hands, and she squeezed it so that it became a twisted coil. "O woman," said Kay, "if thou hadst squeezed me thus none could ever again set their affections on me. Evil love were this." They entered into the house and were served; and soon after they all went forth to amuse themselves. Then the woman opened a stone chest that was before the chimney-corner, and out of it rose a youth with yellow, curling hair. Said Gurhyr, "It is a pity to hide this youth. I know that it is not his own crime that is thus visited upon him." "This is but a remnant," said the woman. "Three and twenty of my sons has Yspadaden Penkawr slain, and I have no more hope of this one than of the others." Then said Kay, "Let him come and be a companion with me and he shall not be slain unless I also am slain with him." And they ate. And the woman asked them. "Upon what errand come you here?" "We come to seek Olwen for this youth." Then said the woman, "In the name of heaven, since no one from the castle hath yet seen you, return again whence you came." "Heaven is our witness that we will not return until we have seen the maiden. Does she ever come hither, so that she may be seen?" "She comes here every Saturday to wash her head, and in the vessel where she washes she leaves all her rings, and she never either comes herself or sends any messenger to fetch them." "Will she come here if she is sent to?" "Heaven knows that I will not destroy my soul, nor will I betray those that trust me; unless you will pledge me your faith that you will not harm her I will not send to her." "We pledge it," said they. So a message was sent, and she came.

The maiden was clothed in a robe of flame-colored silk, and about her neck was a collar of ruddy gold, on which were precious emeralds and rubies. More yellow was her head than the flower of the broom,[1] and her skin was whiter than the foam of the wave, and fairer were her hands and her fingers than the blossoms of the wood-anemone amidst the spray of the meadow fountain. The eye of the trained hawk was not brighter than hers. Her bosom was more snowy than the breast of the white swan, her cheek was redder than the reddest roses. Whoso beheld her was filled with her love. Four white trefoils sprung up wherever she trod. And therefore was she called Olwen.

She entered the house and sat beside Kilwich upon the foremost bench; and as soon as he saw her he knew her. And Kilwich said unto her, "Ah! maiden, thou art she whom I have loved; come away with me lest they speak evil of thee and of me. Many a day have I loved thee." "I cannot do this, for I have pledged my faith to my father not to go without his counsel, for his life will last only until the time of my espousals. Whatever is to be, must be. But I will give thee advice, if thou wilt take it. Go ask me of my father, and that which he shall require of thee, grant it, and thou wilt obtain me; but if thou deny him anything, thou wilt not obtain me, and it will be well for thee if thou escape with thy life." "I promise all this, if occasion offer," said he.

She returned to her chamber, and they all rose up, and followed her to the castle. And they slew the nine porters, that were at the nine gates, in silence. And they slew the nine watch-dogs without one of them barking. And they went forward to the hall.

"The greeting of heaven and of man be unto thee, Yspadaden Penkawr," said they. "And you, wherefore come you?" "We come to ask thy daughter Olwen for Kilwich, the son of Kilydd, the son of Prince Kelyddon." "Where are my pages and my servants? Raise up the forks beneath my two eyebrows, which have fallen over my eyes, that I may see the fashion of my son-in-law." And they did so. "Come hither to-morrow, and you shall have an answer."

They rose to go forth, and Yspadaden Penkawr seized one of the three poisoned darts that lay beside him, and threw it after them. And Bedwyr caught it,

---

[1] The romancers dwell with great complacency on the fair hair and delicate complexion of their heroines. This taste continued for a long time, and to render the hair light was an object of education. Even when wigs came into fashion they were all flaxen. Such was the color of the hair of the Gauls and of their German conquerors. It required some centuries to reconcile their eyes to the swarthy beauties of their Spanish and Italian neighbors.

and flung it, and pierced Yspadaden Penkawr griev-ously with it through the knee. Then he said, "A cursed ungentle son-in-law, truly! I shall ever walk the worse for his rudeness, and shall ever be without a cure. This poisoned iron pains me like the bite of a gad-fly. Cursed be the smith who forged it, and the anvil on which it was wrought! So sharp is it!"

That night also they took up their abode in the house of the herdsman. The next day, with the dawn, they arrayed themselves and proceeded to the castle, and entered the hall; and they said, "Yspadaden Penkawr, give us thy daughter in consideration of her dower and her maiden fee, which we will pay to thee, and to her two kinswomen like-wise." Then he said, "Her four great-grandmothers, and her four great-grandsires are yet alive; it is needful that I take counsel of them." "Be it so," they answered; "we will go to meat." As they rose up, he took the second dart that was beside him, and cast it after them. And Meneu, the son of Gawedd, caught it, and flung it back at him, and wounded him in the centre of the breast. "A cursed ungentle son-in-law, truly!" said he; "the hard iron pains me like the bite of a horse-leech. Cursed be the hearth whereon it was heated, and the smith who formed it! So sharp is it! Henceforth, whenever I go up hill, I shall have a scant in my breath, and a pain in my chest, and I shall often loathe my food." And they went to meat.

And the third day they returned to the palace. And Yspadaden Penkawr said to them, "Shoot not at me again, unless you desire death. Where are my attendants? Lift up the forks of my eyebrows, which have fallen over my eyeballs, that I may see the fashion of my son-in-law." Then they arose, and, as they did so, Yspadaden Penkawr took the third poisoned dart and cast it at them. And Kilwich caught it, and threw it vigorously, and wounded him through the eyeball. "A cursed ungentle son-in-law, truly! As long as I remain alive, my eyesight will be the worse. Whenever I go against the wind, my eyes will water; and perad-venture my head will burn, and I shall have a giddiness every new moon. Like the bite of a mad dog is the stroke of this poisoned iron. Cursed be the fire in which it was forged!" And they went to meat.

And the next day they came again to the palace, and they said, "Shoot not at us any more, unless thou desirest such hurt and harm and torture as thou now hast, and even more." Said Kilwich, "Give me thy daughter; and if thou wilt not give her, thou shalt receive thy death because of her." "Where is he that seeks my daughter? Come hither, where I may see thee." And they placed him a chair face to face with him.

Said Yspadaden Penkawr, "Is it thou that seekest my daughter?"

"It is I," answered Kilwich.

"I must have thy pledge that thou wilt not do toward me otherwise than is just; and when I have gotten that which I shall name, my daughter thou shalt have."

"I promise thee that, willingly," said Kilwich; "name what thou wilt."

"I will do so," said he. "Seest thou yonder red tilled ground?"

"I see it."

"When first I met the mother of this maiden, nine bushels of flax were sown therein, and none has yet sprung up, white or black. I require to have the flax to sow in the new land yonder, that when it grows up it may make a white wimple for my daughter's head

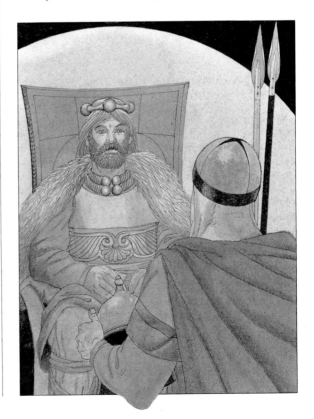

on the day of thy wedding."

"It will be easy for me to compass this, although thou mayest think it will not be easy."

"Though thou get this, there is yet that which thou wilt not get,—the harp of Teirtu, to play to us that night. When a man desires that it should play, it does so of itself; and when he desires that it should cease, it ceases. And this he will not give of his own free will, and thou wilt not be able to compel him."

"It will be easy for me to compass this, although thou mayest think that it will not be easy.

"Though thou get this, there is yet that which thou wilt not get. I require thee to get me for my huntsman Mabon, the son of Modron. He was taken from his mother when three nights old, and it is not known where he now is, nor whether he is living or dead."

"It will be easy for me to compass this, although thou mayest think it will not be easy."

"Though thou get this, there is yet that which thou wilt not get,—the two cubs of the wolf Gast Rhymhi; no leash in the world will hold them, but a leash made from the beard of Dillus Varwawc, the robber. And the leash will be of no avail unless it be plucked from his beard while he is alive. While he lives, he will not suffer this to be done to him, and the leash will be of no use should he be dead because it will be brittle."

"It will be easy for me to compass this, although thou mayest think it will not be easy."

"Though thou get this, there is yet that which thou wilt not get,—the sword of Gwernach the Giant; of his own free will he will not give it, and thou wilt never be able to compel him."

"It will be easy for me to compass this, although thou mayest think it will not be easy."

"Though thou get this, there is yet that which thou wilt not get. Difficulties shalt thou meet with, and nights without sleep, in seeking this, and if thou obtain it not, neither shalt thou obtain my daughter."

"Horses shall I have, and chivalry; and my lord and kinsman, Arthur, will obtain for me all these things. And I shall gain thy daughter, and thou shalt lose thy life."

"Go forward. And thou shalt not be chargeable for food or raiment for my daughter while thou art seeking these things; and when thou hast compassed all these marvels, thou shalt have my daughter for thy wife."

CHAPTER XXX

KILWICH AND OLWEN, CONTINUED

ALL that day they journeyed until the evening, and then they beheld a vast castle, which was the largest in the world. And lo! a black man, larger than three of the men of this world, came out from the castle. And they spoke unto him, and said, "O man, whose castle is that?" "Stupid are ye, truly, O men! There is no one in the world that does not know that this is the castle of Gwernach the Giant." "What treatment is there for guests and strangers that alight in that castle?" "O chieftain, heaven protect thee! No guest ever returned thence alive, and no one may enter therein unless he brings with him his craft."

Then they proceeded towards the gate. Said Gurhyr Gwalstat, "Is there a porter?" "There is; wherefore dost thou call?" "Open the gate." "I will not open it." "Wherefore wilt thou not?" "The knife is in the meat, and the drink is in the horn, and there is revelry in the hall of Gwernach the Giant; and except for a crafts-man who brings his craft, the gate will not be opened tonight." "Verily, porter," then said Kay, "my craft bring I with me." "What is thy craft?" "The best burnisher of swords am I in the world." "I will go and tell this unto Gwernach the Giant, and I will bring thee an answer."

So the porter went in, and Gwernach said to him, "Hast thou news from the gate?" "I have. There is a party at the door of the gate who desire to come in." "Didst thou inquire of them if they possessed any art?" "I did inquire," said he, "and one told me that he was well skilled in the burnishing of swords." "We have need of him then. For some time have I sought for some one to polish my sword, and could find no one. Let this man enter, since he brings with him his craft."

The porter thereupon returned and opened the gate. And Kay went in by himself, and he saluted Gwernach the Giant. And a chair was placed for him opposite to Gwernach. And Gwernach said to him, "O man, is it true that is reported of thee, that thou knowest how to burnish swords?" "I know full well how to do so," answered Kay. Then was the sword of Gwernach brought to him. And Kay took a blue whet-stone from under his arm, and asked whether he would have it burnished white or blue. "Do with it as it seems good to thee, or as thou wouldst if it were thine own." Then Kay polished one half of the blade, and put it in his hand. "Will this please you?" asked he. "I would rather than all that is in my dominions that the whole of it were like this. It is a marvel to me that such a man as thou should be without a companion." "O noble sir, I have a companion, albeit he is not skilled in this art." "Who may he be?" "Let the porter go forth, and I will tell him whereby he may know him. The head of his lance will leave its shaft, and draw blood from the wind, and will descend upon its shaft again." Then the gate was opened, and Bedwyr entered. And Kay said, "Bedwyr is very skilful, though he knows not this art."

And there was much discourse among those who were without, because that Kay and Bedwyr had gone in. And a young man who was with them, the only son of the herdsman, got in also; and he contrived to admit all the rest, but they kept themselves concealed. 166▷ The sword was now polished, and Kay gave it unto the hand of Gwernach the Giant, to see if he were pleased with his work. And the Giant said, "The work is good; I am content therewith." Said Kay, "It is thy scabbard that hath rusted thy sword; give it to me, that I may take out the wooden sides of it, and put in new ones." And he took the scabbard from him, and the sword in the other hand. And he came and stood over against the giant, as if he would have put the sword into the scabbard; and with it he struck at the head of the giant, and cut off his head at one blow. Then they despoiled the castle, and took from it what goods and jewels they would. And they returned to Arthur's court, bearing with them the sword of Gwernach the Giant.

And when they told Arthur how they had sped, Arthur said, "It is a good beginning." Then they took counsel, and said, "Which of these marvels will it be best for us to seek next?" "It will be best," said one, "to seek Mabon, the son of Modron; and he will not be found unless we first find Eidoel, the son of Aer, his kinsman." Then Arthur rose up, and the warriors of the island of Britain with him, to seek for Eidoel; and they proceeded until they came to the castle of Glivi, where Eidoel was imprisoned. Glivi stood on the summit of his castle, and he said, "Arthur, what requirest thou of me, since nothing remains to me in this fortress, and I have neither joy nor pleasure in it, neither wheat nor oats? Seek not, therefore, to do me harm." Said Arthur, "Not to injure thee came I hither, but to seek for the prisoner that is with thee." "I will give thee my prisoner, though I had not thought to give him up to any one, and therewith shalt thou have my support and my aid."

His followers said unto Arthur, "Lord, go thou home; thou canst not proceed with thy host in quest of such small adventures as these." Then said Arthur, "It were well for thee, Gurhyr Gwalstat, to go upon this quest, for thou knowest all languages, and art familiar with those of the birds and the beasts. Thou, Eidoel, oughtest likewise to go with thy men in search of thy cousin. And as for you, Kay and Bedwyr, I have hope of whatever adventure ye are in quest of, that ye will achieve it. Achieve ye this adventure for me."

They went forward until they came to the Ousel of Cilgwri. And Gurhyr adjured her, saying, "Tell me if thou knowest aught of Mabon, the son of Modron, who was taken when three nights old from between his mother and the wall?" And the Ousel answered, "When I first came here, there was a smith's anvil in this place, and I was then a young bird; and from that time no work has been done upon it, save the pecking of my beak every evening; and now there is not so much as the size of a nut remaining thereof; yet during all that time I have never heard of the man for whom you inquire. Nevertheless, I will do that which is fitting that I should for an embassy from Arthur. There is a race of animals who were formed before me, and I will be your guide to them."

So they proceeded to the place where was the Stag of Redynvre. "Stag of Redynvre, behold, we are come to thee, an embassy from Arthur, for we have not heard of any animal older than thou. Say, knowest thou aught of Mabon, the son of Modron, who was taken from his mother when three nights old?" The Stag said, "When first I came hither there was a plain all around me, without any trees save one oak sapling, which grew up to be an oak with an hundred branches; and that oak has since perished, so that now nothing remains of it but the withered stump; and from that day to this I have been here, yet have I never heard of the man for whom you inquire. Nevertheless, being an embassy from Arthur, I will be your guide to the place where there is an animal which was formed before I was, and the oldest animal in the world, and the one that has travelled most, the Eagle of Gwern Abwy."

Gurhyr said, "Eagle of Gwern Abwy, we have come to thee, an embassy from Arthur, to ask thee if thou knowest aught of Mabon, the son of Modron, who was taken from his mother when he was three nights old?" The Eagle said, "I have been here for a great space of time, and when I first came hither there was a rock here from the top of which I pecked at the stars every evening; and it has crumbled away, and now it is not so much as a span high. All that time I have been here, and I have never heard of the man for whom you inquire, except once when I went in

166

search of food as far as Llyn Llyw. And when I came there I struck my talons into a salmon, thinking he would serve me as food for a long time. But he drew me into the water, and I was scarcely able to escape from him. After that I made peace with him. And I drew fifty fish-spears out of his back, and relieved him. Unless he know something of him you seek I cannot tell who may. However, I will guide you to the place where he is."

So they went thither; and the Eagle said, "Salmon of Llyn Llyw, I have come to thee with an embassy from Arthur, to ask thee if thou knowest aught of Mabon, the son of Modron, who was taken away at three nights old from his mother." "As much as I know I will tell thee. With every tide I go along the river upward, until I come near to the walls of Gloucester, and there have I found such wrong as I never found elsewhere; and to the end that ye may give credence thereto, let one of you go thither upon each of my two shoulders." So Kay and Gurhyr Gwalstat went upon the two shoulders of the Salmon, and they proceeded until they came unto the wall of the prison; and they heard a great wailing and lamenting from the dungeon. Said Gurhyr, "Who is it that laments in this house of stone?" "Alas! it is Mabon, the son of Modron, who is here imprisoned; and no imprisonment was ever so grievous as mine." "Hast thou hope of being released for gold or for silver, or for any gifts of wealth, or through battle and fighting?" "By fighting will whatever I may gain be obtained."

Then they went thence, and returned to Arthur, and they told him where Mabon, the son of Modron, was imprisoned. And Arthur summoned the warriors of the island, and they journeyed as far as Gloucester, to the place where Mabon was in prison. Kay and Bedwyr went upon the shoulders of the fish, whilst the warriors of Arthur attacked the castle. And Kay broke through the wall into the dungeon, and brought away the prisoner upon his back, whilst the fight was going on between the warriors. And Arthur returned home, and Mabon with him at liberty.

On a certain day as Gurhyr Gwalstat was walking over a mountain he heard a wailing and a grievous cry. And when he heard it he sprung forward, and went towards it. And when he came there he saw a fire burning among the turf, and an ant-hill nearly surrounded with the fire. And he drew his sword, and

smote off the ant-hill close to earth, so that it escaped being burned in the fire. And the ants said to him, "Receive from us the blessing of heaven, and that which no man can give we will give thee." Then they fetched the nine bushels of flaxseed which Yspadaden Penkawr had required of Kilwich, and they brought the full measure, without lacking any, save one flaxseed, and that the lame pismire brought in before night.

Then said Arthur, "Which of the marvels will it be best for us to seek next?" "It will be best to seek for the two cubs of the wolf Gast Rhymhi."

"Is it known," said Arthur, "where she is?" "She is in Aber Cleddyf," said one. Then Arthur went to the house of Tringad, in Aber Cleddyf, and he inquired of him whether he had heard of her there. "She has often slain my herds, and she is there below in a cave of Aber Cleddyf."

Then Arthur went in his ship Prydwen by sea, and the others went by land to hunt her. And they surrounded her and her two cubs, and took them, and carried them away.

As Kay and Bedwyr sat on a beacon-cairn on the summit of Plinlimmon, in the highest wind that ever was, they looked around them and saw smoke afar off. Then said Kay, "By the hand of my friend, yonder is the fire of a robber." Then they hastened towards the smoke, and they came so near it that they could see Dillus Varwawc scorching a wild boar. "Behold, yonder is the greatest robber that ever fled from Arthur," said Bedwyr to Kay. "Dost thou know him?" "I do know him," answered Kay; "he is Dillus Varwawc, and no leash in the world will be able to hold the cubs of Gast Rhymhi save a leash made from the beard of him thou seest yonder. And even that will be useless unless his beard be plucked out alive, with wooden tweezers; for if dead it will be brittle." "What thinkest thou that we should do concerning this?" said Bedwyr. "Let us suffer him to eat as much as he will of the meat, and after that he will fall asleep." And during that time they employed themselves in making the wooden tweezers. And when Kay knew certainly that he was asleep, he made a pit under his feet, and he struck him a violent blow, and squeezed him into the pit. And there they twitched out his beard completely with the wooden tweezers, and after that they slew him altogether. And from thence

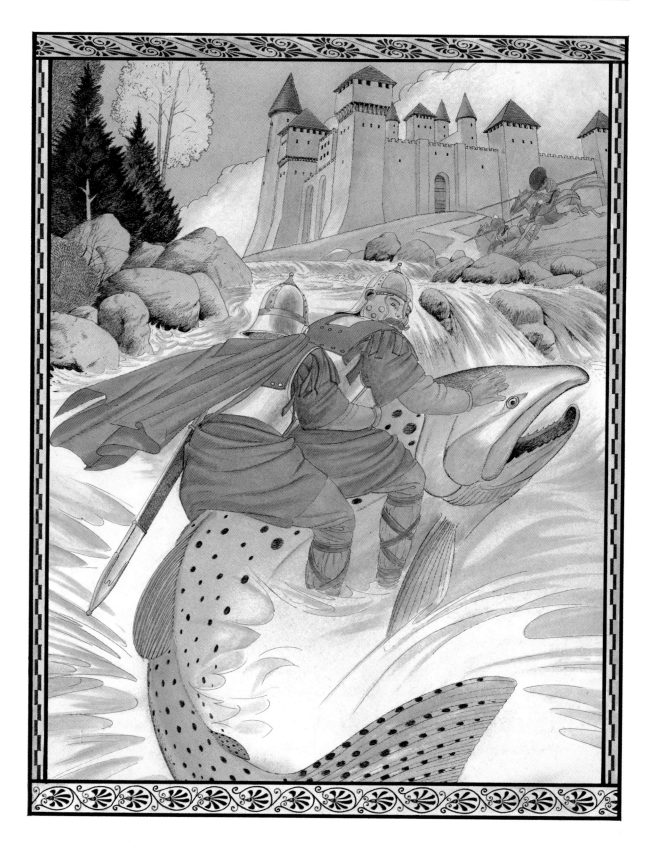

they went, and took the leash made of Dillus Varwawc's beard, and they gave it into Arthur's hand.

Thus they got all the marvels that Yspadaden Penkawr had required of Kilwich; and they set forward, and took the marvels to his court. And Kilwich said to Yspadaden Penkawr, "Is thy daughter mine now?" "She is thine," said he, "but therefore needest thou not thank me, but Arthur, who hath accomplished this for thee." Then Goreu, the son of Custennin, the herdsman, whose brothers Yspadaden Penkawr had slain, seized him by the hair of his head, and dragged him after him to the keep, and cut off his head, and placed it on a stake in the citadel. Then they took possession of his castle, and of his treasures. And that night Olwen became Kilwich's bride, and she continued to be his wife as long as she lived.

CHAPTER XXXI

PEREDUR, THE SON OF EVRAWC

ARTHUR was in Caerleon upon the Usk; and he went to hunt, and Peredur[1] went with him. And Peredur let loose his dog upon a hart and the dog killed the hart in a desert place. And a short space from him he saw signs of a dwelling, and towards the dwelling he went, and he beheld a hall, and, at the door of the hall he found bold swarthy youths playing at chess. And when he entered he beheld three maidens sitting on a bench, and they were all clothed alike, as became persons of high rank. And he came and sat by them on the bench; and one of the maidens looked steadfastly at Peredur and wept. And Peredur asked her wherefore she was weeping. "Through grief that I shall see so fair a youth as thou art slain." "Who will slay me?" inquired Peredur. "If thou art so daring as to remain here tonight I will tell thee." "How great soever my danger may be from remaining here I will listen unto thee." "This palace is owned by him who is my father," said the maiden, "and he slays every one who comes hither without his leave." "What sort of a man is thy father that he is able to slay every one thus?" "A man who does violence and wrong unto his neighbors, and who renders justice unto none." And hereupon he saw the youths arise and clear the chessmen from the board. And he heard a great tumult; and after the tumult there came in a huge black one-eyed man, and the maidens arose to meet him. And they disarrayed him, and he went and sat down; and after he had rested and pondered awhile, he looked at Peredur, and asked who the knight was. "Lord," said one of the maidens, "he is the fairest and gentlest youth that ever thou didst see. And for the sake of heaven, and thine own dignity, have patience with him." "For thy sake I will have patience, and I will grant him his life this night." Then Peredur came towards them to the fire, and partook of food and liquor, and entered into discourse with the ladies. And being elated with the liquor, he said to the black man, "It is a marvel to me, so mighty as thou sayest thou art, who could have put out thine eye?" "It is one of my habits," said the black man, "that whosoever puts to me the question which thou hast asked shall not escape with his life, either as a free gift, or for a price." "Lord," said the maiden, "whatsoever he may say to thee in jest, and through the excitement of liquor, make good that which thou saidest and didst promise me just now." "I will do so, gladly, for thy sake," said he. "Willingly will I grant him his life this night." And that night thus they remained.

And the next day the black man got up and put on his armor, and said to Peredur, "Arise, man, and suffer death." And Peredur said unto him, "Do one of two things, black man; if thou wilt fight with me, either throw off thy own armor, or give arms to me,

---

[1]Peredur, the son of Evrawc, is the Welsh for Perceval, a part of whose story in the preceding pages is taken from the Mabinogeon.

that I may encounter thee?" "Ha! man," said he, "couldst thou fight if thou hadst arms? Take then what arms thou dost choose." And thereupon the maiden came to Peredur with such arms as pleased him; and he fought with the black man and forced him to crave his mercy. "Black man, thou shalt have mercy, provided thou tell me who thou art, and who put out thine eye." "Lord, I will tell thee. I lost it in fighting with the Black Serpent of the Carn. There is a mound which is called the Mound of Mourning; and on the mound there is a carn, and in the carn there is a serpent, and on the tail of the serpent there is a stone, and the virtues of the stone are such that whosoever should hold it in one hand, in the other he will have as much gold as he may desire. And in fighting with this serpent was it that I lost my eye. And the Black Oppressor am I called. And for this reason I am called the Black Oppressor, that there is not a single man around me whom I have not oppressed, and justice have I done unto none." "Tell me," said Peredur, "how far is it hence?" "The same day that thou settest forth thou wilt come to the Palace of the Sons of the Ring of the Tortures." "Wherefore are they called thus?" "The Addanc[1] of the Lake slays them once every day. When thou goest thence thou wilt come to the Court of the Countess of Achievements." "What achievements are these?" said Peredur. "Three hundred men are there in her household, and unto every stranger that comes to the Court the achievements of her household are related. And this is the manner of it,—the three hundred men of the household sit next unto the Lady; and that not through disrespect unto the guests, but that they may relate the achievements of the household. And the day that thou goest there thou wilt reach the Mound of Mourning, and round about the mound there are the owners of three hundred tents guarding the serpent." "Since thou hast indeed been an oppressor so long," said Peredur, "I will cause that thou continue so no longer." So he slew him.

Then the maiden spoke, and began to converse with him. "If thou wast poor when thou camest here henceforth thou wilt be rich through the treasure of the black man whom thou hast slain. Thou seest the many lovely maidens that there are in this court, thou

shalt have her whom thou likest best for the lady of thy love." "Lady, I came not hither from my country to woo; but match yourselves as it liketh you with the comely youths I see here; and none of your goods do I desire, for I need them not." Then Peredur rode forward, and he came to the Palace of the Sons of the King of the Tortures; and when he entered the palace he saw none but women; and they rose up and were joyful at his coming; and as they began to discourse with him he beheld a charger arrive, with a saddle upon it, and a corpse in the saddle. And one of the women arose, and took the corpse from the saddle and anointed it in a vessel of warm water, which was below the door, and placed precious balsam upon it; and the man rose up alive, and came to the place where Peredur was, and greeted him, and was joyful to see him. And two other men came in upon their saddles, and the maiden treated these two in the same manner as she had done the first. Then Peredur asked the chieftain wherefore it was thus. And they told him there was an Addanc in a cave, which slew them once every day. And thus they remained one night.

And next morning the youths arose to sally forth, and Peredur besought them, for the sake of the ladies of their love, to permit him to go with them; but they refused him, saying, "If thou shouldst be slain thou hast none to bring thee back to life again." And they rode forward and Peredur followed after them; and after they had disappeared out of his sight he came to a mound, whereon sat the fairest lady he had ever beheld. "I know thy quest," said she; "thou art going to encounter the Addanc, and he will slay thee, and that not by courage but by craft. He has a cave, and at the entrance of the cave there is a stone pillar, and he sees every one that enters, and none sees him; and from behind the pillar he slays every one with a poisonous dart. And if thou wouldst pledge me thy faith, to love me above all women, I would give thee a stone, by which thou shouldst see him when thou goest in, and he should not see thee." "I will, by my faith," said Peredur, "for when first I beheld thee I loved thee; and where shall I seek thee?" "When thou seekest me seek towards India." And the maiden vanished after placing the stone in Peredur's hand.

And he came towards a valley, through which ran a river; and the borders of the valley were wooded,

[1]The Addanc was a mighty aquatic monster.

and on each side of the river were level meadows. And on one side of the river he saw a flock of white sheep, and on the other side a flock of black sheep. And whenever one of the white sheep bleated one of the black sheep would cross over and become white; and when one of the black sheep bleated one of the white sheep would cross over and become black. And he saw a tall tree by the side of the river, one-half of which was in flames from the root to the top, and the other half was green and in full leaf. And nigh thereto he saw a youth sitting upon a mound, and two greyhounds, white-breasted and spotted, in leashes, lying by his side. And certain was he that he had never seen a youth of so royal a bearing as he. And in the wood opposite he heard hounds raising a herd of deer. And Peredur saluted the youth, and the youth greeted him in return. And there were three roads leading from the mound; two of them were wide roads and the third was more narrow. And Peredur inquired where the three roads went. "One of them goes to my palace," said the youth. "And one of two things I counsel thee to do, either to proceed to my palace, which is before thee, and where thou wilt find my wife, or else to remain here to see the hounds chasing the roused deer from the wood to the plain. And thou shalt see the best greyhounds thou didst ever behold, and the boldest in the chase, kill them by the water beside us; and when it is time to go to meat my page will come with my horse to meet me, and thou shalt rest in my palace tonight." "Heaven reward thee; but I cannot tarry, and onward must I go." "The other road leads to the town, which is near here, wherein food and liquor may be bought; and the road which is narrower than the other goes towards the cave of the Addanc." "With thy permission, young man, I will go that way."

172▷ And Peredur went towards the cave. And he took the stone in his left hand, and his lance in his right. And as he went in he perceived the Addanc, and he pierced him through with his lance, and cut off his head. And as he came forth from the cave, behold the three companions were at the entrance; and they saluted Peredur, and told him that there was a prediction that he should slay the monster.

And Peredur gave the head to the young man, and they offered him in marriage which ever of the three sisters he might choose, and half their kingdom with her. "I came not hither to woo," said Peredur, "but if peradventure I took a wife, I should prefer your sister to all others." And Peredur rode forward, and he heard a noise behind him. And he looked back, and saw a man upon a red horse, and red armor upon him; and the man rode up by his side, and wished him the favor of heaven and of man. And Peredur greeted the youth kindly. "Lord, I come to make a request unto thee." "What wouldst thou?" "That thou shouldst take me as thy attendant." "Who should I take as my attendant if I did so?" "I will not conceal from thee what kindred I am of. Etlym Gleddyv Coch am I called, an earl from the East Country." "I marvel that thou shouldst offer to become attendant to a man whose possessions are no greater than thine own; for I have but an earldom like thyself. But now thou desirest to be my attendant, I will take thee joyfully."

And they went forward to the Court of the Countess, and all they of the Court were glad at their coming; and they were told it was not through disrespect they were placed below the household, but that such was the usage of the Court. For whoever should overthrow the three hundred men of her household would sit next the Countess, and she would love him above all other men. And Peredur, having overthrown the three hundred of her household, sat down beside her, and the Countess said, "I thank heaven that I have a youth so fair and so radiant as thou, since I have not obtained the man whom best I love." "Whom is he whom best thou lovest? By my faith, Etlym Gleddyv Coch is the man whom I love best, and I have never seen him." "Of a truth, Etlym is my companion; and behold here he is, and for his sake did I come to joust with thy household. And he would have done so better than I had it pleased him." "Heaven reward thee, fair youth, and I will take the man whom I love above all others." And the Countess became Etlym's bride from that moment.

And the next day Peredur set forth toward the Mound of Mourning. "By thy hand, lord, but I will go with thee," said Etlym. Then they went forward till they came in sight of the mound and the forts. "Go unto yonder men," said Peredur to Etlym, "and desire them to come and do me homage." So Etlym went unto them, and said unto them thus: "Come and do homage to my lord." "Who is thy lord?" said

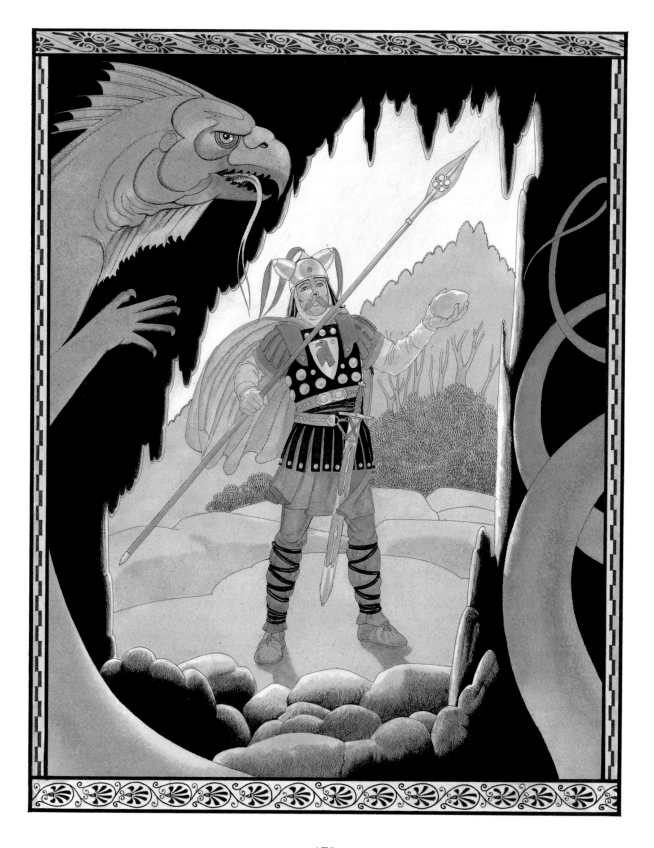

they. "Peredur, with the long lance, is my lord," said Etlym. "Were it permitted to slay a messenger, thou shouldst not go back to thy lord alive, for making unto kings and earls and barons so arrogant a demand as to go and do him homage." On this Peredur desired him to go back to them, and to give them their choice, either to do him homage or to do battle with him. And they chose rather to do battle. And that day Peredur overthrew the owners of a hundred tents. And the next day he overthrew the owners of a hundred more; and the third day the remaining third took counsel to do homage to Peredur. And Peredur inquired of them wherefore they were there. And they told him they were guarding the serpent until he should die. "For then should we fight for the stone among ourselves, and whoever should be conqueror among us would have the stone." "Wait here," said Peredur, "and I will go to encounter the serpent." "No, no, lord," said they; "we will go all together to encounter the serpent." "Verily," said Peredur, "that will I not permit; for if the serpent be slain, I shall derive no more fame therefrom than one of you." Then he went to the place where the serpent was, and slew it, and came back to them, and said, "Reckon up what you have spent since you have been here, and I will repay you to the full." And he paid to each what he said was his claim. And he required of them only that they should acknowledge themselves his vassals. And he said to Etlym, "Go back unto her whom thou lovest best, and I will go forwards, and I will reward thee for having been my attendant." And he gave Etlym the stone. "Heaven repay thee and prosper thee," said Etlym.

And Peredur rode thence, and he came to the fairest valley he had ever seen, through which ran a river; and there he beheld many tents of various colors. And he marvelled still more at the number of windmills and of water-mills that he saw. And there rode up with him a tall, auburn-haired man, in a workman's garb, and Peredur inquired of him who he was. "I am the chief miller," said he, "of all the mills yonder." "Wilt thou give me lodging?" said Peredur. "I will, gladly," he answered. And Peredur came to the miller's house, and the miller had a fair and pleasant dwelling. And Peredur asked money as a loan from the miller, that he might buy meat and liquor for himself; and for the household, and he

promised him that he would pay him ere he went thence. And he inquired of the miller wherefore such a multitude were there assembled. Said the miller to Peredur, "One thing is certain: either thou art a man from afar, or thou art beside thyself. The Empress of Cristonobyl the Great is here; and she will have no one but the man who is most valiant; for riches she does not require. And it was impossible to bring food for so many thousands as are here, therefore were all these mills constructed." And that night they took their rest.

And the next day Peredur arose, and he equipped himself and his horse for the tournament. And among other tents he beheld one which was the fairest he had ever seen. And saw a beauteous maiden leaning her head out of a window of a tent, and he had never seen a maiden more lovely than she. 174 ▷ And upon her was a garment of satin. And he gazed fixedly on the maiden and began to love her greatly. And he remained there, gazing upon the maiden from morning until midday, and from midday until evening; and then the tournament was ended; and he went to his lodging and drew off his armor. Then he asked money of the miller as a loan, and the miller's wife was wroth with Peredur; nevertheless the miller lent him the money. And the next day he did in like manner as he had done the day before. And at night he came to his lodging, and took money as a loan from the miller. And the third day, as he was in the same place, gazing upon the maiden, he felt a hard blow between the neck and the shoulder from the edge of an axe. And when he looked behind he saw that it was the miller; and the miller said unto him, "Do one of two things: either turn thy head from hence or go to the tournament." And Peredur smiled on the miller, and went to the tournament; and all that encountered him that day he overthrew. And as many as he vanquished he sent as a gift to the Empress, and their horses and arms he sent as a gift to the wife of the miller, in payment of the borrowed money. And the Empress sent to the Knight of the Mill, to ask him to come and visit her. And Peredur went not for the first nor for the second message. And the third time she sent one hundred knights to bring him against his will, and they went to him, and told him their mission from the Empress. And Peredur fought well with them, and caused them to be bound like stags, and thrown into the mill dyke. And the Empress sought advice of a wise man. "With thy permission, I will go to him myself." So he came to Peredur and besought him, for the sake of the lady of his love, to come and visit the Empress. And they went together with the miller. And Peredur went and sat down in the outer chamber of the tent, and she came and placed herself at his side. And there was but little discourse between them. And Peredur took his leave and went to his lodging.

And the next day he came to visit her, and when he came into the tent there was no one chamber less decorated than the others. And they knew not where he would sit. And Peredur went and sat beside the Empress, and discoursed with her courteously. And while they were there they beheld a black man enter with a goblet full of wine in his hand. And he dropped upon his knee before the Empress, and besought her to give it to no one who would not fight him for it. And she looked upon Peredur. "Lady," said he, "bestow upon me the goblet." And Peredur drank the wine, and gave the goblet to the miller's wife. And while they were thus, behold there entered a black man, of larger stature than the other, with a wild beast's claw in his hand, wrought into the form of a goblet, and filled with wine. And he presented it to the Empress, and besought her to give it to no one but the man who would fight with him. "Lady," said Peredur, "bestow it upon me." And she gave it to him. And Peredur drank the wine, and sent the goblet to the wife of the miller. And when they were thus, behold a rough-looking crisp-haired man, taller than either of the others, came in with a bowl in his hands full of wine; and he bent upon his knee, and gave it into the hands of the Empress, and he besought her to give it to none but him who would fight with him for it, and she gave it to Peredur, and he sent it to the miller's wife. And that night Peredur returned to his lodging; and the next day he accoutred himself and his horse, and went to the meadow, and slew the three men. Then Peredur proceeded to the tent, and the Empress said to him, "Goodly Peredur, remember the faith thou didst pledge me when I gave thee the stone, and thou didst kill the Addanc." "Lady," answered he, "thou sayest truth, I do remember it." For she was the maiden who had been sitting on the mound when Peredur had gone in search of the Addanc.

CHAPTER XXXII

TALIESIN

GWYDDNO GARANHIR was sovereign of Gwaelod, a territory bordering on the sea. And he possessed a weir upon the strand between Dyvi and Aberystwyth, near to his own castle, and the value of an hundred pounds was taken in that weir every May eve. And Gwyddno had an only son named Elphin, the most helpless of youths, and the most needy. And it grieved his father sore, for he thought he was born in an evil hour. By the advice of his council his father had granted him the drawing of the weir that year, to see if good luck would ever befall him, and to give him something wherewith to begin the world. And this was on the twenty-ninth of April.

The next day, when Elphin went to look, there was nothing in the weir but a leather bag upon a pole of the weir. Then said the weirward unto Elphin, "All thy ill-luck aforetime was nothing to this; and now thou hast destroyed the virtues of the weir, which always yielded the value of an hundred pounds every May eve; and tonight there is nothing but this leathern skin in it." "How now," said Elphin, "there may be therein the value of a hundred pounds." Well! they took up the leathern bag, and he who opened it saw the forehead of an infant, the fairest that was ever seen; and he said, "Behold a radiant brow!" (in the Welsh language, *taliesin*.) "Taliesin be he called," said Elphin. And he lifted the bag in his arms, and, lamenting his bad luck, placed the boy sorrowfully behind him. And he made his horse amble gently, that before had been trotting, and he carried him as softly as if he had been sitting in the easiest chair in the world. And presently the boy made a Consolation and praise to Elphin; and the Consolation was as you may here see:

"Fair Elphin, cease to lament!
Never in Gwyddno's weir
Was there such good luck as this night.
Being sad will not avail;
Better to trust in God than to forebode ill;
Weak and small as I am,

On the foaming beach of the ocean,
In the day of trouble I shall be
Of more service to thee than three hundred salmon."

This was the first poem that Taliesin ever sung, being to console Elphin in his grief for that the produce of the weir was lost, and, what was worse, that all the world would consider that it was through his fault and ill-luck. Then Elphin asked him what he was, whether man or spirit. And he sung thus:

"I have been formed a comely person;
Although I am but little, I am highly gifted;
Into a dark leathern bag I was thrown,
And on a boundless sea I was set adrift.
From seas and from mountains
God brings wealth to the fortunate man."

Then came Elphin to the house of Gwyddno, his father, and Taliesin with him. 176 ▷ Gwyddno asked him if he had had a good haul at the weir, and he told him that he had got that which was better than fish. "What was that?" said Gwyddno. "A bard," said Elphin. Then said Gwyddno, "Alas! what will he profit thee?" And Taliesin himself replied and said, "He will profit him more than the weir ever profited thee." Asked Gwyddno, "Art thou able to speak and thou so little?" And Taliesin answered him, "I am better able to speak than thou to question me." "Let me hear what thou canst say," quoth Gwyddno. Then Taliesin sang:

"Three times have I been born, I know by
    meditation;
All the sciences of the world are collected in my
    breast,
For I know what has been, and what hereafter will
    occur."

Elphin gave his haul to his wife, and she nursed him tenderly and lovingly. Thenceforward Elphin increased in riches more and more, day by day, and in love and favor with the king; and there abode

Taliesin until he was thirteen years old, when Elphin, son of Gwyddno, went by a Christmas invitation to his uncle, Maelgan Gwynedd, who held open court at Christmas-tide in the castle of Dyganwy, for all the number of lords of both degrees, both spiritual and temporal, with a vast and thronged host of knights and squires. And one arose and said, "Is there in the whole world a king so great as Maelgan, or one on whom heaven has bestowed so many gifts as upon him,—form, and beauty, and meekness, and strength, besides all the powers of the soul?" And together with these they said that heaven had given one gift that exceeded all the others, which was the beauty, and grace, and wisdom, and modesty of his queen, whose virtues surpassed those of all the ladies and noble maidens throughout the whole kingdom. And with this they put questions one to another, Who had braver men? Who had fairer or swifter horses or greyhounds? Who had more skilful or wiser bards than Maelgan?

When they had all made an end of their praising the king and his gifts, it befell that Elphin spoke on this wise: "Of a truth, none but a king may vie with a king; but were he not a king, I would say that my wife was as virtuous as any lady in the kingdom, and also that I have a bard who is more skilful than all the king's bards." In a short space some of his fellows told the king all the boastings of Elphin; and the king ordered him to be thrown into a strong prison until he might show the truth as to the virtues of his wife and the wisdom of his bard.

Now when Elphin had been put in a tower of the castle with a thick chain about his feet (it is said that it was a silver chain, as he was of royal blood), the king, as the story relates, sent his son Rhun to inquire into the demeanor of Elphin's wife. Now Rhun was the most graceless man in the world, and there was neither wife nor maiden with whom he held converse but was evil spoken of. While Rhun went in haste towards Elphin's dwelling, being fully minded to bring disgrace upon his wife, Taliesin told his mistress how that the king had placed his master in durance in prison, and how that Rhun was coming in haste to strive to bring disgrace upon her. Wherefore he caused his mistress to array one of the maids of the kitchen in her apparel; which the noble lady gladly did, and she loaded her hands with the best rings that she and her husband possessed.

In this guise Taliesin caused his mistress to put the maiden to sit at the board in her room at supper; and he made her to seem as her mistress, and the mistress to seem as the maid. And when they were in due time seated at their supper, in the manner that has been said, Rhun suddenly arrived at Elphin's dwelling, and was received with joy, for the servants knew him; and they brought him to the room of their mistress, in the semblance of whom the maid rose up from supper and welcomed him gladly. And afterwards she sat down to supper again, and Rhun with her. Then Rhun began jesting with the maid, who still kept the semblance of the mistress. And verily this story shows that the maiden became so intoxicated that she fell asleep; and the story relates that it was a powder that Rhun put into the drink that made her sleep so soundly that she never felt it when he cut off from her hand her little finger, whereon was the signet ring of Elphin, which he had sent to his wife as a token a short time before. And Rhun returned to the king with the finger and the ring as a proof; to show that he had cut it off from her hand without her awaking from her sleep of intemperance.

The king rejoiced greatly at these tidings, and he sent for his councillors, to whom he told the whole story from the beginning. And he caused Elphin to be brought out of prison, and he chided him because of his boast. And he spake on this wise: "Elphin, be it known to thee beyond a doubt, that it is but folly for a man to trust in the virtues of his wife further than he can see her; and that thou mayest be certain of thy wife's vileness, behold her finger, with thy signet ring upon it, which was cut from her hand last night, while she slept the sleep of intoxication." Then thus spake Elphin: "With thy leave, mighty king, I cannot deny my ring, for it is known of many; but verily I assert that the finger around which it is was never attached to the hand of my wife; for in truth and certainty there are three notable things pertaining to it, none of which ever belonged to any of my wife's fingers. The first of the three is, that it is certainly known to me that this ring would never remain upon her thumb, whereas you can plainly see that it is hard to draw it over the joint of the little finger of the hand

whence this was cut. The second thing is, that my wife has never let pass one Saturday since I have known her, without paring her nails before going to bed, and you can see fully that the nail of this little finger has not been pared for a month. The third is, truly, that the hand whence this finger came was kneading rye dough within three days before the finger was cut therefrom, and I can assure your highness that my wife has never kneaded rye dough since my wife she has been."

The king was mightily wroth with Elphin for so stoutly withstanding him, respecting the goodness of his wife; wherefore he ordered him to his prison a second time, saying that he should not be loosed thence until he had proved the truth of his boast, as well concerning the wisdom of his bard as the virtues of his wife.

In the meantime his wife and Taliesin remained joyful at Elphin's dwelling. And Taliesin showed his mistress how that Elphin was in prison because of them; but he bade her be glad, for that he would go to Maelgan's court to free his master. So he took leave of his mistress, and came to the court of Maelgan, who was going to sit in his hall, and dine in his royal state, as it was the custom in those days for kings and princes to do at every chief feast. As soon as Taliesin entered the hall, he placed himself in a quiet corner, near the place where the bards and the minstrels were wont to come, in doing their service and duty to the king, as is the custom at the high festivals, when the bounty is proclaimed. So, when the bards and the heralds came to cry largess, and to proclaim the power of the king, and his strength, at the moment when they passed by the corner wherein he was crouching, Taliesin pouted out his lips after them, and played, "Blerwm, blerwm!" with his finger upon his lips. Neither took they much notice of him as they went by, but proceeded forward till they came before the king, unto whom they made their obeisance with their bodies, as they were wont, without speaking a single word, but pouting out their lips, and making mouths at the king, playing "Blerwm, blerwm!" upon their lips with their fingers, as they had seen the boy do. This sight caused the king to wonder, and to deem within himself that they were drunk with many liquors. Wherefore he commanded one of his lords, who served at the board, to go to them and desire them to collect their wits, and to consider where they stood, and what it was fitting for them to do. And this lord did so gladly. But they ceased not from their folly any more than before. Whereupon he sent to them a second time, and a third, desiring them to go forth from the hall. And the last the king ordered one of his squires to give a blow to the chief of them, named Heinin Vardd; and the squire took a broom and struck him on the head, so that he fell back in his seat. Then he arose, and went on his knees, and besought leave of the king's grace to show that this their fault was not through want of knowledge, neither through drunkenness, but by the influence of some spirit that was in the hall. And he spoke on this wise: "O honorable king, be it known to your grace that not from the strength of drink, or of too much liquor, are we dumb, but through the influence of a spirit that sits in the corner yonder, in the form of a child." Forthwith the king commanded the squire to fetch him; and he went to the nook where Taliesin sat, and brought him before the king, who asked him what he was, and whence he came. And he answered the king in verse:

"Primary chief bard am I to Elphin,
And my native country is the region of the
    summer stars;
I have been in Asia with Noah in the ark,
I have seen the destruction of Sodom and Gomorrah,
I was in India when Rome was built,
I have now come here to the remnant of Troia."

When the king and his nobles had heard the song, they wondered much, for they had never heard the like from a boy so young as he. And when the king knew that he was the bard of Elphin, he bade Heinin, his first and wisest bard, to answer Taliesin, and to strive with him. But when he came, he could do no other than play "Blerwm!" on his lips; and when he sent for the others of the four and twenty bards, they all did likewise, and could do no other. And Maelgan asked the boy Taliesin what was his errand, and he answered him in song:

"Elphin, the son of Gwyddno,
Is in the land of Artro,
Secured by thirteen locks,
For praising his instructor.
Therefore I, Taliesin,
Chief of the bards of the west,
Will loosen Elphin
Out of a golden fetter."

Then he sang to them a riddle:

"Discover thou what is
The strong creature from before the flood,
Without flesh, without bone,
Without vein, without blood,
Without head, without feet;
It will neither be older nor younger
Than at the beginning.
Behold how the sea whitens
When first it comes,
When it comes from the south,
When it strikes on coasts.
It is in the field, it is in the wood,
But the eye cannot perceive it.
One Being has prepared it,
By a tremendous blast,
To wreak vengeance
On Maelgan Gwynedd."

While he was thus singing his verse, there arose a mighty storm of wind, so that the king and all his nobles thought that the castle would fall upon their heads. And the king caused them to fetch Elphin in haste from his dungeon, and placed him before Taliesin. And it is said that immediately he sung a verse, so that the chains opened from about his feet.

After that Taliesin brought Elphin's wife before them, and showed that she had not one finger wanting. And in this manner did he set his master free from prison, and protect the innocence of his mistress, and silence the bards so that not one of them dared to say a word. Right glad was Elphin, right glad was Taliesin.

CHAPTER XXXIII

KING RICHARD AND THE THIRD CRUSADE

THE Crusades were the mightiest or rather the most ambitious undertaking of the chivalry of Europe. From the year 1096 for more than a century the knights of all countries looked to the Holy Land as a field for winning their spurs and obtaining pardon of their sins. And it is most natural

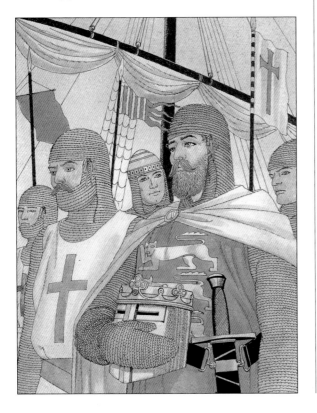

that in giving a picture of English chivalry as it is shown in history that we should give a description of King Richard's exploits in Palestine.

In the last decade of the twelfth century Richard I of England took the cross, which had come to him as a sort of legacy from his father, and sailed for Antioch, which was being besieged by the Christians, to assist in the war in the Holy Land. At the same time Philip Augustus of France and Frederick Barbarossa joined the Crusaders. Frederick was drowned in a river of Cilicia, and his force had so dwindled that when they reached Antioch hardly a tenth of the number were left that had started. Philip of France reached Antioch with his army, and there, as we shall learn later, he fought with the Turk and quarrelled with the Christian for a time, until he finally set sail for France without having accomplished the capture of the Holy City. As for Richard, he was not more successful, and although his deeds were so glorious as to cover him with honor, he was obliged to return home, leaving Jerusalem still in the hands of infidels.

THE EXPLOITS OF KING RICHARD

Now as the ships were proceeding, some being before others, two of the three first, driven by the violence of the winds, were broken on the rocks near the port of Cyprus; the third, which was English, more speedy than they, having turned back into the deep, escaped the peril. Almost all the men of both ships got away alive to land, many of whom the hostile Cypriotes slew, some they took captive, some, taking refuge in a certain church, were besieged. Whatever also in the ships was cast up by the sea fell a prey to the Cypriotes. The prince also of that island coming up, received for his share the gold and the arms; and he caused the shore to be guarded by all the armed force he could summon together, that he might not permit the fleet which followed to approach, lest the king should take again what had been thus stolen from him. Above the port was a strong city, and upon a natural rock, a high and fortified castle. The whole of that nation was warlike and accustomed to live by theft. They placed beams and planks at the entrance of the port, across the passage, the gates, and entrances; and the whole land with one mind prepared themselves for a conflict with the English. God so willed that the cursed people should receive the reward of their evil deeds by the hands of one who would not spare. The third English ship, in which were the women, having cast out their anchors, rode out at sea, and watched all things from opposite, to report the misfortunes to the king,[1] lest haply, being ignorant of the loss and disgrace, he should pass the place unavenged. The next line of the king's ships came up after the other, and they are stopped at the first. A full report reached the king, who, sending heralds to the lord of the island, and obtaining no satisfaction, commanded his entire army to arm, from the first even to the last, and to get out of the great ships into the galleys and boats, and follow him to the shore. What he commanded was immediately performed; they came in arms to the port. The king being armed, leaped first from the galley, and gave the first blow in the war; but before he was able to strike a second he had three thousand of his followers with him striking away at his side. All the timber that had been placed as a barricade in the port was cast down instantly, and the brave fellows went up into the city as ferocious as lionesses are wont to be when robbed of their young. The fight

---

[1]Richard I of England.

was carried on manfully against them, numbers fell wounded on both sides, and the swords of both parties were made drunk with blood. The Cypriotes are vanquished, the city is taken, with the castle besides; whatever the victors choose is ransacked; and the lord of the island is himself taken and brought to the king. He being taken, supplicates and obtains pardon; he offers homage to the king, and it is received; and he swears, though unasked, that henceforth he will hold the island of him as his liege lord, and will open all the castles of the land to him, and make satisfaction for the damage already done; and further bring presents of his own. On being dismissed after the oath, he is commanded to fulfil the conditions in the morning.

That night the king remained peaceably in the castle; and his newly-sworn vassal, flying, retired to another castle, and caused the whole of the men of the land, who were able to bear arms, to be summoned to repair to him, and so they did. The king of Jerusalem, however, that same night landed in Cyprus, that he might assist the king and salute him, whose arrival he had desired above that of any other in the whole world. On the morrow the lord of Cyprus was sought for and found to have fled. The king seeing that he was abused, and having been informed where he was, directed the king of Jerusalem to follow the traitor by land with the best of the army, while he conducted the other part by water, intending to be in the way that he might not escape by sea. The divisions reassembled around the city in which he had taken refuge, and he, having sallied out against the king, fought with the English, and the battle was carried on sharply by both sides. The English would that day have been beaten had they not fought under the command of King Richard. They at length obtained a dear-bought victory, the Cypriote flies, and the castle is taken. The kings pursue him as before, the one by land and the other by water, and he is besieged in the third castle. Its walls are cast down by engines hurling huge stones; he, being overcome, promises to surrender, if only he might not be put in iron fetters. The king consents to the prayers of the supplicant, and caused silver shackles to be made for him. The prince of the pirates being thus taken, the king traversed the whole island, and took all its castles, and placed his constables in each, and constituted justiciaries and sheriffs, and the whole land was subjected to him in everything just like England. The gold, and the silks and the jewels from the treasuries that were broken open, he retained for himself; the silver and victuals he gave to the army. To the king of Jerusalem also he made a handsome present out of the booty.

The king proceeding thence, came to the siege of Acre, and was welcomed by the besiegers with as great a joy as if it had been Christ that had come again on earth to restore the kingdom of Israel. The king of the French had arrived at Acre first, and was very highly esteemed by the natives; but on Richard's arrival he became obscured and without consideration, just as the moon is wont to relinquish her lustre at the rising of the sun.

The king of the English, unused to delay, on the third day of his arrival at the siege, caused his wooden fortress, which he had called "Mate Grifun," when it was made in Sicily, to be built and set up, and before the dawn of the fourth day the machine stood erect by the walls of Acre, and from its height looked down upon the city lying beneath it; and there were thereon by sunrise archers casting missiles without intermission on the Turks and Thracians. Engines also for casting stones, placed in convenient positions, battered the walls with frequent volleys. More important than these, the sappers, making themselves a way beneath the ground, undermined the foundations of the walls; while soldiers, bearing shields, having planted ladders, sought an entrance over the ramparts. The king himself was running up and down through the ranks, directing some, reproving some, and urging others, and thus was he everywhere present with every one of them, so that whatever they all did ought properly to be ascribed to him. The king of the French also did not lightly assail them, making as bold an assault as he could on the tower of the city which is called Cursed.

The renowned Carracois and Mestocus, after Saladin, the most powerful princes of the heathen, had at that time the charge of the besieged city, who, after a contest of many days, promised by their interpreters the surrender of the city, and a ransom for their heads; but the king of the English desired to subdue their obstinacy by force; and wished that the vanquished should pay their heads for the ransom of their bodies,

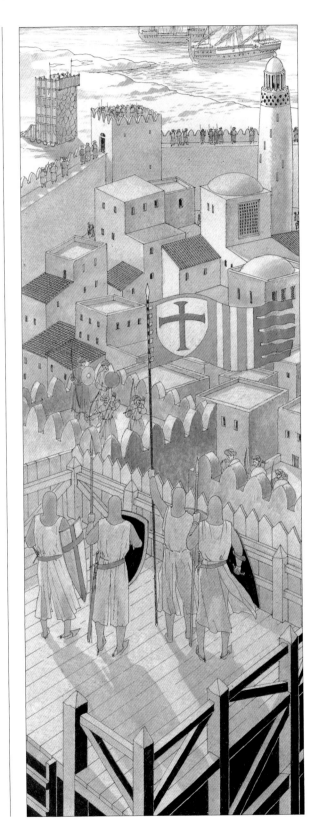

but by the mediation of the king of the French their life and indemnity of limbs only was accorded, if, after the surrender of the city and yielding of everything they possessed, the Holy Cross should be given up.

All the heathen warriors in Acre were chosen men, and were in number nine thousand; many of whom, swallowing many gold coins, made a purse of their stomachs, because they foresaw that whatever they had of any value would be turned against them, even against themselves, if they should again oppose the cross, and would only fall a prey to the victors. So all of them came out before the kings entirely disarmed, and outside the city, without money, were given into custody; and the kings, with triumphal banners, having entered the city, divided the whole with all its stores into two parts between themselves and their soldiers; the pontiff's seat alone its bishop received by their united gift. The captives, being divided, Mestocus fell by lot to the portion of the king of the English, and Carracois, as a drop of cold water, fell into the mouth of the thirsty Philip, king of the French.

Messengers on the part of the captives having been sent to Saladin for their ransom, when the heathen could by no entreaty be moved to restore the Holy Cross, the king of the English beheaded all his, with the exception of Mestocus only, who on account of his nobility was spared, and declared openly, without any ceremony, that he would act in the same way toward Saladin himself.

The king of the English, then, having sent for the commanders of the French, proposed that in the first place they should conjointly attempt Jerusalem itself; but the dissuasion of the French discouraged the hearts of both parties, dispirited the troops, and restrained the king, thus destitute of men, from his intended march on that metropolis. The king, troubled at this, though not despairing, from that day forth separated his army from the French, and directing his arms to the storming of castles along the seashore, he took every fortress that came in his way from Tyre to Ascalon, though after hard fighting and deep wounds.[1]

On the Saturday, the eve of the Nativity of the blessed Virgin Mary, at earliest dawn, our men armed

themselves with great care to receive the Turks, who were known to have preceded their march, and whose insolence nothing but a battle could check. The enemy had ranged themselves in order, drawing gradually nearer and nearer; and our men also took the utmost care to place themselves in as good order as possible. King Richard, who was most experienced in military affairs, arranged the army in squadrons, and directed who should march in front and who in the rear. He divided the army into twelve companies, and these again into five divisions, marshalled according as the men ranked in military discipline; and none could be found more warlike, if they had only had confidence in God, who is the giver of all good things. On that day the Templars formed the first rank, and after them came, in due order, the Bretons and men of Anjou; then followed King Guy, with the men of Pictou; and in the fourth line were the Normans and English, who had the care of the royal standard, and last of all marched the Hospitallers: this line was composed of chosen warriors, divided into companies. They kept together so closely that an apple, if thrown, would not have fallen to the ground without touching a man or a horse; and the army stretched from the army of Saracens to the seashore. There you might have seen their most appropriate distinctions,—standards, and ensigns of various forms, and hardy soldiers, fresh and full of spirits, and well fitted for war. Henry, count of Champagne, kept guard on the mountain side, and maintained a constant lookout on the flank; the foot-soldiers, bowmen, and arbalesters were on the outside, and the rear of the army was closed by the post horses and wagons, which carried provisions and other things, and journeyed along between the army and the sea, to avoid an attack from the enemy.

This was the order of the army, as it advanced gradually, to prevent separation; for the less close the line of battle, the less effective was it for resistance. King Richard and the duke of Burgundy, with a chosen retinue of warriors, rode up and down, narrowly watching the position and manner of the Turks, to correct anything in their own troops, if they saw occasion, for they had need, at that moment, of the utmost circumspection.

It was now nearly nine o'clock, when there appeared a large body of the Turks, ten thousand

---

[1]The preceding narrative is taken from the Chronicle of Richard of Devizes. What follows is from the Chronicle of Geoffrey de Vinsauf.

producing a horrible noise and clamor. The earth vibrated from the loud and discordant sounds, so that the crash of thunder could not be heard amidst the tumultuous noise of horns and trumpets. They did this to excite their spirit and courage, for the more violent their clamor became, the more bold were they for the fray. Thus the impious Turks threatened us, both on the side towards the sea and from the side of the land; and for the space of two miles not so much earth as could be taken up in one hand could be seen, on account of the hostile Turks who covered it. Oh, how obstinately they pressed on, and continued their stubborn attacks, so that our men suffered severe loss of their horses, which were killed by their darts and arrows. Oh, how useful to us on that day were our arbalesters and bowmen, who closed the extremities of the lines, and did their best to repel the obstinate Turks.

The enemy came rushing down, like a torrent, to the attack; and many of our arbalesters, unable to restrain the weight of their terrible and calamitous charge, threw away their arms, and, fearing lest they should be shut out, took refuge, in crowds, behind the dense lines of the army; yielding through fear of death to sufferings which they could not support. Those whom shame forbade to yield, or the hope of an immortal crown sustained, were animated with greater boldness and courage to persevere in the contest, and fought with indefatigable valor face to face against the Turks, whilst they at the same time receded step by step, and so reached their retreat. The whole of that day, on account of the Turks pressing them closely from behind, they faced around and went on skirmishing, rather than proceeding on their march.

Oh, how great was the strait they were in on that day! how great was their tribulation! when some were affected with fears, and no one had such confidence or spirit as not to wish, at that moment, he had finished his pilgrimage, and had returned home, instead of standing with trembling heart the chances of a doubtful battle. In truth our people, so few in number, were so hemmed in by the multitudes of the Saracens, that they had no means of escape, if they tried; neither did they seem to have valor sufficient to withstand so many foes,—nay, they were shut in like a flock of sheep in the jaws of wolves, with nothing but the sky above, and the enemy all around them. O

strong, coming down upon us at full charge, and throwing darts and arrows as far as they could, while they mingled their voices in one horrible yell. There followed after them an infernal race of men, of black color, and bearing a suitable appellation, expressive of their blackness. With them also were the Saracens, who live in the desert, called Bedouins; they are a savage race of men, blacker than soot; they fight on foot, and carry a bow, quiver, and round shield, and are a light and active race. These men dauntlessly attacked our army. Beyond these might be seen the well-arranged phalanxes of the Turks, with ensigns fixed to their lances, and standards and banners of separate distinctions. Their army was divided into troops, and the troops into companies, and their numbers seemed to exceed twenty thousand. They came on with irresistible charge, on horses swifter than eagles, and urged on like lightning to attack our men; and as they advanced they raised a cloud of dust, so that the air was darkened. In front came certain of their admirals, as it was their duty, with clarions and trumpets; some had horns, others had pipes and timbrels, gongs, cymbals, and other instruments,

Lord God! what feelings agitated that weak flock of Christ! straitened by such a perplexity, whom the enemy pressed with such unabating vigor, as if they would pass them through a sieve. What army was ever assailed by so mighty a force? There you might have seen our troopers, having lost their chargers, marching on foot with the footmen, or casting missiles from the arbalests, or arrows from bows, against the enemy, and repelling their attacks in the best manner they were able. The Turks, skilled in the bow, pressed unceasingly upon them; it rained darts; the air was filled with the shower of arrows, and the brightness of the sun was obscured by the multitude of missiles, as if it had been darkened by a fall of winter's hail or snow. Our horses were pierced by the darts and arrows, which were so numerous that the whole face of the earth around was covered with them, and if any one wished to gather them up, he might take twenty of them in his hand at a time.

The Turks pressed with such boldness that they nearly crushed the Hospitallers; on which the latter sent word to King Richard that they could not withstand the violence of the enemy's attack, unless he would allow their knights to advance at full charge against them. This the king dissuaded them from doing, but advised them to keep in a close body; they therefore persevered and kept together, though scarcely able to breathe for the pressure. By these means they were able to proceed on their way, though the heat happened to be very great on that day; so that they labored under two disadvantages,—the hot weather and the attacks of the enemy. These approved martyrs of Christ sweated in the contest; and he who could have seen them closed up in a narrow space, so patient under the heat and toil of the day and the attacks of the enemy, who exhorted each other to destroy the Christians, could not doubt in his mind that it augured ill to our success from their straitened and perilous position, hemmed in as they were by so large a multitude; for the enemy thundered at their backs as if with mallets, so that, having no room to use their bows, they fought hand to hand with swords, lances, and clubs, and the blows of the Turks, echoing from their metal armor, resounded as if they had been struck upon an anvil. They were now tormented with the heat, and no rest was allowed them. The battle fell heavy on the extreme line of the Hospitallers, the more so as they were unable to resist, but moved forward with patience under their wounds, returning not even a word for the blows which fell upon them, and advancing on their way because they were not able to bear the weight of the contest.

Then they pressed on for safety upon the centre of the army which was in front of them, to avoid the fury of the enemy who harassed them in the rear. Was it wonderful that no one could withstand so continuous an attack, when he could not even return a blow to the numbers who pressed on him? The strength of all Paganism had gathered together from Damascus and Persia, from the Mediterranean to the East; there was not left in the uttermost recesses of the earth one man of fame or power, one nation's valor, or one bold soldier, whom the sultan had not summoned to his aid, either by entreaty, by money, or by authority, to crush the Christian race; for he presumed to hope he could blot them from the face of the earth; but his hopes were vain, for their numbers were sufficient, through the assistance of God, to effect their purpose. The flower of the chosen youth and soldiers of Christendom had indeed assembled together, and were united in one body, like ears of corn on their stalks, from every region of the earth; and if they had been utterly destroyed, there is no doubt that there were some left to make resistance.

A cloud of dust obscured the air as our men marched on; and, in addition to the heat, they had an enemy pressing them in the rear, insolent, and rendered obstinate by the instigation of the devil. Still the Christians proved good men, and secure in their unconquerable spirit, kept constantly advancing, while the Turks threatened them without ceasing in the rear; but their blows fell harmless upon the defensive armor, and this caused the Turks to slacken in courage at the failure of their attempts, and they began to murmur in whispers of disappointment, crying out in their rage, "that our people were made of iron and would yield to no blow." Then the Turks, about twenty thousand strong, rushed again upon our men pell-mell, annoying them in every possible manner; when, as if overcome by their savage fury, brother Garnier de Napes, one of the Hospitallers, suddenly exclaimed with a loud voice, "O excellent St. George! will you leave us to be thus put to confusion? The whole of Christendom is now on the point of perishing, because it fears to return a blow against this impious race."

Upon this the master of the Hospitallers went to the king, and said to him, "My lord the king, we are violently pressed by the enemy, and are in danger of eternal infamy, as if we did not dare to return their blows; we are each of us losing our horses one after another, and why should we bear with them any further?" To whom the king replied, "Good master, it is you who must sustain their attack; no one can be everywhere at once." On the master returning, the Turks again made a fierce attack on them from the rear, and there was not a prince or count amongst them but blushed with shame, and they said to each other, "Why do we not charge them at full gallop? Alas! alas! we shall forever deserve to be called cowards, a thing which never happened to us before, for never has such a disgrace befallen so great an army, even from unbelievers. Unless we defend ourselves by immediately charging the enemy we shall gain everlasting scandal, and so much the greater the longer we delay to fight." O, how blind is human fate! On what slippery points it stands! Alas, on how uncertain wheels doth it advance, and with what ambiguous success doth it unfold the course of human things! A countless multitude of the Turks would have perished if the aforesaid attempt had been orderly conducted; but to punish us for our sins, as it is believed, the potter's ware produces a paltry vessel instead of the grand design which he had conceived. For when they were treating on this point, and had come to the same decision about charging the enemy, two knights, who were impatient of delay, put everything in confusion. It had been resolved by common consent that the sounding of six trumpets in three different parts of the army should be a signal for a charge, viz., two in front, two in the rear, and two in the middle, to distinguish the sounds from those of the Saracens, and to mark the distance of each. If these orders had been attended to, the Turks would have been utterly discomfited; but from the too great haste of the aforesaid knights the success of the affair was marred.

They rushed at full gallop upon the Turks, and each of them prostrated his man by piercing him through with his lance. One of them was the marshal of the Hospitallers, the other was Baldwin de Carreo, a good and brave man, and the companion of King Richard, who had brought him in his retinue. When the other Christians observed these two rushing forward, and heard them calling with a clear voice on St. George for aid, they charged the Turks in a body with all their strength; then the Hospitallers, who had been distressed all day by their close array, following the two soldiers, charged the enemy in troops, so that the van of the army became the rear from their position in the attack, and the Hospitallers, who had been the last, were the first to charge.

The count of Champagne also burst forward with 186 ▷ his chosen company, and James d'Avennes with his kinsmen, and also Robert count of Dreux, the bishop of Beauvais and his brother, as well as the earl of Leicester, who made a fierce charge on the left towards the sea. Why need we name each? Those who were in the first line of the rear made a united and furious charge; after them the men of Pictou, the Bretons, and the men of Anjou, rushed swiftly onward, and then came the rest of the army in a body: each troop showed its valor, and boldly closed with the Turks, transfixing them with their lances, and casting them to the ground. The sky grew black with the dust that was raised in the confusion of that encounter. The Turks, who had purposely dismounted from their horses in order to take better aim at our men with their darts and arrows, were slain on all sides in that charge, for on being prostrated by the horse-soldiers they were beheaded by the foot-men. King Richard, on seeing his army in motion and in encounter with the Turks, flew rapidly on his horse at full speed through the Hospitallers, who had led the charge, and to whom he was bringing assistance with all his retinue, and broke into the Turkish infantry, who were astonished at his blows and those of his men, and gave way to the right and to the left.

Then might be seen numbers prostrated on the ground, horses without their riders in crowds, the wounded lamenting with groans their hard fate, and others drawing their last breath, weltering in their gore, and many lay headless, whilst their lifeless forms were trodden under foot both by friend and foe. Oh, how different are the speculations of those who meditate amidst the columns of the cloister from

the fearful exercise of war! There the king, the fierce, the extraordinary king, cut down the Turks in every direction, and none could escape the force of his arm, for wherever he turned, brandishing his sword, he carved a wide path for himself; and as he advanced and gave repeated strokes with his sword, cutting them down like a reaper with his sickle, the rest, warned by the sight of the dying, gave him more ample space, for the corpses of the dead Turks which lay on the face of the earth extended over half a mile. In fine, the Turks were cut down, the saddles emptied of their riders, and the dust which was raised by the conflict of the combatants proved very hurtful to our men, for on becoming fatigued from slaying so many, when they were retiring to take fresh air, they could not recognize each other on account of the thick dust, and struck their blows indiscriminately to the right and to the left; so that unable to distinguish friend from foe they took their own men for enemies and cut them down without mercy. Then the Christians pressed hard on the Turks, the latter gave way before them: but for a long time the battle was doubtful; they still exchanged blows, and either party strove for the victory; on both sides were seen some retreating, covered with wounds, while others fell slain to the ground.

Oh, how many banners and standards of different forms, and pennons and many-colored ensigns, might there be seen torn and fallen on the earth; swords of proved steel, and lances made of cane with iron heads, Turkish bows, and maces bristling with sharp teeth, darts and arrows covering the ground, and missiles enough to load twenty wagons or more! There lay the headless trunks of the Turks who had perished, whilst others retained their courage for a time until our men increased in strength, when some of them concealed themselves in the copses, some climbed up trees, and, being shot with arrows, fell with a fearful groan to the earth; others, abandoning their horses, betook themselves by slippery footpaths to the seaside, and tumbled headlong into the waves from the precipitous cliffs that were five poles in height. The rest of the enemy were repulsed in so wonderful a manner that for the space of two miles nothing could be seen but fugitives, although they had before been so obstinate and fierce, and puffed up with pride; but by God's grace their pride was humbled, and they continued still to fly, for when our men ceased the pursuit fear alone added wings to their feet. Our army had been ranged in divisions when they attacked the Turks; the Normans and English also, who had the care of the standard, came up slowly towards the troops which were fighting with the Turks,—for it was very difficult to disperse the enemy's strength, and they stopped at a short distance therefrom, that all might have a rallying point. On the conclusion of the slaughter our men paused; but the fugitives, to the number of twenty thousand, when they saw this, immediately recovering their courage, and armed with maces, charged the hindmost of those who were retiring, and rescued some from our men who had just struck them down.

Oh, how dreadfully were our men then pressed! for the darts and arrows, thrown at them as they were falling back, broke the heads, arms, and other limbs of our horsemen, so that they bent, stunned, to their saddle-bows; but having quickly regained their spirits and resumed their strength, and thirsting for vengeance with greater eagerness, like a lioness when her whelps are stolen, they charged the enemy, and broke through them like a net. Then you might have seen the horses with their saddles displaced, and the Turks, who had but just now fled, returning, and pressing upon our people with the utmost fury; every cast of their darts would have told had our men kept marching, and not stood still in a compact, immovable body. The commander of the Turks was an admiral, named Tekedmus, a kinsman of the sultan, having a banner with a remarkable device; namely, that of a pair of breeches carved thereon, a symbol well known to his men. He was a most cruel persecutor, and a persevering enemy of the Christians; and he had under his command seven hundred chosen Turks of great valor, of the household troops of Saladin, each of whose companies bore a yellow banner with pennons of a different color. These men, coming at full charge, with clamor and haughty bearing, attacked our men, who were turning off from them towards the standard, cutting at them, and piercing them severely, so that even the firmness of our chiefs wavered under the weight of the pressure; yet our men remained immovable, compelled to repel force by force. And the conflict grew thicker, the blows were redoubled, and the battle waxed fiercer than before: the one side labored to crush, the other to repel; both exerted their strength, and although our men were by far the fewest in numbers, they made havoc of great multitudes of the enemy; and that portion of the army which thus toiled in the battle could not return to the standard with ease, on account of the immense mass which pressed upon them so severely; for thus hemmed in they began to flag in courage, and but few dared to renew the attack of the enemy. In truth, the Turks were furious in the assault, and greatly distressed our men, whose blood poured forth in a stream beneath their blows. On perceiving them reel and give way, William de Barris, a renowned knight, breaking through the ranks, charged the Turks with his men; and such was the vigor of the onset that some fell by the edge of his sword, while others only saved themselves by rapid flight. For all that, the king, mounted on a bay Cyprian steed, which had not its match, bounded forward in the direction of the mountains, and scattered those he met on all sides; for the enemy fled from his sword and gave way, while helmets tottered beneath it, and sparks flew forth from its strokes. So great was the fury of his onset, and so many and deadly his blows that day, in his conflict with the Turks, that in a short space of time the enemy were all scattered, and allowed our army to proceed; and thus our men, having suffered somewhat, at last returned to the standard, and proceeded on their march as far as Arsur, and there they pitched their tents outside its walls.

While they were thus engaged a large body of the Turks made an attack on the extreme rear of our army. On hearing the noise of the assailants, King Richard, encouraging his men to battle, rushed at full speed, with only fifteen companions, against the Turks, crying out, with a loud voice, "Aid us, O God! and the Holy Sepulchre!" and this he exclaimed a second and a third time; and when our men heard it they made haste to follow him, and attacked, routed, and put them to flight; pursuing them as far as Arsur, whence they had first come out, cuffing them down and subduing them. Many of the Turks fell there also. The king returned thence from the slaughter of the fugitives to his camp; and the men, overcome with the fatigue and exertions of the day, rested quietly that night.

Whoever was greedy of gain, and wished to plunder the booty, returned to the place of battle, and loaded himself to his heart's desire; and those who returned from thence reported that they had counted thirty-two Turkish chiefs who were found slain on that day, and whom they supposed to be men of great influence and power from the splendor of their armor and the costliness of their apparel. The Turks also made search for them to carry them away as being of the most importance; and besides these the Turks carried off seven thousand mangled bodies of those who were next in rank, besides of the wounded, who went off in straggling parties; and when their strength failed lay about the fields and died. But by the protection of God we did not lose a tenth, nor a hundredth part so many as fell in the Turkish army. Oh, the disasters of that day! Oh, the trials of the warriors! for the tribulations of the just are many. Oh, mournful calamity and bitter distress. How great must have been the blackness of our sins to require so fiery an ordeal to purify it, for if we had striven to overcome the urgent necessity by pious long-suffering, and without a murmur, the sense of our obligations would have been deeper.

And again the Christians were put in great peril, in the following manner. At the siege of Joppa a certain depraved set of men among the Saracens, called Menelones of Aleppo and Cordivi, an active race, met together to consult what should be done in the existing state of things. They spoke of the scandal which lay against them, that so small an army, without horses, had driven them out of Joppa, and they reproached themselves with cowardice and shameful baseness, and arrogantly made a compact among themselves that they would seize King Richard in his tent, and bring him before Saladin, from whom they would receive a most munificent reward.

So they prepared themselves in the middle of the night to surprise the king, and sallied forth armed, by the light of the moon, conversing with one another about the object they had in hand. Oh, hateful race of unbelievers! they are anxiously bent upon seizing Christ's steadfast soldier while he is asleep. They rush on in numbers to seize him, unarmed and apprehensive of no danger. They were not far from his tent, and were preparing to lay hands on him, when, lo! the God of mercy, who never neglects those who trust in Him, and acts in a wonderful manner even to those who know Him not, sent the spirit of discord among the aforesaid Cordivi and Menelones. The Cordivi said, "You shall go in on foot to take the king and his followers, whilst we will remain on horseback to prevent their escaping into the castle." But the Menelones replied, "Nay it is your place to go in on foot, because our rank is higher than yours; but this service on foot belongs to you rather than us." Whilst thus the two parties were contending which of them were the greatest, their combined dispute caused much delay; and when at last they came to a decision how their nefarious attempt should be achieved, the dawn of the day appeared, viz., the Wednesday next following the feast of St. Peter *ad vincula*. But now by the providence of God, who had decreed that his holy champion should not be seized whilst asleep by the infidels, a certain Genoese was led by the divine impulse to go out early in the morning into the fields, where he was alarmed by the noise of men and horses advancing, and returned speedily, but just had time to see helmets reflecting back the light which now fell upon them. He immediately rushed with speed into the camp, calling out, "To arms! to arms!" The king was awakened by the noise, and leaping startled from his bed, put on his impenetrable coat of mail, and summoned his men to the rescue.

God of all mercies! lives there a man who would not be shaken by such a sudden alarm? The enemy rushed unawares, armed against unarmed, many against few, for our men had no time to arm or even to dress themselves. The king himself, therefore, and many others with him, on the urgency of the moment, proceeded without their cuishes to the fight, some even without their breeches, and they armed themselves in the best manner they could, though they were going to fight the whole day. Whilst our men were thus arming in haste, the Turks drew near, and the king mounted his horse, with only ten other knights with him. These alone had horses, and some even of them had base and impotent horses, unused to arms; the common men were drawn skilfully out in ranks and troops, with each a captain to command them. The knights were posted nearer to the sea, having the church of St. Nicholas on the left, because the Turks had directed their principal attack on that quarter, and the Pisans and Genoese were posted beyond

the suburban gardens, having other troops mingled with them. Oh, who could fully relate the terrible attacks of the infidels? The Turks at first rushed on with horrid yells, hurling their javelins and shooting their arrows. Our men prepared themselves as they best could to receive their furious attack, each fixing his right knee in the ground, that so they might the better hold together and maintain their position; whilst there the thighs of their left legs were bent, and their left hands held their shields or bucklers; stretched out before them in their right hands they held their lances, of which the lower ends were fixed in the ground, and their iron heads pointed threateningly towards the enemy.

Between every two of the men who were thus covered with their shields, the king, versed in arms, placed an arbalester, and another behind him to stretch the arbalest as quickly as possible, so that the man in front might discharge his shot whilst the other was loading. This was found to be of much benefit to our men, and did much harm to the enemy. Thus everything was prepared as well as the shortness of the time allowed, and our little army was drawn up in order. The king ran along the ranks, and exhorted every man to be brave and not to flinch. "Courage, my brave men," said he; "and let not the attack of the enemy disturb you. Bear up against the powers of fortune, and you will rise above them. Everything may be borne by brave men; adversity sheds a light upon the virtues of mankind, as certainly as prosperity casts over them a shade; there is no room for flight, for the enemy surround us, and to attempt to flee is to provoke certain death. Be brave, therefore, and let the urgency of the case sharpen up your valor; brave men should either conquer nobly or gloriously die. Martyrdom is a boon which we should receive with willing mind; but before we die, let us, whilst still alive, do what we may to avenge our deaths, giving thanks to God that it has been our lot to die martyrs. This will be the end of our labors, the termination of our life and of our battles. These words were hardly spoken, when the hostile army rushed with ferocity upon them, in seven troops, each of which contained about a thousand horses. Our men received their attack with their right feet planted firm against the sand, and remained immovable. Their lances formed a wall against the enemy, who would have assuredly broken through, if our men had in the least given way.

The first line of the Turks, perceiving, as they advanced, that our men stood immovable, recoiled a little, when our men plied them with a shower of missiles, slaying large numbers of men and horses. Another line of Turks at once came on in like manner, and were again encountered and driven back. In this way the Turks came on like a whirlwind, again and again, making the appearance of an attack, that our men might be induced to give way, and when they were close up they turned their horses off in another direction. The king and his knights, who were on horseback, perceiving this, put spurs to their horses, and charged into the middle of the enemy, upsetting them right and left, and piercing a large number through the body with their lances; at last they pulled up their horses, because they found that they had penetrated entirely through the Turkish lines. The king, now looking about him, saw the noble earl of Leicester fallen from his horse, and fighting bravely on foot. No sooner did he see this, than he rushed to his rescue, snatched him out of the hands of the enemy, and replaced him on his horse. What a terrible combat was then waged! A multitude of Turks advanced, and used every exertion to destroy our small army; vexed at our success, they rushed toward the royal standard of the lion, for they would rather have slain the king than a thousand others. In the midst of the mêlée the king saw Ralph de Mauleon dragged off prisoner by the Turks, and spurring his horse to speed, in a moment released him from their hands, and restored him to the army; for the king was a very giant in the battle, and was everywhere in the field,—now here, now there, wherever the attacks of the Turks raged the hottest. So bravely did he fight, that there was no one, however gallant, that would not readily and deservedly yield to him the pre-eminence. On that day he performed the most gallant deeds on the furious army of the Turks, and slew numbers with his sword, which shone like lightning; some of them were cloven in two, from their helmet to their teeth, whilst others lost their heads, arms, and other members, which were lopped off at a single blow. While the king was thus laboring with incredible exertions in the fight, a Turk advanced towards him, mounted on a foaming steed. He had been sent by Saphadin of Archadia, brother to Saladin, a liberal and munificent man, if he had not rejected the Christian faith. This man now sent to the king, as a token of his well-known honorable character, two noble horses, requesting him earnestly to accept them, and make use of them, and if he returned safe and sound out of that battle, to remember the gift and recompense it in any manner he pleased. The king readily received the present, and afterwards nobly recompensed the giver. Such is bravery, cognizable even in an enemy; since a Turk, who was our bitter foe, thus honored the king for his distinguished valor. The king, especially at such a moment of need, protested that he would have taken any number of horses equally good from any one even more a foe than Saphadin, so necessary were they to him at that moment. Fierce now raged the fight, when such numbers attacked so few; the whole earth was covered with the javelins and arrows of the unbelievers; they threw them, several at a time, at our men, of whom many were wounded. Thus the weight of battle fell heavier upon us than before, and the galley-men withdrew in the galleys which brought them; and so, in their anxiety to be safe, they sacrificed their character for bravery. Meanwhile a shout was raised by the Turks, as they strove who should first occupy the town, hoping to slay those of our men whom they should find within. The king, hearing the clamor, taking with him only two knights and two crossbow-men, met three Turks, nobly caparisoned, in one of the principal streets. Rushing bravely upon them, he slew the riders in his own royal fashion, and made booty of two horses. The rest of the Turks who were found in the town were put to the rout in spite of their resistance, and dispersing in different directions, sought to make their escape, even where there was no regular road. The king also commanded the parts of the walls which were broken down to be made good, and placed sentinels to keep watch lest the town should be again attacked.

These matters settled, the king went down to the shore, where many of our men had taken refuge on board the galleys. These the king exhorted by the most cogent arguments to return to the battle, and share with the rest whatever might befall them. Leaving five men as guards on board each galley, the king led back the rest to assist his hard-pressed army; and he no sooner arrived than with all his fury he fell upon the thickest ranks of the enemy, driving them back and routing them, so that even those who were at a distance and untouched by him were overwhelmed by the throng of the troops as they retreated. Never was there such an attack made by an individual. He pierced into the middle of the hostile army, and performed the deeds of a brave and distinguished warrior. The Turks at once closed upon him, and tried to overwhelm him. In the meantime our men, losing sight of the king, were fearful lest he should have been slain, and when one of them proposed that they should advance to find him, our lines could hardly contain themselves. But if by any chance the disposition of our troops had been broken, without doubt they would all have been destroyed. What, however, was to be thought of the king, who was hemmed in by the enemy, a single man opposed to so many thousands? The hand of the writer faints to see it, and the mind of the reader to hear it. Who ever heard of such a man? His bravery was ever of the highest order, no adverse storm could sink it; his valor was ever becoming, and if we may from a few instances judge of many, it was ever indefatigable in war. Why then do we speak of the valor of Antæus, who regained his strength every time he touched his mother earth, for Antæus perished when he was lifted up from earth in the long wrestling match. The body of Achilles also, who slew Hector, was invulnerable, because he was dipped in the Stygian waves; yet Achilles was mortally wounded in the very part by which he was held when they dipped him. Likewise Alexander, the Macedonian, who was stimulated by ambition to subjugate the whole world, undertook a most difficult enterprise, and with a handful of choice soldiers fought many celebrated battles, but the chief part of his valor consisted of the excellence of his soldiers. In the same manner the brave Judas Maccabeus, of whom all the world discoursed, performed many wonderful deeds worthy forever to be remembered, but when he was abandoned by his soldiers in the midst of a battle, with thousands of enemies to oppose him, he was slain, together with his brothers. But King Richard, inured to battle from his tenderest years, and to whom even famous Roland could not be considered equal, remained invincible, even in the midst of the enemy; and his body, as if it were made of brass, was impenetrable to any kind of weapon. In his right hand he brandished his sword, which in its rapid descent broke the ranks on either side of him. Such was his energy amid that host of Turks that, fearing nothing, he destroyed all around him, mowing men down with his scythe as reapers mow down the corn with their sickles. Who could describe his deeds? whoever felt one of his blows had no need of a second. Such was the energy of his courage that it seemed to rejoice at having found an occasion to display itself. The sword wielded by his powerful hand cut down men and horses alike, cleaving them to the middle. The more he was himself separated from his men, and the more the enemy sought to overwhelm him, the more did his valor shine conspicuous. Among other brave deeds which he performed on that occasion he slew by one marvellous stroke an admiral, who was conspicuous above the rest of the enemy by his rich caparisons. This man by his gestures seemed to say that he was going to do something wonderful, and whilst he reproached the rest with cowardice he put spurs to his horse and charged full against the king, who, waving his sword as he saw him coming, smote off at a single blow not only his head, but his shoulder and right arm. The Turks were terror-struck at the sight, and, giving way on all sides, scarcely dared to shoot at him from a distance with their arrows.

The king now returned safe and unhurt to his friends, and encouraged them more than ever with the hope of victory. How were their minds raised from despair when they saw him coming safe out of the enemy's ranks! They knew not what had happened to him, but they knew that without him all the hopes of the Christian army would be in vain. The king's person was stuck all over with javelins, like a deer pierced by the hunters, and the trappings of his horse were thickly covered with arrows. Thus, like a brave soldier, he returned from the contest, and a bitter contest it was, for it had lasted from the morning sun to the setting sun. It may seem wonderful and even incredible, that so small a body of men endured so long a conflict; but by God's mercy we cannot doubt the truth of it, for in that battle only one or two of our men were slain. But the number of the Turkish horses that lay dead on the field is said to have exceeded fifteen hundred; and of the Turks themselves more than seven hundred were killed, and yet they did not carry back King Richard, as they had boasted, as a present to Saladin; but, on the contrary, he and his horse performed so many deeds of valor in the sight of the Turks that the enemy shuddered to behold him.

In the meantime our men having by God's grace escaped destruction, the Turkish army returned to Saladin, who is said to have ridiculed them by asking where Melech Richard was, for they had promised to bring him a prisoner? "Which of you," continued he, "first seized him, and where is he? why is he not produced?" To whom one of the Turks that came from the furthest countries of the earth replied, "In truth, my lord, Melech Richard, about whom you ask, is not here; we have never heard since the beginning of the world that there ever was such a knight, so brave and so experienced in arms. In every deed of arms he is ever the foremost; in deeds he is without a rival, the first to advance and the last to retreat; we did our best to seize him, but in vain, for no man can escape from his sword; his attack is dreadful; to engage with him is fatal, and his deeds are beyond human nature."

CHAPTER XXXIV

ROBIN HOOD OF SHERWOOD FOREST

In this our spacious isle I think there is not one,
But he of ROBIN HOOD hath heard and Little John;
And to the end of time the tales shall ne'er be done
Of Scarlock, George a Green, and Much the miller's son,
Of Tuck, the merry friar, which many a sermon made
In praise of ROBIN HOOD, his outlaws and their trade.

Drayton

EVERY reader of "Ivanhoe," at the mention of Richard the Crusader, will be reminded of Robin Hood, the noble outlaw of Sherwood Forest, and his band of merry bowmen. With these we next concern ourselves, and if the reader will pardon the dry outlines of the historian before proceeding to the more interesting and imaginative story of the ballad-singer, we will at first state what so careful an antiquary as Mr. Ritson considers to be truly trustworthy in Robin Hood's history.

Robin Hood was born at Locksley, in the county of Nottingham, in the reign of King Henry II, and about the year of Christ 1160. His extraction was noble, and his true name Robert Fitzooth, which vulgar pronunciation easily corrupted into Robin Hood. He is frequently styled, and commonly reputed to have been, earl of Huntingdon; a title to which, in the latter part of his life at least, he actually appears to have had some sort of pretension. In his youth he is reported to have been of a wild and extravagant disposition, insomuch that, his inheritance being consumed or forfeited by his excesses, and his person outlawed for debt, either from necessity or choice he sought an asylum in the woods and forests, with which immense tracts, especially in the northern part of the kingdom, were at that time covered. Of these he chiefly affected Barnsdale, in Yorkshire; Sherwood in Nottinghamshire, and, according to some, Plompton Park in Cumberland. Here he either found or was afterwards joined by a number of persons in similar circumstances, who appear to have considered and obeyed him as their chief or leader. . . . Having for a long series of years maintained a sort of independent sovereignty, and set kings, judges, and magistrates at defiance, a proclamation was published, offering a considerable reward for bringing him in either dead or alive; which, however, seems to have been productive of no greater success than former attempts for that purpose. At length the infirmities of old age increasing upon him, and desirous to be relieved, in a fit of sickness, by being let blood, he applied for that purpose to the prioress of Kirkley nunnery in Yorkshire, his relative (women, and particularly religious women, being in those times somewhat better skilled in surgery than

the sex is at present), by whom he was treacherously suffered to bleed to death. This event happened on the 18th November, 1247, being the thirty-first year of King Henry III; and if the date assigned to his birth be correct, about the eighty-seventh year of his age. He was interred under some trees at a short distance from the house; a stone being placed over his grave, with an inscription to his memory.

There are some who will have it that Robin Hood was not alive in the reign of Richard I, and who will have it that he preferred other forests to Sherwood. But the stories that we have chosen are of the Robin Hood of Sherwood Forest and of King Richard the Lion-hearted.

LITTLE JOHN

THE lieutenant of Robin Hood's band was named Little John, not so much from his smallness in stature (for he was seven feet high and more), as for a reason which I shall tell later. And the manner in which Robin Hood, to whom he was very dear, met him was this.

Robin Hood on one occasion being hunting with his men and finding the sport to be poor, said: "We have had no sport now for some time. So I go abroad alone. And if I should fall into any peril whence I cannot escape I will blow my horn that ye may know of it and bear me aid." And with that he bade them adieu and departed alone, having with him his bow and the arrows in his quiver. And passing shortly over a brook by a long bridge he met at the middle a stranger. And neither of the two would give way to the other. And Robin Hood being angry fitted an arrow to his bow and made ready to fire. "Truly," said the stranger at this, "thou art a fine fellow that you must draw your long bow on me who have but a staff by me." "That is just truly," said Robin; "and so I will lay by my bow and get me a staff to try if your deeds be as good as your words." And with that he went into a thicket and chose him a small ground oak for a staff and returned to the stranger.

"Now," said he, "I am a match for you, so let us play upon this bridge, and if one should fall in the stream the other will have the victory." "With all my heart," said the stranger; "I shall not be the first to give out. " And with that they began to make great play with their staves. And Robin Hood first struck the stranger such a blow as warmed all his blood, and from that they rattled their sticks as though they had been threshing corn. And finally the stranger gave Robin such a crack on his crown that he broke his head and the blood flowed. But this only urged him the more, so that he attacked the stranger with such vigor that he had like to have made an end of him. But he growing into a fury finally fetched him such a blow that he tumbled him from the bridge into the brook. Whereat the stranger laughed loudly and long, and cried out to him, "Where art thou now, I prythee, my good fellow?" And Robin replied, "Thou art truly a brave soul, and I will have no more to do with thee today; so our battle is at an end, and I must allow that thou hast won the day." And then wading to the bank he pulled out his horn and blew a blast on it so that the echoes flew throughout the valley. And at that came fifty bold bowmen out of the wood, all clad in green, and they made for Robin Hood, and said William Stukely, "What is the matter, my master? you are wet to the skin?" "Truly, nothing is the matter," said Robin, "but that the lad on the bridge has tumbled me into the stream." And on that the archers would have seized the stranger to duck him as well, but Robin Hood forbade them. "No one shall harm thee, friend," said he. "These are all my bowmen, threescore and nine, and if you will be one of us you shall straightway have my livery and accoutrements, fit for a man. What say you?" "With all my heart," said the stranger; "here is my hand on it. My name is John Little, and I will be a good man and true to you." "His name shall be changed," said William Stukely on this. "We will call him Little John, and I will be his godfather."

So they fetched a pair of fat does and some humming strong ale, and there they christened their babe Little John, for he was seven feet high and an ell round at his waist.

FRIAR TUCK

Now Robin Hood had instituted a day of mirth for himself and all his companions, and wagers were laid amongst them who should exceed at this exercise and who at that; some did contend who should jump farthest, some who should throw the bar, some who should be swiftest afoot in a race five miles in length; others there were with which Little John was most delighted, who did strive which of them should draw the strongest bow, and be the best marksman. "Let me see," said Little John, "which of you can kill a buck, and who can kill a doe, and who is he can kill a hart, being distant from it by the space of five hundred feet." With that, Robin Hood going before them, they went directly to the forest, where they found good store of game feeding before them. William Scarlock, that drew the strongest bow of them all, did kill a buck, and Little John made choice of a barren fat doe, and the well-directed arrow did enter in the very heart of it; and Midge, the miller's son, did kill a hart above five hundred feet distant from him. The hart falling, Robin Hood stroked him gently on the shoulder, and said unto him, "God's blessing on thy heart, I will ride five hundred miles to find a match for thee." William Scarlock, hearing him speak these words, smiled and said unto him, "Master, what needs that? Here is a Curtal Friar[1] not far off, that for a hundred pound will shoot at what distance yourself will propound, either with Midge or with yourself. An experienced man he is, and will draw a bow with great strength; he

will shoot with yourself, and with all the men you have, one after another."

"Sayest thou so, Scarlock?" replied Robin Hood. "By the grace of God I will neither eat nor drink till I see this Friar thou dost speak of." And having prepared himself for his journey, he took Little John and fifty of his best archers with him, whom he bestowed in a convenient place, as he himself thought fitting. This being done, he ran down into the dale, where he found the Curtal Friar walking by the water side. He no sooner espied him, but presently he took unto him his broadsword and buckler, and put on his head a steel bonnet. The Friar, not knowing who he was, or for what intent he came, did presently arm himself to encounter with him. Robin Hood, coming near unto him, alighted from his horse, which he tied to a thorn that grew hard by, and looking wistfully on the Friar, said unto him, "Carry me over the water, thou Curtal Friar, or else thy life lies at the stake." The Friar made no more ado, but took up Robin Hood and carried him on his back; deep water he did stride; he spake not so much as one word to him, but having carried him over, he gently laid him down on the side of the bank; which being done, the Friar said to Robin Hood, "It is now thy turn; therefore carry me over the water, thou bold fellow, or sure I shall make thee repent it." Robin Hood, to requite the courtesy, took the Friar on his back, and not speaking the least word to him, carried him over the water, and laid him gently down on the side of the bank; and turning to him, he spake unto him as at first, and bade him carry him over the water once more, or he should answer it with the forfeit of his life. The Friar in a smiling manner took him up, and spake not a word till he came in the midst of the stream, when, being up to the middle and higher, he did shake him from off his shoulders, and said unto him, "Now choose thee, bold fellow, whether thou wilt sink or swim."

[1] "The Curtal Friar," Dr. Stukely says, "is Cordelier, from the cord or rope which they wore round their waist, to whip themselves with. They were," adds he, "of the Franciscan order. Our Friar, however, is undoubtedly so called from his Curtal dogs, or curs, as we now say." *Thoms. Early Prose Romances:* in which, by the way, may be found many of the tales of Robin Hood printed here, and much more besides of interest.

Robin Hood, being soundly washed, got him up on his feet, and prostrating himself, did swim to a bush of broom on the other side of the bank; and the Friar swam to a willow tree which was not far from it. Then Robin Hood, taking his bow in his hand, and one of his best arrows, did shoot at the Friar, which the Friar received in his buckler of steel, and said unto him, "Shoot on, thou bold fellow; if thou shootest at me a whole summer's day I will stand your mark still." "That will I," said Robin Hood, and shot arrow after arrow at him, until he had not an arrow left in his quiver. He then laid down his bow, and drew out his sword, which but two days before had been the death of three men. Now hand to hand they went with sword and buckler; the steel buckler defends whatsoever blow is given; sometimes they make at the head, sometimes at the foot, sometimes at the side; sometimes they strike directly down, sometimes they falsify their blows, and come in foot and arm, with a free thrust at the body; and being ashamed that so long they exercise their unprofitable valor and cannot hurt one another, they multiply their blows, they hack, they hew, they slash, they foam. At last Robin Hood desired the Friar to hold his hand, and to give him leave to blow his horn.

"Thou wantest breath to sound it," said the Friar; "take thee a little respite, for we have been five hours at it by the Fountain Abbey clock." Robin Hood took his horn from his side, and having sounded it three times, behold where fifty lusty men, with their bended bows, came to his assistance. The Friar, wondering at it, "Whose men," said he, "be these?" "They are mine," said Robin Hood; "what is that to thee?" "False loon," said the Friar; and making a little pause, he desired Robin Hood to show him the same courtesy which he gave him. "What is that?" said Robin Hood. "Thou soundest thy horn three times," said the Friar; "let me now but whistle three times." "Ay, with all my heart," said Robin Hood; "I were to blame if I should deny thee that courtesy." With that the Friar set his fist to his mouth, and whistled three

times so shrilly that the place echoed again with it; and behold three and fifty fair ban-dogs (their hair rising on their back, betokening their rage), were almost on the backs of Robin Hood and his companions. "Here is for every one of thy men a dog," said the Friar, "and two for thee." "That is foul play," said Robin Hood. He had scarce spoken that word but two dogs came upon him at once, one before, another behind him, who, although they could not touch his flesh (his sword had made so swift a despatch of them), yet they tore his coat into two pieces. By this time the men had so laid about them that the dogs began to fly back, and their fury to languish into barking. Little John did so bestir himself, that the Curtal Friar, admiring at his courage and his nimbleness, did ask him who he was. He made him answer, "I will tell the truth, and not lie. I am he who is called Little John, and do belong to Robin Hood, who hath fought with thee this day, five hours together; and if thou wilt not submit unto him, this arrow shall make thee." The Friar, perceiving how much he was overpowered, and that it was impossible for him to deal with so many at once, did come to composition with Robin Hood. And the articles of agreement were these: That the Friar should abandon Fountain Dale and Fountain Abbey, and should live with Robin Hood, at his place not far from Nottingham, where for saying of mass, he should receive a noble for every Sunday throughout the year, and for saying mass on every holy day, a new change of garment. The Friar, contented with these conditions, did seal the agreement. And thus by the courage of Robin Hood and his yeomen, he was enforced at the last to submit, having for seven long years kept Fountain Dale, not all the power thereabouts being able to bring him on his knees.

But Friar Tuck was the only man of the clergy with whom Robin had friendly dealings. As a rule these churchmen fared as did the bishop of Hereford in the following ballad, which we add for the sake of an example of the manner in which this True History of Robin Hood has come down to us from the year 1245:

THE BISHOP OF HEREFORD'S ENTERTAINMENT BY ROBIN HOOD AND LITTLE JOHN
AND THEIR COMPANY, IN MERRY BARNSDALE

Some they will talk of bold Robin Hood,
  And some of barons bold;
But I'll tell you how he served the
    Bishop of Hereford,
  When he robbed him of his gold.

As it befell in merry Barnsdale,
  All under the greenwood tree,
The Bishop of Hereford was to come by,
  With all his company.

"Come, kill me a venison," said bold
    Robin Hood,
  "And dress it by the highway side,
And we will watch the bishop narrowly,
  Lest some other way he should ride."

Robin Hood dressed himself in
    shepherd's attire,
  With six of his men also;
And, when the Bishop of Hereford
    came by,
They about the fire did go.

"O, what is the matter?" then said the
    bishop,
  "Or for whom do you make this ado?
Or why do you kill the king's venison,
  When your company is so few?"

"We are shepherds," said bold Robin
    Hood,
  "And we keep sheep all the year;
And we are disposed to be merry this
    day,
  And to kill of the king's fat deer."

"You are brave fellows," said the bishop,
  "And the king of your doings shall
    know;
Therefore make haste, and come along
    with me,
  For before the king you shall go."

"O pardon, O pardon," said bold
    Robin Hood,
  "O pardon, I thee pray;
For it becomes not your lordship's coat
  To take so many lives away."

"No pardon, no pardon," said the
    bishop,
  "No pardon I thee owe;
Therefore make haste, and come along
    with me,
  For before the king you shall go."

Then Robin he set his back against a
    tree,
  And his foot against a thorn,
And from underneath his shepherd's
    coat
  He pulled out a bugle horn.

He put the little end to his mouth,
  And a loud blast did he blow,
All threescore and ten of bold Robin's
    men
  Came running all in a row:

All making obeisance to bold Robin
    Hood;
  'Twas a comely sight for to see.
"What is the matter, master," said
    Little John,
  "That you blow so lustily?"

"O here is the Bishop of Hereford,
  And no pardon we shall have,"
"Cut off his head, master," said Little
    John,
  "And throw him into his grave."

"O pardon, O pardon," said the bishop,
  "O pardon, I thee pray;
For if I had known it had been you,
  I'd have gone some other way."

"No pardon, no pardon," said bold
    Robin Hood,
  "No pardon I thee owe;
Therefore make haste, and come along
    with me,
  For to merry Barnsdale you shall go."

Then Robin he took the bishop by the
    hand,
  And led him to merry Barnsdale;
He made him stay and sup with him
    that night,
  And to drink wine, beer, and ale.

"Call in a reckoning," said the bishop,
  "For methinks it grows wondrous
    high."
"Send me your purse, master," said
    Little John,
  "And I'll tell you bye and bye."

Then Little John took the bishop's
    cloak,
  And spread it upon the ground,
And out of the bishop's portmantua
  He told three hundred pound.

"Here's money enough, master," said
    Little John,
  "And a comely sight 'tis to see;
It makes me in charity with the bishop,
  Though he heartily loveth not me."

Robin Hood took the bishop by the
    hand,
  And he caused the music to play;
And he made the old bishop to dance in
    his boots,
  And glad to get so away.

CHAPTER XXXV

ROBIN HOOD AND HIS ADVENTURES

"They say he is already in the forest of Arden, and a many merry men with him;
and there they live like the old Robin Hood of England … and fleet the time carelessly as they did in the golden world."

As You Like It

As has been already said, some of the ballad makers have so far erred from the truth as to represent Robin Hood as being outlawed by Henry VIII, and several stories are told of Queen Katherine's interceding with her husband for the pardon of the bold outlaw.[1] However this may be, it is known that Robin Hood once shot a match on the queen's side against the king's archers, and here is the story:

Robin Hood on one occasion sent a present to Queen Katherine with which she was so pleased that she swore she would be a friend to the noble outlaw as long as she might live. So one day the queen went to her chamber and called to her a page of her company and bade him make haste and prepare to ride to Nottinghamshire to find Robin Hood in Sherwood Forest; for the queen had made a match with the king, her archers against his archers, and the queen proposed to have Robin Hood and his band to shoot on her side against the king's archers.

Now as for the page, he started for Nottingham and posted all the way, and inquired on the road for Robin Hood, where he might be, but he could not find any one who could let him know exactly. So he took up his quarters at an inn at Nottingham. And in the room of the inn he sat him down and called for a bottle of Rhenish wine, and he drank the queen's health out of it. Now at his side was sitting a yeoman of the country, clad in Lincoln green, with a long bow in his hand. And he turned to the page and asked him, "What is thy business, my sweet boy, so far in the north country, for methinks you must come

---

[1]This seems to have been the opinion of the author from whom we draw the following account of our hero's life,—to show how the doctors will disagree even on a topic as important as Robin Hood:

THE NOBLE BIRTH AND THE ACHIEVEMENTS OF ROBIN HOOD

"Robin Hood was descended from the noble family of the Earl of Huntingdon, and being outlawed by Henry VIII for many extravagancies and outrages he had committed, he did draw together a company of such bold and licentious persons as himself, who lived for the most part on robberies committed in or near unto Sherwood Forest in Nottinghamshire. He had these always ready at his command, so that if need did require he at the winding of his horn would have fifty or more of them in readiness to assist him. He whom he most affected was called Little John by reason of his low stature, though not inferior to any of them in strength of body and stoutness of spirit. He would not entertain any into his service whom he had not first fought with himself and made sufficient trial of his courage and dexterity how to use his weapons, which was the reason that oftentimes he came home hurt and beaten as he was; which was nevertheless no occasion of the diminution of his love to the person whom he fought with, for ever afterwards he would be the more familiar with him, and better respect him for it. Many petitions were referred to the king for a pardon for him, which the king (understanding of the many mad pranks he and his associates played) would give no ear unto; but being attended with a considerable guard, did make a progress himself to find him out and bring him to condign punishment. At last, by the means and mediation of Queen Katherine the king's wrath was qualified, and his pardon sealed, and he spent his old age in peace, at a house of his own, not far from Nottingham, being generally beloved and respected by all."

from London?" So then the page told him that it was his business to find Robin Hood the outlaw, and for that he asked every yeoman that he met. And he asked his friend if he knew anything which might help him. "Truly," said the yeoman, "that I do. And if you will get to horse early tomorrow morning I will show you Robin Hood and all his gay yeomen.

So the next morning they got them to horse and rode out into the forest, and the yeoman brought the page to where were Robin Hood and his yeomen. And the page fell down on his knee and said to Robin Hood, "Queen Katherine greets you well by me, and hath sent you this ring as a token. She bids you post up to London town, for that there shall be some sport there in which she has a mind you shall have a hand." And at this Robin took off his mantle of Lincoln green from his back and sent it by the page to Queen Katherine with a promise that he and his band would follow him as soon as they might.

So Robin Hood clothed all his men in Lincoln green and himself in scarlet, and each man wore a black hat with a white feather stuck therein. And thus Robin Hood and his band came up to London. And Robin fell down on his knees before the queen, and she bade him welcome with all his band. For the match between the queen's archers and the king's was to come off the next day in Finsbury fields.

Here first came the king's archers marching with bold bearing, and then came Robin Hood and his archers for the queen. And they laid out the marks there. And the king laid a wager with the queen on the shooting. Now the wager was three hundred tun of Rhenish, and three hundred tun of good English beer, and three hundred fat harts. So then the queen asked if there were any knights with the king who would take her side. But they were unwilling, for said they, "How shall we bet on these men whom we have never seen, when we know Clifton and the rest of the king's archers, and have seen them shoot?" Now this Clifton was one of the king's archers and a great boaster. And when he had reached the shooting field he had cried out, "Measure no marks for us, my lord the king, for we will shoot at the sun and moon." But for all that Robin Hood beat him at the shooting. And the queen asked the bishop of Herefordshire to back her archers. But he swore by his mitre that he would not bet a single penny on the queen's archers for he

knew them not. "What will you bet against them," asked Robin Hood at this, "since you think our shooting is the worse?" "Truly," said the bishop, "I will bet all the money that may be in my purse," and he pulled it up from where it hung at his side. "What is in your purse?" asked Robin Hood. And the bishop tossed it down on the ground, saying, "Fifteen rose-nobles, and that's an hundred pound." So Robin Hood tossed out a bag beside the bishop's purse on the green.

And with that they began shooting, and shot three bouts and they came out even; the king's and the queen's. "The next three shots," said the king, "shall pay for all." And so the king's archers shot, and then Robin Hood, and Little John and Midge the miller's son shot for the queen, and came every man of them nearer the prick in the willow wand than did any of the king's men. So the queen's archers having beaten, Queen Katherine asked a boon of the king, and he granted it. "Give me, I pray you," said the queen, "safe conduct for the archers of my party to come and to go home and to stay in London here some time to enjoy themselves." "I grant it," said the king. "Then you are welcome, Robin Hood," said the queen, "and so is Little John and Midge the miller's son and every one of you." "Is this Robin Hood?" asked the king, "for I had heard that he was killed in a quarrel in the north country." And the bishop too asked, "Is this Robin Hood? If I had known that I would not have bet a penny with him. He took me one Saturday evening and bound me fast to a tree, and there he made me sing a mass for him and his yeomanry about." "Well, if I did," said Robin Hood, "surely I needed all the masses that I might get for my soul." And with that he and his yeomanry departed, and when their safe conduct was expired they journeyed north again to Sherwood Forest.

ROBIN HOOD AND THE BEGGAR

BUT Robin Hood, once having supplied himself with good store of money, which he had gotten of the sheriff of Nottingham, bought him a stout gelding, and riding on him one day towards Nottingham, it was his fortune to meet with a poor beggar. Robin Hood was of a frolic spirit, and no accepter of persons; but observing the beggar to have several sorts of bags, which were fastened to his patched coat, he did ride up to him, and giving him the time of day, he demanded of him what countryman he was. "A Yorkshireman," said the beggar; "and I would desire of you to give me something." "Give thee!" said Robin Hood; "why, I have nothing to give thee. I am a poor ranger in the forest, and thou seemest to be a lusty knave; shall I give thee a good bastinado over thy shoulders?" "Content, content," said the beggar; "I durst lay all my bags to a threaden joust, thou wilt repent it." With that Robin Hood alighted, and the beggar, with his long quarterstaff, so well defended himself, that, let Robin Hood do what he could, he could not come within the beggar, to flash him to a remembrance of his overboldness; and nothing vexed him more than to find that the beggar's staff was as hard and as obdurate as iron itself; but not so Robin Hood's head, for the beggar with all his force did let his staff descend with such a side blow, that Robin Hood, for all his skill, could not defend it, but the blood came trickling down his face, which, turning Robin Hood's courage into revenge and fury, he let fly at him with his trusty sword, and doubled blow upon blow; but perceiving that the beggar did hold him so hard to it that one of his blows was but the forerunner of another, and every blow to be almost the Postilion of Death, he cried out to him to hold his hand. "That will I not do," said the beggar, "unless thou wilt resign unto me thy horse, and thy sword, and thy clothes, with all the money thou hast in thy pockets." "The change is uneven," said Robin Hood, "but for once I am content."

So, putting on the beggar's clothes, the beggar was the gentleman, and Robin Hood was the beggar, who, entering into Nottingham town with his patched coat and several wallets, understood that three brethren were that day to suffer at the gallows, being condemned for killing the king's deer, he made no more ado, but went directly to the sheriff's house, where a young gentleman, seeing him to stand at the door, demanded of him what he would have. Robin Hood returned answer that he came to crave neither meat nor drink, but the lives of these three brothers who were condemned to die. "That cannot be," said the young gentleman, "for they are all this day to suffer according to law, for stealing of the king's deer, and they are already conveyed out of the town to the place of execution." "I will be with them presently," said Robin Hood, and coming to the gallows he found many making great lamentation for them. Robin Hood did comfort them, and assured them they should not die; and blowing his horn, behold on a sudden a hundred brave archers came unto him, by whose help, having released the prisoners, and killed the hangman, and hurt many of the sheriff's officers, they took those who were condemned to die for killing the king's deer along with them, who, being very thankful for the preservation of their lives, became afterwards of the yeomanry of Robin Hood.

ROBIN HOOD AND KING RICHARD

Now King Richard, hearing of the deeds of Robin Hood and his men, wondered much at them, and desired greatly himself to see him, and his men as well. So he with a dozen of his lords rode to Nottingham town and there took up his abode. And being at Nottingham, the king one day with his lords put on friars' gowns every one, and rode forth from Fountain Abbey down to Barnsdale. And as they were riding there they saw Robin Hood and all his band standing ready to assail them. The king, being taller than the rest, was thought by Robin to be the abbot. So he made up to him, and seized his horse by the head, and bade him stand. "For," said he, "it is against such knaves as you that I am bound to make war." "But," said the king himself, "we are messengers from the king, who is but a little away, waiting to speak with you." "God save the king," said Robin Hood, "and all his well-wishers. And accursed be every one who may deny his sovereignty." "You are cursing yourself," said the king, "for you are a traitor." "Now," said Robin Hood, "if you were not the king's messenger, I would make you rue that word of yours. I am as true a man to the king as lives. And I never yet injured any honest man and true, but only those who make their living by stealing from others. I have never in my life harmed either husbandman or huntsman. But my chief spite lies against the clergy, who have in these days great power. But I am right glad to have met you here. Come with me, and you shall taste our greenwood cheer." But the king and his lords marvelled, wondering what kind of cheer Robin might provide for them. And Robin took the king's horse by the head, and led him towards his tent. "It is because thou comest from the king," said he, "that I use you in this wise; and hadst thou as much gold as ever I had, it should be all of it safe for good King Richard's sake." And with that he took out his horn, and blew on it a loud blast. And thereat came marching forth from the wood five score and ten of Robin's followers, and each one bent the knee before Robin Hood. "Surely," thought the king, "it is a goodly sight to see; for they are more humble to their master than my servants are to me. Here may the court learn something from the greenwood." And here they laid a dinner for the king and his lords, and the king swore that he had never feasted better. Then Robin Hood, taking a can of ale, said, "Let us now begin, each man with his can. Here's a health to the king." And they all drank the health to the king, the king himself, as well as another.

And after the dinner they all took their bows, and showed the King such archery that the king said he had never seen such men as they in any foreign land. And then said the king to Robin Hood, "If I could get thee a pardon from King Richard, wouldst thou serve the king well in everything?" "Yes, with all my heart," said Robin. And so said all his men.

And with that the king declared himself to them, and said, "I am the king, your sovereign, that is now before you." And at this Robin and all his men fell down on their knees; but the king raised them up, saying to them that he pardoned each one of them, and that they should every one of them be in his service. So the king returned to Nottingham, and with him returned Robin Hood and his men, to the great joy of the townspeople, whom they had for a long time sorely vexed.

"And they are gone to London court,
    Robin Hood and all his train;
He once was there a noble peer,
    And now he's there again."

THE DEATH OF ROBIN HOOD

BUT Robin Hood returned to Sherwood Forest, and there met his death. For one day, being wounded in a fight, he fled out of the battle with Little John. And being at some distance, Robin Hood said to his lieutenant, "Now truly I cannot shoot even one shot more, for the arrows will not fly. For I am sore wounded. So I will go to my cousin, the abbess, who dwelleth near here in Kirkley Hall, and she shall bleed me, that I may be well again." So Robin Hood left Little John, and he went his way to Kirkley; and reaching the Hall, his strength nearly left him, yet he knocked heavily at the door. And his cousin came down first to let him in. And when she saw him she knew that it was her cousin Robin Hood, and she received him with a joyful face. Then said Robin, "You see me, my cousin, how weak I am. Therefore I pray you to bleed me, that I may be whole again." And his cousin took him by the hand, and led him into an upper room, and laid him on a bed, and she bled him. But the treacherous woman tied not up the vein again, but left him so that his life began to flow from him. And he, finding his strength leaving him, thought to escape; but he could not,

for the door was locked, and the casement window was so high that he might not leap down from it. Then, knowing that he must die, he reached forth his hand to his bugle horn, which lay by him on the bed. And setting the horn to his mouth, he blew weakly, though with all his strength, three blasts upon it. And Little John, as he sat under the tree in the greenwood, heard his blowing, and he said, "Now must Robin be near death, for his blast is very weak."

And he got up and ran to Kirkley Hall as fast as he might. And coming to the door, he found it locked; but he broke it down, and so came to Robin Hood. And coming to the bed, he fell upon his knees, and said, "Master, I beg a boon of thee,—that thou lettest me burn down Kirkley Hall and all the nunnery." "Nay," quoth Robin Hood; "nay, I cannot grant you your boon; for never in my life did I hurt woman, or man in woman's company, nor shall it be done when I die. But for me, give me my long bow, and I will let fly an arrow, and where you shall find the arrow, there bury me. And make my grave long and broad, that I may rest easily; and place my head upon a green sod, and place my bow at my side." And these words Little John readily promised him, so that Robin Hood was pleased. And they buried him as he had asked, an arrow-shot from Kirkley Hall.

CHAPTER XXXVI

CHEVY CHASE

"The Perse out of Northumberlande,
 And a vowe to God mayde he,
That he wold hunte in the mountayns
 Off Chyviat within days thre,
In the mauger of doughtè Dogles,
 And all that ever with him be."

Percy, *Reliques of Ancient Poetry*

SCARCELY less famous than Robin Hood as a subject for ballad makers was the battle of Chevy Chase. This battle was one of the many struggles rising out of the never-ending border quarrels between Scotland and England, of which poets are never tired of singing. Sometimes the earl of Douglas, the great Scotch border-lord, would make an incursion into Northumberland, and then to revenge the insult Lord Percy would come riding over the Tweed into Scotland.

In the battle of Chevy Chase it would seem as if Earl Percy was the aggressor. As a matter of fact it mattered little which began the quarrel at any particular time. The feud was ever smouldering, and needed little to make it burst forth.

THE BALLAD OF CHEVY CHASE

God prosper long our noble king,
 Our lives and safetyes all;
A woefull hunting once there did
 In Chevy Chase befall.

To drive the deere with hound and horne,
 Erle Percy took his way,
The child may rue that is unborne
 The hunting of that day.

The stout Erle of Northumberland
 A vow to God did make,
His pleasure in the Scottish woods
 Three summer days to take;

The cheefest harts in Chevy Chase
 To kill and bear away.
These tidings to Erle Douglas came,
 In Scotland where he lay,

Who sent Erle Percy present word
 He would prevent his sport.
The English Erle not fearing that,
 Did to the woods resort,

With fifteen hundred bowmen bold;
 All chosen men of might,
Who knew full well in time of neede
 To ayme their shafts aright.

The gallant greyhounds swiftly ran
 To chase the fallow deere:
On Monday they began to hunt
 Ere daylight did appear;

And long before high noon they had
 An hundred fat buckes slaine;
Then having dined the drovyers went
 To rouse the deer again.

The bowmen mustered on the hill,
 Well able to endure;
Their backsides all, with special care,
 That day were guarded sure.

The hounds ran swiftly through the woods
 The nimble deere to take,
That with their cryes the hills and dales
 An eccho shrill did make.

Lord Percy to the quarry went,
 To view the slaughtered deer;
Quoth he, Erle Douglas promised
 This day to meet me heere;

But if I thought he would not come,
 Noe longer would I stay.
With that a brave young gentleman
 Thus to the Erle did say:

Loe, yonder doth Erle Douglas come,
 His men in armour bright;
Full twenty hundred Scottish speres
 All marching in our sight;

All men of pleasant Tivydale,
 Fast by the river Tweede:
O cease your sports, Erle Percy said,
 And take your bowes with speede.

And now with me, my countrymen,
 Your courage forth advance;
For there was never champion yett
 In Scotland or in France,

That ever did on horseback come,
　But if my hap it were,
I durst encounter man for man,
　With him to break a spere.

Erle Douglas on his milk-white steede,
　Most like a baron bold,
Rode foremost of his company,
　Whose armour shone like gold.

Show me, sayd he, whose men you be,
　That hunt so boldly heere,
That without my consent doe chase
　And kill my fallow deere.

The first man that did answer make
　Was noble Percy he;
Who sayd, We list not to declare,
　Nor show whose men we be.

Yet we will spend our deerest blood,
　Thy cheefest harts to slay.
The Douglas swore a solempne oathe,
　And thus in rage did say,

Ere thus I will outbraved be.
　One of us two shall dye:
I know thee well, an erle thou art;
　Lord Percy, soe am I.

But trust me, Percy, pittye it were
　And great offence to kill
Any of these our guiltless men,
　For they have done no ill.

Let thou and I the battell trye,
　And set our men aside.
Accurst be he, Erle Percy sayd,
　By whom this is denyed.

Then stept a gallant squier forth,
　Witherington was his name,
Who said, I wold not have it told
　To Henry our king for shame,

That ere my captaine fought on foot
　And I stood looking on.
You be two erles, sayd Witherington,
　And I a squier alone:

Ile doe the best that doe I may,
　While I have power to stand:
While I have power to wield my sword,
　Ile fight with hart and hand.

Our English archers bent their bowes
　Their harts were good and trew;
At the first flight of arrowes sent,
　Full fourscore Scots they slew.

Yet bides Erle Douglas on the bent,
　As cheeftain stout and good,
As valiant captain, all unmoved,
　The shock he firmly stood.

His host he parted had in three,
　As leader ware and tryd,
And soon his spearmen on his foes
　Bare down on every side.

To drive the deere with hound and horne,
　Douglas bade on the bent:
Two captaines moved with mickle might
　Their speares to shivers went.

Throughout the English archery
　They dealt full many a wound;
But still our valiant Englishmen
　All firmly kept their ground:

And throwing straight their bowes away,
　They grasped their swords so bright:
And now sharp blows, a heavy shower,
　On shields and helmets light.

They closed full fast on every side,
　No slackness there was found;
And many a gallant gentleman
　Lay gasping on the ground.

O Christ! it was a griefe to see,
　And likewise for to heare,
The cries of men lying in their gore,
　And scattered here and there.

At last these two stout erles did meet,
　Like captaines of great might;
Like lyons wood, they layd on lode
　And made a cruell fight:

They fought until they both did sweat,
　With swords of tempered steele;
Until the blood, like drops of rain,
　They trickling down did feele.

Yield thee, Lord Percy, Douglas sayd;
　In faith I will thee bringe,
Where thou shalt high advanced be
　By James our Scottish king:

Thy ransome I will freely give,
　And this report of thee:
Thou art the most courageous knight
　That ever I did see.

Noe, Douglas, quoth Erle Percy then,
　Thy proffer I do scorne;
I will not yield to any Scott,
　That ever yet was borne.

With that there came an arrow keene,
　Out of an English bow,
Which struck Erle Douglas to the heart,
　A deepe and deadly blow:

Who never spake more words than these,
　Fight on, my merry men all;
For why, my life is at an end;
　Lord Percy sees my fall.

Then leaving liffe, Erle Percy tooke
　The dead man by the hand;
And said, Erle Douglas, for thy life
　Wold I have lost my land.

O Christ, my very hart doth bleed
  With sorrow for thy sake;
For sure a more redoubted knight
  Mischance cold never take.

A knight among the Scotts there was
  Who saw Erle Douglas dye,
Who streight in wrath did vow revenge
  Upon the Lord Percy.

Sir Hugh Montgomery was he called,
  Who, with a spear most bright,
Well mounted on a gallant steed,
  Ran fiercely through the fight;

And past the English archers all,
  Without all dread and feare;
And through Erle Percy's body then
  He thrust his hatefull speare;

With such a vehement force and
    might
  He did his body gore,
The staff ran through the other side
  A large cloth-yard or more.

So thus did both these nobles dye,
  Whose courage none could staine:
An English archer then perceived
  The noble erle was slaine;

He had a bow bent in his hand,
  Made of a trusty tree;
An arrow of a cloth-yard long
  Up to the head drew he:

Against Sir Hugh Montgomery,
  So right the shaft he sett,
The grey goose-wing that was thereon,
  In his hart's blood was wett.

This fight did last from break of day
  Till setting of the sun;
For when they rang the evening-bell
  The battle scarce was done.

With stoute Erle Percy there was slaine
  Sir John of Egerton,
Sir Robert Ratcliff, and Sir John,
  Sir James that bold barron:

And with Sir George and stoute Sir James
  Both knights of good account,
Good Sir Ralph Raby there was slaine,
  Whose prowese did surmount.

For Witherington my hart is woe,
  That ever he slain should be;
For when his legs were hewn in two
  He knelt and fought on his knee.

And with Erle Douglas there was slaine
  Sir Hugh Montgomery,
Sir Charles Murray, that from the field
  One foot wold never flee.

Sir Charles Murray, of Ratcliff too,
  His sister's sonne was he;
Sir David Lamb, so well esteem'd,
  Yet savéd cold not be,

And the Lord Maxwell in like case
  Did with Erle Douglas dye:
Of twenty hundred Scottish speres
  Scarce fifty-five did flye.

Of fifteen hundred Englishmen,
  Went home but fifty-three;
The rest were slaine in Chevy Chase,
  Under the greene woode tree.

Next day did many widowes come,
  Their husbands to bewayle;
They washed their wounds in brinish
    teares,
  But all wold not prevayle.

Theyr bodyes, bathed in purple gore,
  They bore with them away;
They kist them dead a thousand times,
  Ere they were cladd in clay.

The newes was brought to Eddenborrow,
  Where Scotland's king did raigne,
That brave Erle Douglas suddenlye
  Was with an arrow slaine.

O heavy newes, King James did say,
  Scotland may witness be,
I have not any captain more
  Of such account as he.

Like tydings to King Henry came,
  Within as short a space,
That Percy of Northumberland
  Was slaine in Chevy Chase:

Now God be with him, said the king,
  Sith it will noe better be;
I trust I have within my realme,
  Five hundred as good as he.

Yet shall not Scotts nor Scotland say,
  But I will vengeance take;
He be revengéd on them all
  For brave Erle Percy's sake.

This vow fall well the king performed
  After at Humbledowne;
In one day fifty knights were slaine,
  With lords of great renowne;

And of the rest of small account,
  Did many thousands dye:
Thus ended the hunting of Chevy
    Chase
  Made by the Erle Percy.

God save our king, and bless this land
  With plentye, joy, and peace;
And grant henceforth that foule debate
  'Twixt noblemen may cease.

CHAPTER XXXVII

THE BATTLE OF OTTERBOURNE

It fell about a Lamass-tide,
When husbands wynn their hay,
The doughty Douglas bound him to ride
In England to take a pray.

ANOTHER famous battle in the border-warfare between England and Scotland was fought at Otterbourne. This is a town in Northumberland, and here, as in Chevy Chase, the Douglas and the Percy matched their strength. Earl Douglas was killed in the fight, and Sir Henry Percy, called Hotspur, was taken prisoner. The story as it is told here is from the works of that most entertaining and long-winded historian of chivalry, Sir John Froissart.

We begin *in medias res* with a Scotch foray, in which the Douglas, with the earl of March and Dunbar and the earl of Moray, has penetrated as far into England as the city of Durham and is now returning to Scotland.

The three Scots lords, having completed the object of their expedition into Durham, lay before Newcastle three days, where there was an almost continual skirmish. The sons of the earl of Northumberland, from their great courage, were always the first at the barriers, where many valiant deeds were done with lances hand to hand. The earl of Douglas had a long conflict with Sir Henry Percy, and in it, by gallantry of arms, won his pennon, to the great vexation of Sir Henry and the other English. The earl of Douglas said, "I will carry this token of your prowess with me to Scotland, and place it on the tower of my castle at Dalkeith, that it may be seen from afar." "By heaven, earl of Douglas," replied Sir Henry, "you shall not even bear it out of Northumberland: be assured you shall never have this pennon to brag of." "You must come then," answered Earl Douglas, "this night and seek for it. I will fix your pennon before my tent, and shall see if you will venture to take it away."

As it was now late the skirmish ended, and each party retired to their quarters to disarm and comfort themselves. They had plenty of everything, particularly flesh meat. The Scots kept up a very strict watch, concluding from the words of Sir Henry Percy they should have their quarters beaten up this night; they were disappointed, for Sir Henry Percy was advised to defer it.

On the morrow the Scots dislodged from before Newcastle; and, taking the road to their own country, they came to a town and castle called Ponclau, of which Sir Raymond de Laval, a very valiant knight of Northumberland, was the lord. They halted there about four o'clock in the morning, as they learned the knight to be within it, and made preparations for the assault. This was done with such courage that the

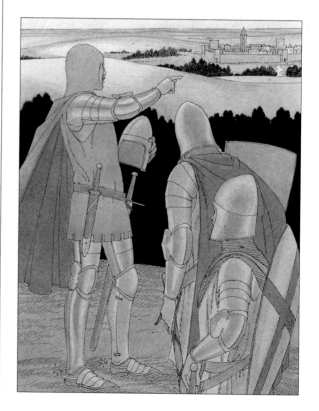

place was won, and the knight made prisoner. After they had burnt the town and castle, they marched away for Otterbourne, which was eight English leagues from Newcastle, and there encamped themselves. This day they made no attack; but very early on the morrow their trumpets sounded, and they made ready for the assault, advancing towards the castle, which was tolerably strong, and situated among the marshes. They attacked it so long and so unsuccessfully that they were fatigued, and therefore sounded a retreat. When they had retired to their quarters, the chiefs held a council how to act; and the greater part were for decamping on the morrow, without attempting more against the castle, to join their countrymen in the neighborhood of Carlisle. But the earl of Douglas overruled this by saying, "In despite of Sir Henry Percy, who the day before yesterday declared he would take from me his pennon, that I conquered by fair deeds of arms before Newcastle, I will not return home for two or three days; and we will renew our attack on the castle, for it is to be taken: we shall thus gain double honor, and see if within that time he will come for his pennon; if he do it shall be well defended." Every one agreed to what Earl Douglas had said; for it was not only honorable, but he was the principal commander; and from affection to him they quietly returned to their quarters. They made huts of trees and branches, and strongly fortified themselves. They placed their baggage and servants at the entrance of the marsh on the road to Newcastle, and the cattle they drove into the marsh lands.

I will return to Sir Henry and Sir Ralph Percy, who were greatly mortified that the earl of Douglas should have conquered their pennon in the skirmish before Newcastle. They felt the more for this disgrace because Sir Henry had not kept his word; for he had told the earl that he should never carry his pennon out of England, and this he explained to the knights who were with him in Newcastle. The English imagined the army under the earl of Douglas to be only the van of the Scots, and that the main body was behind; for which reason those knights who had the most experience in arms, and were best acquainted with warlike affairs, strongly opposed the proposal of Sir Henry Percy to pursue them. They said, "Sir,

many losses happen in war: if the earl of Douglas has won your pennon he has bought it dear enough; for he has come to the gates to seek it, and has been well fought with. Another time you will gain from him as much if not more. We say so, because you know as well as we do that the whole power of Scotland has taken the field. We are not sufficiently strong to offer them battle; and perhaps this skirmish may have been only a trick to draw us out of the town; and if they be, as reported, forty thousand strong, they will surround us, and have us at their mercy. It is much better to lose a pennon than two or three hundred knights and squires, and leave our country in a defenceless state." This speech checked the eagerness of the two brothers Percy, for they would not act contrary to the opinion of the council, when other news was brought them by some knights and squires who had followed and observed the Scots, their numbers, disposition, and where they had halted. This was all fully related by knights who had traversed the whole extent of country the Scots had passed through, that they might carry to their lords the most exact information. They thus spoke: "Sir Henry and Sir Ralph Percy, we come to tell you that we have followed the Scottish army, and observed all the country where they now are. They first halted at Ponclau, and took Sir Raymond de Laval in his castle; thence they went to Otterbourne, and took up their quarters for the night. We are ignorant of what they did on the morrow, but they seem to have taken measures for a long stay. We know for certain that their army does not consist of more than three thousand men, including all sorts." Sir Henry Percy on hearing this was greatly rejoiced, and cried out, "To horse! to horse! for by the faith I owe my God, and to my lord and father, I will seek to recover my pennon and to beat up their quarters this night." Such knights and squires in Newcastle as learned this were willing to be of the party, and made themselves ready.

The bishop of Durham was expected daily at the town; for he had heard of the irruption of the Scots, and that they were before it, in which were the sons of the earl of Northumberland preparing to offer them combat. The bishop had collected a number of men, and was hastening to their assistance, but Sir Henry Percy would not wait; for he was accompanied by six hundred spears, of knights and squires, and upwards of eight thousand infantry, which he said would be more than enough to fight the Scots, who were but three hundred lances and two thousand others. When they were all assembled they left Newcastle after dinner, and took the field in good array, following the road the Scots had taken, making for Otterbourne, which was eight short leagues distant; but they could not advance very fast, that their infantry might keep up with them.

As the Scots were supping,—some indeed had gone to sleep, for they had labored hard during the day at the attack of the castle, and intended renewing it in the cool of the morning,—the English arrived, and mistook, at their entrance, the huts of the servants for those of their masters. They forced their way into the camp, which was, however, tolerably strong, shouting out, "Percy! Percy!" In such cases you may suppose an alarm is soon given, and it was fortunate for the Scots that the English had made their first attack on the servants' quarters, which checked them some little. The Scots, expecting the English, had prepared accordingly; for while the lords were arming themselves they ordered a body of infantry to join their servants and keep up the skirmish. As their men were armed, they formed themselves under the pennons of the three principal barons, who each had his particular appointment. In the meantime the night advanced, but it was sufficiently light, for the moon shone, and it was the month of August, when the weather is temperate and serene.

When the Scots were quite ready, and properly arrayed, they left their camp in silence, but did not march to meet the English. They skirted the side of the mountain which was hard by; for during the preceding day they had well examined the country round, and said among themselves, "Should the English come to beat up our quarters we will do so and so," and thus settled their plans beforehand, which was the saving of them; for it is of the greatest advantage to men-at-arms when attacked in the night to have previously arranged their mode of defence, and well to have weighed the chance of victory or defeat. The English had soon overpowered their servants; but as they advanced into the camp they found fresh bodies ready to oppose them, and to continue the fight. The Scots, in the meantime, marched along the mountain side, and fell upon the enemy's flank quite unexpectedly, shouting their cries. This was a great surprise to the English, who however formed themselves in better order and reinforced that part of their army. The cries of Percy and Douglas resounded on either side.

The battle now raged: great was the pushing of lances, and very many of each party was struck down at the first onset. The English being more numerous, and anxious to defeat the enemy, kept in a compact body, and forced the Scots to retire, who were on the point of being discomfited. The earl of Douglas being young, and impatient to gain renown in arms, ordered his banner to advance, shouting, "Douglas! Douglas! "Sir Henry and Sir Ralph Percy, indignant for the affront the earl of Douglas had put on them, by conquering their pennon, and desirous of meeting him, hastened to the place from whence the sounds came, calling out, "Percy! Percy!" The two banners met, and many gallant deeds of arms ensued. The English were in superior strength, and fought so lustily that they drove back the Scots. Sir Patrick Hepburn and his son of the same name did honor to their knighthood and country by their gallantry, under the banner of Douglas, which would have been conquered but for the vigorous defence they made; and this circumstance not only contributed to their personal credit, but the memory of it is continued with honor to their descendants.

The knights and squires of either party were anxious to continue the combat with vigor as long as their spears might be capable of holding. Cowardice was there unknown, and the most splendid courage was everywhere exhibited by the gallant youths of England and Scotland; they were so closely intermixed that the archers' bows were useless, and they fought hand to hand, without either battalion giving way. The Scots behaved most valiantly, for the English were three to one. I do not mean to say the English did not acquit themselves well; for they would sooner be slain or made prisoners in battle than reproached with flight. As I before mentioned, the two banners of Douglas and Percy met, and the men-at-arms under each exerted themselves by

every means to gain the victory; but the English, at this attack, were so much the stronger, that the Scots were driven back. The earl of Douglas, who was of a high spirit, seeing his men repulsed, seized a battle-axe with both his hands like a gallant knight, and to rally his men dashed into the midst of his enemies, and gave such blows on all around him that no one could withstand them, but all made way for him on every side; for there was none so well armed with helmets and plates but that they suffered from his battle-axe. Thus he advanced, like another Hector, thinking to recover and conquer the field, from his own prowess, until he was met by three spears that were pointed at him. One struck him on the shoulder, another on the stomach, and the third entered his thigh. He could never disengage himself from these spears, but was borne to the ground, fighting desperately. From that time he never rose again. Some of his knights and squires had followed him, but not all; for, though the moon shone, it was rather dark. The three English lancers knew that they had struck down some person of considerable rank, but never thought it was Earl Douglas. Had they known it, they would have been so rejoiced that their courage would have been redoubled, and the fortune of the day had consequently been determined to their side. The Scots were ignorant also of their loss until the battle was over, otherwise they would certainly, from despair, have been discomfited.

I will relate what befell the earl afterward. As soon as he fell, his head was cleaved by a battle-axe, the spear thrust through his thigh, and the main body of the English marched over him, without paying any attention, not supposing him to be their principal enemy. In another part of the field, the earl of March and Dunbar combated valiantly; and the English gave the Scots full employment who had followed the earl of Douglas, and had engaged with the two Percies. The earl of Moray behaved so gallantly in pursuing the English, that they knew not how to resist him. Of all the battles that have been described in this history, great and small, this of which I am now speaking was the best fought and the most severe; for there was not a man, knight, or squire who did not acquit himself gallantly, hand to hand with the enemy. It resembled something that of

Cocherel, which was as long and as hardily disputed. The sons of the earl of Northumberland, Sir Henry and Sir Ralph Percy, who were the leaders of this expedition, behaved themselves like good knights in the combat. Almost a similar accident befell Sir Ralph as that which happened to the earl of Douglas; for, having advanced too far, he was surrounded by the enemy and severely wounded, and, being out of breath, surrendered himself to a Scots knight, called Sir John Maxwell, who was under the command and of the household of the earl of Moray.

When made prisoner, the knight asked him who he was, for it was dark, and he knew him not. Sir Ralph was so weakened by loss of blood, which was flowing from his wound, that he could scarcely avow himself to be Sir Ralph Percy. "Well," replied the knight, "Sir Ralph, rescued or not, you are my prisoner; my name is Maxwell." "I agree to it," said Sir Ralph. "But pay some attention to me; for I am so desperately wounded, that my drawers and greaves are full of blood." Upon this the Scots knight was very attentive to him; when suddenly hearing the cry of Moray hard by, and perceiving the earl's banner advancing to him, Sir John addressed himself to the earl of Moray, and said, "My lord, I present you with Sir Ralph Percy as a prisoner; but let good care be taken of him, for he is very badly wounded." The earl was much pleased at this, and replied, "Maxwell, thou hast well earned thy spurs this day." He then ordered his men to take every care of Sir Ralph, who bound up and staunched his wounds. The battle still continued to rage, and no one could say at that moment which side would be the conqueror, for there were very many captures and rescues that never came to my knowledge.

The young earl of Douglas had this night performed wonders in arms. When he was struck down there was a great crowd round him, and he could not raise himself; for the blow on his head was mortal. His men had followed him as closely as they were able, and there came to him his cousins, Sir James Lindsay, Sir John and Sir Walter Sinclair, with other knights and squires. They found by his side a gallant knight, that had constantly attended him, who was his chaplain, and had at this time exchanged his profession for that of a valiant man-at-arms. The whole night he had followed the earl, with his battle-axe in hand, and had by his exertions more than once repelled the English. This conduct gained the thanks of his countrymen, and turned out to his advantage, for in the same year he was promoted to the archdeaconry, and made canon of Aberdeen. His name was Sir William of North Berwick. To say the truth, he was well formed in all his limbs to shine in battle, and was severely wounded at this combat. When these knights came to the earl of Douglas they found him in a melancholy state, as well as one of his knights, Sir Robert Hart, who had fought by his side the whole of the night, and now lay beside him, covered with fifteen wounds from lances and other weapons.

Sir John Sinclair asked the earl, "Cousin, how fares it with you?" "But so so," replied he. "Thanks to God, there are but few of my ancestors who have died in chambers or in their beds. I bid you, therefore, revenge my death, for I have but little hope of living, as my heart becomes every minute more faint. Do you, Walter and Sir John Sinclair, raise up my banner, for certainly it is on the ground, from the death of David Campbell, that valiant squire who bore it, and who refused knighthood from my hands this day, though he was equal to the most eminent knights for courage and loyalty; and continue to shout 'Douglas!' but do not tell friend or foe whether I am in your company or not; for, should the enemy know the truth, they will be greatly rejoiced."

The two brothers Sinclair and Sir James Lindsay obeyed his orders. The banner was raised, and "Douglas!" shouted. Their men, who had remained behind, hearing the shouts of "Douglas!" so often repeated, ascended a small eminence, and pushed their lances with such courage that the English were repulsed, and many killed or struck to the ground. The Scots, by thus valiantly driving the enemy beyond the spot where the earl of Douglas lay dead,—for he had expired on giving his last orders,—arrived at his banner, which was borne by Sir John Sinclair. Numbers were continually increasing, from the repeated shouts of "Douglas!" and the greater part of the Scots knights and squires were now there. The earls of Moray and March, with their banners and men, came thither also. When they were all thus collected, perceiving the English retreat, they renewed the battle with greater vigor than before.

To say the truth, the English had harder work than the Scots, for they had come by a forced march that evening from Newcastle-on-Tyne, which was eight English leagues distant, to meet the Scots, by which means the greater part were exceedingly fatigued before the combat began. The Scots, on the contrary, had reposed themselves, which was to them of the utmost advantage, as was apparent from the event of the battle. In this last attack they so completely repulsed the English, that the latter could never rally again, and the former drove them far beyond where the earl of Douglas lay on the ground. Sir Henry Percy, during this attack, had the misfortune to fall into the hands of the Lord Montgomery, a very valiant knight of Scotland. They had long fought hand to hand with much valor, and without hindrance from any one; for there was neither knight nor squire of either party who did not find there his equal to fight with, and all were fully engaged. In the end, Sir Henry was made prisoner by the Lord Montgomery.

Chapter XXXVIII

Edward the Black Prince "Ich Dien"

THE last hero of English chivalry with whom we have to do is Edward the Black Prince. And as the most characteristic part of the knighthood of this most knightly of English princes, we have selected the battles of Crécy and of Poitiers.

The Battle of Crécy

THE English, who were drawn up in three divisions, and seated on the ground, on seeing their enemies advance, rose undauntedly up, and fell into their ranks. That of the prince[1] was the first to do so, whose archers were formed in the manner of a portcullis or harrow, and the men-at-arms in the rear. The earls of Northumberland and Arundel, who commanded the second division, had posted themselves in good order on his wing, to assist and succor the prince if necessary.

You must know that these kings, earls, barons, and lords of France did not advance in any regular order, but one after the other, or anyway most pleasing to themselves. As soon as the king of France came in sight of the English, his blood began to boil, and he cried out to his marshals, "Order the Genoese forward, and begin the battle, in the name of God and St. Denis." There were about fifteen thousand Genoese cross-bowmen, but they were quite fatigued, having marched on foot that day six leagues, completely armed and with their cross-bows. They told the constable they were not in a fit condition to do

[1]Edward the Black Prince; son of Edward III.

any great things that day in battle. The earl of Alençon, hearing this, said, "This is what one gets by employing such scoundrels, who fall off when there is any need of them." During this time a heavy rain fell, accompanied by thunder and a very terrible eclipse of the sun; and before this rain a great flight of crows hovered in the air over all those battalions, making a loud noise. Shortly afterwards it cleared up, and the sun shone very bright, but the Frenchmen had it in their faces, and the Englishmen in their backs. When the Genoese were somewhat in order, and approached the English, they set up a loud shout, in order to frighten them; but they remained quite still, and did not seem to attend to it. Then they set up a second shout, and advanced a little forward, but the English never moved. They hooted a third time, advancing with their cross-bows presented, and began to shoot. The English archers then advanced one step forward, and shot their arrows with such force and quickness that it seemed as if it snowed. When the Genoese felt these arrows, which pierced their arms, heads, and through their armor, some of them cut the strings of their cross-bows, others flung them on the ground, and all turned about and retreated quite discomfited. The French had a large body of men-at-arms on horseback, richly dressed, to support the Genoese. The king of France, seeing them thus fall back, cried out, "Kill me those scoundrels, for they stop up our road without any reason." You would then have seen the above-mentioned men-at-arms lay about them, killing all they could of these runaways.

The English continued shooting as vigorously and

quickly as before; some of their arrows fell among the horsemen who were sumptuously equipped, and, killing and wounding many, made them caper and fall among the Genoese, so that they were in such confusion that they could never rally again. The valiant king of Bohemia was slain there. He was called Charles of Luxembourg, for he was the son of the gallant king and emperor, Henry of Luxembourg. Having heard the order of the battle, he inquired where his son, the lord Charles, was. His attendants answered that they did not know, but believed he was fighting. The king said to them, "Gentlemen, you are all my people, my friends and brethren at arms this day; therefore, as I am blind, I request of you to lead me so far into the engagement that I may strike one stroke with my sword." The knights replied they would directly lead him forward; and in order that they might not lose him in the crowd, they fastened all the reins of their horses together, and put the king at their head, that he might gratify his wish, and advanced towards the enemy. The lord Charles of Bohemia, who already signed his name as king of Germany, and bore the arms, had come in good order to the engagement; but when he perceived that it was likely to turn against the French, he departed, and I do not well know what road he took. The king, his father, had rode in among the enemy, and made good use of his sword, for he and his companions had fought most gallantly. They had advanced so far that they were all slain; and on the morrow they were found on the ground, with their horses all tied together.

The earl of Alençon advanced in regular order upon the English to fight with them, as did the earl of Flanders in another part. These two lords, with their detachments, coasting, as it were, the archers, came to the prince's battalion, where they fought valiantly for a length of time. The king of France was eager to march to the place where he saw their banners displayed, but there was a hedge of archers before him. He had that day made a present of a handsome black horse to Sir John of Hainault, who had mounted on it a knight of his that bore his banner, which horse ran off with him and forced his way through the English army, and, when about to return, stumbled and fell into a ditch and severely wounded him. He would have been dead if his page had not followed him round the battalions and found him unable to rise. He had not, however, any other hindrance than from his horse; for the English did not quit the ranks that day to make prisoners. The page alighted, and raised him up; but he did not return the way he came, as he would have found it difficult from the crowd.

This battle, which was fought on a Saturday between la Broyes and Crécy, was very murderous and cruel; and many gallant deeds of arms were performed that were never known. Towards evening, many knights and squires of the French had lost their masters. They wandered up and down the plain, attacking the English in small parties. They were soon destroyed, for the English had determined that day to give no quarter, or hear of ransom from any one.

Early in the day, some French, Germans, and Savoyards had broken through the archers of the prince's battalion and had engaged with the men-at-arms; upon which the second battalion came to his aid, and it was time, for otherwise he would have been hard pressed. The first division, seeing the danger they were in, sent a knight in great haste to the king of England, who was posted upon an eminence near a windmill. On the knight's arrival, he said, "Sir, the earl of Warwick, the lord Stafford, the lord Reginald Cobham, and the others who are about your son, are vigorously attacked by the French; and they entreat that you would come to their assistance with your battalion, for, if their numbers should increase, they fear he will have too much to do." The king replied, "Is my son dead, unhorsed, or so badly wounded that he cannot support himself?" "Nothing of the sort, thank God," rejoined the knight; "but he is in so hot an engagement that he has great need of your help." The king answered, "Now, Sir Thomas, return back to those that sent you, and tell them from me, not to send again for me this day, or expect that I shall come, let what will happen, as long as my son has life; and say that I command them to let the boy win his spurs; for I am determined, if it please God, that all the glory and honor of this day shall be given to him, and to those into whose care I have entrusted him." The knight returned to his lords, and related the king's answer, which mightily encouraged them, and made them repent they ever sent such a message.

Late after vespers the king of France had not more about him than sixty men, every one included. Sir John of Hainault, who was of the number, had once remounted the king; for his horse had been killed under him by an arrow. He said to the king, "Sir, retreat whilst you have an opportunity, and do not expose yourself so simply; if you have lost this battle, another time you will be the conqueror." After he had said this, he took the bridle of the king's horse and led him off by force, for he had before entreated him to retire. The king rode on until he came to the castle of la Broyes, where he found the gates shut, for it was very dark. The king ordered the governor of it to be summoned. He came upon the battlements, and asked who it was that called at such an hour. The king answered, "Open, open, governor; it is the fortune of France." The governor, hearing the king's voice, immediately descended, opened the gate, and let down the bridge. The king and his company entered the castle; but he had only with him five barons, Sir John of Hainault and four more. The king would not bury himself in such a place as that, but, having taken some refreshments, set out again with his attendants about midnight, and rode on, under the direction of guides who were well acquainted with the country, until, about daybreak, he came to Amiens, where he halted. This Saturday the English never quitted their ranks in pursuit of any one, but remained on the field, guarding their position, and defending themselves against all who attacked them. The battle was ended at the hour of vespers.

When on this Saturday night, the English heard no more hooting or shouting, nor any more crying out to particular lords or their banners, they looked upon the field as their own, and their enemies as beaten. They made great fires and lighted torches because of the obscurity of the night. King Edward then came down from his post, who all that day had not put on his helmet, and, with his whole battalion, advanced to the prince of Wales, whom he embraced in his arms and kissed, and said, "Sweet son, God give you good perseverance; you are my son, for most loyally have you acquitted yourself this day; you are worthy to be a sovereign." The prince bowed down very low and humbled himself, giving all honor to the king, his father. The English during the night made frequent thanksgiving to the Lord for the happy issue of the day, and without rioting; for the king had forbidden all riot or noise.

At Crécy the Black Prince won his spurs, but the great achievement of his life was his victory at Poitiers,—a battle fought by him alone with his army, when his father, Edward III, was absent from France in England. At the peace of Bretagne, agreed upon after the battle, several provinces were ceded by France to England, and these Edward added to his dominions in Guienne, and formed for himself a separate kingdom, which he ruled until his death. He never came to the throne of England; his son, Richard II, succeeded Edward III.

THE BATTLE OF POITIERS

ON Sunday morning, the king of France, who was very impatient to combat the English, ordered a solemn mass to be sung in his pavilion, and he and his four sons received the communion. Mass being over, there came to him many barons of France, as well as other great lords who held fiefs in the neighborhood, according to a summons they had received for a council. They were a considerable time debating; at last it was ordered that the whole army should advance into the plain, and that each lord should display his banner, and push forward in the name of God and St. Denis. Upon this the trumpets of the army sounded, and every one got himself ready, mounted his horse, and made for that part of the plain where the king's banner was fluttering in the wind. There might be seen all the nobility of France, richly dressed out in brilliant armor, with banners and pennons gallantly displayed; for all the flower of the French nobility was there; no knight nor squire, for fear of dishonor, dared to remain at home. By the advice of the constable and the marshals, the army was divided into three battalions, each consisting of sixteen thousand men-at-arms, who had before shown themselves men of tried courage. The duke of Orléans commanded the first battalion, where there were thirty-six banners and twice as many pennons. The second was under command of the duke of Normandy, and his two brothers, the lord Lewis and lord John. The king of France commanded the third.

Whilst these battalions were forming, the king called to him the lord Eustace de Ribeaumont, the lord John de Landas, and the lord Guiscard de Beaujeu, and said to them, "Ride forward as near the English army as you can, and observe their countenance, taking notice of their numbers, and examine which will be the most advantageous manner to combat them, whether on horseback or on foot." The three knights left the king to obey his commands. The king was mounted on a white palfrey, and, riding to the head of his army, said aloud, "You men of Paris, Chartres, Rouen, and Orléans, have been used to threaten what you would do to the English if you could find them, and wished much to meet them in arms; now that wish shall be granted. I will lead you to them, and let us see how you will revenge yourselves for all the mischief and damage they have done you. Be assured we will not part without fighting." Those who heard him replied, "Sir, through God's assistance we will most cheerfully meet them."

At this instant the three knights returned, and pushing through the crowd, came to the king, who asked what news they had brought. Sir Eustace de Ribeaumont, whom his companions had requested to be their spokesman, answered, "Sir, we have observed accurately the English; they may amount, according to our estimate, to about two thousand men-at-arms, four thousand archers, and fifteen hundred footmen. They are in a very strong position; but we do not imagine they can make more than one battalion; nevertheless, they have posted themselves with great judgment, have fortified all the road along the hedge side, and lined the hedges with part of their archers; for, as that is the only road for an attack, one must pass through the midst of them. This lane has no other entry; for it is so narrow, that scarcely can four men ride abreast in it. At the end of this lane, amidst vines and thorns, where it is impossible to ride or march in any regular order, are posted the men-at-arms on foot; and they have drawn up before them their archers in the manner of a harrow, so that it will be no easy matter to defeat them." The king asked in what manner they would advise him to attack them. "Sir," replied Sir Eustace, "on foot; except three hundred of the most expert, to break, if possible, this body of archers; and then your battalions must advance quickly on foot, attack the men-at-arms

hand to hand, and combat them valiantly. This is the best advice that I can give you, and if any one know a better, let him say it." The king replied, "Thus shall it be, then." And, in company with his two marshals, he rode from battalion to battalion, and selected, in conformity to their opinions, three hundred knights and squires of the greatest repute in his army, each well armed, and mounted on the best of horses. Soon after, the battalion of the Germans was formed, who were to remain on horseback, to assist the marshals; they were commanded by the earls of Salzburg, Neydo, and Nassau. King John was armed in royal armor, and nineteen others like him.

When the battalions of the king of France were drawn up, and each lord posted under his proper banner, and informed how they were to act, it was ordered that all those who were armed with lances should shorten them to the length of five feet, that they might be the more manageable, and that every one should take off his spurs. As the French were on the point of marching to their enemies, the cardinal of Périgord, who had left Poitiers that morning early, came full gallop to the king, making him a low reverence, and entreated him that he might be allowed to go to the prince of Wales, to endeavor to make peace between him and the king of France. The king answered, "It is very agreeable to us; but make haste back again."

So then the cardinal set off, and went in all speed to the prince; but though he spent all this Sunday in riding from one army to another, he could not make terms which were thought honorable alike by the king and by the prince of Wales. That same day, the French kept in their quarters, where they lived at their ease, having plenty of provisions; whilst the English, on the other hand, were but badly off, nor did they know whither to go for forage, as they were so straitly kept by the French they could not move without danger. This Sunday they made many mounds and ditches round where the archers were posted, the better to secure them.

On Monday morning the prince and his army were soon in readiness, and as well arranged as on the former day. The French were also drawn out by sunrise. The cardinal, returning again that morning, imagined that by his exhortations he could pacify both parties; but the French told him to return when he pleased, and not attempt bringing them any more treaties or pacifications, else worse might betide him. When the cardinal saw that he labored in vain, he took leave of the king of France, and set out towards the prince of Wales, to whom he said, "Fair son, exert yourself as much as possible, for there must be a battle; I cannot by any means pacify the king of France." The prince replied, "that such were the intentions of him and his army; and God defend the right." The cardinal then took leave of him, and returned to Poitiers.

The arrangement of the prince's army, in respect to the battalions, was exactly the same as what the three knights before named had related to the king of France, except that at this time he had ordered some valiant and intelligent knights to remain on horseback, similar to the battalion of the French marshals, and had also commanded three hundred men-at-arms, and as many archers on horseback, to post themselves on the right, on a small hill, that was not too steep nor too high, and, by passing over its summit, to get round the wings of the duke of Normandy's battalions, who was in person at the foot of it. These were all the alterations the prince had made in his order of battle; he himself was with the main body, in the midst of the vineyards, the whole completely armed, with their horses near, if there should be any occasion for them. They had fortified and inclosed the weaker parts with their wagons and baggage.

And when the prince of Wales saw, from the departure of the cardinal without being able to obtain any honorable terms, that a battle was inevitable, and that the king of France held both him and his army in great contempt, he thus addressed himself to them: "Now, my gallant fellows, what though we be a small body when compared to the army of our enemies; do not let us be cast down on that account, for victory does not always follow numbers, but where the Almighty God pleases to bestow it. If, through good fortune, the day shall be ours, we will gain the greatest honor and glory in this world; if the contrary should happen, and we be slain, I have a father and beloved brethren alive, and you all have some relations or good friends, who will be sure to revenge our deaths. I therefore entreat of you to exert yourselves, and combat manfully; for, if it please God and St. George, you shall see me this day act like a true knight." By such words and arguments as these the prince harangued his men, as did the marshals, by his orders, so that they were all in high spirits. Sir John Chandos placed himself near the prince, to guard and advise him; and never, during that day, would he, on any account, quit his post

The lord James Audley remained also a considerable time near him; but, when he saw that they must certainly engage, he said to the prince: "Sir, I have ever served most loyally my lord your father, and yourself, and shall continue so to do as long as I have life. Dear sir, I must now acquaint you that formerly I made a vow, if ever I should be engaged in any battle where the king, your father, or any of his sons were, that I would be the foremost in the attack, and the best combatant on his side, or die in the attempt. I beg, therefore, most earnestly, as a reward for any services I may have done, that you would grant me permission honorably to quit you, that I may post myself in such wise to accomplish my vow." The prince granted this request, and, holding out his hand to him, said: "Sir James, God grant that this day you may shine in valor above all other knights." The knight then set off, and posted himself at the front of the battalion, with only four squires whom he had detained with him to guard his person. The lord James was a prudent and valiant knight; and by his advice the army had thus been drawn up in order of battle. The lord James began to advance, in order to fight with the battalion of the marshals. Sir Eustace d'Ambreticourt, being mounted, placed his lance in its rest, and, fixing his shield, struck spurs into his horse and galloped up to this battalion. A German knight, perceiving Sir Eustace quit his army, left his battalion that was under the command of earl John of Nassau, and made up to him. The shock of their meeting was so violent that they both fell to the ground. The German was wounded in the shoulder, so that he could not rise again so nimbly as Sir Eustace, who, when upon his legs, after he had taken breath, was hastening to the knight that lay on the ground; but five German men-at-arms came upon him, struck him down, and made him prisoner. They led him to those that were attached to the earl of Nassau, who did not pay much attention to him, nor do I know if they made him swear himself their prisoner; but they tied him to a car with some of their harness.

The engagement now began on both sides, and the battalion of the marshals was advancing before those who were intended to break the battalion of the archers, and had entered the lane where the hedges on both sides were lined by the archers, who, as soon as they saw them fairly entered, began shooting with their bows in such an excellent manner from each side of the hedge, that the horses, smarting under the pain of the wounds made by their bearded arrows, would not advance, but turned about, and, by their unruliness, threw their masters, who could not manage them; nor could those that had fallen get up again for the confusion, so that this battalion of the marshals could never approach that of the prince. However, <u>there were some knights and squires so well mounted</u>, <u>that by the strength of their horses they passed through and broke the hedge</u>, but, in spite of their efforts, could not get up to the battalion of the prince. The lord James Audley, attended by his four squires, had placed himself, sword in hand, in front of this battalion much before the rest, and was performing wonders. He had advanced through his eagerness so far that he engaged the lord Arnold

d'Andreghen, marshal of France, under his banner when they fought a considerable time, and the lord Arnold was roughly enough treated. The battalion of the marshals was soon after put to the rout by the arrows of the archers and the assistance of the men-at-arms, who rushed among them as they were struck down and seized and slew them at their pleasure. The lord Arnold d'Andreghen was there made prisoner, but by others than the lord James Audley or his four squires, for that knight never stopped to make any one his prisoner that day, but was the whole time employed in fighting and following his enemies. In another part, the lord John Clermont fought under his banner as long as he was able, but being struck down, he could neither get up again nor procure his ransom; he was killed on the spot. In a short time this battalion of the marshals was totally discomfited; for they fell back so much on each other that the army could not advance, and those who were in the rear, not being able to get forward, fell back upon the battalion commanded by the duke of Normandy, which was broad and thick in the front, but it was soon thin enough in the rear; for when they learnt that the marshals had been defeated, they mounted their horses and set off. At this time a body of English came down from the hill, and, passing along the battalions on horseback, accompanied by a large body of archers, fell upon one of the wings of the duke of Normandy's division. To say the truth, the English archers were of infinite service to their army, for they shot so thickly and so well that the French did not know what way to turn themselves to avoid their arrows. By this means they kept advancing by little and little and gained ground. When the English men-at-arms perceived that the first battalion was beaten, and that the one under the duke of Normandy was in disorder and beginning to open, they hastened to mount their horses, which they had ready prepared close at hand. As soon as they were all mounted, they gave a shout of "St. George for Guienne!" and Sir John Chandos said to the prince, "Sir, sir, now push forward, for the day is ours. God will this day put it in your hand. Let us make for our adversary, the king of France; for where he is will lie the main stress of the business. I well know that his valor will not let him fly; and he will remain with us, if it please God and St. George; but he must be well fought with, and you have before said that you would show yourself this day a good knight." The prince replied: "John, get forward; you shall not see me turn my back this day, but I will always be among the foremost." He then said to Sir Walter Woodland, his banner-bearer, "Banner, advance, in the name of God and St. George." The knight obeyed the commands of the prince; and the prince upon this charged the division of the duke of Athens, and very sharp the encounter was, so that many were beaten down. The French, who fought in large bodies, cried out, "Montjoye St. Denis!" and the English answered them with "St. George for Guienne!" The prince next met the battalion of Germans under command of the earl of Salzburg, the earl of Nassau, and the earl of Neydo; but they were soon overthrown and put to flight. The English archers shot so well that none dared to come within reach of their arrows, and they put to death many who could not ransom themselves. Then the above-named earls were slain there, as well as many other knights and squires attached to them. In the confusion, Sir Eustace d'Ambreticourt was

rescued by his own men, who remounted him. He afterwards performed many gallant deeds of arms, and made good captures that day.

When the battalion of the duke of Normandy saw the prince advancing so quick upon them, they bethought themselves how to escape. The sons of the king, the duke of Normandy, the earl of Poitiers, and the earl of Touraine, who were very young, too easily believed what those under whose management they were placed said to them. However, the lord Guiscard d'Angle and Sir John de Saintre', who were near the earl of Poitiers, would not fly, but rushed into the thickest of the combat. The three sons of the king, according to the advice given them, galloped away, with upwards of eighty lances who had never been near the enemy, and took the road to Chavigny.

Now the king's battalion advanced in good order to meet the English; many hard blows were given with swords, battle-axes, and other warlike weapons. The king of France, with the lord Philip, his youngest son, attacked the division of the marshals, the earls of Warwick and Suffolk, and in this combat were engaged many very noble lords on both sides.

The lord James Audley, with the assistance of his four squires, was always engaged in the heat of the battle. He was severely wounded in the body, head, and face; and, as long as his breath permitted him, he maintained the fight and advanced forward. He continued to do so until he was covered with blood. Then, toward the close of the engagement, his four squires, who were his body guard, took him and led him out of the engagement, very weak and wounded, towards a hedge, that he might cool and take breath. They disarmed him as gently as they could, in order to examine his wounds, dress them, and sew up the most serious.

It often happens that fortune in war and love turns out more favorable and wonderful than could have been hoped for or expected. To say the truth, this battle, which was fought near Poitiers, in the plains of Beauvoir and Maupertuis, was very bloody and perilous. Many gallant deeds of arms were performed that were never known, and the combatants on either side suffered much. King John himself did wonders. He was armed with a battle-axe, with which he fought and defended himself, and if a fourth of his people had behaved as well the day would have been his own. The earl of Tancarville, in endeavoring to break through the crowd, was made prisoner close to him, as were also Sir James de Bourbon, earl of Ponthieu, and the lord John d'Artois, earl of Eu. The pursuit continued even to the gates of Poitiers, where there was much slaughter and overthrow of men and horses; for the inhabitants of Poitiers had shut their gates and would suffer none to enter; upon which account there was great butchery on the causeway before the gate, where such numbers were killed or wounded that several surrendered themselves the moment they spied an Englishman; and there were many English archers who had four, five, or six prisoners.

There was much pressing at this time through eagerness to take the king; and those who were nearest to him and knew him, cried out, "Surrender yourself, surrender yourself, or you are a dead man." In that part of the field was a young knight from St. Omer, who was engaged by a salary in the service of the king of England. His name was Denys de Morbeque, who for five years had attached himself to the English on account of having been banished in his younger days from France for a murder committed in an affray at St. Omer. It fortunately happened for this knight that he was at the time near to the king of France when he was so much pulled about. He by dint of force, for he was very strong and robust, pushed through the crowd, and said to the king in very good French, "Sire, sire, surrender yourself." The king, who found himself very disagreeably situated, turning to him, asked, "To whom shall I surrender myself; to whom? where is my cousin, the prince of Wales? if I could see him I would speak to him." "Sire," replied Sir Denys, "he is not here; but surrender yourself to me and I will lead you to him." "Who are you?" said the king. "Sire, I am Denys de Morbeque, a knight from Artois, but I serve the king of England because I cannot belong to France, having forfeited all I possess there." <u>The king then gave him his right-hand glove, and said, "I surrender myself to you."</u> There was much crowding and pushing about, for every one was eager to cry out, "I have taken him." Neither the king nor his youngest son Philip were able to get forward, and free themselves from the throng.

The prince of Wales, who was as courageous as a lion, took great delight that day to combat his enemies. Sir John Chandos, who was near his person and had never quitted it during the whole of the day, nor stopped to take any prisoners, said to him toward the end of the battle, "Sir, it will be proper for you to halt here and plant your banner on the top of this bush, which will serve to rally your forces that seem very much scattered; for I do not see any banners or pennons of the French, nor any considerable bodies able to rally against us; and you must refresh yourself a little, as I perceive you are very much heated." Upon this, the banner of the prince was placed on a high bush; the minstrels began to play, and trumpets and clarions to do their duty. The prince took off his helmet, and the knights attendant on his person and belonging to his chamber were soon ready, and pitched a small pavilion of crimson color, which the prince entered. Liquor was then brought to him and the other knights who were with him. They increased every moment; for they were returning from the pursuit, and stopped there, surrounded by their prisoners.

As soon as the two marshals were come back, the prince asked them if they knew anything of the king of France. They replied, "No, sir, not for a certainty; but we believe he must be either killed or taken prisoner, since he has never quitted his battalion." The prince then, addressing the earl of Warwick and lord Cobham, said, "I beg of you to mount your horses and ride over the field, so that on your return you may bring me some certain intelligence of him." The two barons, immediately mounting their horses, left the prince and made for a small hillock, that they might look about them. From their stand they perceived a crowd of men-at-arms on foot, who were advancing very slowly. The king of France was in the midst of them, and in great danger; for the French and Gascons had taken him from Sir Denys de Morbeque and were disputing who should have him, the stoutest bawling out, "It is I who have got him." "No, no," replied the others, "we have him." The king to escape his peril, said, "Gentlemen, gentlemen, I pray you conduct me and my son in a courteous manner to my cousin the prince; and do not make such a riot over my capture, for I am so great a lord that I can make all sufficiently rich." These words, and others which fell from the king, appeased them a little, but the disputes were always beginning again, and they did not move a step without rioting. When the two barons saw this troop of people, they descended from the hillock, and, sticking spurs into their horses, made up to them. On their arrival, they asked what was the matter. They were answered that it was the king of France, who had been made prisoner, and that upwards of ten knights and squires challenged him at the same time as belonging to each of them. The two barons then pushed through the crowd by main force and ordered all to draw aside. They commanded, in the name of the prince and under pain of instant death, that every one should keep his distance, and not approach unless ordered or desired so to do. They all retreated behind the king; and the two barons, dismounting, advanced to the king with profound reverence, and conducted him in a peaceable manner to the prince of Wales.

Soon after the earl of Warwick and the lord Reginald Cobham had left the prince, as has been above related, he inquired from those knights around him of Lord James Audley, and asked if any one knew what was become of him. "Yes, sir," replied some of the company, "he is very badly wounded, and is lying in a litter held by." "By my troth," replied the prince, "I am sore vexed that he is so wounded. See, I beg of

you, if he be able to bear being carried hither; otherwise I will come and visit him." Two knights directly left the prince, and, coming to Lord James, told him how desirous the prince was of seeing him. "A thousand thanks to the prince," answered Lord James, "for condescending to remember so poor a knight as myself." He then called eight of his servants and had himself borne in his litter to where the prince was. When he was come into his presence, the prince bent down over him and embraced him, saying, "My lord James, I am bound to honor you very much, for by your valor this day you have acquired glory and renown above us all, and your prowess has proved you the bravest knight." Lord James replied, "My lord, you have a right to say whatever you please, but I wish it were as you have said. If I have this day been forward to serve you it has been to accomplish a vow that I had made, and ought not to be so much thought of." "Sir James," answered the prince, "I and all the rest of us deem you the bravest knight on our side in this battle; and to increase your renown and furnish you withal to pursue your career of glory in war, I retain you henceforward forever as my knight, with five hundred marcs of yearly revenue, which I will secure to you from my estates in England." "Sir," said Lord James, "God make me deserving of the good fortune you bestow upon me." At these words he took leave of the prince, as he was very weak, and his servants carried him back to his tent. He could not have been at a great distance when the earl of Warwick and lord Reginald Cobham entered the pavilion of the prince and presented the king of France to him. The prince made a very low obeisance to the king and gave him as much comfort as he was able, which he well knew how to administer. He ordered wine and spices to be brought, which he presented to the king himself, as a mark of great affection.

Thus was this battle won, as you have heard related, in the plains of Maupertuis, two leagues from the city of Poitiers, on the 19th day of September, 1356. It commenced about nine o'clock and was ended by noon; but the English were not all returned from the pursuit, and it was to recall his people that the prince had placed his banner upon a high bush. They did not return till late after vespers from pursuing the enemy. It was reported that all the flower of French

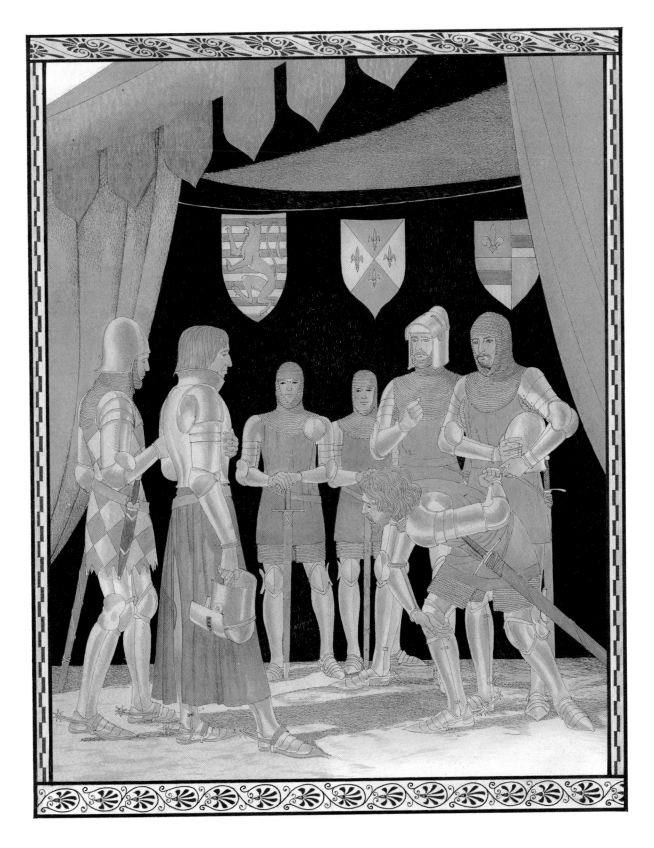

knighthood was slain, and that, with the king and his son the lord Philip, seventeen earls, without counting barons, knights, or squires, were made prisoners, and from five to six thousand of all sorts left dead in the field. When they were all collected, they found they had twice as many prisoners as themselves. They therefore consulted, if, considering the risk they might run, it would not be more advisable to ransom them on the spot. This was done, and the prisoners found the English and Gascons very civil; for there were many set at liberty that day on their promise of coming to Bordeaux before Christmas to pay their ransom.

When all were returned to their banners, they retired to their camp, which was adjoining to the field of battle. Some disarmed themselves and did the same to their prisoners, to whom they showed every kindness; for whoever made any prisoners they were solely at his disposal to ransom or not, as he pleased. It may be easily supposed that all those who accompanied the prince were very rich in glory and wealth, as well by the ransoms of his prisoners as by the quantities of gold and silver plate, rich jewels, and trunks stuffed full of belts that were weighty from their gold and silver ornaments and furred mantles. They set no value on armor, tents, or other things; for the French had come there as magnificently and richly dressed as if they had been sure of gaining the victory.

When the lord James Audley was brought back to his tent after having most respectfully thanked the prince for his gift, he did not remain long before he sent for his brother, Sir Peter Audley, and some more. They were all of his relations. He then sent for his four squires that had attended upon him that day, and, addressing himself to the knights, said:

"Gentlemen, it has pleased my lord the prince to give me five hundred marcs as a yearly inheritance, for which gift I have done him very trifling bodily service. You see here these four squires who have always served me most loyally, and especially in this day's engagement. What glory I may have gained has been through their means and by their valor, on which account I wish to reward them. I therefore give and resign into their hands the gift of five hundred marcs which my lord the prince has been pleased to bestow on me, in the same form and manner that it has been presented to me. I disinherit myself of it and give it to

them simply and without a possibility of revoking it." The knights looked on each other, and said, "It is becoming the noble mind of Lord James to make such a gift;" and then unanimously added: "May the Lord God remember you for it! We will bear witness of this gift to them wheresoever and whensoever they may call upon us." They then took leave of him, when some went to the prince of Wales, who that night was to give a supper to the king of France from his own provisions; for the French had brought vast quantities with them, which were now fallen into the hands of the English, many of whom had not tasted bread for the last three days.

When evening was come, the prince of Wales gave a supper in his pavilion to the king of France and to the greater part of the princes and barons who were prisoners. The prince seated the king of France and his son the lord Philip at an elevated and well-covered table; and with them were some other French lords of high rank. The other knights and squires were placed at different tables. The prince himself served the king's table, as well as the others, with every mark of humility, and would not sit down at it, in spite of all his entreaties for him to do so, saying that he was not worthy of such an honor, nor did it appertain to him to seat himself at the table of so great a king or of so valiant a man as he had shown himself by his actions that day. He added also, with a noble air: "Dear sir, do not make a poor meal because the Almighty God has not gratified your wishes in the event of this day; for be assured that my lord and father will show you every honor and friendship in his power, and will arrange for your ransom so reasonably that you will henceforward always remain friends. In my opinion, you have cause to be glad that the success of this battle did not turn out as you desired; for you have this day acquired such high renown for prowess that you have surpassed all the best knights on your side. I do not, dear sir, say this to flatter you, for all those of our side who have seen and observed the actions of each party have unanimously allowed this to be your due, and decree you the prize and garland for it." At the end of this speech there were murmurs of praise heard from everyone; and the French said the prince had spoken truly and nobly, and that he would be one of the most gallant princes in Christendom if God should grant him life to pursue his career of glory.

INDEX

EDDISON•SADD EDITIONS

Editorial Director Ian Jackson
Editor Cecilia Walters
U.S. Editors Mary Ann Lynch and Betsy Thorpe
Indexer Dorothy Frame

Creative Director Nick Eddison
Art Director Elaine Partington
Mac Designer Brazzle Atkins

Production Charles James